POLITICAL REFORM
IN INDONESIA
AFTER SOEHARTO

The **Institute of Southeast Asian Studies (ISEAS)** was established as an autonomous organization in 1968. It is a regional centre dedicated to the study of socio-political, security and economic trends and developments in Southeast Asia and its wider geostrategic and economic environment. The Institute's research programmes are the Regional Economic Studies (RES, including ASEAN and APEC), Regional Strategic and Political Studies (RSPS), and Regional Social and Cultural Studies (RSCS).

ISEAS Publishing, an established academic press, has issued more than 2,000 books and journals. It is the largest scholarly publisher of research about Southeast Asia from within the region. ISEAS Publishing works with many other academic and trade publishers and distributors to disseminate important research and analyses from and about Southeast Asia to the rest of the world.

HAROLD CROUCH

POLITICAL REFORM
IN INDONESIA
AFTER SOEHARTO

ISEAS

INSTITUTE OF SOUTHEAST ASIAN STUDIES
Singapore

First published in Singapore in 2010 by
ISEAS Publishing
Institute of Southeast Asian Studies
30 Heng Mui Keng Terrace
Pasir Panjang
Singapore 119614

E-mail: publish@iseas.edu.sg
Website: <http://bookshop.iseas.edu.sg>

The responsibility for facts and opinions in this publication rests exclusively with the author and his interpretations do not necessarily reflect the views or the policy of the publisher or its supporters.

ISEAS Library Cataloguing-in-Publication Data

Crouch, Harold A., 1940–
    Political reform in Indonesia after Soeharto.
    1. Indonesia—Politics and government—1998–
    I. Title.
DS644.5 C95   2010

ISBN 978-981-230-920-4 (soft cover)
ISBN 978-981-230-921-7 (E-Book PDF)

Typeset by Superskill Graphics Pte Ltd
Printed in Singapore by Utopia Press Pte Ltd

CONTENTS

PREFACE

Three decades of authoritarian rule in Indonesia came to a sudden halt in 1998. The collapse of the Soeharto regime was accompanied by massive economic decline, widespread rioting, communal conflict, and fears that the nation was approaching the brink of disintegration. Although the fall of Soeharto opened the way towards democratization, conditions were by no means propitious for political reform. This book asks how political reform could proceed despite such unpromising circumstances. It examines electoral and constitutional reform, the decentralization of a highly centralized regime, the gradual but incomplete withdrawal of the military from its deep political involvement, the launching of an anti-corruption campaign despite entrenched corruption in the courts, and the achievement of peace in two provinces that had been devastated by communal violence and regional rebellion.

The focus of this book is on political reforms during the decade after Soeharto's fall. These reforms were initially driven by the need to respond to the national crisis that brought down the New Order regime but were also shaped by specific circumstances and constellations of political forces in the six fields discussed in this book. The book tries to present the "big picture" of political reform but its main contribution most probably lies in the detailed tracing of reform in each of the six policy areas. Although reforms took place more or less simultaneously in an evolving national context, the pace and nature of specific reforms varied considerably. Political reform was not inevitable but depended on a continuing struggle between those who saw benefit in further reform and those who felt disadvantaged by it. Step-by-step political reform during the last decade has made significant advances but, as this book shows, is by no means complete and, in some areas, could still be vulnerable to reversal. It should also be noted that a study of contemporary political reform is inevitably no more than a "work in progress". Even as this manuscript went to press, new developments raised new questions but hopefully will not fatally undermine my main arguments. I hope that readers will find the final product both informative and interesting.

In researching and writing this book, I had the advantage of having spent several decades following, more or less closely, Indonesian political developments under Soeharto. Like many observers towards the end of the New Order, I was both hoping that somehow President Soeharto would leave office but not convinced that it would actually happen soon. And, in any case, I was reluctantly inclined to expect that Soeharto would most probably be succeeded by another general and that a slightly modified New Order would continue to rule Indonesia. In May 1998, however, I shared the euphoria felt by many Indonesian friends and hoped that it was justified.

One evening in the last week of 1999 I picked up the telephone in Canberra and heard the voice of a long-time casual acquaintance, Australia's former foreign minister and then president of the International Crisis Group (ICG), Gareth Evans, who asked whether I knew of anyone who might be interested in setting up an ICG office in Jakarta and, incidentally, whether I might be interested in the job myself. A few months later I arrived in Jakarta and began writing the first of my ICG reports that appeared over the next two years, together with those of my colleagues, Bob Lowry and Diarmid O'Sullivan. That period in Jakarta provided many insights into the enormous challenges faced by those who aspired to bring about political reform in Indonesia. In the following years I visited Indonesia often and continued to use the ICG office in Jakarta, now under the leadership of an old friend, Sidney Jones, whose hospitality and "briefings" I greatly valued. My appreciation of the mood of the times was also enhanced by conversations with Mahlil Harahap, also of ICG. After my return to the Australian National University in 2002, my many visits to Indonesia between 2003 and 2008 were supported by the Australian Research Council to which I remain most grateful.

Another advantage I had in writing about Indonesian politics flowed from my association with the Department of Political and Social Change at the Australian National University, first under the leadership of Jamie Mackie and then Ben Kerkvliet. I also benefited from discussions with my colleagues, Greg Fealy and Ed Aspinall, who shared my interest in the rapid changes taking place in Indonesia. Of particular importance were my graduate students, some of whose theses and other writings on aspects of Indonesian politics after Soeharto are listed in this book's bibliography. Among them are Jun Honna, Ed Aspinall, Marcus Mietzner, Nuraida Mokhsen, Kumiko Mizuno, Chris Wilson, Nankyung Choi, Taufiq Tanasaldy, and Najib Azca.

My understanding of Indonesian politics also owes much to my old "guru", Herb Feith, who arranged my first job at the University of Indonesia in 1968 and was still discussing Indonesian politics with me in Jakarta a fortnight before his untimely death in late 2001.

In Indonesia I conducted numerous interviews and engaged in countless informal conversations with Indonesian politicians, military and police officers, bureaucrats, journalists, think-tank members, academics, and civil society activists. I have not attempted to record individually their contributions to my understanding of a wide range of political issues. Many of them are noted in this book. However, I should mention several with whom I had many conversations over several years and who especially contributed to my own perceptions. Among them are Marsillam Simanjuntak, Agus Widjojo, Marzuki Darusman, Juwono Sudarsono, Ryaas Rasyid, Rizal Sukma, Dewi Fortuna Anwar, Todung Mulya Lubis, Nazaruddin Syamsuddin, Salim Said, and Tatik Hafidz. As a foreign observer of Indonesian politics, I am acutely aware that my knowledge of the issues discussed in this book is much less than theirs.

Finally, the most important advantage that I had in writing this book was the uncomplaining support of my wife and companion, Khasnor, who tolerated my regular short absences in Indonesia and joined me during longer stays in Jakarta and currently in Banda Aceh.

Several chapters in this book develop material previously published. Most of this material, however, has undergone substantial revision so many times that its original form is not easily recognizable. Parts of Chapters 2 and 3 had their origins in "Political Update 2002: Megawati's Holding Operation", in Edward Aspinall and Greg Fealy, eds., *Local Power and Politics in Indonesia: Decentralisation and Democratisation* (Singapore: Institute of Southeast Asian Studies, 2003). Some of the discussion in Chapter 8 evolved from Edward Aspinall and Harold Crouch, *The Aceh Peace Process: Why It Failed* (Washington: East-West Center, 2003). Several International Crisis Group reports analysed matters that foreshadowed parts of several chapters, including "Indonesia's Crisis: Chronic but not Acute", ICG Report, 31 May 2000; "Indonesia: Keeping the Military Under Control", Asia Report No. 9, 5 September 2000; "Indonesia: Impunity Versus Accountability for Gross Human Rights Violations", Asia Report No. 12, 2 February 2001; "Indonesia: The Search for Peace in Maluku", Asia Report No. 31, 8 February 2002; and "Indonesia Backgrounder: A Guide to the 2004 Elections", Asia Report No. 71, 18 December 2003.

Banda Aceh
April 2009

1

INTRODUCTION

Indonesia was in a parlous condition in 1998. Only a few years earlier, in the mid-1990s, it had often been portrayed as one of the Third World's success stories.[1] President Soeharto's military-backed New Order was certainly authoritarian but it had underwritten political stability for almost three decades since the bloody upheaval surrounding the collapse of President Soekarno's Guided Democracy in 1965–66. Over the next three decades, that political stability had provided the foundation for average annual economic growth of 7 per cent that had raised per capita income to over US$1,000 and transformed Indonesia by the mid-1990s into a "near-NIC" on the brink of achieving Newly Industrializing Country (NIC) status.[2] But the Asian Monetary Crisis — spreading from Thailand in July 1997 — brought rapid growth to a sudden halt.[3] Tied to a maze of patronage networks, the Soeharto regime had been much less able than other regional governments to take the firm measures necessary to avert the crisis or at least mitigate its consequences. Indonesia's economy was in disarray with a virtual halt to investment and sharply rising unemployment — aggravated fortuitously by the impact on agriculture of drought caused by El Nino climatic conditions. As beggars re-appeared in large numbers on the streets of Jakarta and other cities, crime rates rose and looting became commonplace, while anti-Chinese rioting spread through Java and on other islands. Finally, massive student demonstrations triggered two days of anti-Chinese rioting in Jakarta in May 1998 that forced the resignation of President Soeharto and marked the end of his New Order.

The timing of the collapse of Indonesia's authoritarian regime was clearly not a direct result of domestic social and political change driven by economic growth but rather the opposite — the sudden interruption and indeed reversal of that growth in response to unexpected external factors. The Indonesian case, however, did not mean that the level of economic development is unimportant for understanding the fall of an authoritarian regime and transformation in the direction of democratization. As argued by Rueschmeyer, Stephens and Stephens, "An agrarian society before or in the incipient stages of penetration by commercial market relations and industrialization is unlikely to gain or sustain a democratic form of government." On the other hand, they note the findings of cross-national statistical comparisons that record "a positive, though not perfect, correlation between capitalist development and democracy."[4] In fact, Indonesian society had already been substantially transformed since the mid-1960s by rapid economic growth under the New Order which resulted in urbanization, the growth of industry, the spread of education and the expansion of the middle class. But, in the judgement of many observers before 1998, the middle class was still too small and the overwhelmingly Chinese business class too dependent on indigenous bureaucratic and military patrons to provide a solid foundation for democratization, while it was feared that the loosening of authoritarian restraints on inter-communal tensions could open the way to violent conflict in a population still divided along ethnic, regional, religious and class lines.[5] In mid-1997, no observer, whether Indonesian or foreign, anticipated that President Soeharto's New Order had already entered its final year. The most common expectation was that President Soeharto would eventually be succeeded by another general heading a regime not very different to the New Order.

Unexpected political transitions are, as O'Donnell and Schmitter point out, characterized by "extraordinary uncertainties" in circumstances where there are "insufficient structural and behavioural parameters to guide and predict the outcome" and "assumptions about the relative stability and predictability of social, economic, and institutional parameters ... seem patently inadequate". These authors therefore turn to political concepts to explain political phenomena. They famously stated that "there is no transition whose beginning is not the consequence — direct or indirect — of important divisions within the authoritarian regime itself, principally along the fluctuating cleavage between hard-liners and soft-liners." Such rivalries continue after the fall of the regime with the result that the transition toward democracy often progresses through a series of negotiated "pacts" in which pro-democracy forces increase their influence but at the same time limit the threat to the basic interests of members of the old regime. Too rapid democratization, which threatens established interests, can endanger the transition process. They note that "an active, militant, and highly mobilized popular upsurge may be an efficacious instrument for bringing down a dictatorship but may make subsequent democratic consolidation difficult and under some circumstances may provide an important motive for regression to an even more brutal form of authoritarian rule." But they also acknowledge that "conditions that are conducive in the short run to an orderly and continuous democratic transition, such as the drafting of interim pacts, may subsequently impede democratic consolidation if their restrictive rules and guarantees produce substantive disenchantment and procedural deadlock". For them, "Political democracy, then, usually emerges from a nonlinear, highly uncertain, and imminently reversible process."[6]

Indonesia's political transition in the aftermath of the fall of Soeharto was clouded by the uncertainty envisaged by O'Donnell and Schmitter as remnants of the New Order regime clung to power in the face of multiple challenges. The authoritarian regime had not been brought down by a committed democratic elite that had mobilized mass support against the government. Certainly, students with the encouragement of part of the educated middle class, had been holding huge demonstrations calling for "democracy" and "reform", but there was no cohesive organized opposition movement waiting in the wings to take over power.[7] The government had instead been confronted by deep popular anger at the regime's failure to ameliorate the social impact of the economic crisis while the military had become reluctant to take the risks of defending what increasingly seemed to be a doomed regime. By the time the regime fell, political protests and disorders in the main cities and the provinces had spread beyond the capacity of the government to repress by conventional authoritarian means. In circumstances where the new government, headed by Soeharto's civilian vice president and protégé, B.J. Habibie, was composed mainly of carry-overs from the authoritarian regime, lacked legitimacy and was internally divided and uncertain of its authority over the military, the new president turned to "democratization" as a more promising alternative.

The transition from authoritarianism toward democratization in Indonesia did not fit comfortably with the patterns commonly proposed by political scientists. In his book on *The Third Wave*, Huntington describes three patterns: transformation, replacement, and transplacement. In "transformation", the authoritarian government itself initiates the reforms that lead to democratization; "replacement" refers to the violent overthrow of the authoritarian regime; in "transplacement" there is a balance between those supporting and opposing democratization with the result that the transition can only proceed through negotiations and compromise. The Indonesian transition had elements of all three.[8] By the 1990s, leading members of the

Soeharto regime, including the president himself, were already giving attention
to the need to civilianize and liberalize the regime and some limited reforms
had been implemented before the crisis hit in mid-1997 but these concessions
fell far short of real "transformation". As in the "replacement" scenario, the
regime fell in response to mass rioting and the threat of further breakdown
of public order, but in the Indonesian case it was only the president and
some of his closest supporters who were replaced while much of the new
government consisted of personnel who had served in similar roles under
Soeharto. In Indonesia, the negotiations and compromises that characterize
"transplacement" did not bring about the change in government but followed
it as powerful survivors of the old regime engaged with new political forces
in political struggles to shape the contours of the new regime. The crucial
condition driving these elite negotiations was the precipitous economic decline
and the consequent mass violence in May 1998 which engendered fears
that renewed violence would exacerbate the economic collapse and political
upheaval. Reform was therefore seen as imperative for elite survival and, in
the view of many, perhaps also for national survival.

The sudden departure of the old president had triggered a scramble
between factions and groups to secure positions in whatever regime was to
emerge in the New Order's wake. A succession of short-lived governments
headed by presidents Habibie, Abdurrahman Wahid and Megawati
Soekarnoputri followed. Deficient in legitimacy and internal cohesion, they
proved unable to guarantee public order and security in many parts of the
country, let alone restore conditions that would encourage a renewal of rapid
economic growth. Although forced to step back from its previously pre-
eminent political role, the deeply entrenched military was able to obstruct
the full imposition of civilian control but was too divided and demoralized
to perform effectively its responsibility to uphold order. In the absence of
strong and legitimate government, the country appeared to be moving toward
national disintegration. The security forces seemed unable to prevent rioting
and looting while criminal gangs (*preman*) operated unhindered by, or in
tandem with, local government in many districts.[9] The fall of Soeharto also
opened the way to the re-invigoration of separatist movements in East Timor,
Aceh and Papua — and East Timor's eventual exit from the Republic after an
internationally endorsed referendum in 1999. Fighting between Muslims and
Christians led to thousands of casualties and much destruction in Maluku
and Central Sulawesi. In West and Central Kalimantan indigenous Dayaks
killed hundreds of migrant Madurese and forced tens of thousands to flee their
homes. In other regions violence between members of ethnic and religious
communities was less devastating but still added to the numbers killed or

maimed. Throughout Indonesia more than a million refugees were unable to return to their homes. At the beginning of the twenty-first century, Indonesia was looking less like a near-NIC than a near-failed state.

Indonesia, however, never descended to the depths of full state failure. The concept of the "failed state" had been applied to several countries in Africa in the 1990s where government barely existed and civil conflict became ubiquitous.[10] After the Bali bombing in 2002 following the attacks on the United States in September 2001, Indonesia was regarded by some as a near-failed state and often identified in the international press as a potential base for Al Qaeda.[11] But central government authority in Indonesia was in fact much stronger than in countries such as Afghanistan or Somalia where effective rule by local warlords over vast tracts of territory was unchallenged. This is not to deny that several regions in Indonesia had acquired some of the characteristics of failed states. In these regions government authority did in fact break down and local conflicts took on the character of civil war. If regions like Maluku, Poso, Aceh, Papua and parts of Kalimantan had existed as independent countries, they may have fitted the description of failed states, but they were small territories within a far larger state which maintained national institutions throughout its territory even when their authority was sometimes quite tenuous.

A more appropriate framework was that of the "weak state" — the concept proposed by Joel Migdal — in which the institutions of government exist but are unable to impose their will on powerful vested interests in a "strong society".[12] Migdal's explanation of state weakness, however, did not fully fit the Indonesian case. The problem in Indonesia under Soeharto was not so much that a reform-minded state lacked the authority to impose its will on powerful vested interests in society as that the state itself had been penetrated by those vested interests.[13] Segments of the state were "captured" by a disparate range of interests, some of which had their origins in business and others in the state itself, including the bureaucracy and the military.[14] As long as the New Order lasted, these competing segments were held together through their personal and institutional links to President Soeharto and his subordinates but his fall opened the way to increasing fragmentation. In place of the relatively unified New Order patronage network, the post-authoritarian governments consisted of rival parties and bureaucratic factions that all fostered their own patronage networks.

Despite internal rivalries among his supporters, Soeharto's authority under the New Order had been such that he was able to foster the formation of a more-or-less cohesive political, social and economic elite during the three decades of his rule and prevent the emergence of serious challengers from within the regime. But the elite's relative cohesion depended on the overriding presence of Soeharto himself and was shown to be brittle when its patron was deposed, even though many of its members survived the "transition" and continued to play major roles in key institutions of the state and associated commercial empires. Richard Robison and Vedi Hadiz argued that "the crisis failed to sweep away the very interests and forces incubated within the Soeharto regime, which underpinned and defined it. These survived to re-establish the economic and political power relationships within new institutional arrangements." Thus, what took place was "the reorganization of the power relations incubated within the Soeharto regime, rather than their fundamental transformation". The difference after 1998, according to Robison and Hadiz, was only that "Authority over the allocation of resources, contracts and monopolies had been shifted from a highly centralized system of state power to a more diffuse and chaotic environment of political parties, parliaments and provincial governments."[15]

This book aims to examine how Indonesia pulled back from the precipice in the years after 1998. How could political reforms be implemented in such unpromising circumstances? Initial political reform was not a case of a carefully planned overhaul of state institutions but primarily a response to the chaotic circumstances of 1998. In the face of huge popular protests, President Habibie felt compelled to embark on the dismantling of the New Order authoritarian regime in which he had long played a prominent role. Restrictions on the press and other freedoms were lifted, new political parties were formed and in 1999 Indonesia's first free general election since the 1950s was held. Members of the New Order political elite, however, continued to occupy key positions in the regime. Soeharto and a few of his cronies were forced out but many ministers, bureaucrats and military officers retained their positions while all the provincial governors owed their appointments to the fallen president. Following Habibie's failure to win re-election in late 1999, the short-lived presidencies of Abdurrahman Wahid and Megawati Soekarnoputri saw a broadening but not replacement of the political elite. The many New Order survivors who retained their positions were forced to make room for new entrants, including earlier critics of the Soeharto regime. Successive post-authoritarian cabinets continued to be made up of uneasy multi-party coalitions, including many ministers who had quite comfortably served in, and benefited from, the New Order government. Meanwhile the military remained under the leadership of officers who had loyally served Soeharto in the past.

In contrast to the view that political reform requires strong political leadership with a unified vision and determination to resist pressures from self-serving sectoral interests, the early post-authoritarian Indonesian state not only lacked capacity to impose policies on a recalcitrant society but was even more than its predecessor thoroughly penetrated by vested interests originating from both outside and within the state itself. How could reform be fostered in, to repeat Robison and Hadiz's characterization, this "diffuse and chaotic environment of political parties, parliaments and provincial governments" where old interests remained entrenched and new interests were emerging? Yet, during the next decade political reform in Indonesia did in fact lead to at least a partial transformation of some key aspects of the political system which, if by no means total, was in many ways quite fundamental and certainly made it very different to the New Order system. This study, therefore, questions whether the "reorganization of power relations" within the old elite necessarily prevented movement toward a more "fundamental transformation". While identifying areas of significant reform, however, it also examines obstacles to, and limitations on, the reform process which sometimes resulted in reform hardly taking place at all.

A central concern of this study is to show how significant reforms were adopted by institutions that were largely dominated by self-interested and often corrupt political forces that in many cases had been closely tied to the Soeharto regime. Grindle and Thomas, in their book on reform in developing countries, distinguish between what they call "crisis-ridden" reforms and those conducted in a "politics-as-usual" environment. They point out that "many reforms emerge and are considered" in circumstances where "policy elites believe that a crisis exists and that they must "do something" about the situation or they will face grave consequences". In crisis-ridden or crisis-driven reform, "concern about national welfare, political stability, and broad coalitions of political support tends to dominate their deliberations". On the other hand, in politics-as-usual reform, "change is considered desirable but the consequences of not acting are not considered threatening to the decision makers or the regime". Thus in politics-as-usual reforms, "concern about bureaucratic and narrow clientelistic relationships is much more apparent".[16]

In the Indonesian cases described and analysed in this book, the reform process was launched in crisis-ridden circumstances. The crisis was so severe that most of the surviving members of the New Order elite were persuaded that in order to save themselves they would have to accept substantial reforms, even when such reforms harmed the immediate interests of that elite itself. The initial reforms were adopted by government leaders, members of legislatures and senior military officers who were convinced that drastic reform offered the only way to avoid the deepening of the crisis. Crisis-ridden reforms, therefore, involved drastic changes of direction. The

New Order's managed electoral facade was abandoned and replaced by a highly competitive system conducted in a free and open atmosphere. An extraordinarily centralized system of regional government was replaced by one that was extraordinarily decentralized. A military institution that was deeply involved in the day-to-day political process stepped back from many of its political functions. As the crisis passed, however, the reform process moved into politics-as-usual mode in which progress was more gradual and sometimes seemed to stop altogether. The earlier sense of urgency was lost as reform measures were taken to the democratically elected legislature where rival political parties manoeuvred to gain advantage and politicians were often tainted by "money politics". Nevertheless, amidst the compromises needed to adopt legislation, the outcomes often — but not always — continued to advance the reform process.

This book consists of a series of case studies that examine reform in different fields. It will describe the pressures toward reform that arose in the wake of the fall of the Soeharto regime and will trace the ways in which surviving New Order elites reacted to demands that threatened to undermine the dominance they had enjoyed during the Soeharto years. It will also discuss how new, or revived, political forces used new circumstances to pursue the interests that they represented. Attention will also be given to "normal" political struggles over particular aspects of the reform programme after the original crisis had passed. Reform did not proceed evenly and simultaneously in all fields but varied according to the nature of proposed reforms and the relative strengths of the interests involved in particular struggles.

This book does not aim to present a comprehensive coverage of all the major areas of political reform but analyses cases that show how the reform process progressed or was delayed or blocked in particular areas. The most drastic reforms in the initial "crisis-ridden" stage involved the formal political structure: the electoral system and centre-regional relations. Under the New Order, Soeharto's electoral system had guaranteed overwhelming majorities for the government party, Golkar, in every general election, while highly centralized regional administration enabled Soeharto to ensure the appointment of loyalists as heads of all provincial and district governments. Faced with a continuing threat of renewed disorder, Habibie's government of New Order holdovers was persuaded that it had little choice but to adopt electoral provisions that would inevitably undermine Golkar's own prospects in the coming elections. No less drastic was the decentralization programme, again introduced by the Habibie government and adopted by the Golkar-dominated parliament in 1999 before its composition was changed as a result of the 1999 election. Amidst growing concerns that the nation was approaching the brink of disintegration, Golkar, together with its military parliamentary allies, now abandoned the extraordinarily centralized system that they had vigorously upheld throughout the New Order era and adopted one of the developing world's most decentralized systems.

In both these cases, however, the willingness of President Habibie and the Golkar-dominated parliament to abandon New Order practices that they had previously upheld was reinforced by self-interested political calculations. As we shall see in Chapters 3 and 4, the Golkar-dominated government was making the best it could of a bad situation to salvage at least some of its influence and power. Although the new election laws were basically damaging to its electoral prospects, it was still able to gain small but significant concessions in its own interest while it appreciated that its long-established nation-wide political machinery would allow it, at least in the short term, to retain a strong position in decentralized regional government.

Another crucial area of reform involved the military which had formed the backbone of the New Order regime but was now unable to insulate itself from the pressures arising from the political crisis. President Habibie, who had been considered a rival by the military leadership during the latter years of the New Order, had little influence in the armed forces so he reached an understanding with the military leaders to allow them to manage their own reform. Fearing that resort to the standard repression of the New Order would only make it more difficult to restore and maintain order, reform-minded generals took the initiative to take substantial steps to reduce their direct political involvement. As the worst of the crisis passed, however, crisis-ridden pressures became less compelling. In contrast to reform of political institutions where the cause of reform was taken up by political parties seeking to expand their own influence, the military mainstream lacked incentives to push for deeper reform after the initial pre-emptive measures. Military reform thus stopped short of the structural overhaul that would have undermined the military's capacity to exercise informal political influence and protect its substantial economic interests. Crisis-ridden reform, therefore, resulted in only partial reform of the military. Post-crisis reform would have to be negotiated both within the military itself and between the military and civilian political forces.

A fourth major institution, the judiciary, escaped much of the brunt of the direct pressure felt in the three areas already discussed. It was almost universally believed by the public that the courts were riddled with bribery but popular protest tended to focus on particular cases of corruption, involving President Soeharto and members of his regime. While blatant failures of the judicial system to uphold justice in particular cases caused public dismay and outrage, the judiciary as such did not become the target of mobs in the streets demanding reform. In contrast to leaders of the legislature and the military who, if not necessarily deeply committed to far-reaching reform, at least understood the need for pre-emptive measures, the courts were barely touched by such awareness. Only a handful of judges identified themselves with the reform movement and the "court mafia" continued to work as usual. As the crisis evolved into politics as usual, political parties in parliament, themselves often deeply involved in "money politics" and vulnerable to corruption allegations, showed little sense of urgency in considering anti-corruption legislation. Judicial reform had to wait for reform measures to be negotiated in politics-as-usual circumstances.

The dynamics of politics-as-usual reform is very different to that of crisis-ridden reform. Re-active reform in response to the compulsion to cope with an immediate crisis soon loses its driving force when it succeeds in averting the feared disaster. The measures taken to avert the disaster, however, can sometimes damage — perhaps fatally — the institutions of the old regime and thus propel a process of further reform. After the way had been opened to free elections, regional autonomy and military re-organization, the prospects of reversing the reform process had become at least very difficult and probably impossible. The barriers to further reform had been breached during the phase of crisis-ridden reform but the pressures to continue were weaker and more varied. Thus there was no certainty that reform would move on to a higher level. At this stage further reform could no longer be driven primarily by fear of looming disaster. As politics becomes more "normalized", mass demonstrations and riots give way to competitive elections, routine negotiations between rival groups and the ordinary mustering of political support for specific measures. The sites of further reform shift to struggles in the national parliament and between bureaucratic groups within state institutions.

What drives politics-as-usual reform? According to the textbook version of democracy, citizens express their political preferences in free elections. In order to retain public support, governments are forced to implement the reforms that the people want or are replaced by new leaders who promise to serve the public interest. Ideally, constitutional and electoral reform should facilitate the formation of governments enjoying broad popular support and expecting to serve a full term in office until the next election. Such a government is likely to consist of either a single party or a more-or-less permanent coalition of like-minded parties which commands majority support in the legislature and is therefore able to ensure that the core of its legislative programme is adopted.

In Indonesia, however, as in many other complex plural societies, the collapse of the old authoritarian regime allowed the emergence of numerous new parties and organizations that had previously been suppressed. Post-authoritarian elections produced parliaments in which a wide range of parties were represented and no single party was even close to dominating the parliament. Governments took the form of uneasy coalitions between rival political forces largely reflecting the make-up of the legislature and lacking a common vision and unity of purpose. Legislation often did not follow a coherent "grand plan" submitted by the government but had a patchwork quality reflecting compromises after long negotiations in which "money politics" was normally important.

How was it possible for significant reforms to be adopted by institutions that were largely dominated by politicians, bureaucrats and military officers, many of whom had resisted reform in the past and were now concerned primarily with securing their own access to new post-authoritarian patronage networks? How was it possible that negotiations involving such groups could eventually arrive at outcomes that, at least to some extent, could reasonably qualify as "reform"? Post-crisis reform did not follow a standard "democratic template" in which freely elected legislators responded to popular pressures and bureaucrats implemented the principles of "good governance" in pursuit of a perception of the long-term "national interest". Rather it was the product of protracted bargaining between largely self-serving parties, both old and new. Committed reformers also contributed proposals but lacked the political power to implement them. Actual reform measures were sometimes adopted grudgingly by beneficiaries of the status quo who anticipated that their own positions might eventually be threatened without at least a semblance of reform. Other reforms were adopted with the support of parties or groups which anticipated concrete benefits from their implementation. The driving force was often the rivalry between political parties and bureaucratic factions seeking relative advantage. Although reformist proposals were often formulated initially by groups or individuals motivated at least in part by idealistic aspirations, their eventual adoption was only possible because they served the interests of key political players in the government and parliament as well as other institutions.

The progress of reform after the initial crisis will also be traced in this study. The most outstanding political reform was the extensive amendment of the constitution that in many respects changed its basic nature after three years of negotiations between parties represented in the People's Consultative Assembly. Similarly, new electoral legislation was adopted as a result of compromises between parties which were not strong enough to impose their own wishes on the parliament but had enough influence to safeguard some of their interests. In the case of centre-region relations, hard bargaining produced new laws on regional autonomy which in some respects restored part of the authority of the central government that it had lost in the earlier crisis-ridden legislation but also, by introducing direct elections of regional heads of government, had a powerful decentralizing impact. New laws were also adopted that formally restricted the military's political role although they failed to deal with the basic structural conditions that undergirded the military's remaining political influence. And, in the sphere of the judiciary, new anti-corruption laws led to the establishment of special courts to hear corruption cases which, under the Yudhoyono presidency, ensnared prominent second-level public officials although corruption remained deeply entrenched in the regular courts.

In contrast to these nation-wide arenas, regional challenges of separatism in East Timor, Papua and Aceh and communal conflict in Maluku and Central Sulawesi were somewhat different. Apart from the case of East Timor which had become an international issue, the government's response in these cases, was not driven primarily by the national crisis but by a series of particular crises occurring in different places and at different times. Although conflicts in these regions undoubtedly disrupted local society, they did not constitute an immediate threat to the life of the nation in the way that the economic crisis, political upheaval and the prospect of national disintegration had in 1997–99. After all, the combined population of the affected regions amounted to no more than about 5 per cent of the total population and there was no coordination between them. What were acute crises in those regions were merely chronic from the perspective of the centre.

In this study the cases of Maluku and Aceh are examined in some detail. The local war between religious communities in Maluku was by far the most severe and long-lasting of Indonesia's post-authoritarian communal conflicts while, after the departure of East Timor, Aceh's separatist movement was the most threatening to national unity. Of the regional crises, the Maluku and Aceh conflicts also attracted the most attention from Jakarta. In Aceh the national military had been directly involved from the beginning. In both fundamental differences between warring forces could not be overcome through local negotiations alone but ultimately required new approaches on the part of the central government. Moreover, in Aceh's case, the central government's peace-making efforts received crucial international support. The central government's intervention in both cases was not crisis-ridden from a national perspective, despite the devastating local crises experienced in the two regions, but occurred in a politics-as-usual context.

As this study will show, political reforms adopted by the post-Soeharto governments left many problems unresolved but could not be dismissed as merely cosmetic. Habibie's early liberalizing and democratizing reforms — the holding of genuinely competitive elections, the freeing of the press and other media, the release of political prisoners, regional autonomy, East Timor's independence — made real differences. The constitutional reforms adopted by the MPR during Megawati's presidency also resulted in substantial changes as shown in the 2004 presidential election. Direct elections of provincial governors and district heads, based on the revised law on regional government adopted at the end of Megawati's tenure and implemented by Yudhoyono significantly changed the nature of local politics. But this study also shows that reform in other areas was less far-reaching. In the case of military reform, the early measures, initiated by the military itself, successfully pulled the military out of formal politics but it retained substantial political influence which enabled it to resist demands for further reform. Judicial reform made even less progress until the Yudhoyono presidency when a more serious anti-corruption campaign was launched. To use Grindle and Thomas's concepts again, early crisis-ridden reform under Habibie drastically changed the contours of Indonesian politics while later politics-as-usual reforms met with more obstacles, proceeded more slowly and involved more compromise.

By 2004, when the first direct presidential election was held following the adoption of significant constitutional reforms, the period of chaotic post-authoritarian politics seemed to have run its course. In terms of democratization theory, 2004 could be seen as marking the end of the democratic transition and further movement toward democratic consolidation. To use a phrase much used by American political scientists, democracy can be considered as "consolidated" when it is accepted by all significant political forces as "the only game in town".[17] The results of democratic elections are accepted by all major parties, no credible group seeks to overthrow the democratic order and the legitimacy of the regime is broadly recognized in the society. Thus a consolidated democracy can be expected to endure. Indonesians who voted in the 2004 election could reasonably expect that they would be voting again in 2009. Aspinall uses the term "normalization" to describe post-2004 politics.[18] Most theorists, however, require several elections before passing firm judgement that democracy has been truly consolidated.[19]

Democratic "consolidation" or "normalization", however, does not mean that "good governance" is assured and that there is no scope for further political reform. As O'Donnell, writing about Latin America, reminds us, it is often not only the formal institutions of democracy that are consolidated but also informal rules and practices that in turn can subvert democratic principles.[20]

This study will note many examples of pervasive money politics in government and both national and regional legislatures; the continuing involvement of the military in its own fund-raising; and the widespread influence of the "court mafia".[21] Despite these "distortions", the study suggests that democratic reform has made government much more responsive to popular aspirations compared to the previous authoritarian regime.

Notes

1. World Bank (1993).
2. GNP per capita reached US$1,135 in 1996. Habibie (2006), p. 220. For an overview of economic growth under the New Order, see Hal Hill (2000).
3. On the Asian Monetary Crisis, see McLeod (1998).
4. Rueschemeyer, Stephens and Stephens (1992), pp. 2, 4.
5. The author was among the pessimists at that time, see for example Crouch (1994). But he was not alone, see for example Liddle (1996).
6. O'Donnell and Schmitter (1986), pp. 3–4, 19, 38–39, 65–66, 70.
7. Aspinall (2005*a*), ch. 1.
8. Huntington (1991), ch. 3. As Huntington himself acknowledges, "historical cases of regime change did not necessarily fit neatly into theoretical categories." Huntington (1991), p. 114.
9. Lindsey (2001); Nordholt and van Klinken (2007).
10. Zartman (1995). Huntington had earlier used the term "praetorianism" to describe what were later called failed states. Huntington (1968), ch. 4.
11. Schuman (2002).
12. Migdal (1988).
13. Crouch (1998).
14. Weber's term, "patrimonialism", has been used to describe this situation. Crouch (1979).
15. Robison and Hadiz (2004), pp. 10, 215, 253. Some observers might of course conclude that this amounted to a "fundamental transformation".
16. Grindle and Thomas (1991), pp. 6, 14.
17. Linz and Stepan (1997), p. 15.
18. Aspinall (2005*b*), p. 154.
19. The unexpected military coup in Thailand in 2006 provides a warning.
20. O'Donnell (1997).
21. It will also note that "money politics" can sometimes be utilized for beneficial purposes, most notably in resolving the Maluku and Aceh conflicts.

2

THE FALL OF THE NEW ORDER AND THE *REFORMASI* GOVERNMENTS

This chapter will provide an overview of national-level political developments from the chaotic conditions that accompanied the fall of President Soeharto to the attainment of a degree of normality under President Susilo Bambang Yudhoyono. Reform was launched after President Habibie had suddenly been catapulted into the presidency by the events of May 1998. Habibie had no reputation as a reformer but he quickly understood that the crisis demanded drastic reforms. His successors, Abdurrahman Wahid and Megawati Soekarnoputri, had been part of the growing moderate opposition to Soeharto but neither was able to form strong coherent governments committed to continuing reform. The "crisis-ridden" reforms forced on Habibie lost momentum after the worst of the crisis had passed. Facing fragmented legislatures — the DPR and MPR — formed after the free 1999 elections, Abdurrahman and Megawati were more concerned with maintaining legislative support than embarking on radical reform. Nevertheless, although Abdurrahman's failure to maintain that support eventually led to his dismissal, significant political reforms were adopted by the DPR and the constitution was overhauled by the MPR during Megawati's tenure. By the time Yudhoyono won the presidency in 2004, the authoritarian political structures of the New Order had been transformed into institutions that met international standards of formal democracy. But, while legislative institutions had been able to reform themselves, major obstacles stood in the way of further reform of the military and the judiciary. Although dubbed the *Reformasi* era, the achievements of the post-Soeharto governments were quite mixed.

THE NEW ORDER AND THE FALL OF SOEHARTO

When President Soeharto was forced from power in May 1998, he had ruled over one of the world's most durable authoritarian regimes for more than three decades. Backed by the military, Soeharto's New Order combined repression with co-optation to prevent the rise of organized political challenges. Blessed by an abundance of natural resources, particularly oil, the Indonesian economy had grown steadily until 1997. By the 1990s it was no longer the "basket case" that it had been in the mid-1960s but moving towards "newly-industrializing-country" status.[1] Indonesian society had been transformed with the emergence of an educated middle class in an increasingly urbanized, although still predominantly non-urban, population. The New Order's political structures, however, had been shaped in the late 1960s and early 1970s and had not kept pace with the rapid economic and social change.

The military provided the backbone of the New Order regime. General Soeharto, the then commander of the army, had forced President Soekarno out of office in a step-by-step military takeover that had begun in response to the assassination of six senior generals in October 1965 and ended with the election by acclamation of Soeharto as president in March 1968.[2] The foundation for the military-dominated regime had been laid by the massacre of as many as half a million supporters of the Communist Party (PKI: *Partai Komunis Indonesia*), the military's main rival before 1965. Military officers dominated both the central and regional administration under the new regime. Officers were appointed to key cabinet posts and as senior bureaucrats in the central government, the majority of the provincial governors and district heads were drawn from the armed forces, and military officers were appointed as members of legislatures at all levels of government. Civilians, however, were not excluded, especially technocrats and bureaucrats who played major roles in formulating the economic policies that were necessary to attract foreign investment and the support of the governments of Western countries and Japan.

Soeharto made a point of adhering to formal constitutional processes while systematically violating their spirit. Legislative elections were held at five-yearly intervals throughout the New Order period but they were always conducted in circumstances that ensured overwhelming victories for the military-created Golkar that served as the government's electoral vehicle. Following each election, the partly elected People's Consultative Assembly

(MPR: *Majelis Permusyawaratan Rakyat*) was convened and invariably re-elected Soeharto unanimously as president. The scope for the non-Golkar political parties to mobilize popular support was severely restricted, their number soon reduced to two through forced mergers, and the amenability of their leaderships guaranteed by the operations of military intelligence and their incorporation into Soeharto's patronage network. Other organizations were controlled by corporatist means through government-endorsed bodies to "represent" business, labour, various professions, veterans, women, youth and so on. Meanwhile the press and other media were kept under tight control and intimidated by occasional banning.[3]

Ultimately, however, the government retained the option of resorting to outright repression. Dissidents of all sorts — student demonstrators, Muslim radicals, trade unionists, dispossessed peasants, journalists and even alienated retired generals — were sometimes jailed while others faced intimidation and other sanctions. Following the initial massacre, tens of thousands of supporters of the PKI were detained without trial well into the 1970s, while those convicted received long sentences or were executed. Following the elimination of the PKI, the focus of repression turned to Muslim groups with potential organizational capacity to challenge the regime. Throughout the New Order period, direct military repression was especially severe in regions where separatist sentiments were strong such as Aceh and Irian Jaya (later called Papua), and East Timor which was invaded by the Indonesian army in 1975.

Patronage distribution was the glue that held the system together. A pyramid of patronage extended from the presidential palace in Jakarta to the villages throughout the country. The entire bureaucracy was permeated with officially encouraged corruption.[4] The formal remuneration of both government officials and military officers fell far short of what was needed to maintain an adequate lifestyle, let alone the luxury enjoyed by senior officials and officers who were given a free hand to find additional sources of income for themselves. At the highest levels, the most common means was for officials and officers, who were almost always indigenous Indonesians, to make arrangements with Indonesian-Chinese businesspeople where Chinese enterprises shared profits in exchange for licences, special privileges and protection when illegal activity was involved. As the regime consolidated, the post-1973 oil boom and the rising inflow of foreign investment provided vastly expanded opportunities for rent-seeking officials.[5]

Rapid economic growth transformed society. The chief beneficiaries of the first decade of the New Order had been military officers and their Chinese partners but by the 1980s a rent-seeking commercial class was expanding.[6]

Many were the sons (and daughters) of military officers and bureaucrats who had obtained higher education but were not normally military officers or bureaucrats themselves. Like the previous generation, they too were integrated into the patronage network and used their political influence on behalf of their Chinese and foreign partners. The prime example was that of the Soeharto children, none of whom joined the military but all of whom were involved in commercial empires that relied on special favours from the state.[7] But the benefits of economic growth spread far beyond the children of the established elite. Expanding educational opportunities had produced a broad educated middle class that aspired less to appointments in the bureaucracy than employment in the booming private sector, especially foreign enterprises. Expanding tertiary education, however, also produced dissidents and student demonstrators who expressed the growing resentment felt more broadly within much of the middle class against the corruption and repression of the regime.

By the 1990s, Soeharto, who turned seventy in 1991, was in full control and seemed destined eventually to die in office. Nevertheless, there were signs of potential, although not necessarily unmanageable, trouble ahead. From the early 1980s, leadership of the military had been passing from Soeharto's generation of military officers who had fought in the revolution against Dutch colonialism in the late 1940s to a new generation of academy-trained officers whose perspectives were gradually becoming more distant from those of the now retired officers who occupied key government positions. Increasingly Soeharto appointed civilians — from the Golkar party and the bureaucracy — as cabinet ministers, provincial governors and district heads, and the share of patronage flowing to civilians increased at the expense of the military. Most alarming from the point of view of the military mainstream which had always been suspicious of political Islam, Soeharto endorsed in 1990 the formation of a new Islamic organization, the Indonesian Muslim Intellectuals' Association (ICMI: *Ikatan Cendekiawan Muslim Se-Indonesia*), which served to channel the aspirations of the Muslim sectors of the new middle class and was seen as a long-term rival to the military.[8] The civilian chairman of ICMI, Dr B.J. Habibie, was a particular focus of military antagonism not only because of his mobilization of the Muslim community, but also his entry into the lucrative military hardware sector which had previously been monopolized by the military itself.[9] At the same time, the president promoted officers with Islamic backgrounds to high positions within the military to balance the previous dominance of the so-called "nationalist" officers.[10]

In this context, Soeharto introduced his "openness" policy that permitted wider public debate in the parliament and the press. "Openness", possibly intended to divide the political elite and dissipate potential long-term challenges, eventually exacerbated elite rivalries to the point where the coherence of the regime was being undermined. The end of "openness" was marked by a crackdown on the press in 1994 and heavy-handed intervention in 1996 to remove Megawati, the daughter of the president whom Soeharto deposed in the mid-1960s, from the leadership of the Indonesian Democracy Party (PDI: *Partai Demokrasi Indonesia*). There was no possibility that the PDI could have outpolled Golkar in the tightly managed general election but a strong vote would have badly damaged the regime's, and Soeharto's personal legitimacy. Instead, the clamp-down on the PDI allowed Golkar to win almost 75 per cent of the votes in the 1997 election, its best result ever.

In mid-1997 Soeharto's position seemed unassailable. The economy was booming, the military was under control, the aspirations of the Muslim community had been assuaged and Golkar had won yet another overwhelming electoral victory. Yet, only a year after the May 1997 election, Soeharto was forced to resign and the New Order had come to an end. In July 1997, the collapse of the Thai baht triggered the "Asian Financial Crisis" which devastated not only the Indonesian economy but also those of Malaysia, South Korea and to a lesser extent the Philippines.[11] Following financial deregulation in the early 1990s, Indonesian companies increasingly looked to foreign loans rather than more expensive rupiah debt with the result that private offshore borrowing rose rapidly. Much of this debt, however, was used to finance mega projects oriented to the domestic market such as industrial and property investments, making borrowers very vulnerable to shifts in exchange rates. When the Thai baht suddenly collapsed, the rupiah soon followed suit. The exchange rate of the rupiah to the U.S. dollar had been Rp 2,400 in mid-1997 but at one point in January 1998 reached 17,000. The rate of economic growth dived from a positive 8 per cent in 1996 to a negative 14 per cent in 1998. Many of Indonesia's largest companies, which had borrowed heavily in foreign currencies, faced bankruptcy while domestic banks were on the point of collapse and unemployment was rising sharply. In September 1997 Indonesia was forced to accept International Monetary Fund (IMF) oversight as part of a rescue package. Many of the conditions imposed by the IMF hit Soeharto's patronage network and thus undermined the foundations of his regime.[12] Despite the economic disaster, however, the MPR convened on schedule in March 1998, unanimously re-elected Soeharto and endorsed his nominee for the vice presidency, B.J. Habibie.

The government seemed powerless to halt the economic decline, partly because of the president's unwillingness to take action that could hurt the

interests of the crony capitalists who constituted the core of the patronage
network, including members of his own family.[13] Rising popular resentment
was marked by the outbreak of anti-Chinese food riots in small towns
throughout Java and elsewhere while continuing student demonstrations
called on the president to resign. The crisis aggravated friction within the
military which was divided between supporters of the new commander-in-
chief, General Wiranto, identified with the nationalist "red-and-white" faction,
and the new commander of the army's strategic reserve (Kostrad: *Komando
Cadangan Strategis Angkatan Darat*), Soeharto's son-in-law Lt. Gen. Prabowo
Subianto, who was aligned with the "green" or Islamic faction. Although
still loyal to Soeharto, both groups were coming to the conclusion that the
looming transition would be smoother if Soeharto could be persuaded to resign
before the situation ran out of control. Meanwhile both were manoevering
to strengthen their positions for the coming struggle once Soeharto had
departed. The military and police seemed reluctant to take firm measures
against both student demonstrators and anti-Chinese rioters for fear that
such action would trigger greater conflagrations while it was widely believed
that some military elements were covertly encouraging both as a means of
applying increased pressure on the president. The government's decision in
early May 1998 to raise the prices of oil products in implementation of the
IMF's programme triggered a big riot in Medan (North Sumatra) and then,
following the police shooting of student demonstrators at Trisakti University
in Jakarta, a massive two-day anti-Chinese riot in the capital, a further riot
in Solo (Central Java), and relatively minor rioting in Surabaya (East Java),
Lampung and Palembang (both in southern Sumatra).[14] It was only when
the military leadership under Wiranto conveyed to Soeharto its inability
to stem the tide of protest that the president reluctantly agreed to resign
and, according to the constitutional procedure, was succeeded by his vice
president, Habibie.[15]

Soeharto's three decades of authoritarian rule had prevented the
development of a coherent mass-based opposition movement that could
challenge the government.[16] Instead, the regime fell unexpectedly as a result
of the economic collapse sparked by events outside Indonesia. The collapse
showed that Soeharto's patronage-based political system rested on shaky
foundations and the "miracle economy" was extremely vulnerable to an
external "shock". But there was no alternative government waiting in the
wings to take advantage of the opportunity provided by the new situation.
Instead, members of Soeharto's own inner circle of confidants indicated to
him that the time had come to go while no rearguard movement attempted
to save him. In the end Soeharto simply resigned and the presidency was

transferred peacefully and constitutionally to his nominated successor on 21 May 1998.

CHAOTIC TRANSITION UNDER HABIBIE

President Habibie was an unlikely reformer. Soeharto had selected Habibie as his vice president not because he saw in him a suitable successor but because he was convinced that Habibie, his longest-serving cabinet minister whom he treated almost like a son, was totally loyal and would never become a rallying point for opposition. Indeed, it was only after Soeharto had made a dismissive remark implying that Habibie might not be capable of coping as president that a deeply offended Habibie had at the last minute agreed to go along with the planned resignation of fourteen economics ministers to press for Soeharto's resignation.[17] The new president did not come to power with the backing of a consensus within the political elite and broad popular support but through his selection as vice president by a president who had every intention of serving a full five-year term. Habibie was an "accidental" president who lacked a strong political base outside the discredited New Order regime and had been thrust unexpectedly into a position for which he was inadequately prepared. It was widely anticipated at the time, therefore, that Habibie's tenure as president would be short.[18] He had inherited the New Order's political structure built on Soeharto's control of the patronage network and his authority over the military. The patronage network, however, had been ravaged by the economic crisis while much of the military mainstream remained hostile to Habibie. Moreover, as the founder of Indonesia's hugely expensive aeroplane industry, he was a leading advocate of the "big leap" into capital-intensive industrialization that was opposed by the orthodox economic technocrats and their international backers in the IMF and World Bank to whom Indonesia had been forced to turn as a result of the economic crisis.

The composition of the new government did not mark a sharp break with the discredited government that it had just replaced. Habibie's cabinet was drawn heavily from Golkar, almost half the ministers having served previously under Soeharto.[19] Although Habibie dropped a few "Soeharto diehards"[20] and gave the government an Islamic flavour by appointing several ICMI activists, the government was not greeted with popular enthusiasm. Habibie, therefore, remained very vulnerable to challenge from rival elements of the New Order regime, especially within the military. The military, however, was internally divided and, no less than Habibie himself, suffered from its close identification with the Soeharto regime. Before Soeharto's resignation, Habibie had been close to the "green" group in the military and included three "green" generals among the five that he appointed to his cabinet, including General Feisal Tanjung, a former commander-in-chief, as Coordinating Minister for Political and Security Affairs.[21] But he retained General Wiranto, the leader of the nationalist camp, as both commander-in-chief and minister of defence and security and suddenly dismissed Wiranto's rival, Prabowo, from the command of Kostrad.[22] That a serious rift had occurred between Habibie and his erstwhile friend, Prabowo, was obvious but accounts of the exact circumstances are not entirely consistent. In his memoir, Habibie described how Wiranto had informed him that Kostrad troops were suspiciously "concentrated" at Habibie's home following his installation as president on 21 May. Apparently fearing Prabowo's intentions, Habibie ordered Wiranto to replace Prabowo as Kostrad commander "before sunset" on 22 May.[23] On the other hand, Prabowo's supporters claimed that Wiranto had intentionally misled Habibie in order to persuade him to dismiss Prabowo.[24] In August, Prabowo's military career came to an end when a military honour council, established by Wiranto, found him responsible for the kidnapping and "disappearance" of radical activists in 1997 and early 1998.[25]

Habibie's rivals in the political elite, including senior retired officers from the nationalist group, were soon plotting to bring him down. The occasion was a special congress of Golkar in July to elect a new party leader. Habibie's candidate, his secretary of state, Akbar Tandjung, was challenged by General (retired) Edi Sudradjat, former ABRI commander-in-chief and minister of defence and security, who had the support of former vice president, General (retired) Try Sutrisno. Edi's prospects seemed good as 22 of Golkar's 27 provincial branches were headed by retired military officers but Habibie, through Feisal Tanjung, was able to prevail on Wiranto to order regional military commanders to put pressure on regional Golkar leaders to back Akbar who eventually won with a comfortable majority of 17 to 10.[26] If Edi Sudradjat had gained control of Golkar, it was highly likely that he would have used the huge Golkar-military majority in the parliament (DPR: *Dewan Perwakilan Rakyat*) to call a special session of the MPR to depose Habibie and replace him with a military candidate, most likely Try Sutrisno. In saving Habibie, however, Wiranto may of course have been saving himself. If he had refused to cooperate with Habibie, he would have risked dismissal himself and, in any case, a new military president would most likely have appointed one of his own protégés as commander-in-chief. Wiranto was also aware that the military had been deeply discredited by its role in the New Order regime and that the replacement of Habibie by a military president could have easily led to a new round of mass demonstrations and rioting that the military would be hard pressed to contain.

The informal alliance between Habibie and Wiranto may have been based on no more than mutual dependence but it lasted for the duration of the Habibie presidency. Neither Habibie nor Wiranto could afford to go along with the complete reform of the New Order regime that was the theme of regular student demonstrations — often on a huge scale — that disrupted the life of Jakarta and other major cities. One of the central student demands was for an end to what they termed KKN (*kolusi, korupsi dan nepotisme*: collusion, corruption and nepotism). In particular they called for the trial of corrupt New Order figures, including the deposed president. Habibie and Wiranto, who were both substantial beneficiaries of Soeharto's largesse and headed their own patronage networks, were hardly in a position to launch a serious drive against KKN which would inevitably undermine their own sources of power and could ultimately ensnare them personally. Moreover, they were both deeply attached emotionally to Soeharto to whom they owed their careers. Although relations between Habibie and Soeharto had soured after Habibie had assented to the push for Soeharto to step down,[27] he continued to revere his patron while Wiranto, at the swearing in of Habibie as president, had stepped forward to pledge that the armed forces would "protect the honour and safety" of former presidents, "including President Soeharto and his family". Another central demand of demonstrators was that the military abandon its Dual Function (*dwi fungsi*) doctrine that provided the ideological justification for its involvement in politics. In fact a small group of military reformers within Wiranto's circle had already envisaged the gradual withdrawal of the military from direct political involvement but their views were not shared by the military mainstream that naturally wanted to retain the privileges officers had enjoyed under the New Order.[28]

The Habibie-Wiranto alliance was formed against a background of deteriorating law-and-order conditions in the wake of the economic collapse. As already noted, a series of anti-Chinese riots had preceded a big anti-Chinese riot in Medan and the collapse of order in Jakarta in May 1998 that resulted in the destruction of the Chinese commercial quarter of the city and the deaths of as many as one thousand people. The economic consequences of the ensuing flight of Chinese capital from Indonesia was compounded by El Nino weather conditions that caused food shortages and aggravated inflation. Increasingly, ordinary people were taking the law into their own hands. Corrupt local government officials came under physical attack, land previously converted to plantations or golf courses was re-occupied by peasants, and lorries carrying produce to urban markets and ports were regularly intercepted by mobs while factories and plantations were often looted. In Aceh and Irian Jaya, separatist movements renewed their resistance to the central government and in Maluku, Central Sulawesi and West Kalimantan, effective government virtually broke down as a result of communal conflict which eventually took thousands of lives and caused the flight of hundreds of thousands of refugees.[29] In these circumstances, it was hardly surprising that neither foreign nor domestic entrepreneurs showed interest in making new investments.

The security forces — both the military[30] and the police — often proved incapable of restoring order and upholding the law. Indeed, poorly paid security personnel were often among those responsible for the spreading unrest. Military officers had been shocked by the sudden fall of the Soeharto regime and dismayed by their own inability to save their patron. They were further humiliated when the military institution came under increasingly devastating criticism in the press and other media of a sort that they had never experienced under the New Order. Soldiers who had been convinced that they were universally respected by the people as members of a "people's army" suddenly found themselves facing an avalanche of condemnation. Their demoralization was further aggravated as the press published a stream of revelations of human rights abuses perpetrated by the military. Responding to popular protests, the DPR sent missions to both Aceh and Irian Jaya where local people detailed the brutal behaviour to which they had been subjected and, in August 1998, the military commander-in-chief himself publicly apologized to the people of Aceh for the behaviour of his troops.[31]

In these unpromising circumstances and faced with a huge legitimacy problem, Habibie opted to move in the direction of "democratic" reform. Although he had never shown strong democratic leanings during his long service in Soeharto's government, he had no choice but to attempt to attract popular support in order to survive in the future.[32] First, as long as popular demonstrations regularly clogged the roads of major cities, the risks of rioting would remain high with unpredictable consequences. And, secondly, Habibie needed to cultivate civilian backing as protection against a possible future reassertion of military power. Although the discredited and demoralized TNI was not in a position to regain control of the government through a coup, it — or at least elements within it — still had the potential to cause trouble for the civilian government. The Habibie government immediately embarked on liberalizing measures. Restrictions on the press and other media were lifted, the law limiting the number of political parties to three was simply ignored, controls on mass organizations such as trade unions were removed, and hundreds of political prisoners were released, including Muslim dissidents and communists and other leftists convicted of involvement in the "coup" of 1965.

Habibie's democratization programme was formalized at a Special Session of the MPR convened in November 1998 which brought forward the next general election from 2002 to "at the latest June 1999". The holding of a general election under new electoral laws was central to Habibie's efforts to acquire legitimacy and met with no opposition in the MPR. Other issues were more controversial. As students outside the MPR demanded the abolition of the military's dwi fungsi, the military members of the MPR insisted on the military's right to representation in both the MPR and DPR. Despite a walk-out by the small Muslim Unity and Development Party (PPP: *Partai Persatuan Pembangunan*), the MPR finally adopted a compromise decree that envisaged only the gradual reduction in the number of military appointees.[33] Another controversial issue was a clause in a decree requiring the government to take firm measures against officials engaged in corruption. While it was difficult in the new atmosphere for any group to oppose such a decree, the controversy focussed on the phrase "including former President Soeharto".[34] A public trial of Soeharto would almost certainly have implicated current leaders of the government and military. But in the end the fear that the removal of the reference to Soeharto would trigger new waves of demonstrations convinced the Golkar-military majority in the MPR to adopt the decree.

Government concerns about future demonstrations and even rioting were not without foundation. The deliberations of the special MPR session were accompanied by mass demonstrations and violence in the streets. Student demonstrators, backed by retired military officers and prominent civilians in what was called the National Front (Barnas: *Barisan Nasional*), called for the replacement of the Habibie government by a presidium of senior leaders.[35] On the other side, Islamic students demonstrated in support of Habibie. Fearing that the session would be disrupted, Wiranto agreed to the mobilization of a Muslim vigilante force (Pam-Swakarsa: *Pengaman Swakarsa*) consisting of 30,000 youths and men largely recruited from rural Islamic schools and militias outside Jakarta. Violent clashes soon broke out including one in which four members of the Pam-Swakarsa were killed. In an atmosphere of heightened tension on the last day of the session, joint military-police troops opened fire on student demonstrators, killing seven. The killing of the students by troops illegally using live ammunition hardened anti-government and anti-military feeling and led to further demonstrations calling for the replacement of the government.[36]

Following the MPR session, the New Order's institutional framework was drastically overhauled. The unreformed Golkar-dominated DPR elected in 1997 understood that it had no choice but to adopt new electoral laws for the general election which was held on 7 June, the first genuinely free election since 1955. Contested by forty-eight parties, instead of the three of the New Order era, the result was a fragmented DPR in which no single party achieved an absolute majority while the law had halved the number of military and police appointees. The leading party was the Indonesian Democracy Party of Struggle (PDI-P: *Partai Demokrasi Indonesia — Perjuangan*), formed by supporters of the Megawati faction of the old PDI, with one third of the votes. Golkar, the electoral vehicle of the Soeharto regime, ran second with 22 per cent — much less than the 75 per cent it received in the last New Order election two years previously. Three Muslim-based parties, won significant support.

Habibie's prospects of re-election in the MPR in October, however, were severely damaged by his endeavour to resolve the long-running war in East Timor. President Soeharto had refused to countenance even limited autonomy for East Timor but in January 1999, after minimum consultation with his cabinet, Habibie announced his intention to hold a "popular consultation" (*jajak pendapat*), in effect a referendum, on the future of East Timor.[37] Amazingly, neither General Feisal Tanjung, as Coordinating Minister for Political and Security Affairs, nor General Wiranto, the commander-in-chief of the military and Minister of Defence and Security, rejected the president's proposal.[38] However, they immediately began to undermine its spirit by supporting the formation of "militias" among pro-Jakarta East Timorese. Armed, trained and backed by the military, these militias aimed to create conditions that would ensure a victory for the pro-Indonesian side in the referendum.[39] Having "secured" overwhelming victories for Golkar in general elections throughout Indonesia during the previous thirty years, the military saw no reason why it could not guarantee a positive vote in the East Timor referendum. The presence of UN officials and the international press in East Timor, however, ensured that murders and other violence perpetrated by militia members received international publicity. When the UN-supervised referendum in August 1999 showed that nearly 80 per cent of the voters favoured independence, the military organized the mass evacuation of about one-third of the population to West Timor and allowed militia units to take their revenge on remaining pro-independence voters, killing more than one thousand. Facing massive international pressure to allow international troops to restore order in East Timor, Habibie and Wiranto relented and later both were widely blamed for the "loss" of East Timor.[40]

It was not only the East Timor debacle that was working against Habibie's prospects for re-election as president at the October 1999 MPR session. The economy had still shown no signs of recovery, separatist and communal violence was breaking out in several regions of the country, and his government was facing accusations of failing to implement the MPR decision on corruption. Not only was Habibie seen as protecting President Soeharto from legal proceedings but he himself seemed to be implicated in a huge corruption scandal involving a bank that had survived the financial crisis in 1997–98.[41] It appeared that a huge sum had been extorted from the Chinese owners of the bank by officials who had connections with Golkar and it was assumed that much of the money was intended to finance Golkar's general election campaign and the re-election of Habibie as president. In the fragmented MPR where no single party was anywhere near to controlling a majority of votes, it was an open secret that money was used to strengthen the commitment of supporters and to induce waverers to change sides.

The atmosphere of the presidential election in the MPR in November 1999 was, of course, totally different to the previous presidential election in March 1998 which had unanimously re-elected Soeharto. This time the incumbent faced strong competition from Megawati, the leader of the PDI-P which had won the most votes in the general election. Golkar's strategy required it to form an alliance with the PPP and the new Muslim parties as well as win the support of the military group. By October, however, Golkar itself was divided over the Habibie presidency and its chairman, Akbar Tandjung, was considering an offer from Megawati to run as her vice presidential candidate. At the beginning of the MPR session, Habibie presented the presidential accountability report that had always been endorsed without dissent by the MPR during the Soeharto presidency. Habibie's report, however, was rejected narrowly by 355 to 322 votes, apparently due in part to "betrayal" by Akbar's supporters.[42] The rejection of the accountability report was an indication that Habibie faced inevitable defeat in the presidential election so he withdrew immediately and his presidency was over.

Despite the chaotic circumstances and the unpromising composition of his government, President Habibie initiated significant reforms during his brief presidency. In the terminology of Grindle and Thomas, the Habibie government's reforms were largely "crisis-ridden". Within days of succeeding to the presidency, Habibie was proposing the release of political prisoners, the reform of the anti-subversion law, the lifting of restrictions on the press, the formation of new political parties and the holding of new general elections.[43] New laws were adopted that transformed the political institutions of the New Order by providing for genuinely competitive elections and the drastic decentralization of regional government. And Habibie, largely on his own initiative and against the wishes of the political elite, embarked on a course that eventually led to the independence of East Timor. Moreover, the first steps toward military reform were taken, although in this case on the initiative of military officers themselves and not the government. But Habibie was also a child of the New Order and inextricably entangled in the patronage network that had been created by his predecessor. His inability to confront the KKN problem, exemplified by his failure to investigate the wealth of Soeharto, his family and cronies, loomed large in the public perception of his presidency. Despite the reforms that he initiated, he continued to be seen by many as no more than an extension of the New Order regime.

THE ERRATIC RULE OF ABDURRAHMAN WAHID

If Habibie was an unlikely reformer, Abdurrahman Wahid was an unlikely president.[44] The "victory" of Megawati Soekarnoputri's PDI-P in the June general election had put her in a strong position to win the presidential election conducted indirectly in the MPR in October 1999. The 700 members of the reconstructed MPR consisted of the 500 members of the DPR (including 38 appointed military and police representatives), 135 provincial representatives and 65 appointed representatives of special interests. Golkar's strong position among the regional representatives, however, meant that the distribution of seats between parties was disproportionate to votes won in the general election. Megawati's PDI-P had won 34 per cent of the votes but held only 27 per cent of the MPR seats, slightly more than Golkar which had won 24 per cent of the votes but gained 26 per cent of the seats. Initially, Abdurrahman Wahid's PKB and Amien Rais's PAN had been inclined to support Megawati but were disappointed by her reluctance to enter coalition negotiations. Apparently convinced that her election to the presidency was certain, Megawati showed little interest in doing deals with other party leaders to ensure their support. In the absence of such initiatives from Megawati, Amien Rais brought together the small Muslim parties, apart from the PKB, in an informal alliance dubbed the Central Axis (*Poros Tengah*) which held 20 per cent of the MPR seats. These parties, which were mainly modernist in orientation, favoured the stronger identification of the state with Islam and rejected Megawati and her party as too secular.[45] Moreover, some argued that Islam did not permit a woman to lead a nation. Although the modernist Amien Rais had long been a rival of the traditionalist Abdurrahman Wahid, he calculated that the only way to bring the traditionalists into the alliance to block Megawati would be to offer support to Abdurrahman for the presidency, an offer which Abdurrahman happily accepted. With Habibie out of the race, Habibie's supporters in Golkar and most of the military group transferred their support to Abdurrahman who defeated Megawati by 373 votes to 313. Thus, Abdurrahman, who had suffered two recent strokes, was effectively blind, could not walk unassisted, and whose party had won only 13 per cent of the votes in the general election and held only 8 per cent of the seats in the MPR, emerged as Indonesia's first democratically elected president.

In contrast to Habibie, Abdurrahman came to the presidency with a reputation as a democrat. He was not only the leader of Indonesia's largest traditionalist Islamic organization but also the head of the small but high-profile Democracy Forum set up to oppose Soeharto's authoritarian rule. The grandson of one of the NU's founders, Abdurrahman was steeped in the practices of traditionalist Islam but at the same time familiar with Western political ideas and culture. He was a staunch opponent of Islamic fundamentalism and committed to inter-faith dialogue. He showed concern for human rights and seemed determined to limit the role of the military while seeking talks with Acehnese and Papuan supporters of independence. His rise to the presidency was therefore widely welcomed by those who had been protesting against authoritarianism and calling for democratization. But Abdurrahman had no modern administrative skills, as those familiar with the NU's headquarters already knew quite well. His administrative style was that of the *kiyai* heading a traditional Islamic school (*pesantren*) whose authority was never questioned. During his years as the leader of the NU he had used his political influence to obtain funds from the government and other financial benefactors which were then distributed in ways that consolidated his political support within the organization. As president, he sometimes seemed to be trying to run the government as if it were the NU writ large.

Despite his disabilities, Gus Dur, as he was usually called, was a wily politician whose victory was built on a complex series of deals with other party leaders and the military. Cabinet positions, especially those entailing wide scope for patronage distribution and party fund-raising, were divided among the parties roughly according to their contribution to the president's election.[46] The result was a disparate thirty-five-member cabinet in which all five major parties and even some of the small parties, as well as the military, were represented. Gus Dur's immediate priority was to win back Megawati and the PDI-P. Megawati, who felt betrayed by her former friend, was persuaded to accept the vice presidency and her party was awarded four cabinet posts. The military was rewarded with six posts, including General Wiranto as Coordinating Minister for Political and Security Affairs, while Golkar got five. The support of the Central Axis was acknowledged with eight posts divided between four parties while Abdurrahman's own PKB received four. The remaining positions went to non-party ministers.

The result was a cabinet that lacked political coherence, a condition that was soon aggravated by the president's erratic behaviour. Within weeks he had sacked the PPP leader, Hamzah Haz, and then the cabinet secretary. General Wiranto followed in February after an official investigation commission held him responsible for post-referendum violence in East Timor. In April Gus Dur dismissed senior PDI-P and Golkar ministers after making unsubstantiated corruption allegations against them.[47] The garrulous Abdurrahman's informal manner and love of political gossip led to rumours that further disrupted trust between ministers.[48] The president was also apt to make controversial policy statements without consulting his cabinet colleagues. Thus, he alienated his original Muslim supporters in the Central Axis by calling for the opening of trade relations with Israel and upset both Muslims and the military by proposing the lifting of the 1966 ban on the PKI. The military was further angered by his intervention in military command appointments and comments that seemed to envisage the holding of a referendum on independence for Aceh as well as his sympathetic approach to those calling for independence in Papua. Discontent culminated in August 2000 when he carried out a major cabinet reshuffle that excluded senior leaders from the PDI-P and Golkar. He thus gratuitously deprived himself of the support of the two largest parties that together held a majority of seats in the DPR.

By the end of his first year in office, Abdurrahman had alienated virtually all the parties — except his own — that had voted for him in October 1999. The president's casual use of government funds made him vulnerable to parliamentary retaliation. Faced with the growing insurgency in Aceh, the president sought funds to win over the support of religious leaders in Aceh. He first looked to the state rice-trading agency, Bulog, which in the past had often been tapped for so-called "non-budgetary" funds by President Soeharto, and then turned to the Sultan of Brunei for an informal loan of US$2 million. In a bizarre turn of events he used his personal masseur as his go-between in his efforts to obtain US$5 million from the Bulog employees' welfare fund. In the end there was no public accounting of the use of either the Bulog or Brunei money and there were doubts about how much had actually been spent in Aceh. The revelations of the "Bulog-gate" and "Brunei-gate" scandals gave the president's opponents in the DPR the grounds they needed to commence "impeachment" proceedings against him. Launched in February 2001, the process ended in July with the dismissal of Abdurrahman and his replacement, in accordance with the constitution, by the vice president, Megawati.[49]

Abdurrahman had believed that his victory in the presidential election entitled him to lead the country for five years and that the presidential system guaranteed that he could not be deposed by the MPR. The relations between president and parliament had indeed worked along these lines under both presidents Soekarno and Soeharto but, although the written constitution remained unchanged, political realities had been transformed by the fall of the New Order. In fact it had not been the constitution that guaranteed five-year terms for Soeharto but the state's repressive apparatus. Without the repressive apparatus the constitution worked in a different way. At first Abdurrahman made little attempt to disguise his contempt for the parties that dominated the parliament — on one occasion provocatively comparing them to a "kindergarten" — and was confident that they could be bought off whenever necessary. But by late 2000 he had alienated many of his former supporters. When in February 2001 the DPR initiated the impeachment process, the desperate president was ready to sacrifice his democratic credentials by attempting in vain to mobilize the repressive apparatus to protect his position. On several occasions in 2001, he called on the military leaders to support a declaration of emergency that would enable him to dissolve the DPR. In contrast to his earlier stand to take the military out of politics, the president now sought to strengthen the military's political position in a last-ditch effort to save himself. Meanwhile he cultivated military support by approving military operations in Aceh and arresting pro-independence leaders in Papua. The military leaders, however, had no desire to attach themselves to a president whose fall by then was already inevitable.

Apart from the erratic personal style of the president, the fundamental weakness of the Abdurrahman presidency lay in its lack of solid parliamentary support in a presidential system with parliamentary features that had become increasingly significant. Abdurrahman, despite his party's small representation, had won the presidency through deal-making in the MPR. His coalition partners joined him not because they shared his political vision but because he offered them patronage opportunities. The president behaved as if he believed that the system was purely presidential and ignored the post-New Order reality that the parliament could in fact initiate proceedings to dismiss the president. His inability to impose his will on his partners led him to dismiss recalcitrant ministers but each dismissal further undermined his support base in the DPR and MPR which ultimately turned against him. Despite its early promise, the democratic contribution of the Abdurrahman presidency to political reform was largely limited to his personal accessibility and willingness to discuss his views publicly. On the other hand his attempt to further military reform backfired badly and his anti-corruption moves were transparently directed against political opponents. During his presidency military repression in Aceh and Papua intensified while the communal conflict in Maluku was in effect neglected.

MEGAWATI'S HOLDING OPERATION[50]

Like Habibie, Megawati reached the presidency as a result of the tumultuous removal of her predecessor. But in contrast to the tumult that continued under Habibie, Megawati's ascendancy was widely greeted with a sense of relief in the expectation that the constant political upheaval that often had its origins in Abdurrahman's own behaviour had ended. Like Abdurrahman's first "rainbow" cabinet but in contrast to his second, Megawati sought to tie all major groups to her government and thus minimize the prospect of a later challenge from the DPR. Her approach was apparent in the election of a new vice president to fill the position that she had vacated. Concerned to avoid circumstances in which she might suffer the fate of Abdurrahman, Megawati chose to support not the most capable potential vice president but one who was least likely to become a threat to her. Thus she directed her party to support the PPP chairman, Hamzah Haz, despite his rejection of her as president in 1999 on the conservative Islamic ground that she was a woman. The other leading candidates, the Golkar leader, Akbar Tandjung, and retired General Susilo Bambang Yudhoyono, were apparently seen as credible potential challengers in contrast to Hamzah whose base of support barely extended beyond his own small party. In selecting her thirty-three-member cabinet she appointed eleven party politicians and several more with close party ties. Her own party, PDI-P, and Golkar each received three posts and the Central Axis parties four. Retired military officers obtained four cabinet seats together with the armed forces commander who was accorded cabinet status while the remaining positions were awarded to non-party technocrats or professional specialists.

The "rainbow" quality of the cabinet served its purpose in ensuring the stability of the government for the remaining three years of the presidential term, but it did little to overcome the lack of coherence of the previous government. Inclusiveness was achieved at the expense of cohesion. Indeed, as the 2004 general election approached, the rival parties in the cabinet seemed more focussed on raising funds to finance their electoral campaigns than working out solutions to Indonesia's problems. In the case of Megawati's presidency the problems arising from political rivalries within the cabinet were compounded by lack of presidential leadership. Megawati seemed content to reign rather than rule. She espoused no clear vision or policy framework and provided little guidance in settling disputes between ministers. She seemed to lack full understanding of complex issues and some former ministers even claimed that she often showed little interest in policy matters.[51] Draft presidential decisions were often delayed for months awaiting her signature. As president, Megawati rarely attempted to provide public explanations of the goals and achievements of her government except when she read from a script on formal occasions.[52]

Megawati's political strength lay not in her presidential leadership qualities but in her role in holding the largest political party together. The party was severely divided between factions engaged in never-ending struggles for the president's favours. Interviews with PDI-P politicians revealed that many were fully aware of her personal limitations but at the same time could not afford to lose her approval. Although the PDI-P was the most successful party in the 1999 elections, the quality of its representatives in the national and regional assemblies was poor. Many were local leaders who saw in the party an opportunity to gain access to the material rewards that had been denied them during the Soeharto years. Others merely shifted their loyalties from the declining Golkar to the ascendant PDI-P. During the post-1999 years the PDI-P gained a reputation for corruption.[53] In the election of regional heads of government, PDI-P candidates often lost because PDI-P members had been bribed to support other candidates.[54] The party's secretary-general, Soetjipto, explained that in the circumstances immediately following the fall of Soeharto and leading to the 1999 election, the party just accepted anyone with the result, as he himself reportedly put it, "the ones we got were recidivists, yes former thieves, yes former whores".[55] The party's deputy secretary general, Pramono Anung Wibowo, used the Javanese term *aji mumpung*, meaning "to make the most of an opportunity", to describe the approach of many party members.[56] The poor quality of regional PDI-P leaders apparently persuaded President Megawati to support in many cases the nomination of retired military officers and former Golkar officials as governors and district heads as the 2004 elections approached. Megawati apparently calculated that the reputation of the PDI-P was so bad that its candidates might be defeated or, even if successful, would probably do further damage to the party's reputation and thus undermine her own campaign to be re-elected as president. While President Megawati herself tended to stand aloof from the wheeler-dealing in her party, her businessman husband, Taufiq Kiemas, played a major role in the party's patronage politics.

Nevertheless, the stability of Megawati's government, in contrast to the nineteen months of upheaval under Abdurrahman, provided space for the MPR and DPR to adopt important legislation. Although hardly driven by the president herself, the MPR adopted fundamental reforms which transformed the constitution. These amendments were not initiated by the Megawati government but emerged as a result of discussions and compromise within the politically fragmented MPR itself. Not only did Megawati not lead the way towards these constitutional changes but she attempted to block the most important among them which provided for the election of the president and vice president directly in place of the old method of indirect election in the MPR. If the president had been elected directly in 1999, it was most likely that Megawati would have won but, apparently sensing that her government had lost much popular support, Megawati and her husband preferred to retain the old system in which money could be used to win over the support of members of the MPR. Although a substantial section of the PDI-P in the MPR (together with military elements) fought a rear-guard action to block the constitutional amendments, another group in the party was in favour and joined other parties in supporting the amendments which were eventually adopted.[57]

Megawati's government also prepared draft legislation which resulted in incremental steps toward reform in other areas. New electoral laws were adopted, the regional autonomy laws were revised, laws on national defence, the police and military were passed and a new anti-corruption commission and court were established. None of these bills were passed intact by the DPR and most underwent substantial amendment before adoption. In contrast to Habibie's "crisis-ridden" reform, the legislative reforms under Megawati emerged from "politics-as-usual", to use Grindle and Thomas' terminology again. The politically fragmented nature of the DPR was matched by the politically fragmented nature of the cabinet leaving broad scope for compromise in a legislature that continued the old practice of taking decisions by consensus rather than majority vote. It should also be noted that much of the most important legislation was adopted only during the last months of the presidential term as Megawati sought re-election. But, while limited legislative steps were taken, the president held back from tackling the main obstacles to reform. She looked to anti-reformist conservative military leaders to back up her regime and showed no interest in tackling the most fundamental obstacles to the development of a modern and professional military force. Corruption in the courts was commonplace as tycoons followed each other in avoiding prosecution, winning exoneration or, in some cases, "absconding" overseas. It was widely assumed that these tycoons had made substantial contributions to the campaign funds of the president, and indeed to some of the other presidential aspirants. Megawati left it largely to her Coordinating Minister for Political and Security Affairs, Gen. Yudhoyono, to deal with the continuing conflicts in Aceh, Papua, Maluku and Poso, and the new challenge of Islamic terrorism. In Maluku and Poso, the main initiative was taken by the Coordinating Minister for People's Welfare, Jusuf Kalla, who succeeded in fostering peace agreements in both regions which eventually resulted in the ending of the conflict in Maluku and a reduction in violence in Poso.

Megawati's government, like that of Abdurrahman, was built on patronage distribution rather than a common platform. Patronage succeeded in holding the government together for more than three years but it did not provide it with achievements that could win popular support in a direct election. Although Megawati was able to preside over a period of political stability, economic growth had risen to only a little more than 4 per cent and was not high enough to bring about the sort of economic "take-off" that would have given a major boost to her re-election chances. The 2004 legislative election saw a drastic decline in support for the PDI-P from 33.8 per cent in 1999 to 18.5 per cent, leaving Golkar as the leading party with 21.6 per cent, also lower than its 1999 support of 22.5 per cent. Following the constitutional change, five candidates contested the first direct presidential election which resulted in the victory of retired General Yudhoyono with a convincing 60.6 per cent compared to Megawati's 39.4 per cent in a run-off round after the elimination of the other three candidates.

POLITICAL CONSOLIDATION UNDER YUDHOYONO

The 2004 presidential election was a landmark in the reform of Indonesia's political institutions. As Aspinall writes, "the elections of 2004 brought to an end the 'transitional period' in Indonesia's politics that began in 1998."[58] Despite dire predictions of communal and political upheaval, Indonesia's first direct presidential election passed with a minimum of violence and produced a result that was widely acknowledged as legitimate. Unlike his three post-Soeharto predecessors, none of whom served the normal five-year term defined by the constitution, Yudhoyono's convincing victory and the constitutional amendment regulating presidential dismissal seemed to assure him of a full term. This did not mean, however, that he would be shielded from all the political difficulties that troubled his predecessors.

Yudhoyono had served in both the Abdurrahman and Megawati cabinets as Coordinating Minister of Political and Security Affairs although he was also dismissed by both — by Abdurrahman when he refused to endorse the president's plan to declare an emergency and by Megawati when it became clear that he planned to run against her in the presidential election. As early as 2001 he had sponsored the formation of the Democrat Party (PD: *Partai Demokrat*), as a potential vehicle for a bid for the presidency in 2004. As a new party, the PD did well when it won 7.5 per cent of the votes in the legislative election but that was hardly sufficient to carry Yudhoyono to the presidency. Despite the conventional wisdom that political success required the backing of entrenched party machines like those of Golkar and the PDI-P, Yudhoyono's personal popularity had risen sharply following his exit from Megawati's cabinet. He had benefited from his high media profile in the earlier cabinets when he had often explained government policies to press and television audiences — a task that was routinely neglected by both the previous presidents. By 2004, Yudhoyono had become one of Indonesia's best-known political leaders. His chances of winning the presidency under the old indirect electoral system would have been poor but the change to the direct system suited him well.

Yudhoyono's lack of his own political machine did not prevent him from winning the presidency but it complicated his role as president. As his vice-presidential running mate, Yudhoyono selected Jusuf Kalla, who had been the Coordinating Minister for People's Welfare in the Megawati government. Kalla had been an aspirant for the Golkar presidential nomination but, calculating that his prospects were not good, opted to join Yudhoyono instead — for which he was expelled from Golkar. Kalla was a long-established businessman from Sulawesi and brought both financial backing and votes from Eastern Indonesia to the Javanese Yudhoyono's campaign. Yudhoyono had initially hoped to form a "limited coalition" rather than the kind of "rainbow coalition" that had undermined the cohesion of previous governments. Such a coalition would allow more room for non-party professionals, technocrats and former military colleagues. He soon found, however, that he needed to recruit party representatives to his cabinet in order to face an opposition coalition in the DPR based on the two largest parties, Golkar and the PDI-P, while his aim to place economic policy in the hands of economic technocrats was undermined by his vice president's insistence on the appointment of another Golkar-linked tycoon, Aburizal Bakrie, as Coordinating Minister for Economic Affairs. The problem of lack of support in the DPR was overcome, however, when Kalla, having being re-admitted to Golkar after becoming vice president, won the party leadership by defeating the incumbent, Akbar Tandjung, at the party congress in December 2004. Golkar, the quintessential patronage machine, had always seen itself as the natural "party of government" and welcomed the opportunity provided by Kalla to join the dominant coalition and, as a result, gave it a solid legislative majority. Yudhoyono thus gained security but relinquished some control over appointments and policy (although he later replaced Aburizal Bakrie with the technocrat, Boediono).

As the military's most prominent reform-minded "intellectual" Yudhoyono had led the move to withdraw the TNI from day-to-day involvement in politics. One of his priorities, therefore, was to ensure that the trend for the military to exercise wider influence during Megawati's presidency was reversed. Even before his installation, he was confronted with his first challenge when in her last days as president, Megawati, still bitter about her defeat in the election, nominated one of her favourites, the arch-conservative General Ryamizard Ryacudu, as the next commander-in-chief. The appointment of the commander-in-chief required the approval of the DPR that was dominated by the still intact Golkar-PDI-P alliance. It is hard to see Megawati's move as driven by anything but pique as a result of her defeat and intended to make things difficult for Yudhoyono. Still lacking majority support in the DPR and keen to avoid a confrontation, Yudhoyono withdrew the nomination of Ryamizard but waited more than a year for his retirement before replacing the incumbent General Endriartono Sutarto with Air Marshal Djoko Suyanto, the first-ever air force officer as commander-in-chief. Meanwhile Yudhoyono appointed one of his own protégés, the reform-minded Djoko Santoso, to Ryamizard's previous position as army chief of staff and then to commander-in-chief at the end of 2007. The president's influence over the military and police was further consolidated by the appointment of class-mates at the military academy as chiefs of staff of the air force and the navy and as well as the chief of police. He also appointed one of his wife's brothers-in-law to command the army's main force, Kostrad, and in 2008 appointed his wife's brother as Commandant-General of Kopassus.

Yudhoyono's control of the TNI was an essential pre-condition for one of the major achievements of his government: the successful resolution of the separatist rebellion in Aceh. The main initiative, however, was taken by Vice President Kalla who had already established contact with the rebel movement during the Megawati presidency. These secret contacts, that only became publicly known after the tsunami that struck Aceh at the end of 2004, led to the negotiations that resulted in a peace agreement in 2005. The talks were regarded as a betrayal by many members of the military and indeed by part of the DPR, but the combination of Yudhoyono's control of the military and Kalla's influence in the legislature smoothed the way not only to the peace but also the election of one of the rebel movement's leaders as governor of the province at the end of 2006.

President Yudhoyono also launched an anti-corruption campaign based on laws that had been adopted by his predecessors but not widely exploited by them. In contrast to Megawati who had delayed investigations by failing to provide the necessary presidential permission to investigate senior officials and members of the legislatures, Yudhoyono promised to prosecute high-profile politicians, bureaucrats and other officials who soon found themselves in courts where many were sentenced to substantial terms of imprisonment. Among those convicted were two of Megawati's cabinet ministers, several provincial governors and retired ambassadors, numerous *bupati* and mayors, high-profile officials in government agencies and several senior police officers. Critics, on the other hand, claimed that the government had been selective in its investigations. Nevertheless, although the anti-corruption campaign had stopped short of the highest levels of the political and business elite, those it had ensnared were by no means politically insignificant and included members of what could be called the "second-level" elite.

The Yudhoyono presidency was also marked by the further democratization of regional government through direct elections of provincial governors and district heads — under a law adopted by the DPR in the dying days of the Megawati government. Like the fears that preceded the first direct presidential election, there was much public speculation about the likelihood of communal and political violence when local leaders were elected in thirty-three provinces and over four hundred districts, but in practice the need to attract majorities encouraged the formation of multi-communal and multi-party coalitions which brought ideologically diverse candidates together in pursuit of public office. The quality of some of the successful candidates might have been questioned but there was widespread acceptance of the results.

Yudhoyono "adopted a cautious, qualified approach to reform, eschewing radical and potentially unsettling political and economic change" and his anti-corruption measures "did little to challenge the systems of patronage and collusion that were entrenched at the centre of power".[59] Cautious by nature, Yudhoyono was careful not to adopt measures that could disturb the alliances, particularly with Golkar and the military, on which his government rested but, at the same time, in tandem with his vice-president he was able to neutralize potential opposition from those quarters, as the achievement of peace in Aceh demonstrated.[60]

The decade after the collapse of the New Order began with the drastic reforms of the brief Habibie presidency but quickly lost their momentum under Abdurrahman and proceeded very slowly under Megawati. Nevertheless the earlier reforms provided an institutional foundation for both consolidation and cautious advance under Yudhoyono. In the following chapters we will trace the evolution of reform in the constitutional and electoral fields, regional government, military-civilian relations and the courts as well as the state's capacity to uphold order in regions where the state had been "failing".

Notes

1. Hill (2000), ch. 2.
2. Crouch (1978).
3. For an overview of New Order politics, see Mackie and MacIntyre (1994).
4. Crouch (1979).
5. Robison (1986).
6. Robison and Hadiz (2004).
7. Schwarz (1994), ch. 6.
8. Hefner (2000), ch. 6; Liddle (1996).
9. On military antagonism toward Habibie, see Crouch (1994), pp. 122–29.
10. Muslims make up 88 per cent of Indonesia's population but many did not identify with "political Islam". In a classic study, the anthropologist Clifford Geertz distinguished between those who adhered to orthodox Islam and those whose practice of Islam was combined with traditional pre-Islamic culture. Geertz (1960).
11. See McLeod and Garnaut (1998); Jomo (1998).
12. Bresnan (1999).
13. The commercial atmosphere in Indonesia in the mid-1990s is well described in O'Rourke (2002), ch. 2.
14. It is commonly reported that the official commission of enquiry into the riot found that more than 1,000 people had been killed in the rioting. In fact the official investigation of the rioting provided four estimates of the number killed ranging from 288 to 1,190. *Laporan Akhir Tim Gabungan Pencari Fakta Peristiwas Tanggal 13–15 Mei 1998*; Part IV. 3. Although the rioting was mainly in Chinese areas, a large majority of the fatalities were *pribumi* (indigenous) Indonesians who had been unable to get out of burning shopping malls.
15. This process is examined by Hafidz (2006), ch. 2 and Mietzner (2004), ch. 3. Gen. Wiranto, the new Commander-in-Chief of the armed forces, records that President Soeharto offered him authority to take any action that was necessary. According to his own account, Wiranto believed that repression of demonstrations would result in "martyrs" and "conditions would get worse and uncontrollable. Therefore, I said that ABRI would not take repressive measures which would lead to casualties among the people". The alternative was a "constitutional resolution which would lead to the replacement of the national leadership". Wiranto (2003), pp. 82, 87. One senior member of Wiranto's staff assumed that Wiranto had not actually requested that Soeharto resign but had provided the President with daily reports that allowed Soeharto to draw his own conclusions. Interview with Maj. Gen. Agus Widjojo, Jakarta, 5 August 1998.
16. Aspinall (2005*a*).
17. In a televised statement following a meeting with nine Muslim leaders on 19 May, Soeharto seemed to be looking for a way to avoid resignation. He

wondered whether his resignation "might not give rise to new problems. We don't want the Vice President also to have to resign". In his memoir, Habibie commented that "the President still doubted that his successor ... could carry out his responsibilities". Habibie (2006), pp. 20, 22. See also Hafidz (2006), pp. 97, 99–100.

18. In his memoir, Habibie noted reports in the domestic and foreign press expecting the Habibie presidency to last only 100 hours. "The slightly more optimistic predicted that I would not last more than 100 days." Habibie (2006), p. 77.

19. The cabinet also included three ministers from the two non-Golkar parties as well as military officers, non-party bureaucrats and technocrats.

20. These included Soeharto's daughter, Siti Hardiyanti Rukmana (usually known as Mbak Tutut), former army chief of staff, General Hartono, and Chinese business crony, Bob Hassan.

21. It needs to be stressed that the "green" generals were not fanatical fundamentalists. Their common bond was their Islamic family and social backgrounds in contrast to the syncretic religious culture of the dominant Javanese officers. One exception was Prabowo Subianto whose Dutch-speaking elite family was very different to that of the typical "green" officer.

22. In his memoir, Wiranto said that he rejected Habibie's initial plan to retain him as minister of defence and security but replace him as commander-in-chief. Wiranto (2003), pp. 93–97. For a general account, see Hafidz (2006), pp. 104–07.

23. Habibie (2006), pp. 81–83. Before Habibie's installation of his cabinet, Prabowo had sent two officers (Kivlan Zen and Muchdi Purwoprandjono) to gain the support of the venerable Senior General Nasution for the appointment of General Subagio Hadi Siswoyo, the current army chief of staff, in place of Wiranto, and Prabowo in Subagio's place. As Nasution's health did not permit him to write the letter, it was drafted by Prabowo's deputy, Maj. Gen. Kivlan Zen, for Nasution to sign. Kivlan Zen (2004), pp. 90–91.

24. Kivlan Zen (2004), pp. 89–91; Fadli Zon (2004), pp. 146–47. Maj. Gen Kivlan Zen was chief of staff of Kostrad. Fadli Zon was a close friend of Prabowo.

25. Nine of the missing activists "reappeared" but at least twelve remained unaccounted for. U.S. Department of State (1999).

26. Dewi Fortuna Anwar (1999), p. 45; Mietzner (1999), pp. 93–96; Crouch (1999), pp. 131–32. Wiranto, however, claimed unconvincingly that he was neutral in the contest. Wiranto (2003), pp. 163–64.

27. Soeharto never forgave Habibie for his "betrayal" and cut off all contact with him. Habibie (2006), pp. 62–67, 133.

28. The leading officer in this group of reformers was Maj. Gen. Susilo Bambang Yudhoyono, who held the position of Assistant to the Chief of Staff for Social and Political Affairs at the time of Soeharto's fall.

29. van Klinken (2007).

30. The military was now called the Indonesian National Military (TNI: *Tentara Nasional Indonesia*).

31. *Kompas*, 8 August 1998.
32. Habibie's memoir, however, suggests that privately he had been unhappy with the "feudal culture" of the New Order and favoured a free press, the lifting of restrictions on the formation of new political parties, and the release of political prisoners. Habibie (2006), p. 57.
33. MPR decree XIV/1998. On the PPP walkout, see *Media Indonesia*, 21 November 1998, reprinted in B.P. Habeahan dkk (1999), pp. 72–75.
34. MPR Decree XI/1998.
35. Barnas was headed by the long-retired Lt. Gen. Kemal Idris, a veteran of the anti-colonial revolution, with Rachmat Witoelar, a former secretary-general of Golkar as its secretary-general. It included supporters of Edi Sudradjat, the losing candidate in the contest for the leadership of Golkar. For a list of participants, see Habibie (2006), pp. 150–51.
36. This shooting became known as the Semanggi incident, after the clover-leaf (*semanggi*) interchange where it occurred.
37. On the development of Indonesian government policy on East Timor, see Mizuno (2003).
38. Alatas (2006), p. 153.
39. The Truth and Friendship Commission established by the governments of Indonesia and Timor Leste (East Timor) in 2005 concluded that "Viewed as a whole, the serious human rights violations against supporters of independence for East Timor were cases of organized violence. Members of militias, the police, local government and the TNI were involved at various stages in violence and political repression carried out against civilians believed to have links with the pro-independence movement." The commission also concluded that the pro-independence side has also committed human rights violation. Komisi Kebenaran dan Persahabatan (KKP) Indonesia-Timor-Leste (2008), pp. 9–10. Former TNI chief of staff for territorial affairs, Lt. Gen. (ret.) Agus Widjojo, was a member of the commission.
40. See Greenlees and Garran (2002).
41. See Chapter 6 below. The bank was Bank Bali.
42. Mietzner (2000).
43. Habibie (2006), pp. 108–30.
44. For a sympathetic biography of Abdurrahman Wahid, see Barton (2002). Abdurrahman had been the leader of Indonesia's largest Islamic organization, the "traditionalist" *Nahdatul Ulama* (NU), on which the National Awakening Party (*Partai Kebangkitan Bangsa* (PKB)) was based.
45. Amien Rais had led the largest "modernist" Islamic Organization, the Muhammadiyah, before founding the National Mandate Party (*Partai Amanah Nasional*: PAN). Modernist Islamic doctrine is derived directly from the Qu'ran and the Hadith. Traditionalist teachings rely on the interpretations made by Islamic scholars since the time of the Prophet Mohamed.
46. Mietzner (2001), pp. 41–42.
47. The dismissed ministers were Laksamana Sukardi, the PDI-P Minister for

Investment and State Enterprises, and Jusuf Kalla, the Golkar Minister of Industry and Trade.

48. For example, the president confided to the author his intention to dismiss his Defence Minister, Juwono Sudarsono, several months before the August 2000 cabinet reshuffle that excluded Juwono. He was also famous for repeating cynical — and often slanderous — rumours about political leaders and government officials, including highly derogatory remarks about his vice president and her husband.

49. The early phases of the impeachment process are traced in two contemporary ICG Indonesia Briefings (21 February 2001 and 21 May 2001). See also Aspinall (2001).

50. For more discussion of Megawati's government, see Crouch (2003).

51. One former minister told the author that he had worked hard to prepare a report on a major issue. He presented the report to the president who just told him that she was confident he could handle the problem. There was no indication that she had read or understood the contents of the report.

52. One of her speech-writers told the author that he doubted that she actually read her speeches before she delivered them.

53. PDI-P cabinet minister, Kwik Kian Gie, admitted publicly that "the largest corruption is committed by my party", *Jakarta Post*, 18 February 2003.

54. In many contests for the positions of governor, bupati or the speakership of local assemblies where the PDI-P was the largest party, the number of votes for PDI-P candidates was considerably less than the number of PDI-P members of the assembly.

55. *Koran Tempo*, 6 March 2003.

56. Interview with Pramono Anung Wibowo, Jakarta, 22 October 2003.

57. Her defeat in the direct presidential election of 2004 proved that Megawati's instincts were correct.

58. Aspinall (2005*b*), p. 119.

59. McGibbon (2006), p. 193.

60. Yudhoyono' alliance with Golkar lasted until the last months of his presidency when Kalla, under pressure from his party, opted to run for the presidency himself.

3

REFORMING THE CONSTITUTION AND THE ELECTORAL SYSTEM

The fall of an authoritarian regime provides the opportunity for democratic reformers to establish democratic institutions. Democratization usually requires the drastic amendment of the old constitution or the drafting of a completely new one while existing electoral laws need to be overhauled. Post-authoritarian regimes, however, are not always dominated by democratic reformers. The implementation of political reforms is not necessarily smooth and must often be adjusted to suit interests surviving from the authoritarian regime and new political forces emerging in the wake of its collapse. In Indonesia's case, as described in Chapter 2, the new Habibie government consisted mainly of carry-overs from the Soeharto regime, while the legislature produced by the "managed" 1997 general election continued to be dominated by Soeharto's Golkar party and its military allies. The path to democratic reform, therefore, was by no means clear, yet it was this government and legislature that initiated the process of democratic transformation leading to Indonesia's first free elections in more than four decades. The 1999 elections, however, did not produce strong and cohesive government but institutions fragmented between competing parties and factions. Reflecting a common view, the Australian legal scholar, Tim Lindsey, noted that "Few believed that the current MPR, an institution with a justified reputation for party political in-fighting and horse trading, could produce the majority necessary to resolve debates that have divided Indonesia since independence in 1945."[1]

These institutions, nevertheless, embarked on further reform which resulted in a fundamental revision of the constitution and further development of the electoral laws. The British political scientist, Andrew Ellis, concluded that "the MPR made decisions of substance, the most important of which being the move to a separation of powers principle and a conventional presidential system".[2] This chapter seeks to explain how substantial reforms were adopted by unpromising institutions. By 2004, when the second post-authoritarian elections were held, most of the arguments between rival parties and factions over the provisions of the constitution and the electoral laws had given way to a consensus that was broadly acceptable to most major groups and conformed to recognized democratic standards. This did not mean, however, that all challenges had been overcome, but the remaining problems lay less in the institutional framework than in the performance of many of the politicians democratically elected to the reformed institutions.

CONSTITUTIONAL LEGACIES

Indonesia's original 1945 Constitution was not explicitly authoritarian but in practice proved to be no obstacle to authoritarian rule — first under President Soekarno and then President Soeharto. Under its unique form of presidentialism, the president and vice president were elected separately for five-year terms by the People's Consultative Assembly (*Majelis Permusyawaratan Rakyat*: MPR) which acted as an electoral college consisting of the members of the parliament (*Dewan Perwakilan Rakyat*: DPR) together with representatives of the regions and social groups. Apart from electing the president and vice president, the MPR, as the repository of the "sovereignty" of the people, had authority to amend the constitution, determine the "Broad Outlines of State Policy" (*Garis-Garis Besar Haluan Negara*) and issue quasi-constitutional decrees (*Ketetapan MPR*).[3] The DPR's main function, as the parliament, was to adopt legislation, including laws in implementation of the broad directives of the MPR. The electoral process during the Soeharto era, however, was such that it was virtually impossible for the president to be removed from office constitutionally. By the early 1970s, the ten legal parties permitted by President Soekarno had been reduced to three — the government party Golkar, the Muslim-based United Development Party (*Partai Persatuan Pembangunan*: PPP) and the Indonesian Democracy Party (*Partai Demokrasi Indonesia*: PDI). Candidates were vetted by military intelligence and criticism of the president and his policies was not permitted during election campaigns.[4] Golkar always won more than 60 per cent of the votes which rose in 1997 to just short of 75 per cent, and was reinforced in the DPR by military appointees who made up one fifth of its members for most of the period. Military representatives were also among the additional appointed members who made up half the MPR's membership. Following the routine unanimous re-election of the president, the MPR would then unanimously elect his nominee to the vice-presidency.

The fundamental constitutional choice — between presidentialism and parliamentarism — was not a controversial issue in Indonesia. Although Indonesia had always had a president since the proclamation of independence in 1945, for most of the 1950s it had practised a Dutch-style parliamentary system in which the president's role was quite limited while the government was led by a prime minister responsible to the parliament. During almost seven years — from the revival of the parliamentary system in 1950 to its collapse in 1957 — six coalition governments had risen and fallen in quick succession while the nation faced a series of regional revolts that threatened its viability.[5] In response to the failure of parliamentary democracy to sustain strong governments, President Soekarno in 1959 decreed the re-introduction of the original presidential constitution that had been abandoned a few months after independence. Soekarno, and later Soeharto, both identified Western "liberal democracy" as the source of many of the country's ills, while the 1945 Constitution was elevated to a central place in the national ideology. By 1998, the negative official perception of parliamentary democracy had become so entrenched that presidentialism was hardly questioned after Soeharto's fall.

Indonesia's "presidential" system, however, did not conform to the standard model. Unlike most presidential systems in which the president is elected in a direct presidential election and cannot be deposed by a parliamentary vote of no-confidence, Indonesia's president was elected by and responsible to the MPR. Authoritarian rule, however, had disguised parliamentary possibilities which only became apparent after Soeharto's fall. During the New Order, manipulated elections and the repression of opposition had ensured that legislative bodies never challenged the president but the free 1999 election produced an assertive MPR representing a wide range of parties that succeeded in deposing two presidents — in 1999 and again in 2001 — and embarked on a programme of constitutional reform. The effective dismissal of two presidents and the initial amendments to the constitution pushed in a "parliamentary" direction despite widespread rejection of parliamentarism as such. It took the second removal of a president in less than two years to convince legislators that they were moving along an unintended path and led to a reaffirmation and strengthening of the constitution's presidential nature when the MPR opted for the direct election of the president in place of the previous indirect election by the MPR itself.

A second important constitutional issue — although not directly regulated in the 1945 Constitution — was the choice of electoral system. The most crucial reforms affecting the conduct of elections were the removal of New

Order provisions that limited to three the number of political parties allowed to contest elections and the lifting of restrictions on the press and other media. Following the Dutch example, proportional representation (PR) was used in the only national election during the brief period of parliamentary democracy in the 1950s and in the manipulated elections throughout the authoritarian New Order. The New Order's electoral laws, however, were intended primarily to ensure the five-yearly unopposed re-election of President Soeharto. After his fall, consideration was given to a majoritarian single-member system (called the "district system" in Indonesia) but, as we shall see, the preferences and electoral calculations of the major parties prevailed and PR was retained although modified in its details.

Under the 1945 Constitution, reform of the constitution and the revision of the electoral laws were the provinces respectively of the MPR and DPR — both products of the very constitution and electoral laws that reformers deemed to be in need of reform. As explained in Chapter 2, the sudden transition from Soeharto to Habibie left existing institutions intact. The fall of Soeharto was not followed by the immediate dissolution of the two legislative institutions that had supported his rule. Eighty per cent of the seats in the DPR, following the last New Order election in 1997, were occupied by Golkar members and their appointed military allies. Indeed, in March 1998, only two months before Soeharto's fall, the MPR had re-elected him unanimously for his seventh presidential term. Nevertheless, as this chapter will show, the DPR and MPR together adopted fundamental reforms that transformed the constitution and the electoral system.

THE BEGINNING OF REFORM AND THE 1999 ELECTIONS

The collapse of the Soeharto regime opened the way to institutional reform but what needed to be reformed and how? While demonstrating students called for "total reform", established political forces rejected radical change. The three New Order parties preferred to retain existing institutions in which they were already ensconced, while new parties anticipated that democratic elections would open the way to their representation in these institutions. In addition, many, particularly military officers and nationalist politicians, felt a deep attachment to the 1945 Constitution that they identified with the nationalist struggle launched in 1945 against Dutch colonialism and which had acquired virtually "sacred" status under the presidencies of Soekarno and Soeharto. Other politicians were more pragmatic and recognized inadequacies that should be "improved" provided that the constitution's essential nature was preserved. Reluctance to amend the constitution was reinforced by fear among nationalists and moderate Muslims that the amendment process might open the way to the re-emergence of divisive issues that had been settled in the past, most notably the minority Muslim demand to establish a state based on Islam.

The impetus to reform came in response to the collapse of the authoritarian regime in the wake of massive rioting and the continuing threat of further violence in the streets. The political elite, including Golkar and the military, the two bastions of the Soeharto regime, had been shocked by the rioting that brought down Soeharto and realized that the new government was vulnerable to its repetition. The sudden transition from Soeharto to Habibie in May 1998 was in accordance with the constitution which provided for the automatic elevation of the vice president in the event of a presidential vacancy, but it left the government structure intact. President Habibie, however, inherited the constitutional institutions of the Soeharto regime but not its repressive capacity. Confronted by waves of demonstrations in Jakarta and other cities and lacking both legitimacy and full control of the military, the new president needed to win public and international acceptance. During his first week in office he decided to hold an early general election on the basis of new electoral legislation and lifted existing restrictions on the formation of new political parties.[6] A Special Session of the MPR was convened in November 1998 to adopt a decree to advance the date of the next election from 2002 to "at the latest June 1999".[7]

To draft new electoral laws, the government appointed Dr Ryaas Rasyid, the rector of the main civil service training institute, as head of a reform-minded team consisting mainly of American-trained political scientists.[8] They proposed a drastic revision of the electoral system from one based on PR to a mixed system in which 420 of the 550 seats in the DPR would be single-member seats while PR would be retained for only 75. The team believed that a system based largely on single-member constituencies would make legislatures more responsive and accountable by providing constituents with easier access to their elected representatives. The draft bills also opened the way for dozens of new parties to contest elections by removing the New Order restriction that allowed only three. The team, however, was mindful of the political fragmentation that had contributed to the instability of coalition governments in Indonesia during the 1950s (and more recently in Thailand in the 1970s) and wanted to deter the excessive proliferation of small parties. Concern about fragmentation lay behind another provision requiring parties to have functioning organizations in nine of the twenty-seven provinces and half of the districts within those provinces. This provision also aimed to encourage the formation of "national" parties rather than parties based on single ethnic groups or regions with separatist inclinations. Another disincentive for small parties was a requirement that parties would need to pass a threshold of 10 per cent in the 1999 election in order to be eligible to contest the following election in 2004; this, however, was later reduced to 2 per cent of the seats in the final law.[9] In contrast to their radical approach to the electoral system, the team was cautious on the sensitive issue of military representation and proposed only a modest reduction in appointed military seats from 75 to 55.

Draft electoral laws drawn up by expert committees, however, are unlikely to be adopted unless they are deemed to serve the interests of dominant groups in the body that adopts the laws. In the Indonesian DPR, Golkar was by far the largest party with 325 of the 500 seats while its military ally had 75. However, it also had to take heed of the "parliament in the streets" and the established New Order parliamentary practice of adopting legislation by consensus rather than voting. Golkar therefore soon agreed to electoral laws that would greatly undermine its prospects in the coming election. Discredited by its role under the New Order and facing the threat of massive opposition in the streets, Golkar was desperately trying to create a new image as a party that supported, or at least accepted, reform. As a result, its real power was much less than its numerical supremacy might have suggested and it felt constrained from using its huge parliamentary majority to ride rough-shod over the interests of the two minority parties, the PPP with 89 seats and the PDI with 11.[10]

In order to complete necessary preparations for the general election in June 1999 as required by the MPR decree, the electoral legislation had to be passed by the end of January 1999. Failure to hold the election on time would have had a disastrous impact on both President Habibie's legitimacy and Golkar's electoral prospects. As the deadline of 28 January for passing the legislation drew closer, President Habibie urged his party to make substantial concessions to the demands of the minority parties, especially the Muslim PPP which threatened to walk out in protest if Golkar had used its majority to impose its will. Golkar leaders feared that such a walk-out would not only undermine its electoral prospects but also trigger further potentially unmanageable opposition in the streets.[11] As Dwight King put it, "Majority rule was trumped by small-party threats to walk out, which would have delegitimized the results."[12]

Golkar finally gave way on three "crucial issues" that remained unresolved until the last week before the deadline.[13] The party had been the chief beneficiary of the old PR system during the New Order and was by no means unanimous in supporting change to a system based predominantly on single-member districts. Moreover, some Golkar members saw such a system as a threat to national unity because it could result in Muslim candidates winning all seats in Muslim-dominated areas while non-Muslims would win all in predominantly non-Muslim areas.[14] However, key leaders including the party chairman Akbar Tandjung, saw political benefits.[15] The party was motivated in part by its hope of acquiring a reformist image but no less important was its calculation that the adoption of a predominantly single-member system would favour the party. In contrast to PR where seats are allocated among all parties in proportion to their votes, Golkar believed that its entrenched nation-wide organization, financial strength and access to government patronage would enable it to win a disproportionately large number of single-member seats. The two minority parties in the DPR, on the other hand, were unwilling to accept a system that might entrench Golkar.[16]

Anxious to shed its domineering New Order image, Golkar initially compromised by dropping its support for the district system but, while accepting PR, cunningly proposed that the constituencies should be based on the 314 administrative districts (kabupaten and municipalities), not the 27 provinces as under the New Order electoral law. As the PPP quickly pointed out, taking into account population, 260 of such constituencies would have only one member anyway — in effect resembling a district system.[17] This was naturally rejected by the PPP and PDI which insisted on province-wide, multi-member constituencies in which they expected to gain better representation. The final compromise resulted in an extraordinarily complex, and indeed virtually unworkable system under which the distribution of seats within province-wide constituencies would be based on PR but individuals would be elected to represent particular districts within the province. The result in practice was that the rules had to be modified after the election and the composition of the national DPR was not finally determined until long after the date of the election.[18] In essence, Golkar, despite its numerical dominance, had to back down and the PR system had been retained despite the preference of the majority party.

Golkar also gave way on a second crucial issue. Part of Golkar's strength lay in its close association with the bureaucracy. It was estimated that around 10,000 civil servants held leadership positions in Golkar at various levels throughout the country and 70 per cent of its officials were civil servants.[19] The minority parties, backed by public opinion outside the DPR, demanded that civil servants be banned from party membership. Golkar was initially reluctant but eventually gave way following the intervention of President Habibie who was concerned about the likely failure to meet the deadline if a concession were not made.[20] Although the president issued a government regulation that allowed civil servants to be suspended temporarily from the bureaucracy in order to retain their party positions, Golkar suffered a major blow when many civil servants resigned from the party.[21]

Golkar, together with its parliamentary ally, the appointed military group, compromised again on military representation. Until 1997, the military had occupied 100 of the 500 seats in the DPR but President Soeharto had reduced the number to 75 in that year. In response to vociferous student demonstrations demanding the entire removal of the military from the legislatures during the Special Session of the MPR in November 1998, the military representatives insisted that their presence should continue but agreed to a "gradual reduction" in their number.[22] In the DPR, both Golkar and PDI supported the military presence but the PPP continued to reject it.[23] The pressure from outside the MPR was reduced, however, when four key reform leaders, Megawati Soekarnoputri of the new Indonesian Democracy Party of Struggle (*Partai Demokrasi Indonesia — Perjuangan*: PDI-P), Abdurrahman Wahid of the National Awakening Party (*Partai Kebangkitan Bangsa*: PKB), Amien Rais of the National Mandate Party (*Partai Amanat Nasional*: PAN) and the Golkar-affiliated Sultan of Yogyakarta issued what was called the Ciganjur Statement in which, among other points, they accepted that the withdrawal of the military from active politics would take place gradually over six years.[24] The final law provided for the reduction of military representation by half to thirty-eight in the DPR and 10 per cent in the provincial and district parliaments.[25]

The legislation was not entirely disadvantageous to Golkar, however. Golkar's quid pro quo lay in the composition of the MPR which was empowered to elect the president and amend the constitution. The new law on the structure of the legislatures provided for the reduction of the membership of the MPR from 1,000 to 700. In addition to the 500 members of the DPR, 135 were regional representatives and 65 "special group" appointees (*utusan golongan*) nominated to represent various non-party organizations and interests. The MPR's regional representatives were elected separately by the provincial legislatures. The distribution of elective seats in both the DPR and MPR had always deviated from the parties' percentages of the national vote because of a deliberate bias against Java where almost 60 per cent of the population lives. This bias was intended to reassure regions outside Java — which had revolted in the 1950s — that their interests would not be neglected. The seats in the DPR were divided more or less evenly between Java-Bali and the rest of the nation which meant that the non-Java regions were over-represented in terms of population. This was greatly accentuated in the MPR in 1999 where each province — regardless of population — had five regional representatives with the result that the representatives from the five relatively populous Java provinces were heavily outnumbered by those from the twenty-two less populous non-Java provinces. The significance of this in party terms was that Golkar was well entrenched in the regions outside Java and was in a position to gain a large share of the regional seats.

The new electoral laws were formulated in crisis-ridden circumstances. Not only had huge demonstrations occurred regularly in Jakarta throughout the year but security forces had fired on demonstrators on the last day of the November 1998 special session of the MPR, killing seven students and wounding many more. The ongoing crisis meant that the DPR's consideration of the new laws was conducted in an atmosphere of urgency in order to meet the end-of-January deadline. Although all the parties accepted the necessity of adopting the legislation in order to permit the June 1999 elections to be held, the actual debates and negotiations in the DPR soon acquired a politics-as-usual quality as the parties bargained over specific electoral provisions in quest of advantage for themselves. Nevertheless, the outcome was a set of electoral laws that permitted an election far more democratic than the manipulated elections of the New Order era.

Although the new electoral laws maintained the basic structure of the New Order electoral system based on PR in province-wide constituencies, there was a fundamental difference. In contrast to the New Order which permitted only three parties to contest elections, the new laws allowed any party that could meet broad criteria to compete and in the end 48 of around 200 parties formed since May 1998 qualified. No less important was the free environment in which the election was held. The Habibie government had lifted the tight New Order restrictions on the press and other media while the military had severed its formal link with Golkar and refrained from openly backing any party.

Despite widespread fears, a largely violence-free election was held on 7 June 1999 in an atmosphere that was quite euphoric.[26] As expected, in the absence of New Order-style government intervention in its favour, Golkar suffered huge losses. Nevertheless, it still emerged as the second largest party with 22.5 per cent of the national votes compared to 74.5 per cent in 1997. The leading party was the PDI-P which won 33.8 per cent. Led by Megawati Soekarnoputri, the PDI-P had broken away from the Soeharto-endorsed PDI and was widely seen as a victim of New Order repression.[27] Three other parties — all Muslim-based — won significant support: the PKB with 12.6 per cent, PPP with 10.7 per cent and PAN with 7.1 per cent while another sixteen small parties also won representation. PDI-P, with 153 seats was by far the largest party in the DPR, well ahead of the next largest party, Golkar, with

120. However, the compromise on the election of regional representatives allowed Golkar to close the gap in the MPR where it obtained 182 seats, almost matching PDI-P's 185.

The MPR convened four months later in October to elect the president. The leading candidates were Megawati Soekarnoputri of the PDI-P who was confident that her party's "victory" in the general election would carry her to the presidency, and Habibie, standing for Golkar. However, a disappointed Habibie withdrew from the contest when his presidential accountability report was rejected by the MPR — partly due to betrayal by a rival Golkar faction. Although few expected that the PKB candidate, Abdurrahman Wahid, who was nearly blind and had suffered two recent strokes, would succeed in mustering the votes needed to win, Habibie's withdrawal opened the way for him. The PKB had won only 12.6 per cent of the votes in the general election with four-fifths of its seats in its home province of East Java and it had only 8.2 per cent of the seats in the MPR. Nevertheless a series of backroom deals involving promises of cabinet appointments and other perquisites gave him victory over Megawati in the presidential election by 373 votes to 313.[28] The huge gap between the level of support for his party in the legislative election and the outcome of the presidential election provided strong impetus for the constitutional reform that was to follow.

THE CONSTITUTIONAL AMENDMENTS

The original 1945 Constitution was a short and incomplete document that had been drawn up hurriedly as nationalist leaders prepared to launch the Indonesian revolution against Dutch colonial rule in 1945. Although initially only a temporary constitution that was soon abandoned, it was reintroduced by President Soekarno in 1959. Elevated as part of the national ideology, it was treated as virtually sacred by both Soekarno and Soeharto and acquired a mystical aura as an embodiment of Indonesian national identity. The MPR was empowered to amend the constitution but until the end of the New Order had never done so. Even after the fall of Soeharto it continued to be revered by nationalist politicians, especially in the PDI-P, and by military officers.

The new MPR that deliberated constitutional reforms during the next three years was by no means fully committed to the thorough democratic overhaul of the constitution.[29] On one side of the debate stood those — particularly representatives of the PDI-P and the military — who emotionally identified the 1945 Constitution with the Indonesian revolution against colonialism and claimed that there was nothing wrong with it in itself although some admitted that that there had been distortions in implementation during the

New Order. Initially, the "nationalist" wing of the PDI-P was reluctant to amend the wording of the historic constitution although they were willing to adopt limited new constitutional practices in the form of MPR decrees. At the other extreme, vocal democratic reformers, some inside but mainly outside the MPR, called for the holding of a constitutional commission or convention along the lines of those in Thailand and the Philippines to draw up a completely new constitution. The MPR, however, was unwilling to surrender power to a new body while there was a general reluctance to revive divisive issues that had been settled in the past.[30]

In the absence of a dominant party or coalition able to impose its will on the MPR, the only way forward was through compromise. The long-established practice of the Guided Democracy and New Order periods of taking decisions by consensus (*musyawarah mufakat*) rather than voting was continued into the *Reformasi* era. In an assembly of minorities, no group expected to win on all questions so each preferred to make concessions on some issues in exchange for securing other interests. A basic three-point consensus soon emerged in which the PDI-P and military agreed to accept "non-core" amendments while other parties acknowledged that the fundamental character of the 1945 constitution should be preserved. This consensus was formalized by the all-party Ad Hoc Committee I (*Panitia Ad Hoc I*: PAH I) established by the MPR's Working Committee following the MPR session in October 1999. PAH I was set up to draft proposed constitutional amendments for consideration at later sessions and chaired by Jacob Tobing, a former Golkar politician who had joined the PDI-P after Soeharto's fall. The consensus identified the constitution's Preamble containing the national ideology, *Panca Sila* (Five Principles), the presidential system, and the unitary state as the constitution's inviolate core values.[31] The three core values reflected a widespread sentiment within the political elite to avoid resurrecting issues that had divided the nation in the past. Panca Sila implied that Indonesia would not become an Islamic state, presidentialism stood opposed to "western" parliamentarism which nationalists blamed for the troubles of the 1950s, and the unitary state negated federalism which was thought to promote national disintegration. During the 1950s Indonesia had moved to the brink of disintegration over Muslim demands to establish an Islamic State, weak and unstable parliamentary government and a series of regional rebellions.

The parties in the MPR broadly accepted the need to "correct" the "distortions" of the New Order period, particularly by limiting the powers of the president and strengthening the DPR. The constitutional amendments proceeded in piecemeal fashion during four MPR sessions between 1999 and 2002. The intention of the MPR to assert its authority over the president was made unambiguously clear at the 1999 session when it in effect dismissed President Habibie by rejecting his presidential accountability report — an event inconceivable during the presidencies of both Soekarno and Soeharto when such reports were normally endorsed unanimously.[32] And, in contrast to the Soeharto era when only one candidate stood in presidential "elections", the MPR exercised its right for the first time to choose between competing candidates when it elected Abdurrahman Wahid in preference to Megawati Soekarnoputri. The MPR then adopted a series of constitutional amendments that further emphasized its authority, the most significant of which limited the president and vice president to two five-year terms — following Soeharto's unlimited six terms — while other amendments changed the language of certain articles to stress the authority of the DPR.[33]

These initial amendments won broad support and were adopted unanimously by the MPR. They were not based, however, on a coherent vision of the direction of change beyond the feeling that the president should take more account of the DPR's views. As the process moved on to more fundamental changes, some groups became concerned that the strengthening of the DPR's role was changing the character of the constitution from its original presidentialism toward parliamentarism which nationalists, remembering the parliamentary constitution of the 1950s, equated with weak and unstable government. A further step in that direction had been taken when the MPR decided in 2000 to hold annual, rather than five-yearly, sessions at which the president would be required to present a progress report. Meanwhile the DPR had exercised its growing authority in 1999 by calling on President Habibie to explain his changed East Timor policy and then a banking scandal, while President Abdurrahman Wahid was forced to come to the DPR in July 2000 to defend his dismissal of two ministers. The parliamentary tendency became even more evident in 2001. From early in his term, President Abdurrahman had steadily alienated not only his political enemies but increasingly many of his political friends, including Vice President Megawati Soekarnoputri. By late 2000, he had lost much of his support in the DPR which at the beginning of 2001 initiated the process that was to lead to his dismissal at a Special Session of the MPR in July of that year. These developments dramatically illustrated the vulnerability of a president who had lost the support of the DPR and faced the prospect of what was in effect the equivalent of a parliamentary-style vote of no-confidence.

In its sessions in 2001 and 2002, the MPR adopted constitutional amendments that sought to redress the balance by reaffirming the presidential nature of the system. The first two rounds of amendments had only prepared the way for tackling fundamental issues in the relations between the president and the MPR/DPR. The most immediate issue, however, was forced onto the MPR's agenda by Abdurrahman's dismissal which highlighted the inadequacy of constitutional provisions for the dismissal of a president or vice president. The 1945 constitution did not include an article covering the dismissal of the president although its Elucidation mentioned briefly that the DPR can call on the MPR to convene a special session to request an explanation from the president if it considers that he or she has "truly violated the national will (*Haluan Negara*) determined by the constitution or the MPR".[34] Although the "sacred" 1945 constitution was never amended before 1999, constitutional flexibility had been provided through decrees adopted by the MPR on constitutional issues, including one in 1978 that adopted an ambiguous, cumbersome and time-consuming four-stage procedure designed in fact to prevent rather than facilitate presidential dismissal. Nevertheless, it was these provisions that guided the drawn-out "impeachment" saga that dominated political life in Indonesia for the first seven months of 2001 and ended with President Abdurrahman's final removal and replacement by his vice president.[35] Thus it was hardly surprising that the formulation of a manageable dismissal procedure was high on the MPR's list of priorities when the amendment process moved into its third round in November 2001. The largest party, the PDI-P, whose leader was now the president, had a particular interest in formulating clear rules that would protect her from an experience like Abdurrahman's.

One of the most serious weaknesses of the old dismissal procedure was the lack of precision in the sole ground for dismissal — "a true violation of the national will". In the case of President Abdurrahman, the debates in the DPR during the impeachment process ranged over many issues far beyond the original allegations of corruption. Such a broad ground for dismissal had strengthened the view that Indonesia's presidential system was being turned into a quasi-parliamentary system where the head of government could be voted out of office not because of specific misdemeanours, but simply because he or she no longer enjoyed the political support of the majority of the legislature. The amendment adopted in 2001 listed specific grounds for dismissal: the president (or vice president) can be dismissed if "proven" to have violated the law in regard to treason, corruption, other serious crimes, "disgraceful behaviour" (*perbuatan tercela*) or "no longer fulfils the requirements for President and/or Vice President" (Article 7A).[36] In contrast to the previous dismissal procedure according to which the DPR brought the charges for judgement to the MPR, most of the members of which were also members of the DPR, the DPR now had to refer its allegations to the new Constitutional Court to "investigate, judge and adjudicate". Only if the court finds that the president or vice president is guilty of the charges can the DPR propose to the MPR that the offender be dismissed.[37] Thus, although the MPR would make what is ultimately a political decision, it could not do so unless the Constitutional Court has found the president or vice president guilty of specific charges defined in the constitution.[38]

The most fundamental and controversial amendments of the constitution were adopted in the third and fourth rounds in 2001 and 2002 and went much further toward reversing the trend toward parliamentarism. Since early 2000, public opinion had been turning toward support for the direct election of the president and vice president in place of the old system through the MPR. It was argued that a president elected directly by a majority of voters would acquire legitimacy that could not be enjoyed by a president whose election was a result of horse-trading between the fragmented parties in the MPR. Moreover, it was widely believed that the election of the president by the 700 members of the MPR opened the way to "money politics" where members were willing to sell their votes.[39] The eventual fate of President Abdurrahman, whose party held only 8 per cent of the seats in the MPR, drove home the point that an indirectly elected president could be very vulnerable to challenge from the legislature and less able to maintain stability. As it seemed impossible that any single candidate could win an absolute majority of votes in a direct presidential election and a president elected with less than half the votes might be considered as lacking legitimacy, it was widely accepted that a second run-off election would most likely be needed.

As the party with the best-organized party machine entrenched throughout the country and strong representation in regional government among governors, mayors and *bupati*, Golkar could see benefits for itself in a direct election. But it was not confident, on the basis of the 1999 general election result, that it could win in the first round of a direct presidential election against Megawati, although it expected that its candidate would have a good chance in a second round run-off after the elimination of smaller parties.[40] To block the prospect of a victory for Megawati in the first round, Golkar initially proposed that the leading candidate would need to obtain not only an absolute majority of votes but also majorities in two-thirds of the provinces. Golkar was, of course, confident that it could win majorities in at least one third of the provinces, thus making it impossible for Megawati to win majorities in two-thirds.[41] Support also came from President Abdurrahman, ever confident of his own personal popularity, who called in March 2000 for a direct presidential election.[42] PPP and PBB also agreed. PAN, apparently accepting that, on the basis of the 1999 results, its leader, Amien Rais, would not be among the top two in the first round of a direct election, proposed that a direct election be limited to two candidates selected by the MPR itself.[43] The PDI-P, however, was ambivalent. Although it had won an impressive victory in the 1999 general election under Megawati's leadership, it hesitated to support the direct election of the president. This was due partly to its ideological identification with the constitution proclaimed by President Soekarno, but also uncertainty about his daughter's prospects if forced to debate with other candidates in a direct election in 2004. Backed by the TNI, the PDI-P justified its reluctance by citing the cost of a separate nation-wide election, the low level of education of the Indonesian people, and the danger that a direct election could spark communal and other conflict.[44] Sensing the shift in the public mood toward direct presidential elections, however, at its first congress in March 2000 it adopted the ambiguous formula of "a direct election conducted within the MPR" without explaining how this might differ from an indirect election.[45] Still hoping to restrict the presidential election to a vote within the MPR, the PDI-P later proposed that the two parties with the most votes in the general legislative election be entitled to nominate presidential candidates with the presidential vote itself conducted within the MPR.[46] On the basis of the 1999 general election result, the PDI-P was confident that it would be among the two top parties.

In accordance with the Indonesian preference for consensual decisions rather than voting, a compromise was eventually reached at the 2001 MPR session. The constitution was amended to provide for the direct election of the president and vice president, running as a team rather than individually as in the past. These teams would be nominated by political parties or coalitions of political parties (but there was no requirement that the candidates should be members of a political party). The amendment required that the winning pair would need to win not only more than 50 per cent of the national votes but also at least 20 per cent of the votes in more than half the provinces.[47] This provision was intended to prevent "Javanese domination". As noted above, previous electoral laws had included built-in biases that gave additional electoral weight to voters outside Java but, in a direct presidential election covering the whole nation, residents of Java would make up nearly 60 per cent of the electorate. The provision that required that the president and vice president run as a team also gave an incentive to include a non-Javanese on the presidential ticket.

The MPR, however, was deadlocked in 2001 on what to do if no pair of candidates, as seemed inevitable, could win in the first round of the election. The PDI-P, supported by the TNI, maintained its view that the second-round election be restricted to the MPR — in effect retaining the core of the existing system. The PDI-P "reached a deal on many of the core issues" with Golkar but consensus could not be reached because of the opposition of the other, mainly Muslim-based parties which argued that the best solution would be simply to hold a second direct election.[48] The positions of the parties were, as usual, expressed in terms of democratic principles and the need to maintain national unity, but in fact reflected electoral calculations. The PDI- P calculated that it would once again be the leading party but still without sufficient support to win in the first round. Expecting a substantial number of seats in the MPR, it preferred to restrict the second-round election to the MPR where, its opponents alleged, the vast financial resources it accumulated as the party of the incumbent president could be used to attract sufficient votes to gain a majority. No less important was the fear in PDI-P circles that President Megawati would not be an effective campaigner in a direct election.[49] On the other hand, by 2002 the most likely challenger was Amien Rais, the speaker of the MPR, who anticipated that his high profile and charismatic qualities would win him more personal votes in a direct presidential election than his party, the Muslim-based PAN, would get in a general election.[50] He would therefore have little chance in a vote in the MPR but, if he managed to come at least second in the first round of a direct presidential election, might be able to muster sufficient anti-Megawati votes from other parties to win in the second round. By the time of this debate in 2002, Golkar's prospects had declined due to the trial of its General Chairman and potential presidential candidate, Akbar Tandjung, on corruption charges but it had not given up all hope.

As the amended constitution stood after the 2001 MPR session, many feared that if the deadlock persisted it would be impossible to hold a presidential election. The constitution stipulated a two-thirds majority in the MPR to amend the constitution but it was not certain that such a majority could be found either to support a second-round direct vote or to revoke the first-round direct election. The old indirect system had been abolished but the new direct system would only work in the unlikely event that one of the candidates succeeded in winning an absolute majority and the required 20 per cent support in half the provinces in the first round. In an attempt to avoid the deadlock before the 2002 session, Golkar proposed that the previous year's amendment be revised by limiting contestants to those nominated by a party or coalition of parties that had won at least 35 per cent of the votes in the preceding general election — thus limiting the number of candidates to two, one of which might be Golkar.[51] But this proposal was rejected by other parties.

As the 2002 session approached, a move was made by PDI-P and military diehards to reverse the previous year's amendment providing for a direct election. A month before the session opened, Megawati told a meeting of PDI-P party leaders that she would prefer to postpone the holding of a direct presidential election until 2009 on the ground that the people "are not yet ready" for such an election in 2004.[52] Megawati's reluctance was backed by the anti-amendment "nationalist" group in the PDI-P which eventually succeeded in obtaining 106 signatures of MPR members, including the president's husband.[53] They not only opposed the direct election of the president but now declared opposition to all substantial amendments of the "sacred" constitution.[54] While they accepted the relatively minor amendments adopted in the first two rounds of the MPR, they regarded the third round as a betrayal of the constitution. In particular, they focussed on the amendment to Article 1 (2) which deprived the MPR of its role as the supreme state institution and thus fundamentally changed the constitution's character.[55] As Ellis explained, the amendments changed "a state with a single all-powerful highest institution of state to become a state with constitutional checks and balances".[56] Of course, as members of the MPR, they also resented the downgrading of their own institution. Another concern was the 2001 amendment establishing a Regional Representative Assembly (*Dewan Perwakilan Daerah*: DPD) which they saw as a step toward federalism and a betrayal of the unitary character of the constitution. This group wanted to rescind the third-round amendments including the one that provided for the direct election of the president.

Opposition to the later constitutional amendments was also widespread within the military and publicly expressed by high-profile retired officers including two former commanders-in-chief, Gen. Try Sutrisno (also a former vice president) and Gen. Edi Sudradjat. Their attitude was shared by the Chief of Staff of the army, Gen. Ryamizard Ryacudu, who was also Try Sutrisno's son-in-law. Indoctrinated for decades during the New Order to believe that the 1945 constitution embodied Indonesia's unique national spirit, they could accept amendments that "improve, clarify and perfect" but not if they in effect created a new constitution.[57] In justifying its reservations, the military also raised the risk of political instability and social conflict during the period between the first and second rounds of the presidential election.[58] Reflecting military concerns, including the possibility of disorder in the event of a deadlock in the MPR, the newly appointed Commander-in-Chief of the TNI, Gen. Endriartono Sutarto, offered two alternatives. First, if the MPR could not reach complete agreement, he proposed that it would be better simply to return to the original 1945 constitution without the earlier amendments. Alternatively, it could be agreed to accept all the amendments on the understanding that the result would be a "Transitional Constitution" until the 2004 election when it would be reviewed "more clearly and objectively".[59] In response to a question from a journalist, he added that the TNI would even support President Megawati if she were to issue a presidential decree to return to the 1945 constitution "if this was the national consensus, and the only way to save the nation, and the nation accepted it".[60]

In the end, however, the parties in the MPR reached a consensus that simply ignored the military's wishes. The anti-amendment faction in the PDI-P had been challenged by another group, headed by the party leader in the MPR, Arifin Panigoro, who believed that the direct election of the president had strong support in the community.[61] Finally, President Megawati was persuaded that it would be in her political interest to accept it. She may have had doubts about whether she could win a direct election but, haunted by the precedent of Abdurrahman's impeachment, she was eventually convinced that she would be less vulnerable as a directly elected president.[62] She therefore opted for a second-round direct vote but her ambivalence was apparent when she explained that "If I were only General Chairwoman of the PDI-P, I would instruct the party to reject the amendments. But because I am at the same time also the president, I must also protect all the political forces."[63] The PDI-P's secretary-general, Soetjipto, explained that the party did not want the constitutional amendments but "is powerless to stop the process".[64] With the president's endorsement, the deadlock was resolved and the anti-amendment groups gave way. Thus the presidential nature of the constitution was in fact strengthened and consolidated. The president would receive his or her mandate directly from the people and be much less vulnerable to the sort of pressures that resulted in the dismissal of President Abdurrahman Wahid. Ironically, the ultra-nationalist anti-amendment group that had opposed the direct election was also among the strongest supporters of the concept of presidentialism.

The direct election of the president together with the new procedures on dismissal halted the post-1999 trend that had seen the strengthening of the legislature at the expense of the president. The quasi-parliamentary character of the formal constitution had been disguised by Soeharto's authoritarian rule but became very apparent in both the election and downfall of President Abdurrahman. The restoration of "pure" presidentialism in 2001 and 2002 necessitated the re-vamping of the MPR's role. In the original constitution, the MPR was the effective source of authority on behalf of "the people", electing and having the power to dismiss the president and determining the "Broad Outlines of State Policy" that in theory were to be implemented by the president and the DPR. After the final round of amendments, the MPR lost its pre-eminent status as the source of sovereignty and no longer elected the president or issued the "Broad Outlines of State Policy". Its role was reduced to three: amending the constitution; formally installing the president and vice president; and dismissing the president and/or vice president "according to the constitution". Its members, as amended in 2002, would consist of the members of the DPR and the new DPD, both of which would be fully elected in general elections. The old regional representatives in the MPR were thus replaced by the members of the DPD while 'special group" representatives were no longer appointed. One consequence of this was that the military, which had been permitted by an MPR Decree in 2000 to retain its representation in the MPR until 2009, would now be excluded after the 2004 election.

Two major institutions were established in the 2001 round of constitutional amendments: the DPD and the Constitutional Court. Initially, Golkar, with its strong base outside Java, wanted the DPD to have extensive powers but this was resisted by the PDI-P, with its strong base in Java, as well as the military. The PDI-P, which had initially rejected the DPD as a step toward federalism, agreed to its formation but only with severe limitations on its powers. Although resembling a senate in a federal system, the DPD was not part of a truly bicameral system in which both houses exercise more or less equivalent powers and it had no power to veto legislation adopted by the DPR. Its role was limited to considering and monitoring regional matters. Each province had an equal number of representatives in the DPD elected at the same time as the DPR. The amended constitution provided that elections to the DPR (and the regional DPRDs) would only be contested by political parties while the DPD elections could only be contested by non-party individuals.[65]

The main function of the new Constitutional Court was to assess whether laws were in accord with the constitution. The Supreme Court, established in the original 1945 Constitution, had never had authority to conduct judicial review of the constitutionality of laws although it had the power to invalidate government regulations conflicting with laws. During the transition process since 1998 the lack of authoritative interpretations of the constitution had on several occasions given rise to political tensions, most dangerously surrounding the dismissal of President Abdurrahman Wahid. The court also had several side functions involving disputes between state institutions, the dissolution of political parties and disputes over the results of general elections, and it was obliged to respond to requests from the DPR to determine whether the behaviour of the president or the vice president merited dismissal. The court would consist of nine judges — three nominated by the Supreme Court, three by the DPR, and three by the president. The constitutional amendments also provided for a Judicial Commission to nominate Supreme Court judges and to investigate abuses allegedly committed by judges.

The reform of the constitution was not limited to the institutional, electoral and judicial changes discussed in this chapter but included important amendments in regard to regional autonomy, defence and security, human rights, and the economy. Of no less significance was the withdrawal of a Muslim proposal in effect to place Muslims under Islamic law.[66]

The four sessions of the MPR between 1999 and 2002 had indeed overhauled the 1945 Constitution. The process was slow and cumbersome partly because the assembly not only lacked a dominant party but even a dominant coalition. As fears of national collapse receded, debate over amendments was often entwined with current political controversies in which the positions adopted by parties reflected short-term party interests. This was most evident during the "impeachment" proceedings against President Abdurrahman and the consideration of the format of the presidential election. Some observers had been very pessimistic about the outcome. Lindsey, for example, believed that it was "almost inconceivable that the current legislature could produced a significant and effective constitutional reform that is clearly so urgently needed" although he conceded that Indonesia might possibly "muddle through".[67] Nevertheless, rival parties eventually reached compromises which were broadly acceptable. As with the election laws in the DPR when agreement was achieved partly because of the need to meet a deadline for holding the 1999 election, the need to complete the constitutional amendments in time for the 2004 election made compromise imperative.[68] In both cases, failure to adopt legislation or constitutional amendments necessary for the holding of elections would have seriously undermined the legitimacy of the government and key institutions. In the end, the constitutional amendment process produced a substantial reform of the constitution that was broadly accepted by all significant political forces.

RENEWING THE ELECTORAL LAWS AND THE 2004 ELECTIONS

The 1999 electoral laws were formulated in the midst of the transition crisis and were, in Grindle and Thomas' terms, "crisis-ridden". By the time that new laws for the 2004 elections were considered by the DPR in 2002 and 2003, the political atmosphere was closer to "politics-as-usual". New laws were needed because the amended constitution provided for a direct presidential election, the election of the newly created DPD and the new composition of the MPR, DPR and DPRDs as a result of the removal of non-elected members, including those representing the military and police. In addition, the parties that held most of the seats in the post-1999 DPR wanted to replace the 1999 electoral laws that had been produced by the "New Order" DPR in which they had not been represented. The new laws, therefore, were not imperative measures to avoid disaster but more a product of normal political competition.

The Department of Home Affairs established a team to draft the new electoral legislation under the leadership of Dr Ramlan Surbakti, a member of the team that drew up the reform-oriented drafts of the laws for the 1999 election. Ramlan's team aimed to make legislators more responsive to their constituents' aspirations by allowing voters to vote for individual candidates on party lists and not just for the party, bringing legislators closer to the constituents by reducing the size of large constituencies, enhancing fairness in the conduct of elections, and promoting democratic practices within parties. It also strengthened measures in the 1999 laws designed to encourage party consolidation by reducing the number of parties.[69] But the final decisions lay, of course, with the DPR itself where debate couched in terms of general democratic principles often only weakly disguised the interests of the main parties. The laws eventually adopted were, as in 1999, the outcome of compromises between the demands of competing parties and public expectations.[70]

Reform groups outside the major political parties had criticized the 1999 laws for failing to provide adequate mechanisms to make members of legislatures accountable to the voters who elected them and claimed that too much power was given to the party machines that nominated candidates. They therefore continued to advocate the adoption of the district system that had been unsuccessfully proposed by Habibie's team in 1999.[71] The drafters of the General Elections bill, however, accepted the reality that the main parties in the DPR would not accept the district system so proposed instead that the "open list" version of PR replace the "closed list" that had been used in 1999 and throughout the New Order period.[72] In the closed list system, voters simply select the party of their choice and seats are distributed between parties in proportion to votes obtained. The seats are then allocated to candidates according to their order on party lists. This system had been criticized by reform groups because in practice it allowed the party machines to determine which candidates were placed high on the list and therefore likely to be elected regardless of whether they enjoyed local support. Legislators, therefore, tended to be clients of the party "bosses" in Jakarta and provincial capitals, and it was commonly believed that candidates of the major parties often "purchased" high positions on party lists.[73] On the other hand, under the proposed version of the "open list" system, voters first select their party and then choose their own preferred candidates from those on the party's list. A major argument in favour of the open list was that it would loosen the grip of unresponsive party "bosses" at the party's headquarters and force candidates to appeal for the support of local voters rather than hide behind party labels. They would need to make themselves accessible to local voters who would hold them individually accountable for their performance. A drawback, however, is that by forcing candidates from the same party to compete against each other, the open list could be expected to aggravate party factionalism. There were also reservations about the practicality of the proposal. If voters, many of whom were relatively uneducated, were required to select a party and individual candidates not only for the DPR but also for the provincial and district DPRDs as well as cast votes in the DPD election, it might take a very long time for each voter to exercise his or her democratic right and the likelihood of mistakes would be high.

The open list system was naturally not appealing to the party "bosses" whose source of power would be undermined. Initially, the two large parties, PDI-P and Golkar, preferred to retain the closed list while smaller parties were more well-disposed to an open list.[74] Later the pragmatic Golkar, after making electoral calculations, switched its position to favour the open list but with the condition that constituencies should be based on the by-now 400 or so administrative districts. This proposal echoed its unsuccessful attempt to have what was called "PR" adopted in single-member constituencies in 1999. As there were 550 seats in the DPR, around three-quarters would have populations too small to merit more than one representative and would in effect be single-member constituencies.[75] Such a system would benefit Golkar with its strong support outside Java where district populations were relatively small and would usually have only one seat which Golkar could expect to win, but would disadvantage parties, such as PDI-P and PKB, with strong bases in the relatively large multi-member constituencies of Java where seats would normally be distributed between several parties. The Golkar proposal was of course not acceptable to the other major parties. In the end, a compromise was reached in which the system, although described in the law as "open list", was not very different in practice to the closed list. In the law as adopted, voters selected their party and had the option of also choosing a single candidate from the party's list, instead of choosing candidates for all seats as in a genuine open list system.[76] The order of remaining candidates, and all the candidates if the voter did not indicate a preference for a particular candidate, would be determined by the party's list. As it turned out, most voters, especially in rural areas, just voted for their party without choosing an individual candidate. In essence, the closed list system continued even if some voters exercised their option to vote for an individual candidate as well as their party. In the final result, only two candidates won sufficient votes to be elected as individuals, leaving 548 drawn from the party lists.[77] In practice, the big parties, anxious to avoid confusion among their supporters, called on voters simply to vote for the party.[78]

Although the DPR in effect rejected the open list, this was balanced by another provision that aimed to make politicians more accountable to voters by drastically reducing the size of the larger constituencies. While national constituencies continued to be based on provinces in less populous regions, the larger provinces were divided into several constituencies. In the DPR elected in 1999, the largest provinces — West Java, Central Java, and East Java — had 82, 60, and 68 seats respectively. Constituents could vote for their preferred party but many would not have known who the candidates were. Under the new law, the number of constituencies was increased to 69 and each constituency contained between 3 and 12 seats with the number varying according to population.[79] This made little difference in the smaller provinces which had less than 12 representatives in any case but it significantly reduced the anonymity of candidates in the big provinces. Of the 32 provinces, 20 continued to form single constituencies while 8 were divided into 2. North Sumatra became 3 constituencies while the 3 big provinces on Java — West, Central and East Java — were each divided into 10. Similar provisions applied to the DPRDs at the provincial and district levels. The exact number of seats for each constituency was left to the Election Commission (*Komisi Pemilihan Umum*: KPU) to decide. It generally opted for larger numbers between 6 and 12 in order to increase the degree of representativeness but it allowed between 3 and 5 seats in several less populous provinces.[80]

The electoral laws sought to discourage party fragmentation in the legislatures. In order to contest elections, parties now needed established organizations in two-thirds of the provinces instead of only one third as in 1999, and the threshold required of parties in the 2004 elections in order to be eligible to contest in 2009 was raised to 3 per cent of seats in the DPR and 4 per cent in the DPRDs with seats in at least half the provinces and districts throughout Indonesia. The impact of these measures, however, was limited as parties that failed to meet the threshold were permitted to merge with other parties or to dissolve themselves and form new parties. In the 1999 election, only six parties qualified to contest in 2004 on the basis of the 1999 result but another eighteen "new" or merged parties met the organizational requirements of the law and were able to contest the 2004 election. In order to promote democratic practices in parties, parties were required to select their candidates "in democratic and open ways in accordance with internal party mechanisms" but no implementing guidelines were issued and no sanctions applied in the case of violations. As in 1999 candidates for election had to be nominated by parties, thus excluding independent non-party candidates.

A new Law on the Election of the President and Vice President was needed after the constitutional amendments. In the debate on this law, the two largest parties, PDI-P and Golkar, had a common interest in restricting the number of contestants. Claiming that too many parties might nominate candidates and thus confuse voters, they initially proposed that only parties gaining at least 20 per cent of the votes in the general election for the DPR would have the right to nominate presidential candidates. This implied theoretically that there could be no more than five candidates but, on the basis of the 1999 election results, more likely only two — namely PDI-P and Golkar. Naturally the other parties resisted this proposal. The large parties backed down and accepted a compromise that limited the right to nominate to parties winning 3 per cent of the seats (i.e., 16 seats) or 5 per cent of the votes, although in later elections the limits would be raised to 15 per cent of seats and 20 per cent of votes.[81] In debating the qualifications required of party candidates, party interests were quite blatant. Golkar proposed that all candidates should be university graduates — a requirement that would have excluded the current president, Megawati Soekarnoputri. The PDI-P backed a provision disqualifying candidates "either charged with, or convicted of, crimes carrying penalties of five or more years' imprisonment". At that time, the Golkar general chairman and likely presidential candidate, Akbar Tandjung, was currently appealing against his conviction in September 2002 on corruption charges carrying a potential sentence of more than five years. Former President Abdurrahman Wahid, the likely PKB candidate, was widely seen as the target of a provision that required candidates to undergo a medical examination to determine their physical and mental capacities to carry out their responsibilities. In the end, compromises were reached which left all but one of the likely candidates still in the race after the KPU issued its own implementing regulations which required a medical examination that resulted in the virtually blind Abdurrahman's disqualification as a candidate.

General elections for the DPR, 32 provincial DPRDs and 416 district DPRDs were conducted on 5 April 2004 and contested by the 24 parties that met the eligibility criteria — half of the number contesting in 1999. All the major parties suffered declines in support. The PDI-P's share of the national votes fell from 33.8 per cent in 1999 to 18.5 per cent, behind Golkar which declined slightly from 22.5 per cent to 21.6 per cent. The three middle-level parties in 1999 also lost ground, with PKB winning 10.6 per cent, PPP

8.2 per cent and PAN 6.4 per cent. Two parties, however, made significant advances. The new Democrat Party (*Partai Demokrat*: PD), formed in 2001 by supporters of the then Coordinating Minister for Political and Security Affairs, retired General Susilo Bambang Yudhoyono, won 7.5 per cent and the Prosperous Justice Party (*Partai Keadilan Sejahtera*: PKS), based on the old PK, obtained 7.3 per cent, a five-fold increase on the PK's result in 1999. Although the number of parties that won seats in the DPR declined from 21 to 16, by another measure the parliament was more fragmented than in 1999. In contrast to the previous election, seven parties won more than 6 per cent compared to five in 1999. In terms of seats, the two leading parties together occupied only 40 per cent compared to 55 per cent in the previous DPR.

As no party won even a quarter of the votes in the general election, electoral logic dictated that presidential candidates should seek vice-presidential partners with different political and geographical bases to themselves who could attract additional votes to the team. Thus, each of the five nominated pairs combined candidates of "nationalist" orientation with partners identified with Islam, and three included candidates from both Java and regions outside Java. In the first round of the presidential election on 5 July, retired General Susilo Bambang Yudhoyono, and incumbent President Megawati emerged as the top vote-winners with 33.6 per cent and 26.3 per cent of the votes respectively and were thus qualified to enter the second round. Yudhoyono, a Javanese Muslim who had formed his own "nationalist-oriented" party ran together with Jusuf Kalla, an Islamic-oriented businessman-politician from South Sulawesi who had failed in his bid to win Golkar's presidential nomination. Megawati, who had grown up in the presidential palace in Jakarta and had impeccable nationalist credentials, selected the leader of Indonesia's largest Islamic organization, the Java-based Nahdatul Ulama (NU), Hasyim Muzadi, as her running mate. The Golkar candidate, retired General Wiranto, who had defeated Akbar Tandjung for the party's nomination, teamed with Solahudin Wahid, another NU official and brother of former president Abdurrahman Wahid, came third with 22.2 per cent, followed by Amien Rais of PAN with 14.9 per cent and Hamzah Haz, the PPP leader and Megawati's vice president, with 3.1 per cent. In the months before the final round on 20 September, the two remaining candidates sought the backing of the parties whose candidates had been eliminated.[82] In the end, Yudhoyono won a decisive victory with 60.6 per cent of the votes compared to Megawati's 39.4 per cent. Yudhoyono was the leading candidate in 28 of the 32 provinces.[83] Indonesia's first direct presidential election thus produced a clear-cut winner who was endorsed by a substantial majority of the voters and therefore acquired high legitimacy.

POLITICAL STABILITY AND CORRUPTION

The holding of a direct presidential election in place of the behind-the-scenes intrigue, manoeuvering and bargaining that characterized the indirect process in the MPR had greatly strengthened the legitimacy of the presidency. The major argument for the adoption of direct presidential elections was that it would enhance political stability but, as political scientists have argued, stability is not necessarily guaranteed by the direct election of the president for a fixed term. In discussing "the perils of presidentialism", Juan Linz points out that "in a presidential system, the legislators, especially when they represent cohesive, disciplined parties that offer clear ideological and political alternatives, can also claim democratic legitimacy" and therefore constitute a serious political challenge "when a majority of the legislature represents a political option opposed to the one the president represents".[84] Scott Mainwaring, on the basis of his study of Latin American presidential systems, argues further that deadlock between president and legislature is particularly likely when parties in the legislature are fragmented.[85] Both scholars note the possibility that such crises can sometimes lead to military coups.

Indonesia's election results in 2004 partly fitted the situation envisaged by these political scientists. Yudhoyono's overwhelming victory was not backed by equivalent support in the DPR where an initial coalition of PDI-P and Golkar together with several smaller parties outnumbered the president's own supporters.[86] Prolonged deadlocks are of course always possible in presidential systems, but it is also possible for presidents to overcome them through negotiation and compromise especially in cases like Indonesia where ideological incompatibility is not usually a major concern for parties which are mainly patronage machines with bases in different sectors of Indonesian society, whether ethnic, geographic or religious.[87] The solution to a potential deadlock, therefore, was to broaden the president's own coalition by extending patronage resources to erstwhile opponents. The president's immediate difficulties with the DPR were soon resolved when Vice President Jusuf Kalla successfully challenged Akbar Tandjung for the Golkar general chairmanship at a party congress in December 2004, only two months after the installation of the new government. Kalla would have had no prospect of defeating the incumbent if he had not already become vice president. The highly pragmatic Golkar members preferred a leader in government rather than one on the outside and immediately abandoned their earlier coalition partners. Backed by an extra 128 members, the president's coalition now enjoyed a comfortable majority in the DPR. Although Golkar obtained no immediate additional cabinet seats, it could be assumed that the flow of government patronage in its direction increased.[88]

Linz also argued that "presidentialism is ineluctably problematic because it operates according to the rule of 'winner-takes-all' — an arrangement that tends to make politics a zero-sum game, with all the potential for conflict such games portend".[89] But, given the cleavages in Indonesian society, Indonesian parties did not expect to gain complete dominance of the government. Their goals were more modest and concerned primarily with ensuring that their supporters were adequately represented and that they obtained an appropriate share of the benefits flowing from government policies. In contrast to the "minimum winning coalition" envisaged by Western political theory, the "rainbow" cabinets of both Abdurrahman and Megawati included virtually all significant parties, thereby exceeding by far what was necessary to provide the government with majority support in the DPR and MPR. Both presidents sought safety in "rainbow" coalitions because, in the context of extreme party fragmentation, they feared that less inclusive coalitions could turn out to be transient. The drawback of "rainbow" cabinets, on the other hand, was their lack of policy coherence. Held together by access to patronage rather than agreement on common policies, cabinets were often divided by rivalries between parties and, indeed, sometimes within parties.[90]

The constitutional amendments establishing a more conventional presidential system as well as his own overwhelming victory in the presidential election put President Yudhoyono into a far stronger position than his post-Soeharto predecessors. Yudhoyono had originally hoped to form what he called a "limited coalition" in which non-party professionals, technocrats and retired military colleagues would hold key portfolios together with the three small parties that had nominated him for the presidency — his own PD, the Muslim PBB, and the "nationalist" PKPI[91] — as well as the Islamist PKS. His vice president, however, who had been a senior leader of Golkar, and the other parties that had joined his coalition in the DPR demanded cabinet posts for their supporters. Eventually 15 of the 35 cabinet positions were allocated to party representatives — 3 to PKS and 2 each to PD, PBB, PAN, PPP and PKB (representing only one wing of a divided party) as well as 2 with Golkar affiliations and 4 retired military officers. Excluding only the PDI-P among the major parties, Yudhoyono's cabinet did not differ drastically from the "rainbow" cabinets of his indirectly elected predecessors. The argument that "Presidentialism usually produces cabinets composed solely of members of the governing party"[92] did not apply to Indonesia's first "purely" presidential cabinet. But political security came with a cost. The president was constrained in selecting his ministers by the need to accommodate, in particular, his vice president's preferences. The vice president's influence became even stronger after Golkar joined the coalition following Kalla's election as its general chairman. The result was that the "rainbow" cabinet was vulnerable to the lack of cohesion that characterized the earlier "semi-presidential" cabinets while the president's rhetoric about far-reaching reform, including a campaign against corruption, seemed more difficult to implement with the strengthening of elements that had benefited from the practices of the past.

The relative ease with which presidents formed coalitions between parties representing diverse ethnic, regional and even religious and ideological interests was facilitated by the culture of "money politics" that permeated Indonesian politics and was particularly apparent in the DPR. Corruption is clearly widespread in the DPR but hard to document.[93] Most of the legislative work of the DPR is done in specialist commissions which discuss bills and prepare them for submission to the plenary session at which stage adoption of the law is usually a mere formality.[94] It is in the commissions and the budget committee that corruption is most rife, particularly in those commissions that deal with so-called "wet" areas (involving large financial stakes as opposed to "dry" areas where the stakes are not so large). Among the commissions considered "wet" are those concerned with such fields as regional government, plantations, logging, transport, telecommunications, public works, trade, state corporations, energy, mining, banking and other financial institutions. Another "wet" area is the DPR's budget committee which examines the allocation of government funds. An alienated member told the press that "it is an open secret that in order for a department's budget to be approved, the members (of the budget committee) must first be 'serviced'."[95] Competition between DPR members is vigorous for appointment to these bodies and especially for the positions of chairman and deputy chairmen. In the "wet" commissions, ordinary members can expect offers of around Rp 50 million (US$5,000) for their support for particular bills while the amount can rise to Rp 150 million (US$15,000) in cases where the stakes are especially high.[96] Commission leaders, of course, can expect more. According to one minister, he had been forced to delay presenting a bill to the DPR because his department could not afford the Rp 2 billion (US$200,000) needed to win the DPR's cooperation.[97]

When commissions were considering matters of significant interest to major enterprises — both private and public — demands were much higher. For example, when the government was planning to divide the state-owned cement company, PT Semen Gresik, into three in order to facilitate its privatization, a respected news magazine reported that members of the relevant DPR commission demanded Rp 500 million to take care of the matter although, after negotiations, the sum was reduced to Rp 280 million.[98] According to Indonesia Corruption Watch (ICW), a state-owned fertiliser corporation was asked to pay Rp 325 million to the commission that was enquiring into corruption allegations. Of that sum, the chairman of the commission allegedly received Rp 10 million, the three deputy chairman Rp 7.5 million each and the ordinary members Rp 5 million each.[99]

It is rare for members of the DPR to openly expose the details of corruption among their colleagues but there were several illuminating cases. One example during the Megawati presidency involved the government's attempt to divest PT Bank Niaga which, like many other bankrupt banks, had been taken over by the Indonesian Bank Restructuring Agency (IBRA) after the financial collapse of 1997–98. The process of divestment had begun in 2000 and IBRA was keen to complete the operation as quickly as it could. The divestment, however, needed the approval of the DPR. Meilono Suwondo and several other alienated PDI-P members of the DPR revealed that IBRA officials had met PDI-P members of the DPR Commission on Banking and Finance at a hotel in mid-2002. At this first meeting, the PDI-P members all received envelopes containing US$1,000. At a later meeting, the amount in the envelopes rose to US$4,000 and, reportedly, a smaller group received US$10,000–15,000.[100] It seems that PDI-P members were not the only target of this operation. Habil Marati, of the PPP, supported Meilono's claims and related that an IBRA official had attempted to bribe him with US$5,000–10,000.[101] Another PDI-P member of the Commission on Banking and Finance said the distribution of envelopes was "normal" at meetings of the commission.[102] Although the police wanted to investigate allegations of corruption, they required the permission of President Megawati to interrogate members of the DPR but such permission was not forthcoming.[103]

A similar case was exposed by DPR members in July 2004. A "special committee" (*Panitia Khusus*: *Pansus*) had been set up to examine a government proposal to amend the 1999 forestry law in order to permit thirteen mining companies to operate in protected forests. In a meeting of the committee one day before the final vote in the plenary session, only the PDI-P members supported the proposal but the next day Golkar and PPP suddenly changed their positions and voted in favour. The proposal was passed in the full DPR by 131 votes to 102. Two members of the committee alleged that payments had been made. Bambang Setyo of PBB said that he had rejected an offer of Rp 50 million to support the proposal. Later a dissident Golkar member, Andas T. Tanri, said that he had been given a note indicating that the chairman of the committee had been offered Rp 150 million while other members would get Rp 100 million. A petition was signed by twenty-nine members of the DPR in which they apologized to the public for failing to prevent the adoption of the proposal.[104]

Another lucrative area for members of the DPR involved the formation of new provinces and kabupaten. Between 1998 and 2004, 8 new provinces were established and more than 200 kabupaten. The formation of a new region required the approval of the original region and the adoption of a law by the DPR. This involved making payments to members of the DPR. The amount depended on the resources that those supporting the new region could mobilize. One of the new provinces needed at least Rp 5 billion (U$500,000) to achieve its goal.[105] Regional governments provided benefits for DPR members in other ways as well. It became the practice for some members of the DPR to act as brokers for regional governments by facilitating the approval of the DPR's budget committee for the release of funds. La Ode Ida, one of the deputy speakers of the DPD, said that he had been told by a regional official that he had to pay 10 per cent of the disbursement to a member of the DPR before it could be released to the region.[106] A member of the DPR budget committee, who had been accused of acting as a broker, claimed that he had received about forty proposals from regional governments but denied receiving fees.[107] However, a bupati claimed that it was normal for DPR members to ask for fees when facilitating disbursements.[108]

Under Yudhoyono, as we shall see in Chapter 6, the government adopted a more vigorous approach to corruption. Among the cases pursued by the recently established Commission to Eradicate the Crime of Corruption (*Komisi Pemberantasan Tindak Pidana Korupsi*: KPTPK but usually abbreviated to KPK) were several that not only exposed corruption in the DPR but also resulted in the arrest of members. Early in his presidency in late 2004 Yudhoyono had given permission to investigate a Golkar member of the DPR who was eventually convicted.[109] Subsequently more DPR members were arrested by the KPK. In 2007 Saleh Djasit, a Golkar member, was arrested and in 2008 convicted in a case relating to his previous role as governor of Riau. In 2008 four members from diverse parties were detained and accused of demanding bribes from public officials — three from regional governments to support the withdrawal of protection from forests in order to allow commercial development and the fourth to win a contract from the Department of Communications for the purchase of patrol boats.[110]

The biggest scandal involving members of the DPR, however, was linked to the Bank Indonesia (BI), the central bank. During its audit of the BI's annual report for 2004, the State Audit Board (*Badan Pemeriksa Keuangan*: BPK) had questioned the governing board's approval in June and July 2003 of payments amounting to around Rp 100 billion (US$10 million) from the BI-sponsored Indonesian Banking Development Foundation (*Yayasan Pengembangan Perbankan Indonesia*). Of that sum Rp 68.5 billion was intended to assist former bank officials facing prosecution in relation to the misuse of bank credit (*Bantuan Likuiditas Bank Indonesia*: BLBI) during the financial crisis of the late 1990s.[111] A further Rp 31.5 billion (about US$3.5 million) was directed to members of the DPR's Commission IX on finance and banking. In this case the DPR members were extorting money from the bank which was trying to win the DPR's support for the amendment of the law on Bank Indonesia and the bank's attempt to find a "political resolution" to the BLBI issue.[112] The bank's governor, Burhanuddin Abdullah, who had only recently been appointed when the decision to make the payments was taken, denied benefiting financially himself but was found responsible and sentenced to five years' imprisonment.[113] Two other senior officials of the bank were sentenced to four years for their roles in handing over payments to two Golkar members of the DPR who were accused of distributing funds to the members of the banking commission. The two Golkar members were also arrested and later tried.[114] One of them, Hamka Yandhu, claimed in his capacity as a witness in the trial of the two BI officials, that all 52 members of the Commission IX had received funds "in cash and without receipts".[115]

One of the most important functions of legislatures is to monitor the government's performance and provide checks and balances on the exercise of its power. The performance of this function requires members who are independent of the government and prepared to challenge it. While the culture of corruption might have helped Indonesia to avoid crises arising from deadlock between the president and the legislature, the distribution of patronage does not always have such a favourable outcome for democratic stability. The transparent search by many DPR members for material rewards clearly undermined the DPR's capacity to perform its "watchdog" function effectively. The impressive capacity of members of ideologically opposed parties to reach the compromises that are so necessary to ensure the effective working of multi-party legislatures lacking permanent majorities often seemed to be the result of financial deals funded by interests that benefit from the adoption of particular legislation. That many members of the DPR perform their duties well is not questioned, but the public perception of the majority has been decidedly negative as revealed by many public opinion polls.[116] If corruption in the DPR is in fact as widespread as anecdotal evidence and occasional trials suggest, it would be unrealistic to expect all its members to perform effectively their duties in the interests of their constituents.[117]

Towards the 2009 Elections

Gradual electoral reform continued as the 2009 elections approached. As had become the practice, a new set of electoral laws was adopted which introduced incremental revisions. The laws were adopted, as usual, on the basis of compromise between the parties in the DPR. Electoral rules, however, were no longer the exclusive preserve of the DPR but also involved a new and somewhat unpredictable factor — a very active Constitutional Court. While the laws adopted by the DPR were essentially "fine tuning", a judgement by the Constitutional Court issued less than four months before the date of the forthcoming legislative elections had implications that were more far-reaching.

The earlier trend toward raising the barrier for small parties to win seats was partly reversed in Law No. 10, adopted in March 2008.[118] The DPR maintained the provision in the previous election law that required small parties to meet a threshold of 3 per cent of seats in the DPR or 4 per cent in provincial DPRDs but, in response to pressure from smaller parties, allowed all parties represented in the current DPR to contest the 2009 election even if they had failed to meet the threshold requirement in 2004. As a result, the number of parties eligible to contest the 2009 election rose from 24 to 38.[119] This provision, however, was invalidated by the Constitutional Court on the ground that it discriminated against parties not already represented in the DPR. But, as the Constitutional Court's judgements are not retroactive, the judgement did not take effect before the 2009 election because the Election Commission had already announced — one day before the Court's judgement — the list of eligible parties. The expansion in the number of parties eligible to contest the general election, however, was balanced by a drastic reduction in the right of parties to nominate presidential candidates. In 2004 the law required that presidential candidates be proposed by parties or coalitions of parties holding at least 3 per cent of the seats in the DPR or winning 5 per cent of the votes. As a result, five pairs of candidates contested the election. After lengthy negotiations a compromise in the DPR raised the requirement to 20 per cent of seats or 25 per cent of votes in the 2009 legislative election making it unlikely that more than two or three candidates would be nominated and increasing the possibility that the election could be decided in the first round.

The most far-reaching reform, however, was not adopted by the DPR but as a result of the Constitutional Court declaring unconstitutional part of the election law adopted in 2008. In response to the effective closed-list PR system maintained in 2004 which resulted in all but two members of the DPR being elected from party lists, Law No. 10/2008 provided for the election of individual candidates who succeeded in winning 30 per cent of the votes in multi-member constituencies while all other seats would be distributed according to the candidates' positions on party lists. On the basis of the 2004 results, it was calculated that this would still mean that a large majority of members would still be drawn from party lists.[120] In the face of demands calling for seats to be distributed according to the number of votes won by individual candidates and not allocated according to party lists, the Constitutional Court declared that allocating seats according to party lists violated "people's sovereignty".[121] It therefore invalidated the "party list" system that had been practised in all Indonesian elections since 1955 and led the way to a genuinely open-list system. The Court's decision, however, opened the way to potentially far-reaching consequences. It undermined the power of party machines to determine likely successful candidates and could be expected to exacerbate rivalry between candidates nominated by the same party. It also greatly complicated the voting process with the prospect that rather than strengthening "people's sovereignty", the new system could lead to many voters failing to caste valid votes or not even voting at all.

CONCLUSION

The election of a president in 2004 by means that were seen almost universally as more-or-less fair, democratic and legitimate was the culmination of more than five years of constitutional and electoral reform. The New Order's authoritarian political structures had not been immediately dismantled but gradually transformed into a constitutional framework that met the standard requirements of a formal democracy. But these reforms were not implemented by a new democratic elite that had suddenly replaced the old authoritarian rulers. The Habibie government consisted largely of ministers drawn primarily from two bulwarks of the New Order, Golkar and the military, while the legislature elected in 1997 was dominated by the same two forces. The free 1999 election brought new parties into the DPR and MPR but forces associated with the New Order remained prominent with Golkar emerging as the second largest party and the military retaining a reduced number of seats. Moreover, both continued to be represented in the Abdurrahman and Megawati cabinets alongside representatives of new political forces, many of whom were either drawn into existing patronage networks or had established their own.

Yet substantial political reforms were in fact implemented during the terms of the first three post-Soeharto governments. How were these unpromising governments and legislatures able to initiate and implement such reforms? The initial impetus did not come primarily from a sudden change of heart on the part of Habibie and his Golkar and military colleagues who had never previously indicated dissatisfaction with Soeharto's authoritarian rule but was a response to the new circumstances that threatened their grip on power. The

massive economic collapse brought on by the Asian Financial Crisis had led
to social disorder and rioting, culminating in the riot in Jakarta that forced
Soeharto's resignation. Lacking the Soeharto regime's repressive capacity and
faced with massive student demonstrations through most of his term, Habibie
drew the conclusion that the only way to gain legitimacy was to hold a
democratic election. That support for Golkar fell from almost 75 per cent in
1997 to 22 per cent in 1999 and President Habibie failed to win re-election
was convincing evidence that the system really had changed.

The Abdurrahman and Megawati governments, however, were unable
to maintain the momentum of reform. Lacking reliable political support in
the DPR, both sought security in coalitions which included all, or virtually
all, major parties as well as the military. But the formation of such broad
coalitions of rival parties sacrificed political cohesion and policy coherence.
Further constitutional and electoral reform originated less from the government
than from the legislatures — the MPR and the DPR. The most far-reaching
change was the adoption of direct presidential elections despite the initial
opposition of significant elements within the largest political party and the
military, and the distinct lack of enthusiasm of the president. The absence
of a single dominant party or a coherent coalition in these bodies ensured
that the process of amending the constitution and formulating new electoral
laws was based on compromise. During both the Soekarno and Soeharto
presidencies, decisions of the DPR and MPR were always unanimous, a
tradition reinforced by the severe sanctions that dissidents could expect to
face if they voted against the government's wishes. This tradition continued
but without an authoritarian government that could impose such sanctions.
Guided by the Speaker of the MPR, Amien Rais (whose party, PAN, held only
7 per cent of the seats in the MPR), and the chairman of the special committee
preparing draft amendments, Jacob Tobing (a former Golkar member who
had switched to PDI-P), all but one of the constitutional amendments were
taken by consensus following much debate and bargaining. A similar process
produced electoral laws in the DPR.

Constitutional and electoral reform can be seen as partly the product of
"political engineering" aiming to strengthen political stability and effective
government. The design of institutions is consciously modified to create
incentives to "induce particular outcomes ... while constraining others". A
major goal is "to encourage the development of broad, aggregative, catch-all
political parties ... while discouraging parties built around narrow, ethnic,
regional or other cleavages". Writing generally about political engineering
in the Asia-Pacific region, Ben Reilly explained that "these reforms sought
to improve government stability, encourage party aggregation, restrict the

enfranchisement of regional or ethnic minorities, and foster majoritarian political outcomes".[122]

The reform process in Indonesia was influenced by this approach. The Indonesian "political engineers" who formulated specific reform proposals were the members of the MPR's Ad Hoc Committee I and later its Commission A in the case of constitutional amendments and special drafting teams appointed by the Department of Home Affairs in the case of the electoral laws. The MPR bodies consisted of politicians, many of whom had become well-versed on the main issues and were assisted by special teams of legal experts.[123] Moreover, much of their deliberations were conducted in relatively non-partisan closed sessions out of the public eye. In the case of the electoral bills, the initial drafts were prepared by teams consisting of academics and bureaucrats.

Whatever the wisdom of proposals formulated by "political engineers", however, they could not be adopted without the backing of the main political forces in the legislatures.[124] The most radical reform proposed by the team drafting the laws for the 1999 election envisaged a system based predominantly on single-member districts. Although this proposal was initially backed by Golkar which stood to gain from its implementation, the party withdrew its support in the extraordinary circumstances of the Habibie presidency rather than face the likely consequences of appearing to ride roughshod over the interests of the two small parties. Similarly, a provision of the draft law for the 2004 election that proposed the open list version of PR failed to win support from the parties in the DPR although a compromise was reached that eventually saw two members of the 550-strong legislature elected as individual party representatives. Party interests were especially obvious at virtually all stages of the constitutional and electoral-law reforms concerning the presidential election from the MPR's initial decision to adopt a direct election to the details of the electoral law passed by the DPR. Not unlike the former communist parties in Eastern Europe which "subsequently reemerged organizationally strong, politically wily, and much more programmatically flexible than observers had expected",[125] Golkar proved particularly adept at forsaking earlier positions in search of present electoral advantage as shown most egregiously in its proposed oxymoronic "single-member PR system".

Nevertheless, despite self-interested motives, significant reforms were adopted in line with measures favoured by "political engineers". Reforms formulated by experts on committees were happily endorsed when they co-incidentally served the interests of major parties. Despite the reservations of the largest party and the incumbent president, other presidential candidates saw benefits in the constitutional amendment that strengthened the legitimacy of the presidency by replacing the old indirect system of electing the president with a direct election. Similarly, all potential presidential candidates and their parties welcomed an amendment that clarified the process by which the president could be dismissed and promised to protect the current and future presidents from the almost ad hoc proceedings that led to Abdurrahman Wahid's dismissal. And the main parties endorsed "political engineering" for both the 1999 and 2004 elections that aimed to limit party fragmentation while encouraging the development of stronger parties. Thus, after opening the opportunity for new parties to contest elections, successive laws were concerned to limit their number not only in the interests of stability and coherence but also the interests of established parties. The number of parties qualified to contest declined from 48 in 1999 to 24 in 2004; a low but gradually rising threshold was intended to deter "hopeless" parties and encourage mergers into larger groups; and the magnitude of the largest constituencies was reduced sharply in 2004 to make it more difficult for small parties to win seats.[126] Other measures that fostered "national" identity by encouraging inter-regional and inter-communal cooperation simultaneously protected established parties from new challenges.

But how did the parties' pursuit of self-interest lead to compromises that furthered the cause of constitutional and electoral reform? In legislatures in which no party had a majority and coalitions were usually temporary in response to particular issues, no party or coalition could impose its will unilaterally. Parties could only advance their interests through bargaining and compromise which took into account the interests of other groups. It was therefore possible to reach eventual agreements that left most participants at least partially satisfied. But there is nothing inevitable about such happy outcomes. Based on his observation of the Abdurrahman and Megawati governments, Dan Slater suggested that "Golkar and PDI-P have taken the lead in devising a system in which these parties share power far more than they fight over it".[127] The result is what he calls "collusive democracy". As shown in this chapter, Golkar and PDI-P did in fact often "fight over power" although ultimately they, together with the other parties, reached consensus on constitutional change and new electoral laws which allowed for considerable sharing of influence and perquisites. These compromises, however, were driven at least as much by party competition as by collusion.

In the end, the amended constitution and electoral laws established institutions of government in conformity with internationally accepted requirements of formal democracy. As a result, renewed political institutions elected in 2004 enjoyed a high level of public acceptance, although public opinion polls soon revealed falling satisfaction with the performance of the government and legislature. The implementation of reforms cannot of course guarantee that they will always work in ways that meet democratic expectations. Nevertheless, although "fine-tuning" of particular provisions is quite likely in the future, the basic contours of the re-invigorated constitution seem to have been established. The initial laws initially adopted for the 2009 national and provincial elections only modified the existing laws and did not mark a sharp break with newly established practice. However, an unexpected judgement of the Constitutional Court provided some potential for opening the way toward more significant change.

Notes

1. Lindsey (2002), pp. 244–45.
2. Ellis (2002), p. 152.
3. 1945 Constitution, chapters 1 and 2.
4. Crouch (1978), ch. 10.
5. The classic study of the era of constitutional democracy in the 1950s is Feith (1962).
6. *Kompas*, 29 May 1998; Habibie (2006), pp. 73–74.
7. MPR Decree No. XIV/1998.
8. Four of the seven members of the team (known as the "Team of Seven") had studied political science with Professor Dwight King at the University of Northern Illinois. Ryaas Rasyid had obtained an MA from Northern Illinois before moving to the University of Hawaii for his doctorate. Dr Andi Mallarangeng and Dr Ramlan Surbakti had obtained doctorates from Northern Illinois while Dr Afan Gaffar obtained his MA there. The other three members were Dr Hamid Awaluddin, a graduate in law of the American University, Djohermansyah Djohan, of the civil service training institute, and Anas Urbaningrum, a former chairman of the largest Muslim students' association (*Himpunan Mahasiswa Islam*: HMI). The team consulted international experts on electoral systems including Donald Horowitz, Andrew Ellis, and Ben Reilly.
9. The team had proposed 5 per cent but the high 10 per cent threshold had been inserted at the insistence of President Habibie himself. McBeth (1998).
10. Interview with Akbar Tandjung, Speaker of the DPR (1999–2004) and General Chairman of Golkar (1998–2004), Jakarta, 19 April 2006.
11. Dwight King (2003), p. 65. During the Special Session of the MPR in November 1998, the PPP members of a commission had already walked out over a procedural issue.
12. Dwight King (2003), p. 68.
13. For detailed discussion, see Dwight King (2003), ch. 3.
14. Interview with senior Golkar leader, Slamet Effendi Yusuf, Jakarta, 11 April 2006.
15. Interview with Marzuki Darusman, leader of Golkar in the 1998 MPR session, Jakarta, 29 November 2005.

16 Interviews with Amien Rais, former general chairman of PAN, Jakarta, 14 December 2005; and drafting team members, Ryaas Rasyid, Jakarta, 22 August 2006, and Ramlan Surbakti, Jakarta, 25 April 2006.

17. *Kompas*, 7 January 1999. See also King (2003), pp. 61–62.

18. According to one of its members, the General Election Commission was forced to use its discretion in allocating seats. He estimated that only about half its decisions were strictly consistent with the law. Interview with Dr Ramlan Surbakti, Jakarta, 25 April 2006. The final result was only determined after President Habibie "unilaterally declared the results of the election valid, bypassing the stalemated election commission." Ziegenhain (2008), pp. 106, 113.

19. *Kompas*, 8 January 1999. In addition, virtually all of Indonesia's five million civil servants were affiliated with Golkar through the state employees' association, KORPRI (*Korps Pegawai Republik Indonesia*).

20. Interview with Marzuki Darusman, Jakarta, 29 November 2005; interview with Akbar Tandjung, Jakarta, 19 April 2006.

21. Dwight King (2003), p. 69. King goes so far as to say that "Restrictions on the political rights of civil servants was the most intractable and difficult issue in the entire package of laws, and for good reason. It probably contributed more than any other single factor to the subsequent electoral defeat of the reigning Golkar party by the Indonesian Democratic Party of Struggle", p. 222.

22. Decree MPR No. XIV/1998. The leader of the military delegation was Lt. Gen. Susilo Bambang Yudhoyono, the military's chief of staff for social and political affairs.

23. The PPP had voted in November against the MPR decree on the election because of the decree's recognition of military representation. *Kompas*, 14 November 1998.

24. *Kompas*, 12 November 1998.

25. According to Akbar Tandjung, Golkar had initially been prepared to support high military representation but realized that the military itself was not ready to fight hard on this issue. Interview with Akbar Tandjung, Jakarta, 19 April 2006.

26. The 1999 general election was Indonesia's first free election since 1955. The term *pesta demokrasi* (festival of democracy) was widely used and seemed appropriate.

27. Megawati had been elected, in defiance of government pressure, to lead the PDI in 1993 but was deposed at a government-backed congress in 1996 which was followed by a military-organized attack on her headquarters in Jakarta on 27 July 1996. See Aspinall (2005), ch. 7.

28. For a detailed account of these backroom deals, see Mietzner (2000).

29. For detailed discussions of the constitutional amendments, see Lindsey (2002) and Ellis (2002). See also Majelis Permusyawarahan Rakyat Republik Indonesia (2003).

30. On the eventual fate of the proposed constitutional commission, see Ellis (2002), pp. 143–45.

31. *Kompas*, 7 March 2000. The consensus also included two procedural matters: the Elucidation appended to the original constitution would be eliminated and its substantive elements added to the text of the constitution itself (there had always been ambiguity about whether the explanations in the appended Elucidation were binding); and, following American practice, amendments would not involve the re-writing of clauses in the constitution but would be listed in appendices.

32. The exceptions were the last two reports of President Soekarno in 1966 and 1967 when the military, led by General Soeharto, was preparing the way for his dismissal.

33. For example, "The president has authority to establish laws with the agreement of the DPR" was changed to "The president has the right to submit bills to the DPR" (Article 5).

34. "*Haluan Negara*" is usually translated as "State Policy" in the expression "Broad Outlines of State Policy". My translation here as "National Will" captures the sense better in the present context. The Elucidation, however, did not elaborate on what would follow if the MPR were not satisfied with the president's explanation. Nevertheless, these imprecise guidelines had been followed to dismiss President Soekarno in 1966–67. See Crouch (1978), ch. 8.

35. For a contemporary account of the development of the "impeachment saga", see International Crisis Group (2001*a* and 2001*b*). The term "impeachment" was commonly used in Indonesia although it involved no trial.

36. The provisions on "disgraceful behaviour" and no longer fulfilling requirements of course open a wide range of discretionary grounds for dismissal.

37. The Chief Justice of the new Constitutional Court later pointed out that the court's powers are limited to determining whether the charges are valid. It has no power to impose penalties on an offender other than recommending dismissal. Because of double jeopardy, an offender cannot be charged again even if found guilty of a criminal offence. Conversation with Professor Jimly Asshidique, Chief Justice of the Constitutional Court, Jakarta, 7 September 2004.

38. The MPR was particularly concerned to remove grounds for a "parliamentary" interpretation of the constitution. The amendment itself specifically explains that in expressing its opinion that the president has violated the law or no longer fulfills the requirements to be president, the DPR is merely carrying out its normal role of "monitoring" the government. Article 7B(2).

39. Interview with Amien Rais, Speaker of the MPR 1999–2004, Jakarta, 3 December 2005.

40. Interview with Akbar Tandjung, Jakarta, 19 April 2006.

41. *Kompas*, 21 June 2000.

42. *Kompas*, 10 April 2000.

43. *Kompas*, 21 June 2000; *Republika*, 3 August 2000.

44. Suharizal, pp. 145–48.

45. *Kompas*, 10 April 2000.

46. *Kompas*, 21 June 2000.
47. This requirement followed the example of Nigeria.
48. Ellis (2007), p. 28.
49. Megawati's presidency was marked by her reluctance to be questioned publicly on policy issues, leading to a belief that she would not be able to debate effectively with other candidates during an election campaign. One indication of the PDI-P's worries on this score was its reluctance to accept public debates between presidential candidates.
50. In 1999, PAN won only 7.1 per cent.
51. *Kompas*, 10 June 2002.
52. *Koran Tempo*, 22 June 2002; *Jakarta Post*, 3 July 2002.
53. *Kompas*, 3 August 2002. In addition, 58 members of the appointed "special social groups" representatives and 41 PKB members circulated their own petitions opposing particular aspects of the amendments. The "special social group" representation would be eliminated if all members of the DPR were to be elected.
54. *Koran Tempo*, 5 August 2002; *Tempo*, 5 August 2002.
55. The original wording of Article 1(2) read: "Sovereignty is in the hands of the people and fully exercised by the People's Consultative Assembly." As amended, it read: "Sovereignty is in the hands of the people and exercised according to the constitution."
56. Ellis (2002), p. 140.
57. *Kompas*, 15 May 2002.
58. *Tempo*, 29 July 2002.
59. In proposing a "clear and objective review" of the constitutional amendments, Endriartono had in mind the establishment of an expert Constitutional Commission with powers to revise the constitution. This proposal was opposed by the parties in the MPR and eventually withdrawn by the TNI/Police group. *Tempo*, 12 August 2002.
60. *Kompas*, 31 July 2002. The mention of a presidential decree referred to the decree issued by Megawati's father in 1959 to re-activate the 1945 constitution as the foundation of Guided Democracy.
61. *Kompas*, 9 July 2002.
62. Interview with Heri Akhmadi, a leading member of Arifin Panigoro's faction in the PDI-P, Jakarta, 17 April 2006. Megawati reportedly had sought guarantees from other parties before she agreed to Abdurrahman's impeachment and her own accession to the presidency. Blair King (2004), p. 117. Amien Rais assured her that he would do all he could to ensure stability when she succeeded Abdurrahman. Interview with Amien Rais, Jakarta, 14 December 2005. However, according to Heri Akhmadi, she did not trust Amien Rais.
63. *Tempo*, 11 August 2002.
64. *Koran Tempo*, 10 April 2002.
65. On the role of the DPD, see Sherlock (2006).

66. In 2002 two Muslim parties, the Crescent and Star Party (*Partai Bulan Bintang*: PBB) and PPP, proposed an amendment to recognize the "Jakarta Charter" which requires Muslims to adhere to syariah. Although there was no possibility that the amendment would win majority support, the MPR speaker, Amien Rais, allowed them to state their position after which they withdrew their proposed amendment. Interview with Amien Rais, Jakarta, 14 December 2005.

67. Lindsey (2002), pp. 275–76.

68. President Megawati took office in 2001 but she was considered to be completing President Abdurrahman's five-year term which was due to expire in 2004.

69. Interview with Ramlan Surbakti, Jakarta, 25 April 2006. The team had initially proposed a preferential system (Alternative Vote) in place of proportional representation.

70. The "package" of electoral laws was made up of four separate laws — the Law on Political Parties (No. 31/2002) adopted in December 2002, the General Elections Law (No. 12/2003) adopted in March 2003, the Law on the Composition and Position of the MPR, DPR, DPD and DPRDs (No. 22/2003) and the Law on the Election of the President and Vice President (No. 23/2003), both adopted in July 2003.

71. The most prominent NGO concerned with electoral reform was the Centre for Electoral Reform (CETRO).

72. Interview with Ramlan Surbakti, Jakarta, 25 April 2006.

73. An article in *Kompas* referred to "commercialisation of political offices". "It is said that to become a DPR candidate placed high enough on the list to win will cost hundreds of millions of rupiah — although relatively less for provincial or district DPRDs." *Kompas*, 10 March 2004.

74 *Kompas*, 5 September 2002. It may seem strange that the president's own party rejected a proposal put forward by her own government. Her Home Affairs minister explained that Megawati usually did not interfere in the work of her ministers. Thus his department was able to submit a bill drawn up by a departmental team but opposed by the president's party. Interview with former Minister of Home Affairs, Gen. Hari Sabarno, Jakarta, 27 April 2006.

75. *Kompas*, 23 January 2003.

76. In reading reports of the debate over the electoral system, it is hard to avoid the impression that many participants did not have a full understanding of the implications of the different proposals.

77. The two successful individual candidates were the PKS leader, Hidayat Nur Wahid, and the former governor of Riau, Saleh Djasit, of Golkar.

78. If the individual candidate selected by a confused voter was not from the party of his/her choice, the vote would be invalid.

79. The law provided that each member of the DPR would represent populations ranging between 325,000 and 425,000. Thus the largest twelve-seat constituency could represent more than five million people while the smallest three-seat constituency could have less than 1 million residents.

80. Ramlan Surbakti (2003). Ramlan was the Deputy Chairman of the KPU.
81. These limits were raised in 2009 to 20 per cent of seats and 25 per cent of votes.
82. One of the unsuccessful presidential candidates in the first round told the author that he was offered a very substantial amount of money to indicate support for Megawati. He rejected the offer. Referring to a different case, *Tempo* magazine reported that a Golkar official had claimed that the PDI-P had offered Rp 100 billion to Golkar in order to obtain its support for Megawati. *Tempo*, 16 August 2004.
83. *Kompas*, 5 October 2004. Megawati won the majority of votes in Bali, Nusa Tenggara Timur, West Kalimantan and Maluku.
84. Linz (1993), p. 110. For this reason, Linz prefers the parliamentary system. "What in a parliamentary system would be a government crisis can become a full-blown regime crisis in a presidential system." Linz (1993), p. 122.
85. Mainwaring (1993).
86. For a discussion of the early Yudhoyono presidency in terms of Mainwaring's framework, see Liddle and Mujani (2006).
87. The main exception was the Islamist PKS but it too was quite pragmatic in choosing its political allies as shown most clearly in regional elections where its allies covered the entire spectrum of the political "rainbow".
88. Yudhoyono's first cabinet included two ex-Golkar dissidents who later rejoined the party. In a reshuffle in December 2005, one extra Golkar minister was appointed. Another was added in May 2007.
89. Linz (1993), p. 113.
90. As Dan Slater points out, in 1999 "it was still not structurally necessary that a 'National Unity Coalition' be formed rather than a cabinet based on a narrower nationalist or reformist coalition" and adds that "it appeared that Wahid had agreed to a quid pro quo in which the price of the presidency was a cabinet he could not control". Slater (2004), pp. 70, 71.
91. The prominence of the PKPI in the initial coalition, despite its solitary seat in the DPR, may have been due to its access to financial support. The chairman of the party, retired General Edi Sudradjat, a former commander-in-chief of the armed forces under Soeharto, had close ties to the military-sponsored conglomerate, Artha Graha, which was managed by a Chinese businessman, Tommy Winata. Lt. Gen (ret.) T.B. Silalahi, a cabinet minister under Soeharto and also closely associated with Artha Graha, was a prominent member of Yudhoyono's "success team" during the presidential election. Another prominent retired officer associated with the party was former vice president and commander-in-chief of the armed forces, General Try Sutrisno.
92. Lijphart (1993), p. 146.
93. The author's informal conversations with members of the DPR strongly support this impression. As one politician put it rather colourfully, it is easy to know that someone has farted but difficult to prove the identity of the culprit. A PDI-P

member estimated that 80 per cent of members took bribes; one PKS member said that corruption was "widespread" in the DPR; and another admitted that "politicians have to be corrupt" in Indonesia.

94. Each commission monitors a group of government departments or agencies concerned with such areas as defence and foreign affairs; law; trade, industry and state corporations; banking and finance, etc. The number increased from nine to eleven after the 2004 election. *Koran Tempo*, 22 October 2004. For details on the structure and procedures of the DPR, see Sherlock (2007).

95. Indira Damayanti Sugono in *Tempo*, 10–16 September 2001. Slamet Effendy Yusuf, a Golkar member of the DPR and chairman of the DPR's Honour Council concerned with the ethics of members, said that he had been told by the secretary of one minister that his department's budget could be increased by a further Rp 8 billion if 15 per cent were paid to one of the members of the budget committee. *Kompas*, 28 October 2005.

96. Discussion with a source close to the presidential palace, 2004.

97. I was told this by a former minister who had been talking to the minister concerned.

98. "Antara Senayan dan Gresik", *Tempo*, 10–16 September 2001.

99. "Tiga Lembar Cek dari Senayan", *Tempo*, 10–16 September 2001.

100. *Koran Tempo*, 21 September 2002.

101. *Koran Tempo*, 28 September 2002.

102. *Koran Tempo*, 28 September 2002.

103. *Koran Tempo*, 14 February 2003.

104. *Kompas*, 24 July 2004, 29 September 2004; *Koran Tempo*, 15 July 2004, 24 July 2004.

105. Discussion with a supporter of the new province.

106. *Jakarta Post*, 22 September 2005.

107. *Kompas*, 23 September 2005.

108. *Jakarta Post*, 23 September 2005.

109. *Koran Tempo*, 4 December 2004. The Golkar member, Adiwarsita Adinegoro, had been chairman of the Indonesian Forestry Business Association (*Asosiasi Pengusaha Hutan Indonesia*).

110. *Kompas*, 21 July 2008. They included representatives of PPP, PBR, PKB and Yudhoyono's own PD.

111. See Chapter 6 below.

112. For a report on how the money was transferred to members of the DPR, see *Tempo*, 26 November 2007 ("*Mengantar Tuan Franklin ke Parlemen*"). It was alleged that Golkar member of the DPR Antony Zeidra Abidin had told bank officials that "if you want to resolve the BLBI problem, there will be expenses". *Kompas*, 6 September 2008.

113. *Kompas*, 30 October 2008.

114. Hamka Yandhu was still a member of the DPR after the 2004 elections while Antony Zeidra Abidin had been elected as deputy governor of Jambi.

115. *Kompas*, 29 July 2008.
116. At the beginning of 2005, only 30 per cent of respondents in a *Kompas* poll considered the recently elected DPR as "free of corruption", but by September the figure had fallen to 3 per cent. *Kompas*, 19 September 2005.
117. For an insightful discussion of the relationship between increasing costs of getting elected and increasing reliance on illegal fund-raising, see Mietzner (2007).
118. Law No. 10/2008.
119. As will be explained in Chapter 8, an additional six "local parties" were permitted to contest at the provincial and district levels in Aceh but not at the national level.
120. According to one estimate, only 89 members of the DPR would have won as "individuals" in 2004. *Kompas*, 22 September 2008.
121. *Kompas*, 24 December 2008.
122. Reilly (2006), pp. 21, 69–70, 174.
123. Ellis noted that "While many PAH I members had already become very familiar with and knowledgeable about the key issues, other MPR members, asked to consider basic issues for the first time, were not yet ready to do so", Ellis (2002), p. 129.
124. As Mark Payne and Juan Cruz Perusia pointed out, "If reforms are to be adopted into law, they must be compatible with the interests of the leading political and social groups. Thus political reform inevitably is shaped in part by the narrow motives of power and privilege", Payne and Perusia (2007), p. 58. Although these writers were surveying the reform of political institutions in Latin America, their comments apply equally to Indonesia.
125. Geddes (1995), p. 47.
126. The trend was slightly reversed in the 2008 law that allowed parties that won seats in 2004 to contest the 2009 elections even though they had failed to meet the electoral threshold. Thus thirty-eight parties were eligible to contest the 2009 national elections.
127. Slater (2004), p. 62.

4

STRUGGLES OVER REGIONAL GOVERNMENT

Since the 1980s, many developing countries have embarked on decentralization in a wide variety of circumstances and for diverse reasons.[1] In some countries decentralization was part of an ongoing programme to raise the efficiency of public administration, but in others it was associated with fundamental changes in the structure of government. The fall of a centralized authoritarian regime, for example, often led not only to constitutional and electoral reform but also the re-structuring of centre-region relations. Democratization extended naturally from the centre to the regional and local levels, although the degree and form of decentralization varied considerably.[2] While most countries decentralized incrementally, Indonesia's initial reform was dubbed a "big bang" that transformed the highly centralized unitary structure of the New Order into one that was highly decentralized.[3] Observers described it as "the most daring decentralization policy in developing countries" based on "the most radical decentralization laws in Asia and the Pacific".[4]

This chapter opens with a brief description of the centralized New Order regime before discussing the drastic "big bang" decentralization measures introduced after Soeharto's fall. Despite their previous support for virtually unfettered central domination of the regions, Golkar and its military partner, which together constituted an overwhelming majority in the unreformed DPR elected in 1997, quickly reversed their position on centre-region relations and supported radical reform legislation proposed by President Habibie. The 1999 regional autonomy laws were adopted in the shadow of a national crisis and the prospect of national disintegration — circumstances that Grindle and Thomas would call "crisis-ridden". But by the time that the 1999 laws were replaced in

2004 concerns about national disintegration had largely abated and "politics-as-usual" had been more or less restored, to borrow another term from Grindle and Thomas.[5] The rushed adoption and implementation of the 1999 laws had led to much confusion and controversy that generated resistance inspired by ideological, pragmatic and interest-based considerations. The revised 2004 laws were the product of "normal" bargaining and compromise between the major parties in the legislature. Although they restored some of the central government's authority, the new laws fell far short of the centralization of the Soeharto regime while further entrenching decentralization by introducing direct elections of provincial and district heads.[6] Finally, the chapter raises the question of the vulnerability of regional governments to elite "capture" and its implications for democratic accountability.

SOEHARTO'S CENTRALIZED GOVERNMENT

Although Indonesia has the world's fourth largest population spread among dozens of distinct ethnic communities occupying thousands of islands stretching more than 5,000 kilometres from east to west, Indonesian nationalists have always rejected federalism. In the negotiations that transferred sovereignty to Indonesia in 1949, the Netherlands succeeded in imposing a federal constitution through which, according to nationalists, the Dutch hoped to maintain their influence, but this was abandoned after only eight months.[7] Since then federalism has been widely perceived as somehow "anti-nationalist" although voices have occasionally been raised in its favour, especially in the Outer Islands.[8] The 1945 Constitution (re-introduced in 1959) is unitary in character and provided the foundation for a government structure that, under the New Order, was highly centralized. Under the military-backed New Order, the provinces and districts were strictly subordinated to Jakarta. Since independence, the military had fought a succession of regionalist and separatist movements and, having taken over the government itself in the mid-1960s, was determined to give no leeway to regional defiance.

The New Order regime imposed a high degree of uniformity on regional government. The Regional Government Law of 1974 established a hierarchical structure under which regional government was essentially an extension of central authority.[9] The central government ruled through 27 level-one regions (provinces) and almost three hundred level-two regions (districts) consisting of urban municipalities (*kotamadya*) and rural districts (*kabupaten*). Beneath the districts were sub-districts (*kecamatan*) and then villages.[10] Just as the central government through the Department of Home Affairs exercised authority over the provincial governments, the provincial governments controlled the district governments to which the sub-districts and villages were subordinated. As Ryaas Rasyid, one of the architects of the 1999 legislation, commented, "These regional structures were uniform across the archipelago, whether in Central Java or Central Papua".[11] Not only did provincial and district government follow the Javanese model but even villages were forced to abandon local traditions and adopt the national pattern.[12]

Regional legislatures (*Dewan Perwakilan Rakyat Daerah*: DPRD) at both provincial and district levels were elected in five-yearly "managed" general elections on the same day as the election of the national parliament (*Dewan Perwakilan Rakyat*: DPR). Like elections for the DPR, elections for the DPRDs were conducted in such a way as to almost always guarantee overwhelming majorities for Golkar, while for most of the period one-fifth of the seats were allocated to military and police officers. Regional heads — governors for provinces, and mayors (*walikota*) for municipalities and *bupati* for *kabupaten* — went through a formal process of election by the appropriate DPRD but in reality were appointed by the central government in the case of governors and the provincial government in the case of mayors and bupati. In an effort to provide a cloak of democratic legitimacy, the DPRDs were permitted to submit the names of five candidates from whom the relevant government selected three to contest the election. The DPRD then voted to select two, leaving the final choice to the Minister of Home Affairs in the case of governors and the relevant governor in the case of districts. In practice, the DPRD members always knew in advance the identity of the government's favoured candidate and normally ensured that that candidate received the most votes. Informally, the favoured candidate was often referred to as the "*calon unggul*" (superior candidate), "*calon jadi*" (real candidate) or "*calon dropping*" (dropped into the election from above), while the other two were called "*calon pendamping*" (accompanying candidates). Until the 1980s, around four-fifths of regional governors were drawn from the ranks of military officers — both active and retired — but the number had fallen to about half in the early 1990s before rising again to 16 out of 27 by May 1998. The proportion of bupati and mayors with military backgrounds had declined to about 40 per cent. Civilian heads of regions were all affiliated with Golkar and virtually all had bureaucratic backgrounds.

During the 1980s and 1990s there were occasional signs of dissatisfaction among regional elites with the manipulated nature of these elections. In several cases, one of the "*calon pendamping*" won more votes than the government's preferred candidate — indicating not only broad public dissatisfaction but also dissension within the government camp itself — as all the DPRDs were controlled by Golkar. In 1985 the Riau DPRD's choice for governor was rejected by the central government and in 1993 troops had to be called out to deal with public protests in Central Kalimantan when an intimidated DPRD dutifully voted for the central government's candidate.[13] Similar disturbances occurred in several districts in response to the election of bupati or mayors.[14] Such open protests were unusual but the sentiments behind them were found in many regions. As long as Soeharto and his military-backed regime remained in power, a thorough overhaul of centre-region relations could not be placed on the agenda.

Central domination was not achieved by military repression alone, however. The New Order's political stability had been accompanied by unprecedented economic growth that was partly financed by exploitation of the vast array of natural resources found mainly in the Outer Islands. While the military prevented or put down open protest, Soeharto used the massive profits from oil, natural gas, mining, timber and other natural resources not only to distribute patronage opportunities in Jakarta but also to regional elites. Soeharto's regional clients, therefore, benefited enormously and were willing to accept central domination in exchange for material riches even though many regions lagged behind in development.[15] The 1997 economic collapse, however, not only led to the fall of Soeharto but also upset centre-regional relations. Jakarta's capacity to service Soeharto's patronage network was badly damaged. Regional elites therefore turned more to their own regions for sustenance, especially in the resource-rich and agricultural-export regions where the drastic fall in the value of the rupiah meant that dollar-denominated exports translated into large windfall profits in rupiah terms. From this new perspective, central dominance was less a source of benefits for regional elites and more an unnecessary burden. Popular resentment against what was seen as central domination and unfair treatment also became widespread. In Aceh and Irian Jaya (later called Papua) armed separatist movements were re-emerging and the East Timor insurgency continued while in several provinces federalist, and occasionally separatist, sentiments began to be expressed openly.

HABIBIE'S REGIONAL AUTONOMY LAWS

As Manor argues, the motives driving decentralization are usually mixed and combine both "statesmanlike considerations" and "hard-nosed calculations of self-interest".[16] The urgent overhaul of centre-state relations in the 1999 regional autonomy laws was conducted in the shadow of a national crisis and the prospect of national disintegration — circumstances that Grindle and Thomas call "crisis-ridden". The new laws were in part a "statesmanlike" response to the crisis but they also involved "hard-nosed calculations" of political interest with the approach of Indonesia's first free election in four decades.

Simmering regional dissatisfaction was transformed into open discontent in the wake of the economic collapse in late 1997 and the signs that the Soeharto era was approaching its end. The burgeoning popular movement to overthrow the Soeharto regime spread throughout the country and simultaneously provided impetus to calls for regional autonomy. The new Habibie government's legitimacy was weak and the loyalty of the factionalized military uncertain. Habibie, therefore, was in no position to crush regional dissension in the manner of the Soeharto regime. Apart from in East Timor, Aceh and Irian Jaya, however, disaffection and sporadic agitation against central rule had yet to develop into organized, let alone armed, movements but the possibility of national disintegration had begun to loom on the horizon. In these circumstances, Habibie, who hailed from Sulawesi and was Indonesia's first non-Javanese president, opted to anticipate and meet regional demands rather than have to repress them later.[17] Many regional leaders took advantage of the sudden weakness of the central government to indicate their support for decentralization. In November 1998 the Special Session of the MPR — still dominated by Golkar — adopted a decree calling for the implementation of regional autonomy.[18]

These developments were taking place in an international environment where what had previously been "unthinkable" had become fact. In particular, the disintegration of the Soviet Union and Yugoslavia conveyed to the Indonesian elite the message that multicultural and multiethnic states do not necessarily hold together. The Indonesian case was by no means identical with those of the Soviet Union or Yugoslavia but the parallels were still too close to ignore. As the prospect of East Timor winning its independence appeared increasingly likely and armed separatist movements revived in Aceh and Irian Jaya, the spectre of national disintegration stimulated public debate on how it could be avoided.[19] While conservatives, especially in the military, the central bureaucracy and nationalist circles, continued to see regional autonomy as the first step toward disintegration, others argued that it was only through regional autonomy that disintegration could be avoided. Violating a New Order taboo, the PAN leader Amien Rais even proposed that federalism should be at least considered.[20]

Deepening resentment of centralized government, however, had not generated widespread support for separatism outside the three regions already experiencing rebellion and a small movement in Riau. The Habibie government's decentralization programme was not so much in response to the mobilization of popular demands as in anticipation of them. During the last decade of the Soeharto regime, some attention had already been given to a very limited degree of decentralization but little progress had been made.[21] However, the idea of regional autonomy was taken up quickly by the Habibie government and Ryaas Rasyid, the newly appointed Director-General for General Governance and Regional Autonomy in the Department of Home Affairs, was put in charge of drawing up new regional autonomy laws.[22] Ryaas, an American-trained political scientist whose origins, like Habibie's, were in Sulawesi, provided many of the radical ideas for the legislation and obtained the backing of Habibie's Minister of Home Affairs, Lt. Gen. Syarwan Hamid, a native of Riau.[23]

The "Big Bang" Approach

Instead of the incremental path taken by many decentralizing countries, the new laws followed the so-called "big bang" approach that transformed centre-region relations in a single blow.[24] Ryaas had long favoured decentralization in principle but in the new post-Soeharto circumstances he believed that a drastic transfer of powers to the regions was needed to cope with the growing threat of disintegration. Indonesia did not have time to adopt a more conventional incremental approach in which powers would be gradually devolved to well-prepared provincial and district governments over a period of several years. Such a gradual approach would have given scope for bureaucratic and political beneficiaries of centralized government to mobilize resistance to the reform. Moreover, it was essential for the laws to be adopted while Golkar retained its large majority in the DPR as there was no certainty that the post-election DPR would be sympathetic. President Habibie also had an immediate political interest in quick decentralization. In the expectation that Golkar would experience a severe setback in the forthcoming general election, the president understood the utility of legislation that would appeal to regional leaders who would be playing a major role in mobilizing voters. The regional autonomy legislation, however, had to be delayed because of the priority given to the even more urgent electoral legislation that was only completed in January 1999.

The Law on Regional Government (No. 22/1999), drafted by the Department of Home Affairs, and the accompanying Law on Fiscal Balance between the Central Government and the Regions (No. 25/1999), drafted by the Department of Finance, permitted a huge transfer of authority and resources directly to the district level, largely by-passing the provinces. Ryaas himself commented that "Their content is in fact not very different to federalism".[25] The regional government law reserved a limited number of fields exclusively for the central government — foreign affairs, defence and security, the courts, monetary and fiscal policy, religion and a number of broad economic-policy areas including macro-developmental planning, state economic institutions, development of human and natural resources, and high technology (Article 7).[26] Specific authority assigned to the provincial governments was limited to the administration of central-government affairs in the regions, cross-district matters, and functions that the district governments were not yet ready to handle themselves (Article 9). District governments were given authority to engage in all fields not specifically reserved for the central or provincial governments but were explicitly "obliged" (*wajib*) to engage in such fields as public works, health, education and culture, agriculture, communications, industry and trade, investment, the environment, land matters, co-operatives and labour (Article 11). These provisions, however, contained potential ambiguities, as we shall see soon.

The existing hierarchical structure of regional government was abolished and simply replaced with provincial and district governments having their own fields of activity. Governors no longer exercised authority over district heads. Both would continue to be elected by their respective DPRDs but without the old practices that ensured that the president's candidates would always win. The role of provincial governors, however, remained somewhat ambiguous as they were entrusted with dual responsibilities as both the central government's representative in the province and head of the province elected by the DPRD. The new law only required that the provincial DPRD "consult" the president about the candidates for governor as "government representative" before voting while bupati and mayors would be simply elected by the district DPRD that was only required to "inform" the governor of the election.

The second Law on Fiscal Balance between the Central Government and the Regions (No. 25/1999) required that 25 per cent of central government revenue be allocated in block grants (*Dana Alokasi Umum*: DAU) to the regions according to a formula taking account of both needs and economic potential. Of DAU, 10 per cent would be allocated to provinces and 90 per cent to districts. In contrast to previous subsidies and grants from the central government which were largely tied to specific purposes, regional governments would now determine how most of the funding was used. In provisions that particularly benefited resource-rich regions, the law also allowed local governments to retain much larger shares of revenues produced in their regions.[27] Fiscal decentralization thus resulted in a huge transfer of funds from the centre to the regions. From 17 per cent in 2000 before the implementation of regional autonomy, the regional share in government spending rose to 32 per cent for 2002.[28] (The two provinces facing separatist insurgencies, Aceh and Papua, were later granted "Special Autonomy" which allowed them to retain much higher proportions of oil and natural-gas revenues.)[29]

A key aspect of the laws was that they largely by-passed the provincial governments by providing greatly expanded functions and resources to the districts.[30] A major goal of decentralization was to undercut potential separatist challenges. Some provinces outside Java had sufficient population, economic resources and sense of communal and ethnic identity to contemplate separation but independence was hardly an option for a kabupaten — the average population of kabupaten outside Java being around 300,000. It was therefore planned initially to abolish the 27 provincial governments and make the more than 300 districts the sole focus of regional autonomy. The districts, which would enjoy the benefits of political autonomy while remaining integrated economically and socially with their neighbours, would be unlikely candidates for independent statehood. Unfortunately for the plan, however, the newly adopted electoral laws had already provided for elections to provincial DPRDs and could not be revised without causing a delay in holding the vital general election. For this reason the plan to dissolve the provincial governments was abandoned.[31] Nevertheless, the law greatly strengthened the role of the districts which were no longer obliged to carry out the instructions of the provincial governors but empowered to determine their own priorities.

Despite their radical nature, the laws passed through the DPR quite smoothly. Submitted to the DPR in February 1999, they were signed by the president in May. The World Bank reported that "the drafting of the law remained largely a bureaucratic process, with little feedback from politicians, and even less from the regions".[32] Ryaas Rasyid noted, "the two decentralization bills attracted relatively little public attention. In the national parliament itself, the bills were passed into law with a minimum of debate and few amendments. Indeed, no substantial changes were made from the government's original draft legislation."[33] The atmosphere of national crisis and fear of possible national disintegration undoubtedly influenced Golkar's and the military's abandonment of centralism. But political considerations reinforced Golkar's approach. It quickly calculated that its own interests could be served by the transfer of power to the regions where it was already deeply embedded in regional government and that uncompromising commitment to existing central domination would be harmful to its electoral prospects in the general election due in June 1999, only a few weeks after the law was adopted.[34] Military officers, many of whom had been suspicious of regional autonomy, also adjusted to the new circumstances and the military group in the DPR did not stand in the way of the legislation. Later General Wiranto said that "it is necessary for the concept of regional autonomy to be realized immediately to overcome the large number of protests in the regions".[35] Apart from the elections, the lack of public attention to the regional autonomy laws in early 1999 was also due to the other pressing political preoccupations at that time, including student demonstrations calling for the trial of Soeharto, ructions in the military, a huge financial scandal involving President Habibie and the referendum on East Timor.

The adoption of the regional autonomy laws seems to have had some effect in ameliorating discontent. Regionalist sentiment had been most worrying from the point of view of Jakarta in the four provinces that had most economic potential to stand alone due to their reserves of oil and natural gas. Of these, armed separatist movements had already long been active for other reasons in Aceh and Papua which were treated as "special cases" by Jakarta. In Riau, which supplied nearly a quarter of Indonesia's exports, a Free Riau (*Riau Merdeka*) movement appeared in March 1999 under the leadership of Tabrani Rab, a medical doctor and professor at the Riau University. In January 2000, a majority of delegates at an unofficial "Riau People's Congress" voted in favour of independence but the resolution, which gained 270 votes, failed to win an absolute majority among the 623 entitled to vote.[36] The Free Riau movement's support, however, was largely limited to Malays who constituted only 38 per cent of the province's population. The decentralization laws appear to have undercut much of the movement's dynamism.[37] Whatever support the movement won seems to have been used to strengthen the province's bargaining position with the central government rather than to fight for independence. In the other major oil and natural-gas producing province, East Kalimantan, regionalist aspirations were taken up by the provincial government itself shortly after Soeharto's fall. The governor, a retired military officer, quickly asked for the return of 75 per cent of oil, natural gas and timber revenues and in November 1999 the DPRD adopted a resolution by acclamation calling for a federal system.[38] However, the local PDI-P, Golkar and TNI, apparently under pressure from their respective headquarters in Jakarta, quickly called for a review of the resolution.[39] Eventually, apparently satisfied by the deal that the province received under the decentralization laws, East Kalimantan withdrew its support for federalism.

Confused Implementation

The new autonomy laws, which began to be implemented on 1 January 2001, were in part statements of broad intent and lacked detail on many important issues. The government therefore needed to issue numerous regulations during the twenty months between the law's adoption and its implementation. Preparations for implementation were further complicated by a struggle between the "radical" Ryaas Rasyid, whom President Abdurrahman Wahid appointed as Minister of State for Regional Autonomy, and the "conservative" Lt. Gen. (ret.) Surjadi Surdirdja, the Minister of Home Affairs. This struggle ended in victory for Surjadi in August 2000 when responsibility for regional government was transferred to an expanded Department of Home Affairs and Regional Autonomy under Surjadi while Ryaas was left with the State Ministry for Administrative Reform. On the day after the implementation of the laws commenced, a frustrated Ryaas resigned from the cabinet.[40]

Administrative preparations for autonomy proceeded very slowly. Ryaas estimated that effective decentralization would require 120 legal instruments — 5 laws, 47 government regulations, 7 presidential degrees and various other regulations.[41] By the time that the one-year deadline imposed by the law for the completion of necessary regulations had been reached, only one had been issued and many had still not appeared by 1 January 2001, the date of the law's implementation.[42] The failure to provide essential implementing regulations, together with ambiguities in the law itself, caused much confusion among both central and regional officials about what was expected of them and led to many disputes when powers seemed to be overlapping. Thus, for example, Article 7 reserving certain fields for the central government was sometimes understood as limiting the central government to those fields.[43] On the other hand, Article 11, which listed "obligatory" responsibilities for the districts, was interpreted by district officials as giving them exclusive authority in these areas. In fact this article was not intended to exclude the central government totally. According to a World Bank study, the law's drafters had thought it unnecessary to state that districts were bound by national laws because they considered such a stipulation too obvious.[44]

As Kent Eaton remarked in his discussion of decentralization in Argentina and the Philippines, "Rather than being a one-shot deal, the decision to decentralize opens up a new and contentious arena for political struggle."[45] The confusion resulting from the implementation of the laws was exacerbated by competing interests between the central and regional bureaucracies, and within regional bureaucracies. Resistance to decentralization was, of course, not just a matter of technical arguments over which fields of activity were more efficiently managed by the central, provincial or district governments. In a bureaucracy where official salaries fell far short of the daily needs of civil servants and where senior officials exercised extensive discretion in making decisions, corruption was the norm. Officials routinely extracted unofficial payments for the awarding of contracts, the granting of licences, the allocation of development funds, and any other benefit that required a signature. Within the bureaucracy itself, recruits normally had to pay for their initial appointments and later promotions. The decentralization of authority, therefore, inherently involved the decentralization of corruption.

In a discussion paper written in 2002, I Made Suwandi, an official of the Department of Home Affairs, explained that the source of conflict was often "the tendency of struggles over authority between levels of government to be related to access to financial sources originating from that authority. Authorities that produce revenues lead to many problems [due to rivalries] while authorities that do not produce revenue are avoided". Among areas in dispute, the paper noted matters involving land, harbours, airports, forestry, plantations, mining and management of natural resources.[46] Among the central departments and agencies that were most reluctant to transfer authority to the regions were those responsible for such fields as logging, mining, land and transport, which were all potentially very lucrative from the point of view of the supervising bureaucrats.[47] Those who held power to allocate benefits in the past — such as senior officials in the central bureaucracy and governors in provinces — naturally resented the loss of these powers and often resisted the process.[48] At the same time, of course, the new beneficiaries in the regions fought to keep their new opportunities. Although the laws provided wide authority to the regions, the beneficiaries of the old system sought to win back some of their authority through new laws and implementing regulations.

Even before the implementation of the regional autonomy laws on 1 January 2001, several central departments had taken steps to quarantine important powers from the scope of decentralization.[49] Only a few months after Law No. 22 on Regional Government was adopted by the DPR, the same legislature with the same membership adopted Law No. 41 on Forestry which had been proposed by the Department of Forestry. While the regional government law excluded forestry from the fields reserved for the central government, the law on forestry gave authority to the central government "to regulate and manage everything related to forests, forested areas and forest products" (Article 2).[50] Thus, the Forestry Department "deliberately pulled back much of the authority decentralized" by the regional government law.[51] In the same vein, President Abdurrahman's Minister of Mining and Energy, Lt. Gen. Susilo Bambang Yudhoyono, declared that the strategic nature of mining, oil and gas, and power meant that they should remain under his department, as provided by 1967 legislation.[52] Thus, the mining sector "was exempted at the last minute from the regional autonomy arrangements. The central government still retains the right to award lucrative mining contracts and set the terms, including how the profits and royalties or fees should be shared out".[53] Similarly, Law No. 43/1999 on the Civil Service competed with provisions of the decentralization law adopted a few months earlier. In another example, the regional autonomy law gave authority over capital investment to districts (Article 11.2) although Law No. 1/1967 (Article 28) granted authority over foreign investment to the central government. And Presidential Decision No. 62/2001 provided that "some of the responsibilities" of the National Land Agency in the regions would continue to be undertaken by the central government despite "land matters" being explicitly included among the regional responsibilities in Law No. 22 and despite the normal practice that laws should take precedence over presidential decisions.

Disputes between different authorities, therefore, were rife. Some districts wanted to require fishermen from outside their district to obtain fishing permits because control over the sea up to four miles from the shore was given to districts, between four and twelve miles from the shore to provinces, and beyond twelve miles to the centre.[54] Disputes arose over the management of water when several district governments demanded royalties for water "exported" to cities.[55] Some disputes involved activities shared by different levels of government in the same field, particularly in the lucrative timber industry where corruption was routine. For example, a dispute arose between the provincial government of West Kalimantan and the kabupaten of Pontianak over the export of logs. In West Java the provincial government and the state forestry enterprise, PT Perhutani, both claimed authority to manage forests under different laws. One observer commented, "This can happen because both sides see the activities of timber companies as sugar" (referring to a common Indonesian remark that "where there is sugar, there must be ants").[56] Similar disputes arose over land issues, another area offering much opportunity for extra-legal payments. The central government requested district governments to withdraw regulations establishing regional Land Agencies (*Dinas Pertanahan*) but "some Local Governments refused to do so as they argued that the authority for land affairs has been given to Local Government under Law 22/1999".[57] In the Kutai Kertanegara kabupaten in East Kalimantan, competing officials of both the National Land Board and the district Land Agency even occupied the same office.[58] It was only in 2001 that government regulations were issued determining control of airports and harbours after some local authorities had laid claim to harbours.[59] Ryaas Rasyid mentioned "the hundreds — possibly even thousands — of new mining, forestry, fishing and trading licences that violate existing laws, or the new taxes and charges local governments have frequently imposed on business in order to generate revenue".[60] Personal relations between officials were also affected. Many governors now felt affronted when district heads took major decisions without consultation and even failed to send monthly reports or absented themselves from meetings.

Central government departments which previously had extensive responsibilities in the regions naturally resented the transfer of powers to the provinces and districts. Decentralization had involved the transfer of 2.4 million central civil servants to the regions.[61] This did not mean the physical re-location of personnel from Jakarta but the transfer of those already working in regions to regional payrolls under regional authority. Two-thirds of the transferred personnel were in the field of education and another 6 per cent in health.[62] It also involved regional take-over of many of the functions of the offices of central government departments.

In Indonesian jurisprudence, inconsistencies between laws should be resolved on the basis of three principles: higher laws take precedence over lower regulations (e.g., national laws are "higher" than government regulations or presidential decisions);[63] later laws take precedence over earlier laws; and specific laws take precedence over general laws. The central Department of Forestry, therefore, argued that Law No. 41/1999 on Forestry, which was adopted in September 1999 and dealt with the specific question of forestry, took precedence over the general regional autonomy laws adopted in May. On the other hand, the Department of Mining and Energy argued that the specific 1967 mining law, although adopted several decades earlier, took precedence over the later regional autonomy law. In the case of authority over land, a "lower" presidential decision somehow took precedence in practice over a "higher" law. Thus there was much scope for legal argument about which was the general and which the specific law. In practice, officials usually adopted whichever interpretation best suited their interests. In many cases, the result was confusion as both central and regional authorities competed for control and issued their own contradictory regulations.[64]

Financial Decentralization

The law on Fiscal Balance aimed to distribute funds between the centre and the regions in a way that was "proportional, democratic, just and transparent taking into account the potential, conditions and needs of the regions".[65] A major concern was to alleviate discontent in potentially separatist resource-rich regions by allowing them to keep a larger share of income derived from their natural resources and thus temper separatist aspirations. At the same time it was necessary to ensure that resource-poor regions continued to be subsidized by the centre. It was generally assumed that, apart from the large provinces in Java, only the oil producers, Riau, East Kalimantan, Papua and

Aceh could survive without central subsidies while only seventeen of more than three hundred districts were believed to be self-financing.[66]

In the past most provincial finance had come in the form of a direct subsidy and special grants from the central government. In the 1999 law, the subsidy and grants were replaced by the DAU amounting to at least 25 per cent of the central government's revenue. The DAU was purportedly designed to "equalize (*pemerataan*) financial capacity between regions".[67] The distribution between the regions was based on a formula that took into account both economic potential and needs. The larger the gap between needs and potential, the larger the allocation.[68] The new law also included provisions that explicitly favoured resource-rich regions. Revenues from timber, fisheries, general mining, natural gas and petroleum were to be shared between producing regions and the central government in varying proportions.[69] Apart from natural-resource revenues, the law also provided for the sharing of land and building taxes and property transfer taxes between the central and regional governments.

The regions were also given scope to raise local revenue (*Pendapatan Asli Daerah*: PAD) in the form of local taxes (*pajak*), user-charges (*retribusi*) and income from government-owned enterprises. Many regional governments, especially those lacking in natural resources, quickly looked for new local sources of revenue without giving much consideration to long-term economic consequences or to the welfare of neighbouring regions. Taxes and charges were imposed on the movement of goods or agricultural produce into and out of regions. The province of Lampung, for example, exploited its geographical location as the last province in Sumatra through which produce was transported on its way to Java to place taxes on goods being transported through the province. District governments tapped all sorts of other revenue sources such as taxes and charges on storage of cement or coal, the use of agricultural machinery, cutting down trees outside forests, ownership of chain saws or health inspections of cattle.[70] In Bali, non-Balinese had to pay for special identity cards. In Ciamis (West Java), a user-charge was imposed on school enrolments from kindergarten to high school. One region taxed advertisements on Coca Cola bottles. The Indonesian Chamber of Commerce and Industry (Kadin) complained that 1,006 regulations impeded business[71] while the World Bank referred to "nuisance taxes". One survey of business perceptions suggested that it was poorer regions where PAD amounted to less than 15 per cent of total revenues that "tend to impose regional regulations on levies and charges that are unfriendly to the business community".[72]

In regions endowed with natural resources such as timber and minerals, illegal exploitation was common. As Ida Resosudarmo notes, "Nowhere has the disorderly and sudden nature of the changes brought about by decentralization been more apparent than in the management of Indonesia's forest resources."[73] Even before the decentralization laws were passed, local governments were already distributing timber licences both to acquire big increases in local revenues and do corrupt deals with timber companies. Discussing timber in Kalimantan, John McCarthy recorded that "When district government agencies used their enhanced discretionary powers under decentralization to create district regulatory regimes, they ignored some laws and chose to base district regulations only on those higher laws that suited their agenda."[74] Resosudarmo, also writing about Kalimantan, concluded that "Almost everywhere the picture is the same: of local governments, motivated by necessity and opportunity, attempting to generate revenue from forest resources without adequately considering the social and environmental consequences."[75] One consequence was a rise in illegal logging.[76] Regional governments were also involved in illegal mining, as the case of coalmining in West Sumatra illustrates.[77]

The regional governments, however, were still subject to some central controls. Law No. 22 on regional government required that regional regulations should not contradict existing national laws and regional regulations and did not conflict with the "public interest" (Article 70), and Law No. 34/2000 required that all regional regulations be submitted for approval by the Department of Home Affairs within fifteen days and also required the department to make its decision on their validity within one month. According to a study by the Asia Foundation, by mid-2003, some 6,000 regional regulations had been submitted,[78] but Turner and Podger reported that "The central agencies are unable to cope efficiently and effectively with the deluge of regulations."[79] The most controversial were the new taxes and user-charges. The 2003 Asia Foundation assessment claimed that some 1,000 district regulations on taxes and user charges had yet to be assessed partly because the Home Affairs Department had to refer technical regulations to other departments.[80] The Department of Home Affairs announced in November 2003 that it had examined 3,312 regulations of which 237 were cancelled by the Department of Home Affairs and another 206 by the Department of Finance.[81] Among the reasons for cancellation of financial regulations were that some taxes overlapped with central taxes, some charges were not really user-charges, and some duplicated existing taxes or charges. Other reasons related to the public good, such as that they obstructed the movement of goods and produce, contributed to "a high-cost economy" and in effect increased government subsidies.[82]

Despite the equalizing rhetoric of Law No. 25/1999, inequality between regions remained high. The per capita revenue of the richest district had risen to fifty times that of the poorest. Per capita revenue in the wealthiest ten per cent of district governments was six times larger than in the lowest 10 per cent.[83] Of all district budgets in 2002, 79 per cent came from DAU, 12 per cent from natural-resource revenue and 5 per cent from PAD.[84] However, the overall figure disguised large disparities between districts. The typical wealthy district obtained large natural-resource and PAD revenues while depending on DAU for less than half its budget. On the other hand, DAU provided more than 90 per cent of revenues in poor districts which lacked natural resources and sources for PAD taxes and user-charges. Such poor districts made up more than half the regions.[85] Kutai Kartanegara, the centre of East Kalimantan's oil and natural gas industries, for example, experienced rapid development and was able to abolish all fees in primary and secondary schools, provide all head teachers with motorcycles and supplement teachers' salaries by Rp 250,000 per month.[86] In 2004, Kutai Kertanegara's budget of Rp 2,943 trillion exceeded by far that of its neighbour, Kutai Timur, which expected revenues of only Rp 690 billion, and was only slightly less than the East Kalimantan provincial budget of Rp 3 billion.[87] Badung, the centre of Bali's tourist industry, obtained Rp 225 billion in PAD compared to Rp 5 billion in Jembrana and Rp 3 billion in Bangli, both in the same province.[88] The total revenue of Pacitan, one of the poorest districts in Java, was Rp 214 billion — less than Badung's PAD revenue alone — while Pacitan's PAD revenue amounted to only Rp 5.5 billion. Pacitan depended on DAU for 92 per cent of its revenue.[89] In the poor provinces, most of the DAU was spent on salaries and basic services in education and health.

Despite the term "regional autonomy", the regions continued to remain financially dependent on the central government which retained the major sources of revenue such as income tax and the largest share of oil and natural-gas revenues. Moreover, the central government retained the right to veto regional budgets and regulations considered to conflict with the "public interest". On the other hand, resources transferred to the regions increased vastly and the regions now had much wider scope to determine how revenues would be used.

REVISING THE LAWS

The rapid transfer of new powers and resources not only to twenty-six provinces but more importantly to more than three hundred districts had led to a kind of unrestrained euphoria and what central officials regarded as unintended "excesses".[90] In August 2000, even before the regional autonomy laws were implemented, the MPR adopted a decree that described regional autonomy as "experiencing much failure and not achieving its declared goals". Implying the restoration of hierarchy, the decree recommended a "fundamental revision" of the two laws including the "provision of levels of autonomy (*otonomi bertingkat*) to provinces, kebupaten/municipalities, villages, etc".[91] This was reinforced by an amendment to the constitution that allowed the regions "the widest autonomy" (*otonomi seluas-luasnya*) but with a proviso excluding "government activities determined by law as Central Government activities".[92] In February 2001, only a month after implementation of the laws had begun, Abdurrahman's Minister of Home Affairs, Surjadi, announced that they would be reviewed.[93]

The Early Debate on Revision

In contrast to the critical conditions faced by the Habibie government when it launched its regional autonomy programme in 1999, the debate over revising the regional autonomy laws was conducted in less urgent circumstances and stretched from 2001 to 2004. Following the 1999 election, the DPR was no longer dominated by Golkar but included a wide range of parties, among which the centralist-inclined PDI-P was the largest. As no party or coalition dominated the DPR, the process was marked by drawn-out bargaining involving parties and the bureaucrats of the Department of Home Affairs. The advocates of revision did not seek a return to Soeharto-era centralism but were disturbed by the "excesses" of the 1999 laws. They argued for the restoration of hierarchy and an overhaul of the distribution of powers between different levels of government.

The criticism of the 1999 laws was both ideological and pragmatic. The ideological argument was prominent in the statements of President Megawati and some PDI-P leaders, and found support among officials of the Department of Home Affairs.[94] They focused on the preservation of the unitary state that was seen as essential to defend national unity and to uphold the vision of Indonesians as a united people. The president was among those who felt uneasy about the laws which, she said, involved "our statehood and nationhood". The laws needed to be amended "to strengthen our national unity and the integrity of the unitary state of the Republic of Indonesia".[95] Dr Soedarsono Hardjosoekarto, the Director-General for General Governance and Regional Autonomy in the Department of Home Affairs and head of the "revision team", argued that "we should realize that the autonomy concept deviates from the unitary state principle stipulated in the 1945 Constitution". He expressed his concern that "The regions (*kabupaten*) and mayoralties (*kotam*) have increasingly become sovereign entities with their own authority separate from that of the central government ...We don't want to see regions developing into independent entities within the Indonesian state".[96]

A major source of conflict and disputation, critics argued, was the abolition of the hierarchical relationship between the central government, the provinces and districts with the consequence that regional governments could act independently of the centre. While still vice president, Megawati had complained that "We're already seeing signs of 'rebellion' by the regencies (i.e., kabupaten) toward the provincial government, which should have authority over the regencies."[97] Megawati and other critics were also disturbed by policies adopted by some regional governments which favoured local ethnic communities and discriminated against people from other regions.[98] Looking ahead, Soedarsono even saw the autonomy laws as leading potentially to the breakup of the country: "We are deeply concerned by the loss of hierarchy between provinces and regencies or mayoralties, the arrogance of resource-rich regions and their egoism and racist policies. Under the current autonomy law, rich regions could easily demand separation from Indonesia."[99]

On the pragmatic level, a wide range of critics claimed that the autonomy laws had been introduced too hastily without proper preparations. The failure to issue sufficient implementing regulations resulted in a chaotic situation, as discussed earlier, in which regional officials were able to adopt their own interpretations of the laws which often conflicted with the interpretations of others. Business organizations protested about the adverse consequences of uncertainty on the investment climate while senior officials complained about the discretion enjoyed by regional DPRDs to manage their own finances which led to most of their budgets being spent on salaries and facilities for DPRD members such as housing, cars, overseas tours and so on.[100]

Soedarsono's team completed their proposed amendments in late 2001. Ideologically, the new draft rejected Law 22's use of the term "authority" (*kewenangan*) to describe the powers transferred to the regional governments and instead proposed that regional governments "organize and manage government activities" (*mengatur dan mengurus urusan pemerintahan*) at the regional level. The new language implied that the regional governments would simply perform certain activities or functions under the "authority" of the national government. An accompanying "academic paper" argued that in a unitary state regional and central governments are "interdependent and hierarchical".[101] The Minister of Home Affairs, Hari Sabarno, said that the provincial governors would exercise more authority by "supervising, monitoring, evaluating and facilitating" district governments.[102] Among specific changes aiming to restore hierarchy between the levels of government, the draft proposed granting the president power to dissolve regional assemblies if an assembly "obstructs the implementation of governance so that the regional government cannot carry out its duties and obligations".[103] The draft also transferred authority to appoint provincial secretaries from the provincial governments to the Minister of Home Affairs.[104]

The draft quickly ran into strong opposition from Golkar which was well represented among regional government heads and in regional DPRDs at both provincial and district levels, especially in the regions outside Java. Golkar warned that the draft tended to restore centralism and was particularly concerned by the proposed granting of authority to the president to dissolve regional assemblies.[105] The Speaker of the MPR and leader of PAN, Amien Rais, warned against "spontaneous" revision of the laws which, he said, "require deep thought because of their extensive consequences".[106] While Golkar district heads, especially from outside Java, tended to be strongly opposed to the proposed bill, PDI-P bupati in Java were often quite ambivalent, on one hand supporting their party's centralist stand while at the same time, as district leaders, preferring more autonomy.[107]

Strong opposition to the draft was also expressed by the associations representing district governments. The chairman of the association of kabupaten governments (APKASI — *Asosiasi Pemerintah Kabupaten Seluruh Indonesia*), Syaukani HR, who was the bupati of oil-rich Kutai Kertanegara in East Kalimantan and a local Golkar leader, claimed that 60 per cent of the draft "moved in the direction of centralism".[108] In a policy paper in 2003, APKASI stated that regional autonomy had already reached "a point of no return" and warned against "systematic endeavours by various interested groups to obstruct the implementation of regional autonomy, as can be seen by various government authorities that should be transferred to the regions but have been pulled back to the Centre for various reasons".[109] APKASI's stand was supported by the association of municipal governments (APEKSI — *Asosiasi Pemerintah Kota Seluruh Indonesia*) and the association of municipal parliaments (ADEKSI — *Asosiasi DPRD Kota Seluruh Indonesia*).[110] On the other hand, the association representing provincial governments (APPSI — *Asosiasi Pemerintah Provinsi Seluruh Indonesia*), headed by the Jakarta governor, Lt. Gen. (ret.) Sutiyoso, was more positive toward the draft which promised to restore authority to the provincial governors.[111]

In response to growing criticism from regional governments, particularly but not only at the district level, the central government announced in May 2002 that it would prepare a new draft. It is not unlikely that the PDI-P-led government was worried that the opposition of Golkar and some of the Muslim parties together with the associations representing the district heads and legislatures might have adverse consequences for the PDI-P in the general election due in 2004.[112] It may have also worried about ambivalence among PDI-P's own bupati, especially in Java.[113] Although the initial draft was withdrawn, the government remained committed to revising the 1999 law, particularly by restoring the authority of provincial governors.[114] The two largest parties in the DPR-D, the PDI-P and Golkar, both supported this view.[115]

The central government did not abandon its goal of curbing the powers of the districts and restoring some semblance of "hierarchy" but pursued its objective in a more incremental way. In July 2002, the Department of Home Affairs issued regulations that provided nineteen new "authorities" to provincial governors, including authority to supervise licensing, coordinate information and conduct "repressive supervision of district regulations and decisions of district heads and DPRDs".[116] Later in the year, governors were made responsible for city and district planning, licences for logging and mining, supervision of local budgets, maintenance of security, and the supervision of foreign investments or agreements.[117] Early in 2003, a regulation sought to impose uniformity on the structure of local government by limiting the number of separate departments within a region and requiring that their heads had the same bureaucratic status. Another regulation gave the governors more scope to appoint officials in the districts.[118] A presidential decision in 2004 also centralized all investment permits "under one roof" at the central Capital Investment Coordination Agency (*Badan Kordinasi Penanaman Modal*: BKPM) instead of under the authority of governors and district heads.[119]

The New Law

The Department of Home Affairs was very slow in drafting the new version of the law and it seemed likely that some of its provisions would be controversial in the DPR and lead to further delay. Thus, there were doubts that the new law could be adopted before the DPR's current five-year term expired at the end of September 2004. The parties in the DPR, however, wanted to ensure that new provisions for direct elections of governors and district heads would be in force when a new round of regional elections commenced in 2005 after a moratorium imposed for the presidential election. In 2003, the DPR had already adopted a new Law on the Composition and Position of the MPR, DPR, DPD and DPRDs which created a vacuum by removing the provisions that required governors, bupati and mayors to be elected by the appropriate DPRD. Rather than wait for the uncertain adoption of the department's comprehensive bill, the DPR itself took the initiative to draw up its own bill devoted only to regional elections in case the department's new bill missed the deadline. This move was backed by all the parties, especially those that were confident of winning executive positions, particularly PDI- P and Golkar. The Department of Home Affairs, which was expecting that its new bill would face substantial opposition in the DPR, then took the opportunity presented by the DPR's bill to finalize its draft and amalgamate it with the DPR's draft.[120] With the parties in the DPR focusing primarily on the issue of regional elections and showing less interest in the Department of Home Affairs' revisions, the combined bill was sent to the DPR in May and finally passed on 29 September 2004, one day before the expiry of the DPR's term.

A major goal of the central government had been to re-establish its own authority over the regions. In contrast to the 1999 law which opened all fields to the regional governments except for a short list of powers reserved for the central government, the new Law on Regional Government No. 32/2004 preserved the short list of central powers but described all other "government activities" (*urusan pemerintahan*) as "concurrent" with some potentially falling within the scope of the central government, while others could be placed under regional government. Regional governments were permitted to propose to the central government that certain matters should be transferred to particular regions. Among the criteria were the extent to which the impact of the activity is limited to the district or provincial levels or extends to the national level; the extent to which accountability is facilitated by the direct involvement of the level of government in administering the activity; and whether the activity could be carried out efficiently at the proposed level.[121] The central government could determine that certain activities are "obligatory" for regional governments such as the provision of such basic services as primary education, health, minimal living requirements and basic infrastructure (Article 13.4).

The new law re-established the hierarchy of regional government. It linked the governor upwards to the central government and downwards to the district governments. The 1999 law made governors responsible to the president in their capacity as the central "government representative" (*wakil Pemerintah*) in the province and also responsible to the DPRD in their capacity as head of the region (*kepala daerah*), but they had no authority over district governments. In contrast to the earlier law, the new law explicitly made them responsible for guiding (*pembinaan*), supervising (*pengawasan*) and coordinating the district governments (Articles 38.1). The law also provided that the provincial secretary (head of the provincial bureaucracy), who had previously been appointed by the governor with the approval of the DPRD, would now be appointed by the president on the advice of the governor, while the district secretaries would be appointed by the governor on the advice of the bupati or mayor (Article 122). In practice, this meant that the regional governments would submit three names to the governor or president who would make the final choice.[122]

In carrying out their responsibilities, governors and heads of district governments issued regional regulations with the approval of the DPRD. The law provided for governors to take over the central government's responsibility to assess district regulations, while provincial regulations continued to be assessed by the centre. As under the previous law, regulations could be invalidated if they conflicted with higher laws or regulations (such as national laws, government regulations, etc.) or were considered to be opposed to "the public interest".[123] Most significantly, regulations concerning financial matters had to be evaluated before implementation in contrast to non-financial regulations that could be invalidated after implementation.[124] The law, therefore, in effect gave the central government a veto over provincial budgets and taxes.[125] In practice, this meant that the provincial government had to send delegations to Jakarta to negotiate budget details.[126] The accompanying Law on Fiscal Balance explicitly forbade regional governments from adopting regional regulations that resulted in "a high-cost economy", or restricted the mobility of the population, trade or services, as well as imports and exports.[127]

The part of the law derived from the bill initiated by the DPR also strengthened the position of governors and district heads in dealing with their local DPRDs. Since the free 1999 election, most DPRDs were no longer dominated by Golkar and usually consisted of many parties, none of which had absolute majorities. As a result, regional heads often faced hostile legislatures that rejected their annual reports and sometimes attempted to depose them. Following the spirit of the constitutional amendment regulating the dismissal of the president, the new law restricted the grounds for dismissal of regional heads to specific violations which required not only the agreement of two-thirds of the DPRD, but also the approval of the Supreme Court. By restricting the grounds of dismissal and requiring clear procedures, the law provided protection to regional heads from dismissal attempts arising from normal political rivalries. Most importantly, it also provided for the direct election of regional heads.

All the parties, as well as the Department of Home Affairs, agreed that direct elections should be held but they differed over details. As usual, the positions taken by the parties were determined mainly by their assessments of their electoral prospects. Rather than follow the national example requiring a candidate to obtain more than 50 per cent of the votes in order to win in the first round, the larger parties with realistic hopes of first-round victories — such as PDI-P, Golkar and PKB — favoured the lowering of the requirement to 25 per cent. They also calculated that their chances of such victories would be enhanced if the number of candidates were reduced. They therefore not only rejected independent candidates, but wanted to limit contestants to those nominated by parties or coalitions of parties that held at least 15 per cent of the seats in the DPRD. Unexpectedly, the conservative Department of Home Affairs adopted a liberal view towards independents and proposed in the draft bill that non-party candidates would be permitted to run if they were able to demonstrate that they had the support of at least 1 per cent of the voters.[128] In the end, the law adopted the 25 per cent requirement, restricted party candidates to those nominated by a party or coalition of parties winning either 15 per cent of the seats in the DPRD or 15 per cent of the votes in the general election, and rejected the Home Affairs proposal to allow non-party independents to be nominated.[129]

Overall, the new law shifted the balance of authority from the regions towards the central government. The hierarchy abolished by Law No. 22/1999 was restored and, in a formal sense, ultimate authority was now placed in the hands of the central government in accordance with the concept of the unitary state. In contrast to Law No. 22 under which residual powers not assigned exclusively to the central government were — somewhat ambiguously — left open to the regional governments, Law No. 32/2004 firmly stated that all authority rested with the central government which delegated the administration of particular "activities" to the regional governments. It strengthened the role of the governor as the centre's "representative" at the expense of the districts. The central government also acquired the power to select provincial secretaries and received strengthened authority to veto regional regulations. Regional budgets now had to be approved by the central government before their adoption by the DPRD. Thus the new law gave the centre substantial legal powers that could potentially be used at the regional level. But regional interests that had emerged since the fall of the New Order were by now too deeply entrenched to be brushed aside. In reality, the new law was far from marking a full return to the centralistic structure of the Soeharto era. In practice, the central government left most administration in the hands of the regions which continued to control a vastly increased share of public expenditure. Most importantly, the amalgamation of the DPR's bill with that of the Department of Home Affairs incorporated the DPR's proposal to introduce direct elections of governors and district heads in place of the old system under which they were elected by members of the DPRDs. Although the law gave governors authority to guide, supervise and coordinate bupati and mayors, elections resulted in governors having to bargain with district heads, including those from different parties to that of the governor.[130] The enhanced local legitimacy of regional heads acquired through direct elections balanced the centralizing tendencies of other parts of the law.

The deliberation of Law No. 32/2004 took place as Indonesia moved from "crisis-ridden" to "politics-as-usual" circumstances. Unlike the rushed 1999 laws that were driven by deep uncertainties about the viability of the Indonesian state itself, as well as President Habibie's aspiration to retain the presidency in the forthcoming elections, the revision process was spread over more than three years of bargaining within both the DPR as well as the Department of Home Affairs. As the threat of national disintegration receded, political rivalries increasingly came to the fore and parties sought to advance their own interests in the new legislation. Lacking the support of a dominant coalition, the government gave considerable scope to the DPR itself to determine the details of the law which was finally adopted on the eve of its dissolution at the end of its five-year term. In the usual Indonesian way, the law was adopted unanimously after compromises between the main parties that provided at least something for everyone.

LOCAL DEMOCRACY:
MONEY POLITICS AND ELECTIONS

The reform of regional government overhauled the highly centralized New Order structure and promised a foundation for local democracy. The "good governance" argument for regional autonomy is that local government is closer to the people and will therefore be more responsive to their needs and expectations. Reformers expected that, with the lifting of the authoritarian political controls of the New Order, local "civil society" and a free press would emerge to monitor the performance of regional governments, ensure transparency, openness to criticism and sensitivity to local needs, and make elected politicians accountable to the voters. The Indonesian reformers did not see decentralization as a discrete programme but an integral part of the democratization that emerged after the fall of the Soeharto regime. Indeed, the teams that drafted the initial election and regional autonomy laws were both headed by the same man, Ryaas Rasyid. In response to those who claimed that decentralization would only transfer powers from corrupt central officials to corrupt regional officials, a combative Ryaas Rasyid responded: "That means that you think the DPRD is stupid, the journalists are stupid, the NGOs are stupid, the parties are stupid because they can be fooled by the corrupt head of a region. I don't believe that. How can you be corrupt if you are abused every day, your name is in the newspapers, you are faced with demonstrations, and the DPRD can bring you down when you are wrong?"[131]

In reality, however, the performance of regional government fell far short of Ryaas's expectations. Like the national election laws, the introduction of the regional autonomy laws introduced significant procedural changes but did not change the political milieu in which they would operate. In the regions, the dominant political elites of the New Order period were not swept away and replaced by leaders of the democratization movement.[132] Instead, most retained their existing positions but, in contrast to the Soeharto period when the authoritarian regime guaranteed their continued tenure, they now found themselves facing challengers. In some cases, committed reformers won election as heads of regions or as members of DPRDs, but in many other cases, as Vedi Hadiz puts it, the "predatory interests nurtured under the Soeharto regime's formerly vast, centralized system of patronage … have reconstituted themselves through new alliances, nationally and locally, and captured the institutions of Indonesia's democracy to further their own objectives".[133] The post-authoritarian competitors for local power, according to Hadiz, "include ambitious political fixers and entrepreneurs, wily and still-predatory state bureaucrats, and aspiring and newly ascendant business groups, as well as a wide range of political gangsters, thugs and civilian militia".[134]

The 1999 general election had provided the opportunity for citizens to elect new legislatures at all levels, but many politicians who had been involved in the corrupt practices of the New Order were re-elected while not a few new members seemed to be motivated by the desire to emulate their predecessors. During the following years, corruption in local government became pervasive. Illustrating his argument with a discussion of politics in North Sumatra, Hadiz describes how Golkar candidates were successful in almost all contests for bupati or mayor, despite Golkar's failure to retain its dominance in the 1999 general elections. In elections for regional heads conducted in the DPRDs, support was routinely "bought" by Golkar candidates.[135] But it was not only Golkar, the most successful party in regional elections outside Java, that carried over "normal" practices from the previous regime. The "reformist" PDI-P, the biggest party in Java, as well as smaller parties were no less engaged in money politics. It could hardly be expected, therefore, that the DPRDs both at the provincial and district levels would play the role Ryaas Rasyid expected of them by adequately supervising the performance of regional heads. This failure was particularly obvious when regional heads presented "accountability reports" to the DPRD and when new heads of regions were elected.

Law No. 22 required regional heads to present a report to the DPRD at the end of every budget year. If the report were rejected by the DPRD, the official would be allowed to present an "improved" version, but if the report were rejected a second time, the DPRD could recommend dismissal. Even before the implementation of the law in 2001, DPRDs had responded to the new atmosphere by rejecting "accountability reports" by the governors of West Kalimantan, Aceh and Jakarta and several district heads.[136] It was widely believed that the threat of rejection of an accountability report by the DPRD was often motivated by the hope that the regional head would be willing to pay members of the DPRD to withdraw their threat. As the legal scholar, Satya Arinanto, put it, the DPRD's "bargaining position was largely identical with money".[137] A member of the national Election Commission, Hamid Awaluddin, described "accountability reports" as "no more than fields for extortion by members of legislatures".[138]

Payments were also routinely made to DPRD members when regional heads were elected. In many cases, rumours of "money politics" emerged when the successful candidate was not from the party that held the most seats in the assembly. Although such results were quite possible when minority parties formed coalitions to defeat the candidate of the majority party, suspicions were aroused when the number of votes for the majority party's own candidate fell far short of the number of seats held by that party. The PDI-P, despite the success of many of its candidates in Java and Bali, also experienced losses that seemed inexplicable in normal terms. Cornelis Lay, a political scientist from Yogyakarta's Gajah Mada University and a prominent member of the PDI-P, complained that "it is very clear in a number of cases that leaders who had been selected as candidates for the position of bupati through very democratic procedures at conferences from the lowest level to the branch level suddenly failed to win votes because they were betrayed by members of their own party in the DPRD only because of money".[139] Typical examples of PDI-P losses were in Medan (North Sumatra) where the party held 16 seats but its candidate won only 4 votes; Boyolali (Central Java) where it held 18 seats but won only 11 votes, and Jembrana (Bali) where it held 17 seats but won only 11 votes. In Kebumen (Central Java), the PDI-P candidate, Ms Rustriningsih, ensured victory by "quarantining" all eighteen members of her party in a hotel where they were subjected to "extra-tight security and supervision".[140] It was not only the PDI-P, however, that suffered such embarrassing defeats. Golkar and PKB candidates, among others, experienced similar fates. In one reported case, five unsuccessful candidates in Sibolga (North Sumatra) demanded their money back.[141] Afan Gaffar, a political scientist attached to the office of the Minister of State for Regional Autonomy, estimated that candidates for the position of bupati or mayor would need at least Rp 1 billion (US$100,000) for the purchase of votes.[142]

Blatant vote-buying became so ubiquitous that it had begun to undermine the legitimacy of Indonesia's new democracy. Signs of a changing mood appeared in 2000 when the MPR amended the constitution to provide for "the democratic election" of governors and district heads, implying that the current method was less than fully democratic.[143] But it was only in 2004, as already discussed, that indirect elections were abandoned in favour of direct popular votes. This reform, however, was not driven so much by regional DPRDs, but was a by-product of the MPR's decision to introduce direct election for the presidency, as discussed in Chapter 3. In fact, many members of DPRDs were unhappy with the reform of a system that had brought substantial material benefits to them personally, but their parties' representatives in the DPR recognized that the much publicized "money politics" in regional assemblies had damaged their reputations at the national level.[144]

Regional elections began to be held under the new provisions in 2005. Despite fears that direct elections would spur ethnic, religious and political tensions, the few disturbances were minor and usually organized by disappointed candidates. Rather than provoking high emotions and uncontrolled mobilization, the non-voting rate in 2005 was 31.3 per cent — higher than in the national elections of the previous year.[145] In several cases, the non-participation rate was higher than the percentage won by the successful pair of candidates.[146] One factor that minimized electoral violence was the realization on the part of candidates in multi-ethnic and multi-religious regions that their prospects of success would not be good unless they supplemented their own social bases of support with running mates who could attract votes from other communities. It became common for ideological differences to be trumped by tactical calculations, with the result that alliance patterns in the regions were very different to that at the national level. Thus, while Golkar, through Vice President Jusuf Kalla, was a key component of the dominant alliance in the DPR where PDI-P placed itself in opposition, Golkar and PDI-P were allies in some regions but rivals in others. Similarly, candidates from President Yudhoyono's PD sometimes fought local elections on the same ticket as the PDI-P, but on other occasions against it. The secular PDI-P and the Islamist party PBB both joined the coalition that won the governorship in West Sumatra. Another Islamist party, PKS, was prepared to form coalitions with almost any other party, even including the Christian PDS. In Poso kabupaten which had been torn by fighting between Muslims and Christians since 1999, all five pairs of candidates comprised a Christian and a Muslim.[147] The Constitutional Court's decision to allow parties not represented in DPRDs to pool their votes with other parties to meet the 15 per cent requirement resulted in some alliances consisting of a dozen or so parties. In at least several districts, alliances of small parties elected the district head.[148]

The ease with which "unlikely" alliances were formed indicated that ideological considerations carried little weight. The Golkar deputy chairman, Agung Laksono, said "There are no limits on forming coalitions with anyone. Provided that a candidate who joins a coalition with a Golkar candidate has strong selling points, is acceptable to the society, meets low resistance, and doesn't have 'problems'."[149] In selecting candidates, parties did not always require candidates to have a serious track record of support for the party, but were willing to offer party nomination in exchange for financial contributions — what was commonly called "hiring a boat". In some cases, candidates who failed to win the nomination of their own party, turned to other parties for nomination.[150] Political observer, Irman Lanti, noted that "Many party officials in various regions eventually became pure political entrepreneurs offering their services to those who sought nomination by a party".[151] Many candidates, as Mietzner pointed out, were drawn from the political elite of the New Order period and had previous or existing connections with Golkar, either as Golkar officials, civil servants, Golkar-linked businesspeople or military or police officers. In North Sulawesi, for example, all five gubernatorial candidates had previous direct or indirect affiliations with Golkar.[152] The introduction of direct elections meant that increased funds were needed to win an election. A senior government official estimated that about Rp 6 billion (US$600,000) was spent by one successful gubernatorial candidate.[153]

Due to the complexity of alliance patterns it was difficult to interpret the results in party terms. PDI-P and Golkar were the most successful parties, sometimes in alliance, but also as members of competing alliances.[154] The elections showed, however, that voters were often discriminating in casting their votes. For example, in six of seven gubernatorial elections in 2005 (the seventh was in a new province), incumbents did not perform well. In West Sumatra, the former governor could not find a party to nominate him. The incumbent governor of Bengkulu had to turn to an alliance of minor parties for his nomination but was defeated. Similarly the incumbent in South Kalimantan had to seek a new coalition of sponsors but still failed to regain his post. In Central Kalimantan and North Sulawesi, incumbents were at least able to secure the nomination of their own party, but also lost. At the district level, incumbents were more successful in the first round of elections in June 2005. Of 103 elections, incumbents succeeded in 65 while 38 lost.[155] By mid-2006, more than 40 per cent of incumbent governors, bupati and mayors in 224 regions had been defeated.[156]

Regional government after 2005 continued to be dominated by politicians from much the same backgrounds as those who had been dominant before the change to direct elections. But the process became more competitive and candidates had to take more account of public opinion. On the other hand, "money politics" remained pervasive. Instead of bribing DPRD members to win their support as in the pre-2004 DPRDs, candidates were usually forced to "rent a boat". Both before and after the reform, regional heads were left with debts to benefactors or even just to banks which had to be repaid. Local government, therefore, could not escape the influence of Hadiz's "predatory interests" and remained in various degrees "captured" by local elites, but direct election made it necessary to take more account of non-elite interests and provided at least some avenues for the emergence of reform-minded or performance-oriented candidates.

CONCLUSION

Regional government reform became imperative in the wake of the economic crisis of 1997 and the political crisis that led to the collapse of President Soeharto's government in May 1998. The widespread disaffection expressed in demands for the democratization of political institutions was also channeled into calls, especially in the provinces outside Java, for "real" regional autonomy and even federalism. As law-and-order deteriorated throughout the country and the spectre of national disintegration loomed on the horizon, the new Habibie government was convinced that drastic measures were needed. Although the pressure for wider regional autonomy was still largely limited to spontaneous agitation during the early months of the Habibie presidency, the government took the initiative to forestall the spread of organized demands by launching its own decentralization programme. In this respect the policy succeeded as separatist demands virtually disappeared, except in the regions already experiencing armed rebellion.

Political calculations were also important. Golkar, the party of Soeharto's New Order, quickly abandoned the centralized system that it had upheld for three decades and supported the passage of regional autonomy laws. Its policy reversal certainly had its roots in widespread popular dissatisfaction with the centralized system, especially in regions outside Java, and the broader concern about the possible break-up of the nation. But the party also calculated that its own interests could be served by the transfer of power to the regions, where it was already deeply embedded in regional government. And it was aware that dogged insistence on maintaining Soeharto's centralized system could lead to electoral disaster in the forthcoming general elections. Golkar's partner in administering the centralized system — the military — was pre-occupied with its own problems, as will be discussed in Chapter 5, and raised no serious objections to the new regional laws. These laws were rushed through the DPR partly in response to the continuing national crisis but also to take advantage of the window of opportunity provided by Golkar's domination of the unreconstructed DPR which was unlikely to survive the coming general election.

The government opted for what was called a "big bang" approach that made Indonesia's unitary state more decentralized than many federal states. A more cautious, incremental approach may well have been obstructed after the election as the predominantly Java-based and more centralist-inclined PDI-P was expected to become the largest party. But the speed of the transformation led to much disruption and confusion. The legislation was adopted hurriedly and the next government failed to issue essential implementing regulations. The result was much conflict over which level of government had authority in which field. At the same time, district governments quickly used new powers to raise local revenues in ways that often harmed neighbouring districts and imposed costs that hindered economic recovery. Even strong supporters of decentralization had to admit that the process had not gone smoothly and within months of its implementation calls were being made for a revision of the laws. In contrast to the initial regional autonomy law in 1999 that was widely accepted as a necessary response to a national crisis, the revised law was formulated in a more "normal" atmosphere and shaped by bargaining between rival bureaucratic and political interests. In a notoriously corrupt bureaucracy, the transfer of functions from the centre to the regions also meant the transfer of material resources with the result that central bureaucrats fought to restore some of their lost "territory", while those in the regions fought to retain what they had recently gained. A parallel battle was being played out in the DPR where the two leading parties, PDI-P and Golkar, bargained particularly over the contours of regional elections. The drafting of new legislation was long delayed but the law was eventually passed after compromises between the PDI-P, Golkar and the other parties. The new law returned significant authority to the centre and re-established the hierarchy that had been abolished by the 1999 law, but the core of decentralization proved to be irreversible and no demands were made to restore New Order-style centralization.

The limited recentralization tendency of the 2004 law was balanced by the introduction of direct elections of governors and regional heads, following the precedent set in the presidential election. After 1998, regional leaders had continued to be elected by regional DPRDs but, with the loosening of central controls and the introduction of genuine competition between candidates, the process had become extremely corrupt as DPRD members demanded payments for their votes. The introduction of direct elections, however, did not eliminate "money politics" in regional elections. Instead of purchasing the support of members of DPRDs, candidates now found themselves needing to purchase the support of political parties which, according to the law, had the sole authority to nominate candidates. Nevertheless, direct elections increased the degree of transparency in local politics and led to vigorous competition among candidates for the popular vote. As few candidates could hope to attract enough votes to win on the basis of support mobilized by their own party alone and from their own religious or ethnic community, it was necessary for form alliances with other parties and to reach out for support from other communities. One consequence of regional autonomy was that in forming alliances for regional elections, parties were under no compulsion to conform with alliances formed at the national level. Alliances reflected local conditions with the result that the pattern of alliances varied drastically from region to region.

The new regional government law provided a foundation for local democracy, just as the constitutional amendments and revised electoral laws had created a political system that largely met the standard international criteria of democracy. But like those at the national level, the new structures of government at the regional level could not guarantee a better quality of government.[157] As in the centre, "money politics" was ubiquitous. Writing about decentralization more generally, Manor argued that "Many [politicians] saw decentralization not as an alternative to patronage systems, but as [a] device to extend and renew those systems."[158] Nevertheless, the outlook in Indonesia was by no means entirely bleak. The very fact of open competition between parties, especially after the introduction of direct elections, allowed the emergence of new types of local leader whose success depended, to some extent at least, on meeting public expectations.

Notes

1. See "Explaining the Latest Wave of Decentralizations" in Manor (1999), Part III.
2. In Latin America, for example, the decentralization of centralized regimes was "triggered in most cases by the national democratic transitions that took place in the region during the 1990s". Daughters and Harper (2007), p. 213.
3. For an assessment of decentralization in East Asia that classifies newly democratized Indonesia and the Philippines as "fast starters" in contrast to "incrementalists" (China and Vietnam) and "cautious movers" (Cambodia and Thailand), see World Bank (2005), pp. 6–7.
4. Asia Foundation (2003), p. 6; Turner et al. (2003), p. xii.
5. Grindle and Thomas (1991), ch. 4. Grindle and Thomas argue that "Certain

kinds of policy issues ... tend to get on decision makers' agendas only when crisis conditions exist. Other kinds of policies — to decentralize, for example — emerge almost uniquely under politics-as-usual circumstances" (p. 73). Indonesia's "big bang" decentralization in 1999 was an exception to that rule.

6. Like the cases of Argentina and the Philippines, "there is an intermediate outcome in which the decision to decentralize is neither fully reversed nor implemented as designed". Eaton (2001), p. 123.

7. For details, see Kahin (1952), ch. XIV; Feith (1962), ch. II.

8. See for example, Nazaruddin (2002). Nazaruddin Sjamsuddin was an Acehnese professor of political science at the University of Indonesia. He was chairman of the national Electoral Commission in 2004.

9. Law No. 5/1974 on Regional Government.

10. The term "region" refers to both provinces and districts. The term "district" covers both municipalities and *kabupaten*. Sub-districts were administrative, not political, units and therefore did not have regional assemblies. They were headed by civil servants from the Department of Home Affairs.

11. Ryaas Rasyid (2003), p. 67.

12. The 1979 law on village government declared its intention "to make the position of village government as far as possible uniform". Law No. 5/1979 on Village Government, article 10(1).

13. Malley (1999), pp. 87–93.

14. Malley (2003), p. 108. For cases in Aceh, see Kell (1995), pp. 36–40.

15. As Manor argues, "It should be remembered that patronage systems that evolved in some less developed countries actually worked after a fashion (or at least appeared to) in those years." Manor (1999), p. 22.

16. Manor (1999), p. 37.

17. Not referring specifically to Indonesia, Manor explained that "the effect of this political awakening was not to create mass pressure from the grass roots for decentralization, but rather to persuade leaders atop political systems to consider decentralization, in order to cope more effectively with emerging social forces." Manor (1999), p. 32.

18. MPR Decree No. XV/1998.

19. The leading weekly, *Tempo*, even asked readers "to imagine a new Indonesia without Aceh and without Papua. We could no longer sing 'From Sabang to Merauke' [a famous nationalist song] but this does not mean the end of the world". *Tempo*, 3–9 January 2000. Sabang, in Aceh, is on the northwestern tip of Indonesia and Merauke, in Papua, is on the southeastern edge.

20. *Jakarta Post*, 18 November 1999. On 24 October 1999, a few days after his election as president, Abdurrahman Wahid addressed the "Indonesia Next" conference organized by Van Zorge, Heffernan and Associates in Bali. Asked about federalism, he said that "Actually we would like to have a federal system"

but acknowledged that the term "federalism" was politically sensitive. "Doing things without naming them is the Indonesian way", he explained. The author participated in the conference.

21. For details, see Nuraida Mokhsen (2003).
22. As noted in Chapter 3, Ryaas Rasyid also headed the team that drew up the 1999 electoral laws.
23. Lt. Gen. Syarwan Hamid had served as ABRI's chief of staff for social and political affairs before becoming one of the Deputy Speakers of the DPR in 1997. After leaving the cabinet he said "We don't think too far ahead like calling for independence, federalism is enough because it is still in the framework of unity." *Kompas*, 15 November 1999.
24. The term "big bang" seems to have been coined by the World Bank. World Bank (2003), ch. 1. According to World Bank economist, Anwar Shah, the defining characteristics of a "Big Bang" approach are that it is "holistic (comprehensive)" and "implemented at lightning speed". Anwar Shah and Theresa Thompson (2004), p. 317.
25. *Gatra*, 17 November 1999.
26. Authority over religion was included at the insistence of the Department of Religion which was concerned about possible discrimination against local religious minorities in particular regions if power were transferred to district governments. Interview with Ryaas Rasyid, Jakarta, 20 April 2004.
27. Local governments were permitted to keep 80 per cent of revenues from forestry, fisheries and general mining, 30 per cent from natural gas and 15 per cent from oil.
28. World Bank (2003), p. 2; World Bank (2005), p. 86.
29. See Chapter 8 on Aceh.
30. The concept of transferring more functions to the districts had been floated earlier by General (ret.) Rudini, who served as Minister of Home Affairs in 1988–93. Rudini's plan, however, was not implemented. Nuraida Mokhsen (2003), pp. 152–59.
31. World Bank (2003), p. 3.
32. Ibid.
33. Ryaas Rasyid (2003), p. 63. This was in sharp contrast to the election laws also drawn up by a team headed by Ryaas.
34. The significance of pressing political incentives is demonstrated by comparison with the other East Asian "fast starter" country, the Philippines (note 3 above), where the Local Government Code bill was submitted to the congress in 1987 but only passed in 1991, "reflecting the ambivalence of many legislators to decentralization". Eaton (2001), pp. 117–18.
35. *Gatra*, 17 November 1999. According to Ryaas Rasyid, the TNI commander-in-chief, General Wiranto supported reform in general but did not give special attention to regional autonomy. The only senior general to express open doubts

was Lt. Gen. Susilo Bambang Yudhoyono, the TNI chief of staff for Social and Political Affairs, who thought the laws were "too drastic". Interview with Ryaas Rasyid, Jakarta, 20 April 2004.

36. *Jakarta Post*, 2 February 2000. Of those entitled to vote, 199 supported autonomy and 146 preferred federalism. The total attendance at the congress was more than 2,000.

37. Ford (2003), pp. 138–40. In 2003 Tabrani was one among twenty candidates seeking Golkar's nomination for the 2004 presidential election.

38. Malley (2001), pp. 359–61.

39. A leading Golkar figure in East Kalimantan and later bupati of Kutai Kertanegara, Syaukani HR, had been a strong advocate of federalism but was warned by Golkar leaders in Jakarta and local military officials against repeating his demand. Interview with Syaukani, Kutai Kertanegar, 27 April 2004.

40. Two years later, Ryaas complained, "Whatever I planned was abandoned by the then Minister of Home Affairs, Surjadi Surdirdja. Even my staff who had supported the preparation of the laws were no longer used". *Kompas*, 5 February 2003. For more on the differences between Ryaas and Surjadi, see Ryaas Rasyid (2004), p. 72.

41. Turner et al. (2002), p. 48.

42. World Bank (2003), p. 4.

43. A senior Home Affairs official complained that the "regions tend to interpret (these articles) literally and think that all authorities that are not (specifically) central authorities are regional authorities". Made Suwandi (2002), p. 8.

44. World Bank (2003), p. 10. See also Hofman and Kaiser (2002).

45. Eaton (2001), p. 102.

46. Made Suwandi (2002), p. 19.

47. Interview with Ryaas Rasyid, 29 August 2001. See also *Kompas*, 26 June 2001.

48. Andi Mallarangeng, who had assisted in drawing up the 1999 laws (and later became one of President Yudhoyono's official spokesmen), claimed that the main motive for such resistance was the desire of central officials to regain access to the economic rents arising from control of issuing licences. *Koran Tempo*, 3 April 2002.

49. According to two World Bank officials, "The key line ministries were outright obstructionists. They felt they had everything to lose from decentralization, as the laws would abolish their deconcentrated apparatus, and with it their control over projects, resources and perks". Hofman and Kaiser (2004), p. 19.

50. This law put the involvement of regional governments in forestry at the discretion of the central government. According to the Law No. 41/1999 on Forestry, "In managing forestry the (central) government can transfer part of its authority to regional governments" (Article 66(1)). For details on the struggle between the Department of Forestry and districts in Kalimantan, see Resosudarmo (2003).

51. Turner et al. (2003), p. 16. One pro-autonomy former minister claimed in an interview that the Department of Forestry had bribed members of the DPR to adopt Law No. 41/1999.
52. *Jakarta Post*, 21 December 1999.
53. *Jakarta Post*, 16 February 2001.
54. See comments by the Minister of Home Affairs, Lt. Gen. Hari Sabarno. *Jakarta Post*, 25 September 2001. President Megawati even complained that she could not issue fish with identity cards!
55. For example, Semarang and Solo in Central Java both obtained their water supplies from neighbouring districts. *Kompas*, 2 September 2001.
56. *Koran Tempo*, 16 June 2001; *Kompas*, 10 April 2003; *Kompas*, 14 June 2002.
57. See the Statement of the Government of Indonesia on Progress of Decentralization in Indonesia, presented at the Twelfth Meeting of the Consultative Group on Indonesia, Bali, 21–22 January 2003.
58. *Kaltim Post*, 26 April 2004.
59. *Tempo*, 26 May 2003. The Minister for Transportation and Telecommunications, Lt. Gen. (ret.) Agum Gumelar, warned that "Regional administrations must understand (that) operating an airport is not the same as operating a bus station". *Jakarta Post*, 2 February 2002.
60. Ryaas Rasyid (2003), p. 70.
61. Turner et al. (2003), p. 102. After the transfer, the number of regional civil servants rose to 2.8 million of a total 3.9 million civil servants. World Bank (2003), p. 1.
62. Asia Foundation (2003), p. 21.
63. MPR Decree No. III/MPR/2000.
64. "The legal system is in a mess (*kacau*) and anything goes", said Ryaas Rasyid. Interview, Jakarta, 20 April 2004.
65. Law No. 25/1999, Article 1.1.
66. This was the assessment of the technocrat and former cabinet minister, Emil Salim. *Jakarta Post*, 2 August 2000.
67. Law No. 25/1999, Article 1.18.
68. For a detailed analysis, see Fane (2003).
69. *Kompas*, 7 January 2001.
70. A list of sixty-eight taxes and charges was published in *Kompas* on 26, 27, and 28 November 2001.
71. *Koran Tempo*, 6 September 2001.
72. Asia Foundation (2003), p. 59.
73. Resosudarmo (2003), p. 230.
74. McCarthy (2004), p. 1205.
75. Resosudarmo (2003), p. 230.
76. See Obidzinski (2005), pp. 198–200.
77. Erwiza notes that "Illegal mining is a highly organized activity, often with close

links to the criminal underworld." Erwiza (2005), p. 208. See also Erwiza (2007).

78. Asia Foundation (2003), p. 18.
79. Turner et al. (2003), pp. 41, 58.
80. Asia Foundation (2003), pp. 19, 58.
81. *Kompas*, 12 December 2003.
82. *Kompas*, 13 August 2003.
83. Turner et al. (2003), p. 40.
84. Fane (2003), p. 161.
85. Turner et al. (2003), p. 40.
86. *Kompas*, 2 September 2001.
87. *Kaltim Post*, 27 April 2004.
88. *Kompas*, 15 June 2001.
89. *Kompas*, 2 September 2001.
90. The Javanese term, *kebablasan*, was often used to describe these excesses. It conveys the sense of "out of control". The number of provinces had declined from 27 to 26 when East Timor obtained its independence before the law was implemented.
91. Policy Recommendation in Implementing Regional Autonomy, contained in MPR Decree No. IV/MPR/2000.
92. Clause 18.5 of the constitution as amended by the MPR at its session in August 2000.
93. *Jakarta Post*, 16 February 2001.
94. Interviews with Dr Siti Nurbaya Bakar, Secretary-General of the DPD and former Secretary-General of the Department of Home Affairs, Jakarta, 12 September 2006; and Dr Sudarsono Hardjosoekarto, Director-General for National Unity and Politics and former Director-General for General Governance and Regional Autonomy in the Department of Home Affairs, Jakarta, 11 September 2006.
95. *Jakarta Post*, 12 February 2002. Megawati, however, was among the leaders who occasionally showed a poor understanding of the concept of regional autonomy. While still vice president she had declared that Indonesia could never accept the presence of small "states" within its territory. *Jakarta Post*, 17 May 2001.
96. *Jakarta Post*, 4 September 2001. There is little consistency in the English translations of *kabupaten* and *kotamadya*. *Kabupaten* is variously translated as "regency", "district" or even "region". *Kotamadya*, known as *kota* since the adoption of the 1999 law, can be "city", "town", "municipality" or "mayoralty".
97. *Jakarta Post*, 17 May 2001.
98. One of Megawati's advisors, Dr Cornelis Lay, said that Megawati strongly believed that any Indonesian has a right to live anywhere in Indonesia and was disturbed by the tendency for local governments to discriminate against "migrants". Discussion with Cornelis Lay, Canberra, 26 September 2002.
99. *Jakarta Post*, 4 September 2001.

100. Interviews with former Minister for Home Affairs, Lt. Gen. Hari Sabarno, Jakarta, 23 August 2006; and former Secretary-General of the Department of Home Affairs, Dr Siti Nurbaya Bakar, Jakarta, 12 September 2006.

101. *Kompas*, 9 February 2002.

102. *Koran Tempo*, 11 April 2002.

103. Clause 41.1.b. of the draft. *Kompas*, 9 February 2002.

104. Clause 74.2 of the draft. *Kompas*, 9 February 2002. The regional secretary is the head of the regional bureaucracy with powers that often rival those of the regional head.

105. *Kompas*, 9 February 2002. Ferry Baldan Mursyidan, a Golkar member of the DPR, asked why have DPRDs if they can be dissolved by the president. Interview, Jakarta, 4 September 2006.

106. *Media Indonesia*, 31 January 2003.

107. According to a Home Affairs official, however, the draft was strongly opposed by "all bupati and mayors regardless of party affiliation". Interview with I Made Suwandi, Director of Regional Government Affairs, Department of Home Affairs, Jakarta, 9 July 2007.

108. *Koran Tempo*, 6 February 2002.

109. Asosiasi Pemerintah Kebupaten Seluruh Indonesia, Policy Paper, Rapat Kerja Nasional III, 24–26 Agustus 2002, Jakarta.

110. Hery Susanto et al. (2003), p. 133.

111. *Kompas*, 1 July 2002.

112. The number of districts had grown from 316 in 1998 to 440 in 2003.

113. At the district level in Java in 2003, PDI-P had 28 out of 35 district heads in Central Java, 4 out of 5 in Yogyakarta, 23 out of 34 in East Java and about half in West Java. It also had 9 out of 11 in Bali. Interview with Pramono Anung Wibowo, Deputy Secretary-General of the PDI-P, Jakarta, 22 October 2003.

114. Interview Lt. Gen. Hari Sabarno, Jakarta, 23 August 2006. Hari Sabarno was the Minister of Home Affairs in 2002.

115. Interview with Ferry Baldan Mursyidan, Golkar member of DPR. Jakarta, 4 September 2006.

116. *Koran Tempo*, 18 July 2002.

117. *Straits Times* (Singapore), 19 December 2002.

118. PP 8/2003 and PP9/2003; *Koran Tempo*, 11 April 2003.

119. *Jakarta Post*, 17 April 2004.

120. The former secretary-general of the Department of Home Affairs, Dr Siti Nurbaya Bakar, said that if the department's proposal had not been merged with the DPR's bill, it may have taken a long time for it to be passed. Interview, Jakarta, 12 September 2006.

121. Law No. 32/2004: Penjelasan part 3.

122. Interview with Siti Nurbaya Bakar, Jakarta, 12 September 2006.

123. Law No. 32/2004: Article 145 and Penjelasan part 7. Regulations considered

against the public interest included "distortive" taxes and charges that hindered business activities.

124. Law No. 32/2004: Penjelasan part 7. By the end of 2008, the Department of Finance had cancelled 2,398 of 11,401 regional financial regulations, and either disallowed or revised 67 per cent of draft regulations. *Kompas*, 12 December 2008.

125. But, as Ferry Mursyidan Baldan, the Golkar deputy chairman of the DPR's special committee on the bill, pointed out, the central government was not empowered to change provincial budgets. It could only require provincial governments to produce a revised budget. Interview with Ferry Mursyidan Baldan, Jakarta, 4 September 2006.

126. According to a senior provincial official, this bargaining provided scope for financial demands on provincial governments in order to facilitate central approval.

127. Law No. 25/2004, Article 7. This law also slightly increased some allocations to the regions: for example, DAU increased from 25 to 26 per cent of the central government's budget, the share in petroleum revenue from 15 to 15.5 per cent and the share in natural gas revenue from 30 per cent to 30.5 per cent. Articles 14 and 27.

128. Department of Home Affairs draft of the Law on Regional Government, 26 January 2004. The liberal attitude of the department to independent candidates was surprising to many observers. One politician suggested that the minister, Lt. Gen. Hari Sabarno, may have been responding to pressure from some of his retired military colleagues who were wanting to contest the elections but could not find a party willing to nominate them. Interview, Jakarta. A senior Home Affairs official said that the minister knew the proposal would be rejected by the DPR anyway. Interview, Jakarta.

129. Later the Constitutional Court upheld a challenge to the law's definition of "political party" which restricted the term to political parties that held seats in the DPRD. The Court ruled that a party was a party whether it had seats or not, so the votes won by small parties without seats could also be counted towards the 15 per cent needed by coalitions to enable them to nominate candidates. *Koran Tempo*, 23 March 2005. In July 2007, the Court went much further by removing the requirement that candidates had to be nominated by parties, thus permitting non-party independents to contest. Mahkamah Konstitusi, Putusan Nomor 5/PUU-V/2007.

130. One official believed that in practice governors exercised only limited control over district heads from their own party, let alone from other parties. Interview with I Made Suwandi, Jakarta, 9 July 2007. Another prominent official agreed that party differences did not matter much because "bargaining normally revolves around money". Interview with Laode Ida, Deputy Chairman of the Regional Representative Assembly (DPD), Jakarta, 7 September 2006.

131. *Kompas*, 19 December 2000.

132. See Malley (2003).
133. Hadiz (2004), p. 711.
134. Hadiz (2003), p. 124.
135. Hadiz (2003).
136. *Kompas*, 17 June 2000, 27 July 2000, 8 January 2001. The central government, however, could still intervene as was demonstrated when the Minister of Home Affairs invalidated the dismissal of the governor of South Kalimantan by the provincial DPRD in August 2002. *Jakarta Post*, 22 August 2002, *Kompas*, 1 March 2003.
137. *Koran Tempo*, 5 September 2002. See also Laode Ida in *Kompas*, 7 September 2002.
138. *Kompas*, 5 February 2003.
139. *Kompas*, 14 March 2000.
140. *Kompas*, 21 March 2000, *Kompas*, 5 April 2000, *Kompas*, 15 August 2000.
141. *Kompas*, 9 March 2000.
142. *Kompas*, 9 March 2000.
143. Second Amendment of the Constitution, Article 18.4.
144. All five major parties elected in 1999 experienced a decline in support in the June 2004 general election.
145. *Kompas*, 22 December 2005. The rate in the general election was 23.3 per cent, in the first round of the presidential election 21.8 per cent and in the second round 26.3 per cent. Kacung Marijan in *Kompas*, 19 July 2005.
146. Of 166 elections in June 2005, a second round was needed for 1 gubernatorial and 7 district elections because no pair reached the required 25 per cent needed to win in the first round. *Kompas*, 5 August 2005.
147. *Jakarta Post*, 22 May 2005.
148. Mohamad Qodari in *Koran Tempo*, 2 July 2005.
149. *Kompas*, 23 February 2005.
150. For example, the incumbent mayor of Semarang, Sukawi Sutarip, who had been elected previously as a PDI-P candidate, was dropped by the party but won re-election on behalf of an alliance that included PAN, PPP, PKB and PKS. *Jakarta Post*, 29 June 2005. In another case, a candidate failed to win the PDI-P's nomination so put together an alliance of eighteen small parties which carried her to victory in Banyuwangi, East Java. *Koran Tempo*, 27 June 2005.
151. *Kompas*, 7 July 2005. Irman Lanti was the Program Director of the Indonesia Institute.
152. Mietzner (2009).
153. Interview with senior official of the Department of Home Affairs, September 2006.
154. In the 29 direct gubernatorial elections held between 2005 and the end of 2008, PDI-P candidates standing alone won seven and were part of winning coalitions in six. Golkar had won two standing alone and six in coalitions, including two coalitions that also included PDI-P. Nine were won by coalitions in which

neither PDI-P nor Golkar was included. The only successful candidate without a coalition partner was a former GAM activist who ran as an independent in Aceh. *Kompas*, 10 December 2008.

155. *Media Indonesia*, 19 July 2005. I am indebted to Marcus Mietzner for this reference.

156. Based on statistics collected by the People's Voter Education Network (*Jaringan Pendidikan Pemilih untuk Rakyat*: JPPR). See McGibbon (2006), p. 199; Ramage (2007), p. 138.

157. For a general discussion of key "governance risks that could mitigate the posited advantages of decentralization", including elite capture, clientelism, capacity constraints, competition between levels of government, and weakness of informational flow, see Campos and Hellman (2005).

158. Manor (1999), p. 44.

5

MILITARY REFORM: WITHDRAWING FROM "PRACTICAL POLITICS" AND STEPS TOWARD CIVILIAN CONTROL

Democratic military reform, following the fall of a military-backed authoritarian regime, involves a series of conceptually distinct steps although in reality they often overlap. First, the military must withdraw from its political role as a dominant or major force in the government and concentrate on its professional military functions. Second, the civil government has to establish control over the military which should loyally carry out the policies determined by that government. And third, if "democratic civilian control" is to be achieved, the military must accept its obligation to be accountable through the government to an elected legislature and public opinion. As Muthiah Alagappa argues, "Ultimately, success in democratic civilian control will hinge as much if not even more on the consolidation of democracy and development of state capacity than on the specific measures instituted to control the military".[1] The actual path towards military reform, however, is always affected by the specific circumstances of the country undergoing reform.

The collapse of Soeharto's New Order and the launching of Reformasi posed huge challenges for civil-military relations. How would the post-Soeharto regime deal with the military and, no less important, how would the military adjust to completely new circumstances? Advocates of military reform often envisage a Western-style professional military that takes its orders from a democratically elected civilian government and is primarily concerned with the defence of the nation against foreign military threats. The Indonesian military, of course, with its origins among the nationalist fighters who conducted the successful guerilla war against the Dutch colonial power in the late 1940s, had never conformed to the apolitical Western model. Like the Dutch colonial military, its main purpose was to maintain order and put down rebellion within it own territory. It was also structured in such a way as to provide political support for the incumbent president. During the New Order, the military was closely integrated with the Soeharto regime and served as the ultimate guarantor of its longevity.

Democratic political reform required that the military be dislodged from the position it held during the New Order. Unlike military-dominated governments in countries where the military had acquired power in a relatively recent coup, the New Order regime had been thoroughly penetrated over several decades by active and retired military officers who occupied key positions at all levels of civil government, stretching from the national cabinet to provincial and district administration. The military's political domination had been backed by its territorial organizational structure which shadowed civil administration throughout the country. Moreover the military's political independence was supported by its practice of raising much of its financial requirements from outside the government budget. Ultimately, therefore, it was accountable to no state institution apart from the presidency itself.

On the day that Soeharto stepped down in the wake of the May 1998 riot, he was simply replaced by his civilian vice president while the military institution, on which he had previously relied for political support and the perpetuation of his rule, remained largely intact. In the chaotic circumstances following Soeharto's resignation, the new Habibie government, was preoccupied with defending itself from multiple challenges and in no position to impose reform on the divided and demoralized military. The task of military reform, therefore, was left to reformers within the military itself who persuaded their brother-officers that things would only get worse if limited reforms were not adopted. The first phase aimed at removing military officers from formal roles in government and insulating the institution from day-to-day political involvement. After discussing these early measures, the chapter will focus on the slow and difficult process that aimed to place the military more fully under the authority of the civilian government and accountable to it. To quote Alagappa again, "advance in effective civilian control over the military in post-authoritarian states is likely to be gradual and subject to protracted struggle and negotiation and, at times, setbacks".[2] Although the reforms in the first decade fell short of establishing full civilian control over military matters, significant progress was made. But first it is necessary to say something about the role of the military under Soeharto's New Order.

THE MILITARY IN THE NEW ORDER

As the ultimate guarantor of the Soeharto regime for three decades, the military supervised political life and regularly took action to suppress the emergence of opposition. Dominated by the army, the armed forces (*Angkatan Bersenjata Republik Indonesia*: ABRI) included not only the navy and air force but also the police.[3] The main army force, the Army Strategic Reserve Command (*Komando Strategis Cadangan Angkatan Darat*: Kostrad), consisted of two conventional divisions, but most of the army was organized on a "territorial" basis in which units were spread out in a hierarchy of commands stretching from Jakarta to the provincial capitals, district towns and sub-district townships.[4] Through this structure the army was able to shadow each level of civil government throughout the entire country. The territorial forces, backed by intelligence agencies, were also responsible for monitoring and controlling the activities of political parties, trade unions, religious organizations, student groups, the press, and non-government organizations to ensure that challenges to the government were nipped in the bud. Territorial troops broke strikes, crushed student protests, removed peasants from their land to make way for development projects, and ensured overwhelming victories for the government party, Golkar, in general elections.

Military officers — both active and retired — occupied key positions in civil government, serving as cabinet ministers, senior civil servants, provincial governors, district *bupatis*, municipal mayors, ambassadors and directors of state corporations.[5] As noted in Chapter 3, they were also appointed to legislatures at the national, provincial and district levels. Until the late 1970s, military officers serving in government were normally still on active service and sometimes returned to military duties after completing their terms in civilian posts, but from the 1980s, as the "1945 Generation" officers reached retirement age, retired officers were increasingly appointed to these positions.[6] Nevertheless, the number of active military officers serving in civil government was still substantial although declining. Throughout the New Order period the military propagated its Dual Function (*Dwi Fungsi*) doctrine to justify and legitimate its broad non-military role. According to the Dwi Fungsi concept, the military had two functions — first as a military force in the fields of defence and security, and second as a socio-political force with the duty of playing an active role in government and society more generally.[7]

President Soeharto's authority was rarely challenged within the military. In the early years of his rule when the army was still dominated by the "1945 Generation", some officers resented the rise of a colleague whose qualities seemed to them to be not especially outstanding. Soeharto, however, quickly removed dissident officers from key military posts — occasionally arresting them but more commonly offering lucrative alternatives which they were only too willing to accept. As the economy grew Soeharto's control of the patronage network ensured that both the rewards of loyalty and the costs of disloyalty were high. By the 1980s the last of the revolutionary fighters were leaving active service and being replaced in top positions by a new generation of academy-trained officers who had already been integrated into the patronage network. During the 1990s there were signs of increasing public resentment against massive corruption, military repression and restrictions on civil liberties, but it was only when the Asian Financial Crisis devastated the economy and exposed the ageing president's obvious inability to find a way out that officers began seriously to consider a future without Soeharto. By then, however, military officers were seen by much of the public as major beneficiaries of the corruption of the regime and responsible for the repression that had kept it in power. After the devastating May 1998 riot in Jakarta that the military could neither prevent nor suppress, the military leadership in effect withdrew its support from the president who, seeing the writing on the wall, resigned, while the military became the target of unrestrained public condemnation that would have been unthinkable when Soeharto was still in power.

THE HABIBIE PRESIDENCY: THE IMPETUS TOWARD MILITARY REFORM

Vice President Habibie took over the presidency without substantial support at either the elite or popular level. He enjoyed some lukewarm backing within Golkar but his friends among military officers were limited mainly to those with Islamic backgrounds originating from regions outside Java. On the other hand, many nationalist-oriented officers had little respect for him and regarded him as a temporary stop-gap president. Habibie's sudden and unexpected elevation to the national leadership allowed him little opportunity to give much attention to military reform. Indeed, his main concern was to make sure that the military made no move to unseat him. In these uncertain circumstances the military on its own initiative began to implement a series of reforms aiming, at least partially, to disengage itself from the political arena. These reforms, however, were not fully accepted by the majority of officers, many of whom in their hearts still hoped for a return to the good old days when the military was in charge.

The initial military reforms were unquestionably crisis-ridden. The military, too, had been caught by surprise in May 1998. The collapse of the Soeharto regime had shocked military officers who were neither able to save their patron nor stop the riot. Indoctrinated to believe that the Indonesian military was a unique "people's army" that, in contrast to the professional militaries of other countries, was duty-bound to participate actively in civil government, they suddenly faced indignant demands that they abandon their most fundamental doctrine, *Dwi Fungsi*, on which their self-image was based. Military personnel who had imagined that they were universally admired by "the people", now experienced daily excoriation in the mass media.[8] Demoralized by widespread public antagonism and their own failure to save the president from an ignominious end, military leaders were sharply divided and unable to devise a strategy to regain their authority. They feared that any attempt on their part to restore the military's predominance would only provoke even bigger demonstrations and further exacerbate military disunity. In the newly liberalized atmosphere, civilians became emboldened to criticize the military which was soon the target — together with the deposed president — of unrestrained condemnation in the mass media. Facing huge student demonstrations and fearing the outbreak of renewed rioting, the demoralized military leaders felt unable to re-assert themselves.

The military's inability to defend itself was also a consequence of its internal divisions which had been exacerbated by the May crisis. The nationalist-oriented mainstream — the so-called "red-and-white" officers — had never been close to Habibie, whose military links were with the so-called "green" Islamic officers.[9] During the months before May 1998, ABRI had been sharply divided between supporters of the new Commander-in-Chief, Gen. Wiranto, and his rival, President Soeharto's son-in-law, Lt. Gen. Prabowo Subianto, the newly appointed commander of the Army Strategic Reserve Command (Kostrad). Wiranto was widely seen as representing the "red-and-white" officers while Prabowo, whose own family was in fact not particularly Islamic, led officers with Islamic backgrounds.[10] The struggle between the two factions, however, was not over ideology but control of the military and its patronage network. Both Wiranto and Prabowo were in fact protégés of Soeharto who played them off against each other — as he had been doing with his top military commanders from the beginning of the New Order. Habibie was in fact much closer to Prabowo and the "green" group but he lacked Soeharto's manipulative skills and experience in handling the military.[11] Suddenly alienated by what he saw as Prabowo's threatening behaviour during the days immediately after Soeharto's fall, he turned to Wiranto who quickly removed Prabowo from his command.[12]

The new president was in no position to establish his authority over the military while, despite the "red-and-white" mainstream's antagonism toward Habibie, Wiranto was not in a position to launch a move to overthrow him. Such action would have further divided the military and could have sparked a renewal of massive rioting not only in Jakarta but throughout Indonesia.[13] During the next months when the beleaguered Habibie felt compelled to introduce fundamental liberalizing reforms that reversed policies with which ABRI had been identified — the lifting of restrictions on the press, the release of political prisoners, the formation of new political parties, the relaxation of labour controls and eventually a free general election and, most remarkably of all, the later referendum on the future of East Timor — the military felt powerless to stand in the way.

The new civilian-led government was too preoccupied with preserving its own limited authority to give attention to working out a programme of military reform. Military reform, therefore, was left to the badly shaken military itself. The Commander-in-Chief, General Wiranto, appreciated that the military could not just return to the New Order system so he entrusted a group of reform-minded "intellectual" staff officers with the task of re-conceptualizing the military's future role.[14] They believed that the military had been excessively involved in day-to-day politics under Soeharto and that this had impaired its capacity to perform its professional duties in the fields of defence and internal security. They were especially resentful of the way that Soeharto had used the military for short-term political purposes and his propensity to select his personal favourites for rapid promotion (including his son-in-law, Prabowo). Wiranto appreciated the talents of these professional-oriented officers who had already been appointed to important staff positions at the ABRI headquarters while Soeharto was still in office and had been discussing among themselves for several years their proposals for the post-Soeharto era.[15] While appreciating the achievements of the Soeharto presidency, they argued that Indonesian society had changed fundamentally since the 1960s when Soeharto had taken over the government and that an approach that worked well at that time was no longer appropriate in a modernizing society with a growing educated middle class. They were, however, by no means radical in outlook and believed that the military could only be reformed gradually.[16]

These officers had been among Wiranto's advisers during the crisis that led to Soeharto's resignation in May 1998 and he entrusted them with organizing a military seminar in Bandung in September 1998 that produced what was called the "New Paradigm". The "New Paradigm" proposed principles to guide the military in the new era. The military would no longer seek to "occupy" positions in the government but only to "influence" government decisions. It would exercise its influence "indirectly" and not "directly". And instead of dominating the government, the military would "share" power with civilian political forces.[17] The "New Paradigm" was by no means a comprehensive blueprint for the overhaul of the military but rather an indication of the direction of change.

During the year following the Bandung seminar, the military implemented a series of measures to reduce its participation in "practical" day-to-day politics. The first step was to dissolve the military's Social and Political Affairs branch through which the Chief of Staff for Social and Political Affairs (*Kepala Staf Sosial Politik*: Kassospol) oversaw a hierarchy of social-political units placed at each level in the territorial structure throughout the entire country. It was through these units that the military "guided" political parties, social organizations, the press and other civilian activities. In November 1998 shortly after the Bandung seminar, the branch, which was then headed by Yudhoyono, was downgraded although Yudhoyono continued to supervise the army's territorial network in his new post as Chief of Staff for Territorial Affairs.[18]

The abolition of the military's Political and Social Affairs Branch was followed by the withdrawal of seconded military officers holding positions in government and the bureaucracy. In early 1999 about 4,000 active officers were occupying positions in the civil bureaucracy.[19] Five of President Habibie's 36 cabinet ministers, 10 of 27 provincial governors and 128 of 306 district heads were active officers.[20] As part of the reform programme, the military leadership decided that from 1 April 1999 all officers wishing to retain or accept such appointments would have to retire from the military. This policy was naturally resented by many officers who were thereby deprived of the money-making opportunities that such posts provided. In practice its impact on senior officers was less onerous as they were approaching retirement in any case, but many middle-ranking officers opted to return to the military. Its most senior "victim" was Lt. Gen. Yudhoyono himself who had initiated the policy. At fifty, the relatively youthful Yudhoyono's military career was involuntarily cut short when he was forced to retire following his appointment to the cabinet in the new Abdurrahman Wahid government in November 1999.

The military reformers also wanted to reduce, and ultimately remove, military representation in legislatures. Military and police officers had been appointed to national and regional legislatures since 1960. In 1998, 75 military officers sat in the national DPR and another 2,800 in the 27 provincial and 306 district parliaments. Thus a large number of officers had an interest in continuing military representation in the legislatures — not only current members but also those who aspired to appointments in the future. By November 1998 when a special session of the MPR was convened, the military reformers had not yet convinced the ABRI leadership to withdraw military representatives from the legislatures. However, confronted by public opinion and massive student demonstrations, the military group in the MPR, led by Yudhoyono, agreed to a compromise that recognized continuing ABRI representation in the DPR and MPR but required a gradual reduction in numbers.[21] In January 1999 the military accepted electoral laws that reduced representation in the DPR by half from 75 to 38 and in the regional legislatures to 10 per cent.

The military also severed its connection with Golkar, the government party of the New Order. During the New Order, the military had been formally integrated into the Golkar structure and many regional branches were headed by military officers. However, even before Soeharto's fall, some officers had been arguing that ABRI should "stand above all groups". As general elections approached in 1999, Gen. Wiranto ordered the military not to support any party. This order was, perhaps, not without calculation as it was obvious that Golkar would not be repeating its overwhelming electoral successes of the New Order era so it made sense for the military to keep its options open by adopting a neutral stance — although retired officers continued to be well represented in Golkar, especially in the regions. Wiranto's order was largely observed by military personnel during the 1999 general election.

The military's withdrawal from "day-to-day" politics was accompanied by measures to distance the army from routine public-order duties. Throughout the New Order era the police had been integrated into the command structure of ABRI and often participated with the army in joint operations against demonstrations, riots and strikes as well as regional rebellions. The military reformers believed that overlapping duties had been harmful for both forces.[22] The police culture had been "militarized" and it tended to adopt military methods in dealing with political protests. Often police were armed with military weapons more suitable for facing an invading army than controlling a demonstration. As the national police chief said at the time, the police philosophy of "fighting crime" should replace the military philosophy of "destroying the enemy".[23] At the same time, the military's reputation was often besmirched as the direct involvement of the military in maintaining public order sometimes resulted in soldiers "destroying the enemy" and perpetrating other abuses of human rights. In practice an internal security force, it had inevitably been drawn into the political arena as an instrument at the disposal of the government to strengthen its political position against opposition. The military leadership accepted the proposals of the reform group and on 1 April 1999 the process of removing the police force from the armed forces began. Although no longer placed under the command of Gen. Wiranto as TNI commander-in-chief, however, it remained temporarily answerable to him in his other capacity as Minister of Defence and Security.[24] At the same time, the military used the occasion of its separation from the police to further distance itself from the New Order by changing its name from ABRI to TNI (*Tentara Nasional Indonesia*, Indonesian National Military), its name during the anti-colonial revolution.

These reforms were taken largely on the initiative of a small group of officers in response to the new circumstances. The reforms were not welcomed by the majority of officers but, in their demoralized state, they were persuaded that things would only get worse if they tried to defend the old system. Nor were they imposed by the new civilian government which was entirely preoccupied with the host of immediate challenges it was facing during the country's sudden transition from authoritarian rule. No major civilian figure in the government had shown significant interest in the internal reform of the military — although not a few were concerned to keep the military out of power. Nor was there heavy pressure for reform from the three pre-election political parties in the parliament — except to reduce military representation in the legislatures. The military reformers, however, were not formulating their proposals in a social and political vacuum. During the months after Soeharto's fall, massive demonstrations had become almost routine in Jakarta and other cities as students and others called for free elections, the complete withdrawal of the military from politics, and trials of those accused of corruption and human-rights abuses — including Soeharto and his "cronies".

All this was taking place at a time when the nation was facing challenges that proved beyond the military's capacity to control. Nothing demonstrated the military's loss of political influence more than its inability to block President Habibie's decision in January 1999 to hold a referendum later in the year on the future of East Timor. At the same time, however, as Mietzner points out, "the most striking evidence for the success of the armed forces in avoiding subordination to civilian control was its independent political operations in East Timor".[25] Making matters worse, the efforts of TNI commanders on the ground in East Timor, with the backing of generals in Jakarta, to ensure "a victory for Indonesia", disgraced Indonesia in the eyes of the international community and resulted in heavy pressure on the Indonesian government to withdraw its forces after the overwhelming vote in favour of independence. In the end the outcome was disastrous for the TNI which was forced to make a humiliating withdrawal from a territory it was sworn to defend and then saw leading officers, including its Commander-in-Chief, accused of gross human rights violations by both an international commission set up by the United Nations and a national commission appointed by the Indonesian government. One consequence of this humiliation, however, was the reinforcement of resentment within the TNI and a strengthening of "hardline" attitudes that eventually led to a backlash against the reformist trend.

Nevertheless, the TNI had taken significant, although still limited, steps toward extricating itself from formal political involvement. The president and his senior civilian ministers had played little direct part in this, preferring to leave defence and security matters to Wiranto as TNI Commander-in-Chief and Minister of Defence and Security.[26] Although hardly an initiator of reform himself, Wiranto understood the need for the military to create a new public image. But he was wary — as indeed was the reformist group itself — of launching reforms that would hurt the fundamental long-term interests of the military institution and lead to excessive disaffection within the officer corps. The military reformers were attempting to overhaul an institution that had benefited enormously from the New Order so progress was inevitably slow. Military officers in general were at best ambivalent and were reluctant to give up the privileges that they had enjoyed in the past but, bewildered and on the defensive, most grudgingly accepted the need to give concessions. As Geoffrey Robinson put it, "even if some among the military leadership in Jakarta appeared to move in the direction of reform, a great many officers and men seemed inclined to resist, or simply ignore, the changes".[27] During the first phase of military reform under the Habibie presidency, significant steps were taken but, as we shall see, the reform movement soon ran out of steam although the early reforms were not reversed.

THE ABDURRAHMAN PRESIDENCY: THE LOSS OF IMPETUS

The election of Abdurrahman Wahid (often called Gus Dur) as president at the 1999 MPR session seemed to offer hope that military reform would continue. Gus Dur, the leader of Indonesia's largest Islamic organization, the rural-based traditionalist *Nahdatul Ulama*, had founded the oppositionist Democracy Forum together with secular intellectuals in the 1990s[28] and seemed determined, as president, to establish the principle of civilian supremacy. Early indications that President Abdurrahman was willing to adopt policies at odds with military views included his attempts to bring about a ceasefire with separatist rebels in Aceh, his personal approaches to separatist leaders in Papua and his efforts to establish warm relations with East Timor soon after the withdrawal of Indonesian troops from that territory. "Wahid, it appeared," wrote Mietzner, "targeted nothing less than the fundamentals of TNI's political and economic influence, and he seemed to have the necessary political will and backing to succeed".[29]

But several factors undermined his efforts to establish and consolidate civilian control. First, his election as president was, in a sense, a "freak" result arising from intensive political bargaining and not reflecting the political balance within the MPR where Gus Dur's party held only 8 per cent of the seats. His political position, therefore, was fragile from the start and not helped by his blatant disregard of the interests of the largest parties. Second, his background as a religious leader and democratic activist had not prepared him to understand the requirements of institutional reform in the military. He was quite adept at dealing with officers on an individual basis but had little interest in the details of military affairs.[30] Third, his personal style relied more on short-term intuition than long-term planning and, hampered by his inability to read due to his near-blindness, he had a tendency to believe the speculation and rumours that he heard from his personal friends, which he often repeated to visitors and journalists. One result was that he became famous for his inconsistent public statements in response to immediate issues.[31] Finally, Gus Dur was a very shrewd politician and ever ready to deal with almost any group if necessary to maintain his political position — including conservative generals. At best, it could be said that Gus Dur had a vision of military reform but he never bothered to work out a consistent long-term strategy to achieve it.

Although wary of the military, Abdurrahman quickly showed his awareness of the need to take account of military interests when he appointed six retired or soon-to-be-retired military officers to his cabinet. Gen. Wiranto was appointed as Coordinating Minister for Political and Security Affairs, one of the three top cabinet posts.[32] The new position, however, deprived him of direct control over the TNI which was transferred to Admiral Widodo Adi Sucipto, the first ever non-army Commander-in-Chief. Widodo's appointment, together with that of Professor Juwono Sudarsono of the University of Indonesia as Indonesia's first civilian defence minister since the 1950s was consistent with the goals of reform in that they reduced the previous army dominance of key positions. Gus Dur's concern to limit Wiranto's influence, however, affected his choice of chief of staff of the army and led him to miss the opportunity to appoint Yudhoyono, the leading military reformer, to that position. Instead he appointed Gen. Tyasno Sudarto, an intelligence officer with no reputation as a reformer but who had opposed Wiranto's bid to win the vice presidency.[33] In

selecting the new army chief of staff, the president had given higher priority
to isolating Wiranto than pushing forward a programme of military reform.
Gus Dur apparently suspected Yudhoyono of being too close to Wiranto so
appointed him to the cabinet as Minister for Mining and Energy, forcing
him to leave military service five years before retirement age.[34]

It was not long, however, before an opportunity arose for the president
to demonstrate his authority over his generals. In January 2000, the Habibie-
appointed Indonesian commission of enquiry into the TNI's behaviour in
East Timor named Wiranto, the then Commander-in-Chief, as ultimately
responsible for gross human rights violations while a parallel UN commission
recommended the establishment of an international tribunal. Gus Dur's move
to dismiss Wiranto, however, was carried out in his usual confusing way and
after much prevarication.[35] But the president's political judgement proved to
be correct in assessing that Wiranto's base of support in the military was not
strong and there was no overt military resistance to his dismissal.[36] Ironically,
he later promoted Yudhoyono to the post of coordinating minister previously
held by Wiranto.

Meanwhile, behind the drama of Wiranto's dismissal, incremental steps
toward demilitarization continued. In February 2000, Admiral Widodo used
in public the term "civilian supremacy" — a term that had previously been
taboo in military circles.[37] And in April the ideological transformation that
had begun with the "New Paradigm" culminated in a statement by Widodo to
a meeting of TNI leaders that the TNI had "abandoned the implementation
of its social-political function".[38] By formally removing the second function
of the dwi fungsi, the military had forsaken the doctrine that had provided
its justification for political involvement. Meanwhile, the military's capacity
to repress political dissent was further reduced by the dissolution of the
Coordinating Agency for the Maintenance of National Stability (*Badan
Kordinasi Bantuan Pemantapan Stabilitas Nasional: Bakorstanas*) and the largely
military-staffed Social and Political Affairs Directorate in the Department of
Home Affairs.[39]

The Wiranto dismissal had given impetus to Gus Dur's endeavour to
establish presidential authority over the military but he soon squandered his
advantage by interfering clumsily in matters that military officers considered
their own prerogative, such as appointments within the military hierarchy.[40] In
particular, he alienated officers by attempting to promote his own favourites
— a presidential practice that had previously engendered resentment
against Soeharto. The most controversial case involved Maj. Gen. Agus
Wirahadikusumah, one of the core members of the reform group on Wiranto's
staff. Unlike his colleagues in the reform group, Wirahadikusumah had openly

questioned established military doctrines and in October 1999 publicly launched a book of "reformist" essays by fellow officers.[41] Wirahadikusmah's high profile and willingness to "wash dirty linen in public" alienated many officers, including his fellow reformers, but it attracted the attention of Gus Dur.[42] In December 1999, Wirahadikusumah, who by then had been transferred by Wiranto to the regional army command in Sulawesi, appeared before a DPR commission where he described the army's territorial structure as an "instrument of power" and called for its gradual dismantling.[43] A few days later he cast implicit aspersions on his fellow senior officers when he asserted that Indonesian soldiers "should not be dedicated to the service of generals but to the TNI as an institution and to the nation and state".[44] He was apparently referring to Wiranto when he claimed — with no supporting evidence — that a plot to depose the new president included "a person whose aspirations to become vice president or become president were not fulfilled".[45] In February 2000, the president in effect laid down a challenge to the military establishment when he persuaded Gen. Tyasno to appoint Wirahadikusumah from his relatively lowly post in Sulawesi to the command of the military's most powerful force, the two-division Kostrad.[46]

Wirahadikusumah's tenure as Kostrad commander, however, was short. His unpopularity within the military reached its peak when he exposed the "disappearance" of Rp 135 billion (about US$14 million) from the Kostrad-owned Mandala Airlines during the tenure of his predecessor and Wiranto ally, Lt. Gen. Djadja Suparman.[47] The public airing of the alleged misuse of funds caused outrage in the officer corps for whom such casual withdrawals of large sums of money was considered normal practice. If Wirahadikusumah's allegations had been allowed to proceed, the issue threatened to engulf not only previous Kostrad commanders but many others. In August the president bowed to military pressure and replaced Wirahadikusmah but soon stirred the pot again by proposing that Wirahadikusumah be appointed as chief of staff of the army. Forty-five senior offices responded by signing a petition in October calling for a Military Honour Council to be established to take disciplinary action against Wirahadikusumah.[48] The council was not formed but Wirahadikusumah's military career had effectively ended.[49]

By the latter half of 2000, military reform was far from the president's mind. His impetuous dismissal of two ministers — one from the PDI-P (Laksamana Sukardi) and the other from Golkar (Jusuf Kalla), the two largest parties in the DPR — began a process that eventually led to his impeachment as president the following year. As he came under increasing political attack, he needed whatever political support he could get, including that of the military members of the DPR and MPR. In 2001, things went from bad to worse as far as military reform was concerned. Far from continuing to push for the further withdrawal of the TNI from direct involvement in politics, Gus Dur now sought its support against the DPR that was considering allegations against him. On 28 January 2001, he proposed to the military leaders that an emergency be declared to enable him to dissolve the DPR. Again on 5 May he revived this proposal but again it was rejected by the military leadership. The new army chief of staff, Gen. Endriartono Sutarto, warned the president "not to plan, or even consider, declaring a state of emergency, which is only used for the dissolution of the house".[50] Having been blocked, he dismissed Yudhoyono from his cabinet and then attempted to replace all the service chiefs of staff and appoint the professional-oriented Lt. Gen. Johnny Lumintang as the new TNI Commander-in-Chief but failed to get the agreement of the proposed new chiefs of staff.[51] Finally, as the MPR was about to begin its session to consider his impeachment, he did not just propose but issued a decree declaring the emergency. However, this was simply ignored by the MPR which went ahead with his impeachment and installed the vice president, Megawati Soekarnoputri, as president on 23 July 2001.

Far from depoliticizing the military, President Abdurrahman had in the end gone to extreme lengths to bring the military back into politics on his side. The military leadership, however, had rejected his entreaties. The TNI leaders were aware that all their efforts to restore the TNI's public image would come to nothing and they would face huge public protests if they intervened to save a president who had lost the confidence of the entire MPR except the small group representing his own party.

THE MEGAWATI PRESIDENCY: THE PERSISTENCE OF THE *DWI FUNGSI* MENTALITY

In contrast to Abdurrahman Wahid who had at least begun his presidency speaking the language of military reform, such aspirations were not prominent in the public comments of President Megawati. The leading military reformer, Susilo Bambang Yudhoyono, who had failed in his bid for election as vice president in place of Megawati, was brought back into the government as Coordinating Minister for Political and Security Affairs — a position from which he had been dismissed by Gus Dur for obstructing his plan to issue an emergency decree. Yudhoyono, now retired from active service, did not have authority to push through further reform of the military in which hardliners were re-emerging. Although Endriartono Sutarto, a relatively professional officer who had resisted Gus Dur's entreaties to support an emergency, was promoted to Commander-in-Chief in 2002, other appointments suggested that further reform was no longer on the agenda. The new army chief of staff, Gen. Ryamizard Ryacudu, and his colleague, the new Kostrad commander, Lt. Gen. Bibit Waluyo, reflected the "New Order mentality"and were openly contemptuous of those who called for reform.[52] As if to reinforce the military's conservative profile, Maj. Gen. Syafrie Syamsudin, the Jakarta regional commander at the time of the May 1998 riot, was appointed as TNI spokesman in February 2002.[53]

It was not so much that President Megawati opposed further reform of the military but rather that she revealed no indication of giving it much thought. Although she kept Yudhoyono in the top political post in her cabinet, she seems to have simply surrendered military affairs to generals who were either conservative professionals unlikely to challenge the status quo — like Endriartono Sutarto — or firmly opposed to reform — like Ryamizard Ryacudu.[54] Symbolizing Megawati's lack of interest in military reform, her civilian minister of defence, Matori Abdul Djalil, who had been expelled from Abdurrahman's party after supporting Megawati against the then president, had no background in military affairs. Her lack of attention to military reform became even more obvious later when Matori was incapacitated by a stroke in August 2003 but not replaced, leaving the Defence Department with a non-active minister for the remaining year of her presidency.

The TNI's loss of authority after 1998 had not been well received by the majority of military officers. They looked back on the achievements of the New Order government with some pride, even if they did not have much idea about how to recover lost ground. They were particularly disturbed by the constraints imposed by the two preceding governments which had refused to give full authority to the military to deal with security challenges. They felt humiliated by Indonesia's forced withdrawal from East Timor, for which they blamed Habibie and what they saw as an "international conspiracy". The only lesson they drew from the East Timor experience was not to give concessions to rebels and they had been dismayed when they saw Gus Dur doing just that in his dealings with the supporters of independence in Aceh and Papua. Concerned about possible charges of human-rights violations in the new *Reformasi* era, officers often complained that they could not deal effectively with separatist rebels or communal rioters without the kind of "legal umbrella" (*payung hukum*) that a state of military emergency would provide but successive governments were reluctant to provide such powers. Military demands for a state of military emergency to deal with communal conflict in Maluku, for example, were rejected by President Habibie and only a civil emergency — in which formal authority remained with the governor — was implemented by President Abdurrahman Wahid. Similar calls for a military emergency in Aceh were resisted by the Abdurrahman government. The military mainstream hoped that Megawati would be more accommodating to their aspirations and eventually, despite the reservations of Yudhoyono, her Coordinating Minister of Political and Security Affairs, a military emergency was declared in Aceh after the collapse of negotiations with the rebel movement, GAM, in May 2003.

The dominant element in the military under Megawati continued to use the language of the New Order.[55] Reflecting the military concern with internal security and the maintenance of national unity, military leaders constantly used the term "NKRI" (*Negara Kesatuan Republik Indonesia*: Unitary State of the Republic of Indonesia) to a point where it seemed to have taken the place of the discredited dwi fungsi as the TNI's core ideological concept. Like dwi fungsi, NKRI seemed to imply that the military would continue to be the custodian of the domestic security and welfare of the nation. These officers, whose overseas experience was often very limited, tended to feel threatened by the outside world — particularly the West — which they believed harboured plans to foster Indonesia's disintegration. The security forces, therefore, had to maintain a high level of vigilance not only against the foreign threat but also against domestic political groups "infected" with Western liberal ideas like democracy and human rights.[56] These officers continued to use the rhetoric of the dwi fungsi era with its emphasis on the organic — almost mystical — "unification of the TNI with the people" (*kemanunggalan TNI dengan rakyat*). The army chief of staff, Gen. Ryamizard Ryacudu, believed that this "unification" meant that the concept of civil-military relations did not apply to Indonesia.[57] He declared that the TNI "cannot be forced to return to the barracks because this would distance us from the people".[58] According to Ryamizard, the military must continue to play a political role because Indonesia is faced by threats to national unity. "It is true", he said, "we do not abstain from matters related to national issues. Because in this country, unlike advanced countries such as the United States, the question of disintegration is still here. So we must all join together to manage this country."[59] These officers, as we shall see in Chapter 8, saw no purpose in negotiation with separatist movements and preferred to call for the "elimination" and "eradication" of rebels.

REVIVING REFORM:
LEGISLATING CIVIL-MILITARY RELATIONS

The initial military reforms during the Habibie presidency were driven by the crisis surrounding the fall of Soeharto when much opprobrium was directed at the TNI's entrenched political role. As Mietzner explained, "The character and scope of reforms proposed by the armed forces in politics thus not surprisingly suggested that the problem of military intervention in politics was limited to the participation of senior officers in political institutions."[60] The "New Paradigm" reforms therefore focussed on the withdrawal of military officers from direct engagement in day-to-day politics and mostly concerned issues that could be decided and implemented unilaterally by the military leadership by means of an instruction from the Commander-in-Chief. The next stage was more complex as crisis-ridden conditions gave way to politics-as-usual and reformers aimed to establish a legislative framework for military professionalism and the advancement of civilian control over the military.[61]

Although much of the initial military-sponsored momentum toward reform under Habibie had been lost during the next two presidencies, a minority of officers continued to aspire to develop a professional military under civilian control and oriented toward national defence. Such views received more support in the navy and air force which, by their very nature, were oriented toward external defence, than in the army which had always been primarily concerned with internal security.[62] Naval and air force officers, along with army colleagues, were well represented in the higher levels of the Department of Defence which became the main institutional base for further professionalization and reform. These professional-oriented officers engaged in discussions with a group of civilian academics and others gathered together in ProPatria, a small "think-tank" concerned with "security-sector" reform.[63]

President Megawati did not play a significant role in these discussions while her defence minister, before his incapacitation in mid-2003, had no expertise in military affairs. In general, the TNI was now under the influence of conservative army officers appointed under Megawati and had little appetite for further reform.

The aspirations of reform-minded officers in the Defence Department, led by Maj. Gen. Sudradjat, the Director-general for Defence Strategy, were presented in a defence White Paper in 2003. It put forward three central objectives. First, the White Paper declared that "As a professional military, the TNI is committed to distancing itself from involvement in practical politics." Second, the TNI would be "placed under the authority of the government that is elected by the people through democratic and constitutional means". And finally the TNI was "to become a professional military in performing the role of an instrument of the state in the field of national defence".[64] These concepts directly challenged the *Dwi Fungsi* attitudes of the officers Megawati had appointed to lead the army.

In contrast to the limited withdrawal from political involvement envisaged in the "New Paradigm" reforms, the next phase required the adoption of new laws by the DPR. The conceptual foundation of military reform had been set out in two decrees of the MPR in August 2000 during the Abdurrahman presidency. Decree No. VI confirmed the institutional separation of the police from the TNI while Decree No. VII delineated their functions and provided the guidelines for further laws which were initiated under Abdurrahman and adopted during Megawati's presidency — the Law on National Defence (No. 3/2002) and the Law on the National Police (No. 2/2002), both promulgated in January 2002. These were followed by the Law on the TNI (No. 34/2004) in October 2004, passed a few days before the expiry of Megawati's presidential term. In contrast to the "New Paradigm" reforms of 1998–99, the next round had to be deliberated by the political parties in the fragmented MPR and DPR. In considering the two laws of 2002 the DPR seemed reluctant to challenge the wishes of the TNI mainstream but was less inhibited in amending the 2004 law on the TNI.

Department of Defence

One major concern of the new legislation was to find a proper balance between civilian supremacy and the professional autonomy of the military. During the New Order, President Soeharto had "politicized" the military by using it to further his own political purposes. After his fall, both officers and civilian politicians joined forces to adopt new procedures aiming to prevent the president appointing personal protégés to key military positions on political rather than professional grounds.[65] MPR Decree No. VII, which required the president to obtain the DPR's approval both in appointing and dismissing the Commander-in-Chief, was followed by the Law on National Defence which restricted the choice to officers who were currently serving or who had previously served as Chief of Staff of one of the services.[66]

Reformers wanted to insulate the TNI further by placing it under the authority of the Minister of Defence rather than directly under the President as ABRI had been during the New Order. This proposal, however, met strong opposition, not from the president but from military leaders. As the August 2000 MPR session approached, Abdurrahman's civilian defence minister, Juwono Sudarsono, proposed that such a transfer should take place gradually over a period of three years while at the same time the police should be transferred to the Department of Home Affairs. Juwono also wanted to move the military intelligence agency (*Badan Intelijen Strategis*: BAIS) from the TNI to the Defence Department.[67] These proposals, however, were rejected by the military leaders. According to Juwono, President Abdurrahman had initially accepted the proposal but later "the president gave in because the TNI and National Police wanted to stand alone."[68] Thus, despite the general mood favouring limitations to the president's authority, the MPR in Decree VII stipulated that the Commander-in-Chief remain directly under the president rather than the Minister of Defence. The DPR too was reluctant to oppose the wishes of the TNI. The Law on National Defence made the Commander-in-Chief responsible directly to the president for "strategic planning" and "military operations" although it acknowledged the Minister of Defence's responsibilities in the fields of broad policy and administration.[69] Reflecting the TNI's independence from the Ministry, the Commander-in-Chief was granted ministerial status and, together with the Chief of Police, participated in cabinet meetings.

The subordinate position of the Defence Department was illustrated in 2003–04 after President Megawati had intervened in the purchase of military aircraft from Russia. The Defence Department's Director-General for Defence Strategy, Maj. Gen. Sudrajat, complained that although the law made the Defence Department responsible for general policy, it had not approved the purchases. "The TNI proposed their own defence programme to the President and secured approval from the latter", he said.[70] The authority of the Department of Defence had been undermined by the failure of the president to appoint a new minister in place of the incapacitated Matori while senior officials were constrained by their status as active military officers and therefore subordinates of the Commander-in-Chief. The purchase of the four Sukhoi fighter aircraft and two Mi-35 helicopters by means of barter trade involved the Minister of Trade and Industry, Rini Soewandi. The lack of transparency in the purchase led to much speculation about possible commissions intended to boost President Megawati's campaign funds for the coming presidential election.

When the long-delayed TNI bill was finally submitted to the DPR in mid-2004, members returned to the question of the status of the Department of Defence. Some, such as the Deputy Chairman of Commission I, Effendy Choirie of the PKB, called for the TNI to be placed directly under the department, while a Golkar member, Harjriyanto Tohari, proposed that "the TNI be placed beneath the president through the minister".[71] But both the TNI and the police remained reluctant to be placed under departmental authority. Gen. Endriartono claimed that the TNI would be willing to transfer to the Department of Defence but only when civilian politicians had proved their "maturity". He was particularly worried that a future minister representing a political party might try to politicize the TNI.[72] One of the reasons for the resistance of the police was the reluctance of many police officers to serve under retired TNI officers who customarily served as Minister of Home Affairs.[73] In any case the proposed moves could not overcome the obstacle of MPR Decree No. VII/2000 which stated clearly that the TNI and the police were "beneath" the President. The reformers won a token victory, however, in the unenforceable "Elucidation" attached to the TNI law which stated that "In order to achieve effectiveness and efficiency in the management of national defence, the institution of TNI will in the future be placed within the Department of Defence."[74]

Deployment of Forces

The first draft of the TNI law had been drawn up by the TNI itself and contained several clauses that disturbed both civilians and reform-minded military officers. In 2003, a public controversy had arisen over the issue of authority to deploy military forces. The 2002 Law on National Defence had confirmed the authority of the president to deploy defence forces to face military threats but also required the approval of the DPR. However, in "pressing circumstances" the president was permitted to act immediately without parliamentary approval, but was required to obtain the DPR's agreement within forty-eight hours.[75] The new controversy arose in response to the TNI's draft of the TNI bill which authorized the TNI to act without presidential approval in an emergency. Clause 19 proposed that "In pressing circumstances the Commander-in-Chief may use TNI force as a preliminary measure to prevent a greater loss for the nation" without reporting to the president for up to twenty-four hours.[76] Clause 19 was quickly dubbed by critics as the "coup clause". The reform-minded Maj. Gen. Sudrajat of the Defence Department commented: "It is dangerous because it means the TNI could carry out a coup and be protected by law."[77] The hardline Chief of Staff of the Army, Gen. Ryamizard quickly emerged as a strong supporter of the clause. Dismissing critics as "depraved" (*bejat*), he said that "If we want to revolt, we can revolt now, why wait for a law?"[78] The Commander-in-Chief, Gen. Endriartono, stressed the need for the TNI to be able to act in emergency situations. If the president were kidnapped, he asked, was the TNI expected to get the permission of the kidnappers in order to contact the president before deploying troops?[79] Meanwhile civilian observers pointed out that in most countries such contingencies did not need to be defined in law but were anticipated in standard operating procedures.[80]

The protest over the "coup clause" led to a delay of more than a year before the bill was submitted to the DPR on 30 June 2004 after review by the Department of Defence and finally the Office of the Coordinating Minister for Political and Security Affairs — then headed by Lt. Gen. Hari Sabarno in an "ad interim" capacity in place of Yudhoyono who had become a presidential candidate. By then political circumstances were very different to those of 2003. The general elections had been held in which PDI-P had lost much support and the two-stage presidential election was about to begin. The struggle between the Department of Defence and the TNI had also been resolved — at least at the procedural level — by the president who determined that it was the responsibility of the Department of Defence to submit the bill without direct involvement of the TNI.[81] Facing Yudhoyono as her main rival in the presidential election, it seemed that Megawati was taking up the cause of civilian rule, implicitly hinting that it might be undermined by the military represented by Yudhoyono. The new draft removed the original Clause 19 and placed "authority and responsibility for the deployment and use of TNI forces" firmly in the hands of the president (Clause 18), while making the Commander-in-Chief "responsible to the President for the operational implementation of deployment and use of TNI forces" (Clause 20).[82] In the DPR, the government representatives — Coordinating Minister Hari Sabarno, Commander-in-Chief Endriartono and the Secretary-General of the Department of Defence, Vice Admiral Suprihadi — argued that the TNI be given authority in the law to take pre-emptive action, for example, against separatist groups before they were capable of launching an armed rebellion. The majority of the political parties in the DPR, however, remained opposed to extending TNI authority. They also criticized the bill's blanket reference to the TNI's duty to deal with "each threat" and succeeded in narrowing it to "each military threat and armed threat".[83]

Reformist Amendments

In the highly politicized atmosphere surrounding the presidential election campaign, the DPR unexpectedly adopted a series of reformist amendments that implicitly criticized the TNI. The "taboo" topic of military finance was addressed specifically in an amendment requiring that the "TNI is funded from the national defence budget" and that its budget should be submitted by the Defence Department (Clause 66), implying that military purchases and other expenditures should no longer be made by the TNI or individual services using their own non-budgetary resources. A clause was also added which required the government within five years "to take over all business activities owned and managed by TNI whether directly or indirectly" (Clause 76). On the territorial structure, the military responsibility to provide "guidance" was removed (Clause 10.e in bill) and the Elucidation attached to the law was amended to require the TNI "to avoid forms of organization that can open opportunities in the interests of practical politics", implicitly targeting the mobilization of the army's territorial network for political purposes.

Another amendment nullified a clause that seemed to reverse the earlier reform that had ended the practice of placing officers in the bureaucracy. Clause 45 of the bill stated that "military personnel can be appointed to positions in departments and non-departmental institutions" while Clause 43 permitted the appointment and dismissal of military personnel outside the structure of the TNI.[84] These clauses came under heavy criticism in the DPR as an attempt to bring back old dwi fungsi practices. The law as adopted reaffirmed the 1998 principle that officers appointed to civilian positions should first retire from the TNI, but made limited exceptions for officers placed in the office of the minister responsible for coordinating political and security affairs, the Defence Department, State Intelligence, the National Defence Council, the National Search and Rescue Service and so on, including the position of Military Secretary to the President.[85]

Finally, the DPR excised, or at least modified, some of the bill's dwi fungsi rhetoric. The TNI's original draft bill declared in typical New Order language that "The TNI is a people's army, with its origins and source in the people, fighting (*berjuang*) together with the people, the protector and defender of the people. Thus the unification (*kemanunggalan*) of the TNI with the people is the strength of the TNI in defending the nation." The language of the final law was considerably "toned down". The "People's Army" is defined simply as an army whose personnel are Indonesian citizens, while the Fighter's Army (*Pejuang*) "fights to uphold the Unitary State of the Republic of Indonesia".[86] Reflecting the outlook of civilian and military reformers, a sub-clause was added referring to a "Professional Army" which supports democracy, civilian supremacy, human rights, national laws and ratified international law (Clause 2).

It is hard not to suspect that the government's willingness to accept amendments to the original bill was related to the current presidential election campaign. In the first round of the presidential election on 5 July, the two top candidates were Yudhoyono and Megawati who therefore became the contenders in the final round on 20 September. Vulnerable to criticism for her government's unimpressive legislative record, President Megawati had sent the long-delayed bill to the DPR on 30 June, just before the first-round election. Although deliberation in the DPR's Working Committee only began on 2 August, it was completed in what for the DPR was extraordinary speed on 30 September, the day the DPR's five-year term expired. As the

Kompas newspaper reported, "The material of the TNI bill produced by the Working Committee virtually overhauled completely the bill proposed by the government."[87] Dwi fungsi language was changed, the clause on secondment of military personnel to civilian jobs was effectively removed, the nature of threats was clarified, the transfer of the TNI to the Defence Department was envisaged and, as will be discussed later, the role of the territorial system was restricted and the closure of military commercial ventures was foreshadowed.[88] In the DPR, PDI-P and Golkar were now allies against Yudhoyono following the elimination of Golkar's candidate (General Wiranto) in the first round of the presidential election. They now took the lead in pushing through reformist amendments of a type that they had not supported earlier. Facing a retired military general in the final round of the presidential election, Megawati tried to portray herself as the civilian candidate resisting the "return of the military" by supporting significant changes to her own government's bill that had originally been seen as "pro-military".

Withdrawal from the MPR

One further legislative change relating to civil-military relations needs to be noted. In early 2000 the TNI Commander-in-Chief, Admiral Widodo, had announced that the TNI was willing to relinquish its representation in the DPR but wanted to remain in the MPR.[89] Debate in the MPR at its August 2000 session eventually resulted in a compromise that allowed military officers to sit in the MPR "until 2009 at the latest". In the earlier discussions in the MPR's Ad Hoc Committee I, only the TNI and a small military-linked group had supported the TNI's bid to retain its MPR seats but in the MPR session itself only three small parties were opposed.[90] The TNI had argued that its representation in the MPR was compensation for its forbearance in not insisting on the right of military and police personnel to vote in elections. The PDI-P leader in the MPR, Sophan Sophiaan, said his party opposed TNI representation "but we could not do it immediately for the sake of national unity".[91] It appears that most of the parties were reluctant to further humiliate the TNI after its experiences in the previous two years.[92] It also seems that, in the context of a very fragmented parliament, parties appreciated that support from the TNI/Polri group could be crucial and were therefore careful not to alienate the military group.[93] The TNI, however, later found itself in a difficult position when moves were launched to impeach President Abdurrahman who, according to the constitution, held supreme authority over the military. Its confusion was clear when its representatives supported the first impeachment resolution in the DPR but abstained on the second before finally supporting the final dismissal in the MPR.[94] The TNI continued to defend its claim to MPR representation until 2002 when, as discussed in Chapter 3, the MPR amended the constitution in a way that provided for a fully elected MPR.[95] By then, it seems, TNI leaders believed that there were more effective ways of having the TNI's voice heard than through its representatives in the MPR which had been largely emasculated by the 2002 constitutional amendments.

The legislation on civil-military relations adopted during the Megawati presidency had proceeded with little presidential guidance and, in the last year, in the effective absence of a defence minister. The draft legislation submitted to the DPR was primarily the outcome of debates within, and between, the Department of Defence and the TNI. However, the DPR was by no means a "rubber stamp" and amended key clauses of the TNI bill in ways that pushed forward the reform programme but at the same time was reluctant to challenge directly TNI prerogatives. Indeed some of the most important amendments were placed in the Elucidation where they only foreshadowed further reform without requiring immediate implementation.[96] It appeared, however, that the reformist amendments may have been driven as much by political calculations as by commitment to reformist principles. The main parties supporting the amendments, PDI-P, Golkar and PKB, were now allies in opposing the bid of a retired military officer for the presidency.

THE YUDHOYONO PRESIDENCY: ENTRENCHED OBSTACLES TO FULL CIVILIAN CONTROL

During the first three presidencies of the Reformasi era, governments had overseen significant reforms which restricted the role of the military in non-military affairs but the TNI continued to exercise substantial autonomy. Presidents Habibie and Abdurrahman had both been able to impose specific policies in the security field that were most unwelcome to military officers but neither succeeded in institutionalizing civilian authority. Thus Habibie thrust aside the military's deep commitment to ensure that East Timor remained part of Indonesia by holding a referendum on self-determination in the province that resulted in a vote for independence. Abdurrahman overrode military objections to negotiations with separatists in Aceh and explored contacts with separatists in Papua. Despite these initial "victories", however, neither president was able to win military support for the implementation of his policies. In East Timor, the military gave strong backing to the pro-Indonesian side, including the formation of militias which were responsible for the killing and destruction that followed the referendum, although in the end, in the face of enormous international pressure, the military withdrew. In the Aceh case, military troops on the ground just continued operations against the rebels despite the formal cease-fire which was eventually abandoned by the government itself. Without the institutional capacity to establish civilian control over the military, Habibie and Abdurrahman found that they could initiate policies but could not implement them successfully in the face of determined military opposition. Under Megawati, a new cease-fire agreement was negotiated for Aceh but she made no serious effort to save it when the military embarked on a course that led to its collapse and the introduction of martial law.

Although reform-oriented military leaders regularly stated that defence and security policy should no longer be determined by the military alone but through "national agreement" (*kesepakatan bangsa*) reached by constitutional processes,[97] the military mainstream retained its conviction that military officers had a special obligation to determine the measures needed to ensure the preservation of the "Unitary State of the Republic of Indonesia". For them, the experience of East Timor and the failed peace negotiations in Aceh had only strengthened that conviction. They believed that peace in Aceh and Papua could only be achieved by "exterminating" members of the Free Aceh Movement (*Gerakan Aceh Merdeka*: GAM) and the Free Papua Organization (*Organisasi Papua Merdeka*: OPM).

The continuing war in Aceh presented the Yudhoyono government with an enormous challenge but also an opportunity. The Aceh negotiations during the Megawati presidency had been supervised by Yudhoyono as her Coordinating Minister for Political and Security Affairs, but in the end, the "dove", Yudhoyono, had to give way to the "hawks" and a huge military operation was launched in 2003. As will be discussed in detail in Chapter 8, Yudhoyono had not abandoned hope of reaching a peace in Aceh and, immediately after his election as president, authorized Vice President Jusuf Kalla to continue his earlier efforts to establish contacts with GAM. Given the attitude of the military mainstream, these contacts had to be conducted in secret, but they soon bore fruit in the tragic circumstances following the devastating tsunami that hit Aceh in December 2004. Many military officers and nationalist politicians regarded negotiations with rebels as a "betrayal of the Republic". Although opposed quietly by many military officers and openly by politicians in the DPR, particularly those representing Megawati's PDI-P and also some from Golkar, formal talks began in Helsinki, Finland, in January 2005.

It had therefore been crucial for the peace process that President Yudhoyono establish his authority over the TNI and win majority support in the DPR. Yudhoyono's control of the TNI, however, had been threatened by President Megawati's last-minute nomination of the military hardliner, Gen. Ryamizard, to succeed Gen. Endriartono as Commander-in-Chief of the TNI. MPR Decree No. VII/2000 and the Law on National Defence required the president to gain the approval of the DPR for the proposed new Commander-in-Chief. In the last days of her presidency following her defeat in the presidential election, the bitterly disappointed Megawati had in effect planted a "time bomb" for Yudhoyono as many members of the DPR favoured Ryamizard. Once in office, Yudhoyono withdrew Ryamizard's nomination but the PDI-P, supported by sections of Golkar and other parties in the DPR, continued to demand the right to decide on Ryamizard's nomination. Rather than risk defeat in a head-on challenge to the DPR, Yudhoyono postponed putting forward his own nomination until after Ryamizard reached retirement age and only nominated the Chief of Staff of the air force, Air Marshal Djoko Suyanto, to succeed Endriartono in January 2006. By then the potential challenge from the DPR had been neutralized at the Golkar party congress in December 2004 when Jusuf Kalla defeated the incumbent party General Chairman, Akbar Tandjung, who had aligned the party with the PDI-P in the DPR. Kalla's victory and the change of orientation in Golkar gave the government majority support in the DPR.

The manoeuvring over the nomination of the Commander-in-Chief of the TNI was crucial for Yudhoyono's strategy to control the TNI. Ryamizard's attitudes on military issues contrasted sharply with those of the president but won much sympathy within the army itself. By appointing an air force officer, the first ever to be appointed as Commander-in-Chief, Yudhoyono further weakened the army's grip on the TNI. Yudhoyono had already begun to replace hard-line army officers with those who shared his own approach. His close ally, General Djoko Susanto, replaced Ryamizard as Chief of Staff of the Army in 2005 and at the end of 2007 was promoted to Commander-in-Chief. Another of Yudhoyono's protégés, General Agustadi Sasongko Purnomo, was appointed as Chief of Staff.[98] Yudhoyono's brother-in-law, Lt. Gen. Erwin Sudjono, was appointed as commander of Kostrad and then TNI chief of staff for general affairs, while another brother-in-law, Brig. Gen. Pramono Edhie Wibowo, was appointed as commandant-general of Kopassus in 2008.[99]

The removal of Ryamizard and other hard-liners from key military positions not only overcame an enormous obstacle to the Aceh peace agreement but also established a crucial precedent for the exercise of presidential authority over the military. Whatever their private thoughts about Aceh, ambitious military officers recognized that their prospects for future promotions and appointments in their last years of service (and possible post-retirement careers) were in the hands of a president whose likely tenure in office would exceed the remaining years that most senior officers could expect to serve before retirement. In contrast to his predecessors as president since 1998, none of whom held office for a full term, Yudhoyono's political legitimacy, derived from his convincing victory in the direct presidential election, greatly enhanced his capacity to deal with dissident officers. It apparently took a retired military officer to establish a degree of civilian control over the military that had never been achieved by the previous civilian presidents. However, although the military's acceptance of the president's Aceh policy was a major step forward to establishing government control of the military, many important issues of military reform remained unresolved.

UNRESOLVED ISSUES

Following the interruption of the Gus Dur presidency, the military reform process focused on the details of legislation. Moderate military reformers, however, were constrained by the conservative officers favoured by President Megawati. Despite the DPR's adoption of new laws regulating the role of the military, fundamental areas of military reform were either left unaddressed or unresolved. While the TNI's primary role in the field of national defence was recognized, some of its precise responsibilities remained in "grey areas" (*wilayah abu-abu*) and awaited proper definition. This debate was linked to the continuing role of the army's embedded territorial structure and the government's inability to supply adequate funding which forced military units and personnel to find their own ways to make ends meet. And finally, the apparent impunity of military officers before the law was not seriously tackled.

"Grey Areas"

The long-term goal of the military reformers was to transform the TNI into a professional defence force. When the MPR convened in 2000, this aspiration was embodied in MPR Decree No. VI which described the TNI unequivocally as responsible for "national defence" while the police force was made responsible for "security" (i.e., internal security). Additionally, the decree required the two forces to cooperate in areas where defence and security overlapped.[100] This clear-cut distinction between "defence" and "internal security", however, was somewhat blurred in Decree No. VII adopted in the same MPR session. While the police force was required "to preserve security and social order, uphold the law, and provide protection and service to society", the TNI's function was "to uphold national sovereignty, the unity of the territory of the Unitary State of the Republic of Indonesia based on Pancasila and the 1945 Constitution, and to protect the entire Indonesian nation from threats and disturbances to national unity."[101] Thus, although Decree No. VI seemed to exclude the TNI from responsibilities in the field of internal security except where internal security was linked to defence, the second decree opened the way to a broader interpretation of "defence" by including the preservation of national unity, the national ideology and the constitution. This decree, therefore, could potentially provide legitimacy for continuing TNI involvement not only in internal-security affairs but also broader political matters.

The sharp distinction in Decree VI between "defence" and "internal security" soon led to a debate over "grey areas". Where exactly was the dividing line? The military hardliners, such as Ryamizard, simply called for internal-security functions to be transferred back to the military.[102] But the reformers, too, were concerned about the rigid distinction between the two areas. According to Yudhoyono, "there is a simplification in that when we talk about defence then it's the TNI's business, while security is for the police". In his view, external defence and internal security were both aspects of the broader concept of "national security".[103] This view was supported by the Minister of Defence, Juwono, who described the MPR decrees as conceptually wrong.[104] Reform-minded military officers accepted that maintenance of public order was a police task but argued that internal conflicts that threatened the unity of the nation were also the responsibility of the military. Moreover, military officers — both reformist and conservative — questioned the capacity of the police to cope with armed separatists in Aceh or communal conflict as in Maluku or severe rioting in cities. They believed that the police force was unable to cope with major challenges to public order without military support.[105] Numbering about 200,000 at the time of the separation, it was commonly estimated that the police would need manpower of about 600,000 before it could fully take over the internal-security role.[106] The police paramilitary force, the Mobile Brigade (*Brigade Mobil*: Brimob) was equipped to deal with rioting but it did not have the equipment or training required to face a serious armed revolt or major communal conflict.[107]

The 2003 Defence White Paper, drawn up by professional-oriented officers in the Department of Defence, contributed further to the blurring of the distinction when it argued for the TNI's continuing role in "overcoming non-traditional security issues that are cross-national including security issues that arise internally" such as terrorism, separatist movements, cross-national crime, "radical actions", communal conflict and the impact of natural disasters.[108] While professional militaries everywhere are giving increasing attention to "non-traditional threats" or, in military jargon, Military Operations Other Than War (MOOTW), the breadth of the White Paper's list in effect asserted the TNI's claim to a continuing internal-security role. Since the Al Qaeda attacks on the US in 2001, and especially the series of terrorist bombings in Indonesia beginning with the Bali bombs in October 2002, rivalry between the TNI and the police had increased over which force should take the lead role. The TNI, through Kopassus, already had a special counter-terrorism unit called Detachment 81 (so named after its successful assault on a hijacked Indonesian aircraft in Bangkok in 1981), but the reluctance of foreign governments to provide aid to Kopassus, due to its human-rights record, led to a sharp growth in police capacity in the form of a new counter-terrorism unit known as Detachment 88.[109] Meanwhile, assisted by foreign police, the Indonesian police took primary charge of investigating terrorist bombings with considerable success. In an effort to improve coordination between different agencies, a Coordinating Desk for the Elimination of Terrorism headed by a police officer was established in the Office of the Coordinating Minister for Political and Security Affairs, at that time Yudhoyono.

An immediate problem was to determine when the TNI could intervene in internal conflict. The Law on the Police No. 28/1997 and the succeeding Law No. 2/2002 gave authority to the relevant regional police chief to request military assistance but with the police retaining "operational authority". Thus, technically the war against GAM in Aceh until 2003 was conducted under the command of the provincial chief of police although in reality it was a military operation. In regions where emergency law had been applied, as in Aceh after 2003, the 1959 Emergency Law gave authority to the governor to ask for military assistance but, in the case of civil emergencies, the military would remain technically under police command. Only in military emergencies or a "state of war" could the military legally take charge. To add to the confusion, following heightened tension between the police and the army in Maluku in May 2002, the Kodam commander, a brigadier-general, had been replaced by a major-general who thus outranked the police chief, a brigadier-general. In order to avoid a situation where an army major-general received orders from a police brigadier-general, a new Operational Command for the Restoration of Security (*Komando Operasi Pemulihan Keamanan*) was established under Maj. Gen. Djoko Santoso with authority over the police — despite the clear requirement of the emergency law that operational command should be in the hands of the chief of police during a civil emergency.[110] As the current law stood — except in emergency conditions — it was up to the local police chief to decide whether he needed reinforcements from the military, but police officers were often reluctant to seek such assistance.

Cooperation between the army and the police has always been a problem in Indonesia. Apart from "normal" rivalry between two forces, tension between the two was aggravated by the presence of both army and police units stationed in every city, town and township throughout the nation. Much of the conflict arose from the government's failure to provide adequate financial resources which resulted in competition for scarce local resources to supplement both the income of personnel and the cost of operations. In some regions understandings were reached over which resources are the "right" of which force to exploit, but in this field too there were "grey areas" over which each force was prepared to defend its stake. In the case of illegal logging for example, an agreement could be reached which allows one force to control the extraction of logs while the other takes care of transporting them to timber companies or across borders to foreign buyers. Control of informal charges at a port might be allocated to one force while "taxes" on road transport are left to the other. And illegal gambling, narcotics networks and prostitution can be divided between them according to local areas. But such arrangements can also break down, sometimes resulting in violent clashes.[111] After the separation of the police from the TNI, such clashes increased in number. Between 1997 and 1999, 28 clashes took place, killing 4 members of each force,[112] but the number reported in 2000 rose to 79 in which 6 participants were killed and 70 seriously wounded before declining to 52 in 2001 with 3 killed and 39 seriously wounded.[113] The reported number of clashes in 2002 and 2003 were approximately 50 and 100.[114] In following years clashes continued to take place regularly although the number of casualties declined.[115]

The Army's Territorial Structure

At the centre of the debate over "grey areas" was the future of the army's territorial structure. The army consists of centralized and territorial commands. The two most important centralized commands are Kostrad with personnel of about 30,000 in two conventional divisions, and the 5,500-strong Kopassus. The territorial commands, on the other hand, are spread throughout the archipelago. Since 2002 there have been twelve regional military commands (*Komando Daerah Militer*: Kodam). Headed by a major-general, a Kodam could cover a single large province or several smaller provinces. Each Kodam is divided into several sub-regional commands (*Komando Resor Militer*: Korem), headed by a colonel and based in major cities and towns. Beneath the Korem are district regional commands (*Komando Distrik Militer*: Kodim), headed by lieutenant-colonels and based in civil-administration districts (kabupaten), and then sub-district military commands (*Komando Rayon Militer*: Koramil) led by captains or lieutenants and based in civil-administration sub-districts (*kecamatan*). At the bottom of the structure are "Village Guidance" non-commissioned officers (*Bintara Pembina Desa*: Babinsa) located in villages. The number of soldiers placed in the territorial structure is around 150,000 or about two-thirds of the army.[116] However, many of these troops are not engaged in territorial functions as some troops are organized in battalions that can be deployed to other regions in emergencies.

The formal rationale for the army's territorial structure is based on the defence doctrine known as the Total People's Defence and Security System (*Sistem Pertahanan Keamanan Rakyat Semesta*: Sishankamrata) which had its origins in the guerilla struggle waged by the nationalist forces in the revolution against Dutch colonial rule between 1945 and 1949. Lacking sophisticated weapons, training and equipment, the post-independence defence strategy assumed that Indonesia would not be able to prevent an invasion by a powerful enemy but could mobilize mass resistance to a foreign occupation along the lines of the successful guerilla war against the Dutch.[117] This doctrine has not been formally abandoned although Indonesia now possesses significant conventional forces in the form of Kostrad, the navy and the air force. However, the probability of a major invasion of Indonesia in the foreseeable future is recognized as very low so in practice little emphasis is now given to the defence rationale for the territorial system.[118] Instead, mainstream military officers argued that the territorial structure is needed to support social and political stability from such "internal" threats as separatist movements, communal conflict, rioting and so on.

Civilian critics were dubious of what they regarded as rationalizations for a structure that facilitated military involvement in local politics and had the potential to undermine democracy. They focussed on the political influence wielded by territorial commanders at the local level and the capacity of territorial troops to repress opposition, as they had during the New Order regime. As long as its forces were deployed territorially, the military retained a structure that could facilitate the reversal of the post-Soeharto decline in its political role.[119] Although military units were no longer mobilized to ensure Golkar victories in elections, local military commanders continued to play roles behind the scenes in local elections. Candidates, whether retired military officers or party politicians, often sought military backing which was given in one form or another, often in exchange for financial benefits.[120] Moreover, troops spread throughout the nation but without adequate financial support inevitably became involved in illegal money-making activities.

In 1999 the reformers within the military itself had begun to question the necessity for the territorial structure — at least in its form at that time. The most public criticism was launched before a DPR commission on 13 December 1999 by Maj. Gen. Agus Wirahadikusumah who called it an "instrument of power".[121] He argued that the territorial command structure was no longer appropriate in developed provinces in Java where security was already established, although he acknowledged that it was still needed in undeveloped regions which were not effectively served by local government.[122] In the developed areas, the army's territorial units were seen as duplicating the responsibilities of the police. Wirahadikusumah proposed that the dismantling of the structure in Java should begin with the lowest levels — the babinsa in the villages and the koramil in the sub-districts.[123] He believed that the unnecessary presence of the territorial units at every level of society was one of the sources of public resentment of the military.[124] In a minimal response to Wirahadikusumah's proposal, the army chief of staff, Gen. Tyasno Sudarto, withdrew some babinsa from urban "villages" in Jakarta and Surabaya and dissolved some koramil but stressed that they were still very much needed in rural areas.[125]

Agus Wirahadikusmah's proposal faced strong opposition within the military and he himself estimated — somewhat optimistically — that only 20 per cent of officers supported him.[126] Over the next two years intermittent discussions took place within the TNI. In August 2001 — coincidentally a few weeks before Agus Wirahadikusumah died of a heart attack — a seminar was held at the TNI headquarters to examine new proposals. Lt. Gen. Agus Widjojo, another of the original group of reformers and now TNI chief of staff for territorial affairs, defended the existence of the territorial structure but argued that it should be focused exclusively on defence responsibilities. He envisaged that only the Kodam and Korem from the old territorial structure would be retained with the purpose of managing and training troops for defence, while broader duties, particularly support for "defence potential" and the maintenance of public order, would be handed over to provincial governments and the police.[127] However, Widjojo anticipated that the implementation of the plan would be gradual, taking more than a dozen years in Java and much longer in less developed regions. A major concern was the need to avoid the disruption that would be caused by a sudden demobilization of territorial troops as a result of the dissolution of the lower levels of the territorial structure.[128] The proposal received only lukewarm endorsement from the army chief of staff, Gen. Endriartiono Sutarto, who described it as a "concept" and said it could not be implemented until regional governments and the police were ready to take over the territorial function of "guidance" (*pembinaan*).[129] Civilian critics, however, asked why it was necessary to meet an external threat by maintaining territorial units in every region of the country rather than concentrating troops in regions potentially most vulnerable to direct enemy incursion.

Agus Widjojo's proposals, like those of Agus Wirahadikusumah before him, came under heavy attack from the conservative military mainstream. The then Kostrad commander, Ryamizard Ryacudu, retorted, "If the Kodams are given up, I am convinced that Irian Jaya will be independent tomorrow" although he conceded it might be possible in "relatively secure" regions.[130] His ally, the then Jakarta regional commander, Lt. Gen. Bibit Waluyo, worried about who would supervise (*mengawas*) isolated districts. Without the babinsa, koramil and kodim, the military would be like "a person without eyes and ears". "If the system is dissolved," he claimed, "the nation will break up." For Bibit, the territorial structure was "'ideal" and constituted the "spirit" of the TNI.[131] The essence of the reactions of these officers was that if the military did not continue to supervise the people closely, the nation would descend into chaos and soon disintegrate. It should be noted, however, that public opinion in rural areas was not strongly opposed to the territorial institutions. A survey conducted in villages in Central Java showed that around 80 per cent of respondents approved the presence of kodim and koramil although the level of acceptance was rather lower in the case of babinsa. Another survey conducted in several regions showed approval rates of more than 50 per cent.[132]

The open debate in August 2001, only a month after Megawati rose to the presidency, marked the end of moves to reform the territorial structure, however. Two months later, Agus Widjojo's position of chief of staff for territorial affairs was abolished but the territorial structure remained intact. In May 2002, two of the staunchest defenders of the territorial system were appointed to key posts — Ryamizard Ryacudu as army chief of staff and Bibit Waluyo as Kostrad commander. Ryamizard continued his strong defence of the territorial structure. "It has been proven over 56 years that the territorial command structure used in Indonesia is able to confront security disturbances and revolts", he said.[133] He declared that "I won't dissolve Kodam; if possible I'll increase them".[134] The "unification of the TNI with the people" could only be achieved through "territorial guidance", he claimed.[135] Ryamizard's main argument was that Indonesia's national unity was still under challenge. "We are not America that has been independent for two hundred years and the question of nationality has been settled", he explained.[136] The rising influence of the conservatives was indicated by what appeared to be a late insertion of a passage in the executive summary of the Defence Department's White Paper, immediately after the passage about the "professional military as an instrument of the state in the field of national defence" quoted earlier. In the classic language of the New Order, the new passage stated: "As a people's army, the TNI must always be close to the people. Therefore, attempts to separate the TNI from the people are a denial of the very nature of the TNI as an army that originated from the people, fought together with the people and for the interests of the people. This is one of the realities of the implementation of the territorial function by the TNI to safeguard its closeness to the people and their territory."[137]

The territorial system came under criticism during the parliamentary debate on the TNI bill in August–September 2004. The military-drafted bill presented by the government to the DPR included among the duties of the TNI the function "to carry out territorial guidance (*pembinaan*)" and "create the unification (*kemanunggalan*) of the TNI with the People".[138] The chairman of the DPR's Commission I, Ibrahim Embong of Golkar, supported the removal of the "kemanunggalan" doctrine from the bill.[139] In line with Agus Widjojo's earlier concept, one of the Commission's deputy chairmen, Effendy Choirie of PKB, proposed that the army's territorial structure be replaced by regional defence commands including officers from the navy and air force,[140] while the PDI-P's spokesman, Permadi, argued that "territorial guidance" should be restricted to regions in conflict and regions with large natural resources.[141] As discussed earlier, amendments to the bill led to the eventual adoption of a law that removed references to both "territorial guidance" and "kemanunggalan" while stressing that the TNI's "posture" should be "in accordance with national defence policy" (Clause 22.2). The Elucidation attached to the Law implicitly criticized the spread of the territorial network throughout the nation by stating that the placement of TNI forces "must prioritize regions where security is disturbed, border areas, regions disturbed by conflict, and isolated islands". It also criticized current practice by calling on the TNI "to avoid forms of organization that can open opportunities in the interests of practical politics" and proposed that troop deployment "should not always follow the structure of government administration".[142]

Although the DPR showed its concern about the potential misuse of the army's territorial structure, the TNI Law did nothing to dismantle it. In 2005, Gen. Endriartono told the DPR that as long as he was Commander-in-Chief, he would not dissolve any territorial command but at the same time would not allow them to be used for political purposes.[143] Meanwhile the new Chief of Staff of the Army, Gen. Djoko Susanto, proposed to form three new Korem and nineteen Kodim on the grounds that the TNI still did not yet have the capacity to defend the nation.[144] Following his election in 2004, President Yudhoyono, called on the TNI to take measures against terrorism, one of the duties listed among "Military Operations Other than War" in the TNI Law. General Endriantono reacted immediately saying that he was ready to "re-activate" the territorial structure down to the village level,[145] but in fact its de-activation had been limited to the elimination of its earlier intelligence role. Djoko Santoso, who would replace Endriartono as Commander-in-Chief at the end of 2007, strongly defended the territorial structure in language reminiscent of the dwi fungsi era when he described the babinsa as our "eyes and ears" in collecting information and combating terrorism.[146] Anti-Terrorism Desks were established in all the Kodam and would be extended to the Korem and Kodim but their role would be limited to "assisting the police to gather information". Making arrests and carrying out investigations would be left to the police.[147]

Despite reservations expressed in the DPR, the territorial structure remained in place.[148] Although some members of the DPR had succeeded in inserting implicit criticisms of the territorial organisation in the TNI law, the consensus within the DPR stopped well short of mandating a thorough reform of the system. As Alagappa has argued, "to be durable, change in role definition has to be accompanied by alteration in force posture, command structure and deployment".[149] Such "alterations" had not been adopted by the DPR while the new Yudhoyono government seemed to have decided that the time was not ripe to introduce the fundamental reforms needed to overhaul the territorial structure.[150] Its hesitance was no doubt related to the importance of the territorial structure's function of providing self-financing opportunities that enabled the army to maintain its growing force which by 2006 had 233,000 personnel.[151]

Military Finance

The greatest obstacle to military reform is the inability of the government to finance its military forces from its official budget. Since its foundation in 1945 as a guerilla force to fight Dutch colonialism, the military was never adequately funded by the national government and always depended on its own capacity to acquire extra-budgetary funds.[152] In effect the guerilla practice of "living off the land" continues to the present although the form has changed.

Self-financing practices had become deeply entrenched during the New Order. Soeharto turned necessity into a virtue that enabled the military to finance its operations and provide for the needs of its personnel. In essence Soeharto presided over a pyramid of patronage that distributed commercial and extractive opportunities to each level of the military. While central funds partly covered basic salaries and administration, military units throughout the country financed themselves by sponsoring commercial enterprises and extracting all manner of "contributions" from local populations. These enterprises received special treatment from the government while the military provided "protection" when activities such as smuggling, illegal logging and extortion were involved. At the same time individual officers themselves made private arrangements with Chinese business partners at every level from Jakarta down to the provinces and districts. The military (but not only the military), therefore, was deeply involved in the corruption that was the norm during the Soeharto years.

The territorial network thus made an essential contribution to this system. As one well-informed observer put it, "The building and maintenance of business networks were crucial in financing the operation of the political role of the territorial units".[153] By spreading military personnel throughout the entire nation, small units and individual soldiers were able to exploit local opportunities in ways that would be impossible if troops were concentrated in centralized barracks. The official salaries of officers were completely inadequate so they were expected to use their positions not only to make up the shortfall but to achieve at least a high level of comfort and, in the case of senior officers, a luxurious life-style. In effect the loyalty of military officers was indirectly bought by giving them the freedom to extort funds from local economies. In these circumstances, ordinary soldiers could hardly be disciplined if they too sought supplements to their incomes. This did not mean, however, that there were no limits at all. Officers were expected to refrain from "excesses" that might provoke popular outrage.

Since the fall of Soeharto, the defence budget has remained very low. It increased in rupiah terms from Rp 8.4 trillion in 2000 to Rp 33.7 trillion in 2008, hovering around 1 per cent of GDP.[154] According to the TNI spokesman, Maj. Gen. Syafrie Syamsuddin, the government budget in 2002 covered only 30 per cent of the military's expenses.[155] In 2005, the Defence Minister guessed that it might be as much as one half.[156] In response, President Megawati declared that "Whatever the cost of improving the armed forces, it is the state that is obliged to meet those costs. We should stop the practice where the TNI and the national Police are compelled to seek funds in order to finance their daily operations, let alone to support their principal duties."[157] However, of necessity, the TNI continues to depend on non-budgetary finances.

Part of the military's non-budget finances were raised through its commercial enterprises. Altogether in 2002 around 270 enterprises were owned by foundations (*yayasan*) sponsored by military units, ranging from the TNI and service headquarters in Jakarta to various units in the regions.[158] The largest was the army's *Yayasan Kartika Eka Paksi* (YKEP) which in 2002 owned 33 enterprises with assets of Rp 315 billion (US$35 million), covering such fields as timber, plantations, property, insurance, steel and construction, a hotel, a shoe factory and a pharmaceutical retailer.[159] It also had a stake in Bank Artha Graha Internasional and its office was located in the Artha Graha building in Jakarta's Sudirman Business District in which it also had an interest.[160] Other army foundations included those owned by Kostrad and Kopassus as well as individual regional commands. The navy and air force also owned foundations, as did the police force.[161] In reality, the companies sponsored by these foundations were not managed directly by military personnel although retired officers were regularly appointed to sinecures as company directors. As an editorial in *Koran Tempo* pointed out, "Lacking the skills needed to operate a business, the military and police only act as brokers. They obtain licences from the government and then sell them to private businessmen who operate them."[162]

The profits of these enterprises, however, were not large and many were poorly managed.[163] Rieffel and Jaleswari explain that "In the case of TNI's business activities, asset stripping has been endemic for decades and represents a main reason for their poor performance".[164] According to the then TNI Commander-in-Chief, Gen. Endriartono, the profits of the *Yayasan Kartika Eka Paksi* were only about Rp 50 billion (about US$6 million) annually and far from sufficient to meet the army's needs.[165] In 2002, the foundation's profit rose to Rp 102 billion (US$11.5 million).[166] To cover the TNI's shortfall, he said, the foundations would need profits of Rp 35 trillion. "What company can make that much of a huge annual profit?" Endriartono asked.[167] The TNI spokesman, Syafrie Syamsoeddin, said that "the contributions of the *yayasan* to the military budget are extremely small, even negligible".[168] In 2001, then former Defence Minister, Juwono Sudarsono, estimated that profits from all military-controlled enterprises covered only about one-third of the gap between budget allocations and actual requirements.[169]

Another major reason for the poor performance of military-sponsored enterprises was the easy access that senior officers had to foundation funds. As noted above, shortly after his appointment as Kostrad commander, Lt. Gen. Agus Wirahadikusumah publicly revealed how his predecessor as commander — in his capacity as chief commissioner of Mandala Airlines, a company owned by Kostrad's *Yayasan Dharma Putra Kostrad* — had simply withdrawn Rp 135 billion (US$14 million) from the company on his own authority. An audit requested by Wirahadikusumah also revealed cases of soldiers' housing and armaments being bought at highly inflated prices, implying kickbacks.[170] An audit of Kostrad finances conducted by the National Audit Board (*Badan Pemeriksa Keuangan*: BPK) in 2000 indicated a similar unrecorded withdrawal of Rp 48 billion.[171] An official of the BPK explained the difficulties faced in conducting audits involving military foundations: "In the structure of the foundation, the position of chairman is held ex officio by the commander (who) makes all the decisions in the foundation. Because the commander is fully in charge, withdrawals are not backed up by good and clear records."[172] Such practices were of course not limited to Kostrad but common everywhere. Withdrawals of funds were normally at the personal discretion of the commander and might be used for a range of purposes such as routine administration, military operations, maintenance of equipment or repair of barracks — as well as "black" political operations. Funds were of course also siphoned off to supplement the incomes of senior officers.

In their study of irregular funding, Rieffel and Jaleswari calculated that net income generated by TNI's off-budget activities for "operational purposes" amounted to only 1.5–3 per cent of the formal defence budget in 2006.[173] But, as they acknowledge, much off-budget funding flows to purposes that are by no means exclusively "operational". They note that "The practice of generating off-budget income is deeply ingrained in the culture of the TNI and Indonesian society in general" and estimate "It will take more than a generation to wean the TNI from illegal activities."[174]

Assuming that the official military budget and the profits of military enterprises together covered not more than half the military's expenses, from where did the rest come? It had long been the practice for regional governments to contribute funds to regional military and police units under the budget heading "public security and order". The link between regional government and the regional military was often close through the regular meetings of the provincial and district leadership bodies (*Musyawarah Pimpinan Daerah*: Muspida) at which the regional government head and the local heads of the army, police, judiciary and prosecutor's office coordinated their activities. During the New Order it was common for a military officer serving as regional head to be succeeded by the regional military commander and it had become natural for local governments to find ways to help meet the needs of the local military. For example, the military rural development programme, Military Enters the Village (*TNI Masuk Desa*), was routinely financed by the relevant local government.[175] Moreover at the district level, especially when the district head was from the military, it was normal for military officers to be appointed to positions in the district bureaucracy which gave access to money, such as the administrators of transportation, the market, the bus terminal, parking and telecommunications. The officers appointed to such positions were expected to divert some of the proceeds to the military itself.[176] Officers could also "facilitate" local entrepreneurs in their dealings with local government. They "could not only guarantee the physical security of their businesses, but could also strengthen their lobbying in struggles over project tenders offered by the local governments".[177] It was also possible for additional contributions to be disguised in the regional head's "contingency" or "emergency" fund (*Dana Rumah Tangga Bupati/Walikota*). Military commanders were also able to insist that "contributions" from investors should not just be given to the head of the regional government but to the local military commander as well.[178]

The huge boost in regional finances following from the implementation of regional autonomy in 2001 provided the opportunity for regional military commanders to get access to more funds. In 2003 and 2004, for example, several provincial governments, including Riau, Papua, Banten and Bangka-Belitung, offered to buy patrol boats to be operated by the navy.[179] More important, however, were the district governments. Mietzner argues that "Decentralization thus offered the armed forces increased opportunities to access the budgets of local governments at the district level where most of the new decentralization funds were concentrated."[180] In the new democratic era, however, the transfer of funds to the TNI was by no means automatic and could be contested in the DPRD.[181] As one observer noted, "The better governance and transparency demanded by the new system had decreased possibilities of financial mismanagement or other covert management, including unclear financial allocations for the defence and security apparatus."[182]

Much of the military's additional funding from private sources was obtained by means that can best be described as "extortion". These funds did not go into the "military budget" as such but were used to finance the operations of individual units or provide direct supplements to the incomes of military personnel. A big source was the kickbacks that accompanied purchases of armaments and other equipment. During the New Order, members of the Soeharto family were major beneficiaries, but military officers were also routinely involved.[183] In written answers to questions posed by the International Crisis Group, Juwono Sudarsono estimated that mark-ups had been as high as 60 per cent on some contracts.[184] After his reappointment as Minister of Defence in the Yudhoyono cabinet, Juwono complained that the Department of Defence and the TNI went their own ways in determining armament purchases, implying that they competed for commissions.[185] He said he hoped to reduce "leakage" from 30 per cent to 10 per cent.[186]

Large contributions were also extracted from foreign corporations in the resources sector, particularly mining, petroleum and natural gas. The former commander-in-chief of the U.S. Pacific Command, Admiral Denis

Blair, said that the Freeport gold and copper mine in Papua had paid "up to US$18 million annually" to the military "to provide security".[187] After the killing of two American schoolteachers at the Freeport mine in 2002, American shareholders in the mine's owner, Freeport McMoRan Copper & Gold Inc, raised the issue of Freeport's payments to the Indonesian military. In response, the corporation revealed for the first time that it had made such payments — specifically US$5.8 million in 2001 and US$7 million in 2002 for "support costs for government-provided security" and $900,000 for "associated infrastructure". Later claims suggested that substantial payments had also been made directly to individual officers.[188] *Newsweek* reported that ExxonMobil paid US$6 million annually for "protection" of its petroleum and natural gas complex in Lhokseumawe, Aceh.[189] These payments were made through the government oil and gas regulatory authority, BP Migas, because of U.S. government restrictions on payments directly to the Indonesian military.[190] In both Papua and Aceh, the presence of armed separatist movements was used by military officers to convince these corporations that military protection was necessary. It was not only vital mining projects in isolated regions experiencing separatist rebellions, however, that were "protected" by the TNI. An audit of the Indonesian Banking Reconstruction Agency (IBRA) showed it had allocated billions of rupiah to military commands to protect its assets.[191] The military and police also earned funds by hiring out personnel as security guards to commercial enterprises such as plantations, mines, banks, hotels, shopping malls, office buildings, entertainment centres and transport companies. In small towns, Chinese traders often paid regular "retainer" fees to local commanders in order to guarantee the availability of soldiers in the event of an anti-Chinese riot. Security guards were also provided for wealthy businesspeople and officials.

Much military fund-raising has been blatantly illegal. Illegal logging has been a huge source of extra funds for military and police regional commands throughout Indonesia.[192] It is usually protected by local military and police units — sometimes cooperating together but sometimes in rivalry. Similarly, illegal mining often receives protection from either military or police personnel.[193] Illegal mining, however, is less lucrative because it is usually conducted on a small scale, unlike logging.[194] Military units, including the navy, have been involved in smuggling. For example, motor vehicles were smuggled into Indonesia while subsidized products, such as oil and sugar, were smuggled out.[195] Naval ships have also protected illegal fishing. Unofficial taxes were imposed on goods moving through ports and along highways. Such extractions were particularly prevalent in "crisis" regions. For example, a World Bank study noted that truck drivers in March 2005 had to make payments to police, soldiers or officials at between seventy and 110 checkpoints along the 375-mile highway from Banda Aceh to Medan.[196] On smaller roads in Aceh, individual military or police personnel supplemented their incomes by charging public transport vehicles Rp 5,000 (U.S. 60 cents) at each checkpoint. During communal violence in Central Kalimantan in 2001, military and police units competed to extract payments from desperate Madurese fleeing attacks by Dayaks. In this case, there was even a shootout between the police and the military fighting to gain access to the refugees.[197] Military personnel were also routinely involved in protecting prostitution, illegal gambling, petty crime and narcotics distribution. In this regard, the financial position of the police was no less dire and, as noted above, police personnel are engaged in much the same practices as the military although mainly at the middle and lower levels.

The fundamental reason for the embedded nature of the involvement of military and police personnel in fund-raising was of course their low salaries as a result of inadequate allocations from the state budget. In 2000, the official basic monthly salary of a major-general was only Rp 1.6 million (at that time about US$200), while a corporal received only Rp 850,000 (about US$100). However, basic salaries are supplemented by various allowances that can amount to considerably more than the basic salary. Officers received special allowances according to their duties, while ordinary soldiers received daily food allowances and other supplements.[198] Nevertheless, as one officer told the *Jakarta Post* in 2003, an ordinary soldier working as a bodyguard could earn about Rp 2.5 million (around US$300) — double the official basic salary of a captain.[199] The then Kostrad commander, Lt. Gen. Ryamizard, explained that "taking second jobs is not allowed for soldiers, but I just permit it. Because we cannot afford to provide them with a proper living. The important thing is that their duties as soldiers are not neglected and that their side-jobs do not involve "backing" gambling and prostitution".[200] Many soldiers, of course, are involved in such "backing". The pressure on soldiers to find additional income begins from the day they join the military. Confronted by a claim by a member of the DPR that recruits at the lowest level had to pay Rp 35 million in order to be accepted, the army chief of staff, Gen. Djoko Santoso, replied: "To be honest, I admit that this happens ... and has even been going on for dozens of years."[201] In the case of the school for training sergeants, "Objective assessments for student recruitment hardly existed. Most candidates could only succeed after three or more tries and after spending lots of money for paying bribes".[202] Rieffel and Jaleswari point out that "It is considered normal for senior officers to "purchase" a posting to a "wet" position with well-developed sources of off-budget funds. Senior officers even pay for the privilege of attending Staff and Command School."[203]

Measures only began to be taken to reform military finances in 2000 in response to pressure from the IMF and the World Bank.[204] The BPK conducted it first audit of military institutions in 2000 and reported many malpractices to the DPR.[205] Although the BPK was empowered to audit government bodies, it had no authority to audit private businesses operating under their control. The army responded in February 2001 by appointing internationally respected auditors, Price Waterhouse Coopers and Ernst & Young, to examine 39 companies controlled at that time by YKEP. The auditors recommended that the companies should be insulated from direct intervention by military officers through the establishment of a holding company on behalf of YKEP to manage them.[206] However, it was only after the TNI Law was adopted at the end of Megawati's presidency requiring the transfer of all military businesses to the government within five years that further measures were taken. Juwono Sudarsono, re-appointed as Defence Minister in the new Yudhoyono government, set up a joint committee representing both the Department of Defence and TNI which recommended the establishment of a state holding company to take over military businesses.[207] An inventory of military enterprises was compiled which revealed a total of 219 enterprises, of which 25 were foundations and 194 were co-operatives.[208] Most of the co-operatives were very small-scale businesses operated by local commands in such fields as poultry, fisheries and credit societies to supplement the incomes of ordinary soldiers. The defence minister said that only six could really be classified as military business enterprises.[209] The army, however, resisted the transfer of assets to the government. Even before the proposed state holding company could be established, YKEP sold its 11 per cent stake in Bank Artha Graha Internasional to two fellow shareholders in 2005.[210] The deputy chief of staff of the army, Lt. Gen. Endang Suwarya, explained that the results from the sale would not be transferred to the government as the bank had not been considered a state asset.[211] The Artha Graha sale was soon followed by the Kostrad foundation's sale of its share in Mandala Airlines in what was described as a "private sale".[212] The state holding company was never established but in April 2008, as the October 2009 deadline for the transfer of TNI business approached, the government established the National Team for the Takeover of TNI's Business Activities (*Tim Nasional Pengambilahlian Aktivitas Bisnis TNI*) under the leadership of Erry Riyana Hardjapamekas, former deputy chairman of the KPK, to make recommendations to the government. It should be borne in mind, however, that the transfer of military commercial enterprises to the government does not of itself curb extortion and other illegal methods of acquiring funding.

Today's officers have spent their entire careers in a system where they are expected to look after themselves. The military did not so much pay its officers and ordinary soldiers as reward them with franchises that allow them to pay themselves. As long as the military (and police) are not provided with adequate funding, this system cannot be changed in fundamental ways. Officers guilty of egregious "excesses" are sometimes dismissed or very rarely taken to court, but the system is in a sense "necessary" for everyone else. It could not be dismantled quickly without provoking dangerous protest from military and police personnel. On the other hand, it has provided senior officers with access to enormous wealth far beyond their official salaries. As a result, they have strong personal interests in preserving the system. The system of unrecorded financing also provides a pool of funds that in the past was often used to finance political projects and could, potentially, be used for such purposes in the future. One consequence of self-financing by military units was that, especially in the past, the central military command in Jakarta has not always been able to maintain effective control of what troops were doing in the regions.[213]

Human Rights, Courts and Military "Impunity"

Throughout the New Order, military personnel were subjected to few constraints in dealing with civilians. Human rights violations were virtually routine, not only in regions where operations were conducted against separatist rebels, but throughout the country.[214] Following the fall of Soeharto, the newly liberated mass media exposed a series of appalling cases that led to public demands for military perpetrators to be brought to justice.[215] The capacity to deal with human rights violations and other crimes perpetrated by military personnel is an important indicator of the extent of government control over the military.

Although military personnel, like civilians, had always been subject to the criminal law (KUHP), they could not be tried by civil courts but only military courts which heard cases involving both violations of military discipline as well as ordinary criminal matters. A soldier could only be brought to court with the approval of his commanding officer while the judges, prosecutors and defending counsel were all military officers.[216] Although there was some ambiguity about whether police could arrest a soldier believed to have committed a criminal offence, in practice such arrests were left to the military police. As the army chief of staff, Gen. Endriartono, said, "Armed contact between law enforcers and soldiers might be unavoidable if the police go to military barracks to arrest suspects".[217]

In the post-New Order atmosphere, civilians questioned the "special treatment" of military personnel involved in criminal cases. In practice, military personnel accused of criminal violations were often "dealt with administratively" rather than charged in military courts. And those convicted often received what appeared to be extraordinarily light sentences. At its session in 2000, the MPR, as part of its decree on the role of the TNI and the Police, stated that TNI personnel "are subject to the authority of military courts in regard to violations of military law and subject to civil courts in regard to violations of general criminal law".[218] However, although some clauses of the decree were deemed to be operative immediately, the implementation of this clause was seen as requiring a new law on military courts which by the end of 2008 had still not been adopted.

Public concern about the apparent "impunity" of military personnel before the law had been heightened by several high-profile trials of military personnel in military courts in the early post-Soeharto period.[219] In the "Trisakti" trial in August 1998, two junior police officers respectively received sentences of ten and four months for their roles in shooting students demonstrating near Jakarta's Trisakti University on 12 May 1998 — an incident that triggered the May riots that led to President Soeharto's resignation. Public dismay was less in reaction to the light sentences than the failure to investigate the suspected involvement of senior officers. Another trial of eleven members of a Kopassus team accused of kidnapping anti-Soeharto protestors during the months before the president's fall resulted in sentences in April 1999 ranging from twelve to twenty-two months. The charges related to only nine of twenty-three people who had been kidnapped. Of the remaining fourteen, one had been found dead and the other thirteen had never reappeared. The claim of the major in charge of the Kopassus team that the kidnappings had been carried out on his personal initiative was widely seen as intended to protect the Kopassus commander at that time, Lt. Gen. Prabowo Subianto, who had been discharged from the military after an enquiry by a Military Honour Council. All eleven soldiers appealed against their convictions and remained free while "awaiting the results of their appeals". The leader of the team, who was dismissed from the military, was later employed by a corporation owned by Lt. Gen. Prabowo.[220] In May 2000, twenty-three soldiers and one civilian were convicted of killing an Acehnese religious teacher, Teuku Bantaqiah, and fifty-six of his followers in July 1999 in a remote village in West Aceh. In this case, the sentences reached by what is called a *koneksitas* court including both military and civilian judges were quite substantial, ranging from eight-and-a-half to ten years. However, the highest-ranking officer was only a captain while most were privates or NCOs. It was announced that their commanding officer, Lt. Col. Sudjono, had "disappeared" and could not be presented to the court.[221]

The violence in East Timor, both before and after the August 1999 referendum that opted for independence, had outraged the international community which demanded that those responsible should be held accountable. In the wake of separate reports by an Indonesian government-endorsed commission and a UN commission, the main pressure for the trials of those responsible came from the international community. While many Indonesians were horrified by what their nation's military had done in East Timor, many others believed that soldiers had valiantly performed their duties in attempting to foil an international plot to deprive Indonesia of part of its territory. International pressure, however, was unambiguous after the UN Secretary-General's International Commission of Inquiry on East Timor called on the UN to "establish an international human rights tribunal … to try and sentence those accused by the independent investigation body of serious violations of fundamental human rights and international humanitarian law which took place in East Timor since January 1999".[222] The Indonesian commission formed by the Indonesian National Commission on Human Rights at the behest of President Habibie had placed the main blame on "the failure of the Commander of the TNI (i.e., General Wiranto) to guarantee security" and had named thirty-three people to be investigated, nearly half of whom were military officers.[223] Desperate to avoid the establishment of an international tribunal and conscious of the lack of credibility that Indonesia's military courts had so convincingly displayed in other cases during 1999, the government was left with little choice but to support the adoption of legislation establishing a special human rights court with retrospective powers.

The establishment of the court was anticipated by military leaders when the MPR, meeting in August 2000, adopted the second round of constitutional amendments. Reacting to the abuses of the Soeharto era, the Ad Hoc Committee of the MPR Working Committee had included a chapter on human rights among the proposed constitutional amendments. The chapter was largely drawn from rights listed in the UN Covenant on Civil and Political Rights which included "the right not to be prosecuted on the basis of a retroactive law", but it did not refer to the covenant's provision that makes an exception of "any act or omission which, at the time when it was committed, was criminal according to the general principles of law recognized by the community of nations".[224] The civilian members of the

Ad Hoc Committee were divided on the "non-retroactive" provision while the military members, showing new-found concern for human-rights principles, were among its most vigorous advocates.

In response to heavy international pressure, the Law on Human Rights Courts (Law No. 26/2000) was adopted by the DPR in November 2000.[225] The law recognized gross violations of human rights, particularly "genocide" and "crimes against humanity" that were not adequately covered in Indonesia's criminal code. Under the criminal code, ordinary soldiers or junior officers who physically perpetrated human rights abuses could be expected to be much more vulnerable than the senior officers who gave the orders. By introducing the concept of "crime of omission" alongside "crime of commission", the new law provided for the prosecution of those in authority who failed to take action to prevent crimes committed by subordinates where military commanders (or civilians in authority) knew "or under the prevailing circumstances ought to have known" that crimes were being committed. However, by defining "crimes against humanity" very broadly as "actions perpetrated as part of a broad or systematic direct attack on civilians", the law provided a loophole that was later exploited by defence lawyers. The ultimate obstacle to convictions, however, lay in the constitutional amendment on "non-retroactivity". In an attempt to get round this obstacle, the law provided for retrospective prosecution if the DPR recommended to the president that special "ad hoc" human rights courts be established to try specific retrospective cases.

Following the necessary recommendation from the DPR for the East Timor cases, President Abdurrahman, who by then was desperately trying to win military support in order to stave off his threatened impeachment, established ad hoc courts but only to try cases that took place after the August 30 1999 referendum, thus excluding the numerous crimes perpetrated before the referendum. Following Abdurrahman's fall, his successor Megawati extended the period slightly to include the month of April 1999 when two particularly shocking massacres had occurred, but at the same time excluded abuses that occurred during the four months between April and the referendum.[226] In 2002 and 2003, eighteen men — ten army officers, four police officers, three civilian officials and one militia leader — were tried by the ad hoc human rights court.[227] The most senior were Maj. Gen. Adam Damiri, the commander of the Kodam covering East Timor, Brig. Gen. Timbul Silaen, the East Timor police chief, and Abilio Soares, the civilian governor of East Timor.[228] Of the eighteen, six — including Adam Damiri, Abilio Soares and the militia leader, Eurico Guterres — were found guilty and sentenced to periods of imprisonment ranging from three to ten years, but remained free while awaiting the results of appeals.[229] The appeals of all were successful except those of the East Timorese civilians, Abilio Soares and Eurico Gutteres. Soares was sentenced to three years and Gutteres to ten years. Following a judicial review by the Supreme Court, however, Soares was released after three months. Gutteres remained in prison until 2008 when he too was freed after a judicial review.

The only other retrospective prosecution was launched in September 2003 to try military personnel accused of shooting dozens of Muslim demonstrators at Tanjung Priok, North Jakarta, two decades earlier in 1984 and torturing detainees. Of four officers charged, two were found guilty in 2004 while two were exonerated. However, both convicted officers and ten convicted soldiers won their appeals the following year to the Jakarta High Court.[230]

The first "ordinary" non-retrospective prosecution before the Human Rights Court tried two police officers in relation to a revenge attack by police after aggrieved Papuans had killed two policemen in Abepura, Papua, in December 2000. The enraged police had then beaten about one hundred Papuans, at least three of whom died, including many who had not been involved in the original attack on the police. The two police officers — the Jayapura chief of police and the Brimob commander in Papua — were found not guilty.[231] The attitude of many senior military officers was expressed by the army chief of staff, Gen. Ryamizard Ryacudu, when four Kopassus officers were convicted in April 2003 of murdering the Papuan pro-independence leader, Theys Eluay, in 2001. While accepting the judgments, Ryamizard said, "Law says they are guilty. OK, they are punished. But to me they are heroes." Their commander, Lt. Col. Hartomo, was sentenced to three-and-a-half years and the others to shorter terms.[232]

Action against military (and police) officers accused of human rights offences since the fall of Soeharto were no more effective than before Soeharto's fall. The innovative Human Rights Courts failed to put a single officer behind bars although, perhaps feeling that their credibility was at stake, they convicted some in later cases and imposed several heavy sentences. However, all those convicted won their appeals or judicial reviews. In the early pre-Human Rights Courts cases, some junior officers and ordinary soldiers were sent to jail, although in one case their senior officer escaped trial by somehow "disappearing". In the 1999 Kopassus case, convicted military personnel were simply released, although, officially, they were waiting for the results of indefinite appeals. The results of their appeals were never made public and it remains unclear whether they actually went to jail. In an effort to show that the government was determined to "win hearts and minds" when it resumed military operations in Aceh under martial law in 2003, the military took quick action to court-martial ordinary soldiers who abused civilians, but when these cases were publicized by foreign journalists, tight controls on reporting — by both Indonesian and foreign journalists — were imposed and no further indications of abuses were revealed in the Indonesian press.[233]

In August 2008, as Yudhoyono's first presidential term approached its final year, another senior officer was put on trial for a human rights offence. Retired Maj. Gen. Muchdi Purwoprandjono, one of the Deputy heads of the State Intelligence Agency (*Badan Intelijen Negara*: BIN) was accused of organizing the murder of the prominent human rights activist, Munir, who died of poisoning during a flight to Europe in September 2004. A Garuda Airlines pilot had already been convicted of the murder but it was assumed that he was acting on orders from a senior official. Muchdi had been the Commandant-General of Kopassus during the months before Soeharto's resignation and had earlier been accused of involvement in the kidnapping of protesters by Kopassus troops, as discussed above.[234] Muchdi, however, was exonerated.[235]

Following the election of President Yudhoyono steps were finally taken to activate the implementation of MPR Decree No. 7/2000 which required that civilian crimes committed by military personnel should be tried in normal civilian, rather than military, courts. Military officers, however, continued to resist the idea of placing military personnel under the jurisdiction of civil courts. An early draft bill defined military offences as offences committed by members of the military, regardless of context[236] and officers in the Department of Defence argued that crimes committed by military personnel during military operations should continue to be tried in military courts.[237] By the end of 2008 the government was seeking a compromise in which such cases would be heard in civilian courts but preliminary investigation would be in the hands of the military police.[238] Behind the delay was the continuing worry that investigation of soldiers by police might aggravate "psychological" problems in the military. In any case, the defence department believed that a transition period of several years would be needed before soldiers could be tried in civil courts.[239]

CONCLUSION

The military was the ultimate guarantor of Soeharto's New Order. Despite gradual "civilianisation", Soeharto had continued to rely heavily on the military institution for routine political support and the perpetuation of his regime which was thoroughly penetrated by both active and retired military officers who occupied important posts at all levels, ranging from the national cabinet to regional and local administration. As popular demands escalated calling for the removal of the president in the wake of the 1997 economic collapse, an increasing number of military officers were belatedly accepting the need to distance themselves from their patron.

In the chaotic circumstances following May 1998, the new Habibie government was pre-occupied with defending itself from multiple challenges and in no position to impose reform on the divided and demoralized military. A section of the military leadership itself therefore took the initiative. While some military "hardliners" would have preferred that the military defend its ground, the recently appointed commander-in-chief, General Wiranto, and a group of reform-minded staff officers believed that matters would only get worse if the military refused to give substantial concessions to public demands. Although General Wiranto doubled as Minister of Defence and Security in the Habibie government, the initial phase of military reform was not guided by the government as such, but by military officers acting on their own initiative in response to the mass protests that had continued after Soeharto's fall. The early reforms aimed to withdraw the military from formal participation in politics and consisted largely of measures that could be taken within the military institution itself without requiring explicit government action. At the same time, the military leadership did not attempt to block the broader democratizing reforms implemented under the Habibie government. By moving the TNI as an institution away from direct involvement in practical politics, the early reforms were a crucial pre-requisite for the broader constitutional and political reforms discussed in Chapters 3 and 4.

Military reform proceeded during the Habibie presidency partly because it was supported by key officers in the military leadership. The initial impetus was lost, however, under the ineffective presidency of Abdurrahman Wahid and was not regained by President Megawati who promoted hardline military conservatives to several key positions. The main political parties in the DPR elected in 1999 similarly showed little enthusiasm for pushing military reform forward. In a fragmented legislature, the appointed military members played a role equivalent to that of a medium-sized political party that was seen as a potential ally by other parties. Moreover, party politicians, in the shadow of the New Order, were reluctant to alienate the military which retained much of its capacity to make life difficult for its antagonists. Nevertheless, reform-minded officers in the Department of Defence, with the assistance of a small group of civilians associated with non-military think-tanks, were able to propose legislation concerned with military matters and produced a defence White Paper that emphasized military professionalism. Legislation was eventually adopted by the DPR delineating the powers of the president, the minister of defence, the commander-in-chief of the TNI and the parliament itself in regard to defence and security matters. Some of this legislation had undergone reform-oriented amendments during drawn-out legislative processes before eventual adoption, although not all were actually implemented.

Despite the TNI's loss of direct political power, many military officers continued to see themselves as endowed with special responsibility to safeguard the nation's destiny and the integrity of the "Unitary State of the Republic of Indonesia". They had been increasingly dismayed by the policies adopted by the Habibie and Abdurrahman governments, such as Habibie's decision to hold a referendum in East Timor and Abdurrahman's willingness to negotiate in Aceh and Papua. In response, the military mainstream set about undermining the government's approach in East Timor by allowing military units and military-backed civilian militias to continue hostilities. The same tactics were used again in Aceh when the government held talks with GAM. And in Papua, the assassins of the leader of a non-violent independence movement were praised as "heroes" by the army chief of staff. Without strong backing from the president and the DPR, the talks over Aceh collapsed in 2003 and the mainstream military's preferred option of a military emergency was adopted. It was only after Yudhoyono's convincing victory in Indonesia's first direct presidential election in 2004 and his rejection of Megawati's candidate for command of the TNI that the new president was able to assert his authority and negotiate a peace agreement for Aceh in 2005.

The new president's success in imposing the peace in Aceh on a reluctant military marked a major step forward toward establishing civilian control over the military. But civilian control was by no means complete. Major areas remained largely unreformed including the army's territorial structure, military financing and the "impunity" of military officers before the law. The remaining limited potential of military units to defy government authority rested in part on their independent sources of funding. In this regard, the retention of the army's territorial structure was a vital military interest. The New Order-style rhetoric of conservative generals about the "unification between the people and the TNI" masked the self-financing reality of the territorial network. Without the territorial structure it would have been impossible to maintain the army at its current size and for the military leadership to exercise political influence beyond the security field.[240] The informal self-financing system had the additional advantage for senior officers in that it operated without formal accounting requirements and therefore enabled them to accumulate much personal wealth.

In Indonesia's post-authoritarian circumstances, however, the likelihood that the military could regain control of the government seems slight. Any move to take over the government in a coup would risk splitting the military itself and almost certainly lead to massive demonstrations in the main cities throughout Indonesia which could only be repressed by violent means which would in turn trigger further domestic protests, not to speak of international condemnation. Indonesia in the early twenty-first century is very different to the Indonesia of 1965–66 when General Soeharto established his regime.[241]

The initial military reforms in the wake of the collapse of the New Order were clearly crisis-ridden. The reforms would not have been accepted by the military mainstream in less drastic circumstances. But the first stage of reforms depended on the presence of reform-minded officers in the military leadership who already aspired to creating a non-political professional military force. As the urgency of the crisis abated, the conservative military mainstream regained top positions under Abdurrahman and especially Megawati and the reform process lost its original impetus. The reform movement had largely succeeded in pulling the military out of direct involvement in day-to-day politics but stopped well short of allowing the government to establish full civilian control over the military. President Yudhoyono's success in imposing the Aceh peace on a reluctant military was a major step toward civilian control but, without strong and reliable political support in the DPR, the government was unwilling to confront the military mainstream which had strong interests in retaining the army's corruption-ridden territorial network and the associated system of "non-budgetary" military financing as well as, of course, the legal impunity of military personnel accused of human rights violations. Reform under the cautious Yudhoyono was not abandoned, but its advance had become very slow.

Notes

1. Alagappa (2001), p. 475.
2. Alagappa (2001), p. 433.
3. In the 1990s the armed forces amounted to about 450,000 personnel, consisting of 211,000 in the army, 42,000 in the navy, 19,000 in the air force and 180,000 in the police. Lowry (1996), pp. 86, 99, 107, 109.
4. Lowry (1996), pp. 91–94.
5. In 1973, military officers served as governors in 22 out of 26 provinces. Indria Samego (1998), p. 106.
6. The "1945 Generation" of officers were those who had participated in the revolution against Dutch colonialism that had started in 1945.
7. The *Dwi Fungsi* doctrine was developed from the experience of the military during the revolution when it was both a guerilla force fighting against the Dutch and the effective government in much of the countryside. See Salim

Said (1991). In 1966 at the beginning of the New Order, the army declared: "The army, which was born in the cauldron of the Revolution, has never been a dead instrument of the government concerned exclusively with security matters. The army, as a fighter for freedom, cannot remain neutral toward the course of state policy, the quality of the government, and the safety of the state based on Panca Sila. The army does not have an exclusively military duty but is concerned with all fields of social life." Cited in Crouch (1978), p. 345.

8. The author recalls reading a letter to a newspaper at that time in which a mother disowned her earlier hope that her daughter would marry a military officer.

9. Red and white are the colours of the national flag while green is associated with Islam. The common perception of the military as sharply divided ideologically along religious lines, however, is mistaken. The "green" officers did not advocate an Islamic programme for Indonesia. Rather they were resentful because they felt that they had been by-passed for promotion because of their Islamic identity during the period when the military was dominated by the Javanese Catholic Gen. Benny Murdani. After Soeharto had dismissed Murdani from the government in 1993, these Muslim officers rose to senior positions under the new Commander-in-Chief, Gen. Feisal Tanjung, a Sumatran Muslim "green". However, Soeharto ensured that the factional balance was preserved. This was shown by the rise of the nationalist "red-and-white" officer, Wiranto, to the position of Commander-in-Chief during a period of "green" pre-eminence.

10. Although identified with the "green" faction, Prabowo did not come from a typical Islamic family background. His family was part of the post-colonial Dutch-educated urban elite and his public image was not overtly Islamic. His father, Professor Sumitro Djojohadikusumo, was Indonesia's most famous economist and had earlier served in Soeharto's cabinet as well as several cabinets during the 1950s.

11. The three "green" officers appointed to his cabinet were former ABRI Commander-in-Chief, General Feisal Tanjung, as Coordinating Minister for Political and Security Affairs; Lt. Gen. Syarwan Hamid, as Minister for Internal Affairs; and Lt. Gen. Yunus Yosfiah, as Minister for Information. The "red-and-white" officers were Gen. Wiranto as Minister for Defence and Security and Lt. Gen. Hendropriyono as Minister for Transmigration.

12. See Habibie's account in Habibie (2006), pp. 82–84, 94–104. Prabowo was eventually "honourably discharged" from the military by a Military Honour Council which found him responsible for the kidnapping by Kopassus troops of radical activists, some of whom "disappeared". For an account sympathetic to Prabowo, see Fadli Zon (2004).

13. For a more detailed discussion of the Habibie-Wiranto relationship, see Crouch (1999).

14. The leading members of this group were the ABRI Chief of Staff for Social and Political Affairs, Lt. Gen. Susilo Bambang Yudhoyono, and two other members of the ABRI general staff, Maj. Gen. Agus Widjojo and Maj. Gen.

Agus Wirahadikusumah. All three had impeccable military pedigrees. Yudhoyono was the son-in-law of Lt. Gen. Sarwo Edhie, who had played a major role in crushing the Communist Party after the 1965 "coup attempt". Agus Widjojo was the son of Brig. Gen. Sutojo Siswomihardjo, one of the six generals killed in the 1965 affair, and Agus Wirahadikusumah was a nephew of Gen. Umar Wirahadikusumah, the Jakarta regional commander in 1965 and later Vice President. In contrast to most officers, all three had undertaken part of their education in the United States.

15. See Honna (2003), chs. 3, 7.

16. In an interview before Soeharto's fall, Yudhoyono stressed that reform should be gradual in a society that was fragile and vulnerable to violent conflict. He believed that the political structure of the New Order was acceptable provided it was implemented properly. He was not in favour of permitting the formation of new parties and believed that the military representatives in the DPR served a useful function. Interview with Susilo Bambang Yudhoyono, 28 November 1997. His colleague, Agus Widjojo, also described Indonesian society as "fragile" and warned that "if political change is too rapid, there is a danger that social conflict could lead to disaster". Interview with Agus Widjojo, 15 October 1997.

17. Markas Besar, Angkatan Bersenjata Republik Indonesia 1998. *TNI Abad XXI, Redefinisi, Reposisi, dan Reaktualisasi Peran TNI dalam Kehidupan Bangsa.*

18. Lt. Gen. Yudhoyono had been appointed as Chief of Staff for Political and Social Affairs by the new Commander-in-Chief, Wiranto, in February 1998. He was later succeeded as Chief of Staff for Territorial Affairs by his colleague, Lt. Gen. Agus Widjojo.

19. One source reports that 6,899 officers had been seconded but this appears to include the 2,800 serving in legislatures. If retired officers appointed to bureaucratic posts are included, the total number in July 1998 was 12,446. Ikrar Nusa Bhakti et al. (1999), p. 143.

20. *Tempo*, 12 April 1999. In addition to the ten governors who were active officers, another five were retired officers.

21. The anti-military atmosphere at that time was exacerbated by military firing on demonstrators on 12 and 13 November which killed nine students and wounded many more. United States Department of State (1999).

22. See Wiranto (2003), pp. 109–15.

23. Police Chief, Lt. Gen. Rusmanhadi in *Forum Keadilan*, 6 October 1998.

24. On 1 July 2000, the police were placed directly under the authority of the president. International Crisis Group (2001*b*), p. 4.

25. Mietzner (2006), pp. 17–18.

26. Mietzner noted the irony that Wiranto, as defence minister, "represented the civilian government vis-à-vis the very military whose institutional interests he was determined to defend". Mietzner (2004), p. 187.

27. Robinson (2001*b*), p. 229.

28. Aspinall (2005), pp. 70–78; Ramage (1995), pp. 157–67.
29. Mietzner (2006), p. 26.
30. One of the president's close advisors told the author that "Gus Dur knows nothing about military matters". Interview with Bondan Gunawan, former State Secretary under President Abdurrahman, 24 August 2000.
31. For example, see Chapter 8 for his successive contradictory comments on the future of Aceh during the month after his election.
32. Wiranto later claimed that Gus Dur had offered him support to become vice president. As the presidential election at the November 1999 special session of the MPR drew closer, Wiranto had appeared to be making approaches to the likely candidates in the hope of gaining the vice presidency although he claimed that they approached him. In his memoir, he says that he received offers from Habibie, Abdurrahman and Akbar Tandjung. Wiranto (2003), pp. 209–19.
33. Tyasno was later forced to resign after his name was mentioned in the trial of a military officer who claimed that he had become involved in a scheme to make counterfeit money on the orders of Tyasno. The counterfeit money was allegedly used to pay militia forces in East Timor. *Jakarta Post*, 13 September 2000.
34. According to former State Secretary, Bondan Gunawan, Gus Dur believed that Yudhoyono was too close to Wiranto. Interview with Bondan Gunawan, 24 August 2000.
35. During a three-week visit overseas, Gus Dur provided the press with a running commentary on the Wiranto case. He would ask Wiranto to resign, he would pardon Wiranto if found guilty by a court, generals were holding secret meetings in Jakarta, Wiranto had once saved Gus Dur when Soeharto ordered Feisal Tanjung to "get rid of him", and so on. Then, on his return to Jakarta he declared that Wiranto would remain in his position but the next day he announced that he had suspended Wiranto from the cabinet. *Tempo*, 14 and 21 February 2000; author's discussion with cabinet secretary, Marsillam Simanjuntak, April 2000.
36. As will be discussed in Chapter 7, it has been suggested that Wiranto's supporters responded by encouraging conflict in Maluku in order to undermine Abdurrahman's presidency.
37. *Kompas*, 12 February 2000. Widodo's statement at that time could also be seen as a response to the current political situation and indicated that the TNI would not obstruct President Abdurrahman's intention of dismissing Gen. Wiranto from his cabinet.
38. *Kompas*, 20 April 2000.
39. Bakorstanas was established in 1988 as the successor to the Operational Command for the Restoration of Security and Order (*Komando Operasi Pemulihan Keamanan dan Ketertiban: Kopkamtib*), the New Order's original agency for the repression of political dissent. The Social and Political Affairs Directorate with offices in all the regions was another instrument of political control.

40. For example, he personally announced the dismissal of Maj. Gen. Sudradjat, the TNI spokesman, whom he considered close to Wiranto.
41. The officers were from the 1993 graduating class of the Academy of the Armed Forces of Indonesia (*Akademi ABRI*: Akabri). Friction within the reform group appeared when Yudhoyono, a member of that class who had originally written an introduction to the book, withdrew it before the book's public launch. See Wirahadidkusumah (1999).
42. The author was present when Wirahadikusumah publicly described the military's core dwi fungsi doctrine as a "bastard child that has already been born" (*anak haram yang sudah terlanjur lahir*). Hotel Borobodur, Jakarta, 8 March 1999.
43. *Kompas*, 14 December 1999.
44. *Kompas*, 17 December 1999.
45. *Detik.com*, 14 December 1999.
46. In March 2000, Abdurrahman confided to the author's Ph.D. student, Marcus Mietzner, that "I'll make him (Wirahadikusumah) Army Chief of Staff soon, and then he can take over as TNI Commander later on." Mietzner (2004), p. 199.
47. *Tempo*, 7 August 2000. Djadja Suparman blamed Wirahadikumah for destroying his military career and claimed that Wirahadikusumah had been manipulated by "socialists" among the president's advisors. Interview with Lt. Gen. Djadja Suparman, Jakarta, 6 September 2004.
48. Dewi Fortuna Anwar (2002), pp. 52, 81–82.
49. The disappointed Agus Wirahadikusumah died of a heart attack a year later at the age of 49 on 30 August 2001.
50. *Jakarta Post*, 15 May, 2001.
51. Dewi Fortuna Anwar (2002), p. 84.
52. On the persistence of the "*Dwi Fungsi* mentality" or "mindset", see Sebastian (2006), especially ch. 5.
53. *Kompas*, 18 February 2002.
54. It is possible that Megawati, having so recently witnessed the downfall of Abdurrahman, calculated that she would be safer if she had backing from the conservative military mainstream. Mietzner referred to such backing as "A kind of life insurance against desertion by political allies and attacks by long-term opponents." Mietzner (2006), p. 35.
55. In this they echoed the views of former Vice President and ABRI Commander-in-Chief, Gen. (ret.) Try Sutrisno. Try believed that the TNI must engage independently in politics because it cannot be placed "beneath civil government". TNI is not the same as militaries in other countries, he said. "The TNI was born from the people. For that reason, the TNI must participate in politics together with the people." *Kompas*, 28 March 2004. Try Sutrisno was the father-in-law of Gen. Ryamizard.
56. Jun Honna has examined this threat perception that was indoctrinated in military officers during the New Order. See Honna (2001); Honna (2003), ch. 5.

57. *Kompas*, 12 November 2002.

58. *Kompas*, 17 October 2002.

59. *Kompas*, 21 February, 2003.

60. Mietzner (2006), p. 13.

61. The level of professionalism among the troops was still very low. When General Endriartono took over as army chief of staff, he commented that "I found that soldiers have poor ability in using military equipment, such as artillerymen who cannot shoot well. I also found that soldiers in some platoons have no idea how many and what kind of rifles are in their unit". *Jakarta Post*, 6 November 2000.

62. When I mentioned "the military's *Dwi Fungsi*" to a naval officer in a conversation shortly before Soeharto's fall, he corrected me by pointing out that I should have said "the army's *Dwi Fungsi*".

63. ProPatria's views are outlined in Andi Widjajanto (2004). Among this group were Dr Ikrar Nusa Bhakti of the Indonesian Institute of Sciences (LIPI), Dr Rizal Sukma, Andi Widjajanto, Dr Kusnanto Anggoro and Dr Edy Prasetyono of the Centre for Strategic and International Studies (CSIS), Dr Cornelis Lay and Dr Fajrul Falaakh of Gajah Mada University, and T. Hari Prihatono. The murdered human rights activist, Munir, had also been a member of the group.

64. *Mempertahankan Tanah Air Memasuki Abad 21* (2003), p. 14.

65. Members of the DPR/MPR were reacting in part to Soeharto's personal control of the military as well as Abdurrahman's rapid promotion of Agus Wirahadikusumah.

66. Law No. 3/2002 on National Defence Clause 17.

67. Interview with Juwono Sudarsono, 11 August 2000.

68. *Kompas*, 26 November 2001.

69. Law on National Defence No. 3/2002, Clauses 16 and 18. Among the minister's responsibilities were "general defence policy", "general policy on the use of TNI forces", policy on international defence cooperation, the management of the budget and general administration. Illustrating the minister's lack of authority over military affairs, Juwono, when asked by journalists in 2000 about the dismissal of Agus Wirahadikusumah as Commander of Kostrad, could only reply "I have just found out about the transfers in the TNI from this morning's newspapers". *Kompas*, 1 August 2000.

70. *Jakarta Post*, 25 March 2004.

71. *Kompas, Koran Tempo*, 3 September 2004.

72. *Kompas*, 9 November 2004.

73. The most recent civilian Minister of Home Affairs was Ipik Gandamana who served under President Soekarno in 1963–64.

74. Elucidation of Law No. 34/2004 on the Indonesian National Military, Clause 3, sub-clause 2.

75. Law on National Defence, Clause 14.

76. "Harmonized" Draft bill, meeting at Defence Department, 3 February 2003. This draft shows differences with the earlier draft prepared by the TNI.

77. *Koran Tempo*, 27 February 2003.

78. *Koran Tempo*, 6 March 2003.

79. *Kompas*, 7 April 2003. Megawati's civilian Minister of Defence, Matori, took the side of his generals by pointing out that "sometimes the discussions of the political elite take too long". *Kompas*, 3 March 2003. Amien Rais, the Chairman of the MPR, thought that the critics were making too much of the issue. "It is too much to think that this sort of authority would tempt the TNI to launch a coup". The Speaker of the DPR, Akbar Tandjung, also supported Clause 19. *Media Indonesia*, 2 March 2003.

80. *Kompas*, 8 March 2003.

81. The Commander-in-Chief now confirmed that the TNI did not have authority to draft the bill which "is the business of the Department of Defence". *Koran Tempo*, 17 July 2004, *Kompas*, 22 July 2004.

82. Draft bill, finalized at meeting at the office of the Coordinating Minister for Political and Security Affairs on 10 June 2004.

83. Clause 11 of act, Clause 12 of bill. The key amendment on the nature of threats was proposed by Panaiarsi Siahaan of PDI-P. *Kompas, Koran Tempo, Jakarta Post*, 7 September 2004.

84. Clause 43 had appeared as Clause 42 in the original TNI version of the bill and itself was taken from the New Order Law No. 2/1988 on military personnel.

85. Clause 47. Most of these positions had in fact already been exempted by a government regulation. *Koran Tempo*, 3 July 2002.

86. The term *"pejuang"* loses its resonance when translated into English as "fighter". The literal translation, "struggler", is even worse although in a sense more accurate as it refers to the "Struggle" for national independence. For military personnel, their self-identification as *"pejuang"* associates them with the sacrifices of national heroes in the struggle for independence against Dutch colonialism in the late 1940s.

87. *Kompas*, 28 September 2004.

88. TNI members of the DPR, now in the last weeks of TNI representation in the DPR, raised no objections to the amendments. According to one retired senior officer, they were more concerned about provisions relating to the age of retirement and pensions. Interview, April 2006.

89. *Jakarta Post*, 26 February 2000.

90. *Kompas*, 13 August 2000. The three were two Muslim parties (PBB, PDU) and the Christian party (PDKB). The core of the military-linked group was the PKP headed by former ABRI Commander-in-Chief, General Edi Sudrajat.

91. *Jakarta Post*, 9 August 2000.

92. Interview with former MPR Chairman, Amien Rais, Jakarta, 3 December 2005.

93. Salim Said (2000).

94. See International Crisis Group (2001*c*) and (2001*d*).

95. See Chapter 3. On 17 June 2002, the day before he was replaced as Commander-in-Chief, Admiral Widodo was still asserting the TNI's claim to representation in the MPR. *Jakarta Post*, 9 July 2002.

96. For this reason, one of the leading members of the group supporting the amendments, Effendy Choirie of the PKB, described the result as really only "half-reform". Interview with Effendy Choirie, Jakarta, 15 May 2008.

97. See the numerous statements by then Chief of Staff for Territorial Affairs, Lt. Gen. Agus Widjojo, for example, *Kompas*, 17 April 2002. The then Army Chief of Staff, Gen. Endriartono, also expressed similar views. *Koran Tempo*, 29 August 2001.

98. *Kompas*, 28 December 2007.

99. Another brother-in-law, retired Colonel Hadi Utomo, was already General Chairman of Yudhoyono's Democrat Party.

100. MPR Decree No. VI/2000.

101. MPR Decree No. VII/2000.

102. *Jakarta Post*, 4 March 2003.

103. *Jakarta Post*, 17 January 2001.

104. *Kompas*, 26 November 2001. Reflecting on past policies, Juwono said that reform ideas in 2000 were "too politically correct" and had been influenced by advisors from the British Department for International Development (DFID). Juwono believed that Indonesia was not yet ready for those ideas at that time. Conversations with author, Canberra, 27 March 2008; Jakarta, 15 May 2008.

105. Interview with Agus Wirahadikusumah, Jakarta, 5 August 1998.

106. By 2004 the number had reached about 280,000, including 33,000 in Brimob. International Crisis Group (2004*c*), p. 7.

107. In 2000, Juwono predicted that for the next five or more years the TNI would have to continue to be involved in internal security. *Kompas*, 21 July 2000. This turned out to be a conservative estimate.

108. *Mempertahankan Tanah Air Memasuki Abad 21* (2003), pp. vii–viii.

109. According to John McBeth in the *Far Eastern Economic Review* (13 November 2002), the unit's name arose from Indonesian confusion with American accents. When American training officers referred to Anti-Terrorist Assistance as "ATA", the Indonesians heard "88". International Crisis Group (2004*c*), p. 6. I am indebted to Bob Lowry for this point.

110. *Kompas*, 28, 29 May 2002; *Koran Tempo*, 30 May 2002. The circumstances leading to that situation are discussed in Chapter 7.

111. After one serious clash in Madiun in East Java, the army Chief of Staff, General Endriartono, commented that "it is no secret that they back illegal businesses", referring to gambling and narcotics. *Jakarta Post*, 20 September 2001.

112. *Koran Tempo*, 20 September 2001.

113. Lela E. Madjiah (2002).

114. *Koran Tempo*, 6 March 2004. A nine-hour battle between the police and the army at Binjai in North Sumatra on 29–30 September 2002 resulted in six police, two soldiers and two civilians killed and many more wounded. *Jakarta Post*, 7 October 2002. The clash involved narcotics. Vice President Hamzah Haz explained that "the main problem is not the separation of the police from the TNI but the backing of criminals, involving the units". *Kompas*, 2 October 2002.

115. As ProPatria member, Dr Rizal Sukma, wrote in 2007, "I have lost count how many times members of our security apparatus, the Indonesian Military (TNI) and the National Police, have engaged in embarrassing clashes". Rizal Sukma (2007).

116. In 2000, there were 266 Kodim, 3,309 Koramil and about 33,000 Babinsa. *Tempo*, 28 May 2000.

117. Nasution (1964).

118. According to the 2003 White Paper, "A traditional security threat in the form of invasion or military aggression by another country against Indonesia is considered very unlikely." *Mempertahankan Tanah Air* ...., p. vii.

119. International Crisis Group (2000*b*), p. 13. Mietzner argues that "the TNI's core institutional interests in the post-Soeharto era are tied to the maintenance of the territorial command structure, which in turn guarantees its independence from civilian control mechanisms". Mietzner (2003), p. 251.

120. Referring to elections in West, Central and East Java during the Megawati presidency, Jun Honna explained that "The three gubernatorial elections in Java all demonstrate the TNI's active political participation." In the absence of orders from the TNI headquarters in Jakarta, "Kodams were given autonomy to support candidates who would maximize the local military interests both politically and economically". Honna (2006), p. 94.

121. *Kompas*, 14 December 1999.

122. Interview with Lt. Gen. Agus Wirahadikusmah, Jakarta, 12 August 2000.

123. *Kompas*, 21 December 1999.

124. Even General Wiranto admitted "it is not easy to change the behaviour of *babinsa* from rough (*kasar*) to polite (*santun*) and gracious (*lemah lembut*)". *Kompas*, 19 April 2000.

125. *Kompas*, 27 April 2000; *Media Indonesia*, 11 June 2000.

126. Rabasa and Haseman reported an informal survey of captains, majors and lieutenant colonels and concluded that "Most of these middle-rank officers have little interest in scrapping the territorial system". Rabasa and Haseman (2002), p. 65. Haseman is a fomer U.S. military attaché in Jakarta.

127. Interview with Agus Widjojo, Jakarta, 23 November 2000. *Kompas*, 22 August 2001. Among the activities that Widjojo envisaged would be transferred were the TNI's village development programmes, provision of labour services for building schools and mosques, and promotion of family planning and health care. *Jakarta Post*, 27 August 2001.

128. *Koran Tempo*, 31 August 2001.

129. *Jakarta Post*, 25 August 2001.

130. *Koran Tempo*, 27 August 2001.

131. *Koran Tempo*, 29 and 31 August 2001; *Kompas*, 29 August 2001.

132. *Kompas*, 23 August 2001. The Central Java survey in September 2000 was conducted by a team from Gajah Mada University in Yogyakarta. The second survey was conducted by *Aliansi Peneliti Muda Hubungan Sipil-Militer* (Alliance of Young Researchers on Civil-Military Relations) in November 2000.

133. *Kompas*, 13 July 2002.

134. *Kompas*, 17 October 2002.

135. *Kompas*, 12 November 2002.

136. *Kompas*, 18 September 2002.

137. Department of Defence, *Mempertahankan Tanah Air Memasuki Abad 21* (2003), p. v. The inclusion of this passage in the "executive summary" is curious because this sort of language is not found in the body of the White Paper. The *Kompas* newspaper mentioned the appearance of a "mysterious" paragraph. *Kompas*, 31 May 2003.

138. These functions are listed in Clause 8 of the draft on the duties of the TNI and Clause 9 on the army.

139. *Koran Tempo*, 6 August, 2004. This suggestion dismayed General Ryamizard. "How could the military be separated from the people?" he asked.

140. *Kompas*, 18 August, 2004.

141. *Kompas*, 27 August 2004.

142. Elucidation, Clause 11.

143. *Kompas*, 9 September 2005.

144. *Kompas*, 31 March 2005.

145. *Kompas*, 6 September 2005.

146. *Kompas*, 28 February 2007. He reminded the DPR that Indonesia had been able to cope with the Aceh tsunami better than the United States managed the New Orleans cyclone because Indonesia had *babinsa*.

147. *Koran Tempo*, 8 November 2005, *Kompas*, 9 November 2005.

148. Defence Minister Juwono believes that territorial forces are necessary to deal quickly with security challenges in any part of the country. Interview with Juwono Sudarsono, Jakarta, 15 May 2008.

149. Alagappa (2001), p. 484.

150. By 2008, even the president was using the language of the conservatives. To a Kostrad audience, he urged them to "Maintain the unification (*kemanunggalan*) of soldiers with the people. Territorial guidance (*pembinaan*) is valid and therefore continue it. Remain close to the people". *Kompas*, 17 September 2008.

151. International Institute of Strategic Studies (2007), p. 352.

152. Crouch (1978), ch. 11; Robison (1986), ch. 8.

153. Mahrozi (2006), p. 63.

154. Department of Defence, *Mempertahankan Tanah Air Memasuki Abad 21*, p. 90;

Human Right Watch (2006), pp. 85–86; *Kompas*, 27 May 2009. These figures do not include allocations to the police for security. However, officials of the Department of Finance acknowledged to Human Rights Watch that "data on military spending has been very unreliable".

155. *Kompas*, 20 June 2002.
156. Human Right Watch (2006), p. 88.
157. *Jakarta Post*, 6 October 2002.
158. *Kompas*, 31 August 2002.
159. *Jakarta Post*, 3 September 2002.
160. The Artha Graha conglomerate was managed by a military-linked Chinese businessman, Tommy Winata.
161. Human Rights Watch (2006), pp. 34–36.
162. *Koran Tempo*, 30 August 2002.
163. Human Rights Watch (2006), pp. 105–108.
164. Rieffel and Jaleswari (2007), p. 72.
165. *Koran Tempo*, 30 August 2002.
166. *Jakarta Post*, 17 September 2002.
167. *Jakarta Post*, 3 September 2003.
168. *Kompas*, 11 October 2004.
169. Interview with Juwono Sudarsono, 29 August 2001. In contrast, the TNI's Assistant for General Planning, Col. Poerwadi, claimed that the contribution of the military foundations covered only from 0.7 to 1 per cent of the military budget. *Kompas*, 26 November 2003. Col. Poerwadi was apparently referring to the defence budget passed by the DPR while Juwono was talking about the real expenditure needed to maintain the TNI.
170. *Tempo*, 7 August 2000.
171. *Kompas*, 4 November 2000. In 2001, a new law on foundations (Law No. 16) required that foundations that use state funds be audited by a public auditor, not the BPK.
172. I Gede Artjana in *Kompas*, 27 July 2000.
173. Rieffel and Jaleswari (2007), p. 7.
174. Rieffel and Jaleswari (2007), p. 49.
175. Mietzner (2003), p. 255.
176. Mahrozi (2006), p. 56.
177. Mahrozi (2006), p. 64.
178. Conversation with foreign military attaché, Jakarta, July 2000.
179. *Tempo*, 8 September 2003, *Kompas*, 24 June 2004.
180. Mietzner (2006), p. 15.
181. Mahrozi (2006), pp. 234–42.
182. Mahrozi (2006), p. 140.
183. *Koran Tempo*, 23 July 2002.
184. International Crisis Group (2001*i*), p. 13.
185. *Koran Tempo*, 8 November 2005.

186. *Koran Tempo*, 24 September 2005.
187. *Jakarta Post*, 20 May 2003. Note that this estimate is much higher than the corporation's own later admissions.
188. Global Witness (July 2005). 2,300 government troops were based at the mine. Perlez and Boner (2005).
189. *Newsweek*, 26 August 2002.
190. *Jakarta Post*, 29 December 2005. About 2,000 government troops were posted at the oil and gas facilities.
191. *Jakarta Post*, 11 October 2002.
192. For an example of military forestry operations in East Kalimantan, see Human Right Watch (2006), pp. 38–44. For Papua, see Telapak (Bogor)/Environmental Investigation Agency (London/New York), 2005.
193. See the case of the Senakin mine in South Kalimantan in Human Rights Watch (2006), pp. 56–63.
194. International Crisis Group (2001*j*), pp. 10–11, 18.
195. On oil smuggling into East Timor, see *Media Indonesia*, 3 February 2003.
196. World Bank (2006).
197. International Crisis Group (2001*e*), p. 10.
198. *Kompas*, 6 May 2000. Senior officers could obtain very high incomes despite low salaries. One source gave the example of a lieutenant general with an official income of Rp 6 million per month who sat on the boards of companies within TNI's business empire which provided him with an additional Rp 90 million — a total annual income equivalent to about US$120 million. Confidential source.
199. *Jakarta Post*, 12 August 2003.
200. *Kompas*, 27 June 2002.
201. *Koran Tempo*, 28 June 2005.
202. Mahrozi (2006), pp. 251–52.
203. Rieffel and Jaleswari (2007), p. 55.
204. See Government of Indonesia and Bank Indonesia Memorandum of Economic and Financial Policies, 17 May 2000. This memorandum is a review of a broad range of economic reforms, including the issue of off-budget funding.
205. *Kompas*, 21 November 2000.
206. Lt. Gen. Kiki Syahnakri in *Jakarta Post*, 14 May 2005.
207. *Koran Tempo*, 25 January 2005.
208. *Kompas*, 6 October 2005. Said Didu, one of the members of the team, said the task had not been easy because "management data was in a mess (*amburadul*)". *Koran Tempo*, 22 December 2005.
209. *Jakarta Post*, 21 June 2007.
210. *Koran Tempo*, 27 August 2005; *Jakarta Post*, 29 September 2005.
211. Mietzner (2006), p. 55.
212. Human Rights Watch (2006), p. 115. The purchaser, Cardig International Group, was owned by PT Bimantara and an air force foundation, Adi Upaya. Van Zorge Report, 25 April 2006.

213. According to the Minister of Defence, Juwono Sudarsono, in 2000, it was not only the generals in Jakarta who were unable to control the troops in the regions, but even the majors and captains in the regions. Interview with Juwono Sudarsono, Jakarta, 11 August 2000.

214. See Amnesty International (1994); Human Rights Watch (1994); and annual U.S. Department of State, Human Rights country reports on Indonesia.

215. Abuses in Aceh received much publicity, including the discovery of mass graves and a "village of widows" whose husbands had "disappeared". Another much publicized case was that of radical activists kidnapped in Jakarta, discussed below.

216. Law No. 31/1997 on Military Courts.

217. *Jakarta Post*, 20 September 2001. When the author asked a senior military officer why the police in a recent case had not arrested a soldier who had stolen a motorcycle, he responded by asking whether I expected that police who went into the military barracks to arrest a soldier would come out alive. Interview with Lt. Gen. Agus Widjojo, Jakarta, June 2003.

218. MPR Decree No. VII/2000, clause 4.a.

219. International Crisis Group (2001*a*), pp. 3–5. I have borrowed from this report of which I was the principal author.

220. *Tempo*, 23 April 2001. In 2007, the TNI Commander-in-Chief, Air Marshal Djoko Suyanto, revealed that three of the convicted officers had "served their sentences" (*menjalani hukuman*) and were now lieutenant colonels, two serving as Kodim commanders and one as chief of staff of a Korem. *Kompas*, 16 May 2007. It was not, however, stated explicitly that they had actually served their sentences in prison.

221. According to Lt. Gen. Agus Wirahadikusumah, he had asked his own intelligence officers to help to find Col. Sudjono but intelligence officers at the regional command headquarters in Medan had warned against looking for him. Interview with Agus Wirahadikusumah, Jakarta, 12 August 2000.

222. Report of the International Commission Inquiry on East Timor to the Secretary General (January 2000).

223. *Ringkasan Eksekutif Laporan Penyelidikan Pelanggaran Hak Asasi Manusia di Timor Timur* (31 January 2000), Clauses 73 and 74.

224. International Covenant on Civil and Political Rights.

225. See International Crisis Group (2001*a*), pp. 11–18.

226. These time limits had the effect of making it difficult to establish that violations had been "systematic" as required by the law.

227. On the poor quality of the indictments, see International Crisis Group (2002*b*).

228. The initial investigation commission concluded that "crimes against humanity" in East Timor had been due to "the failure of the Commander of the TNI to guarantee security" but General Wiranto was not among those charged. According to the Attorney General, Marzuki Darusman, he was expecting that the trials of Wiranto's subordinates would reveal evidence that could later be

used against Wiranto. Interview with Marzuki Darusman, Jakarta, 10 January 2001.

229. *Tempo*, 11 August 2003.

230. The officers were Maj. Gen. (ret.) Rudolf Butar Butar (the Kodim commander in Tanjung Priok), Maj. Gen. (ret.) Pranomo, Maj. Gen. Sriyanto Muntasram and Captain Sutrisno Mascung. The first three had been junior officers in 1984 while Sutrisno was still an NCO. At the time of the trial, Sriyanto was Commander of Kopassus and he was soon promoted to the command of the Siliwangi Kodam in West Java.

231. *Jakarta Post*, 10 September 2005. At the time of the trial, one of them, Brig. Gen. Johny Wainal Usman, was National Commander of Brimob.

232. *Tempointeraktif*, 23 April 2003. Ryamizard said "We are at war against rebels." The elderly Theys Eluay led a pro-independence movement that rejected violence.

233. See Chapter 8 below.

234. *Kompas*, 22 August 2008; *Tempo*, 29 June 2008, 5 October 2008.

235. *Tempo*, 5 January 2009.

236. *Jakarta Post*, 20 June 2005.

237. Brig. Gen. Sugeng Widodo, head of the Legal Bureau of the Department of Defence, argued that if such cases were heard in civil courts, military secrets might be revealed. *Koran Tempo*, 21 February 2005.

238. *Kompas*, 17 October 2008.

239. *Kompas*, 9 February 2007.

240. According to the International Institute of Strategic Studies's 2007 report, the total manpower of the TNI was 302,000 consisting of 233,000 in the army, 45,000 in the navy and 24,000 in the air force. The police had an estimated membership of 280,000. International Institute of Strategic Studies (2007), pp. 352–54.

241. It needs to be remembered that the stability of the Soeharto regime was built on the foundation of a massacre of half-a-million supporters of the Indonesian Communist Party in the midst of the "Cold War".

6

POLITICS, CORRUPTION AND THE COURTS

The experience of many post-authoritarian regimes suggests that judicial reform usually faces huge obstacles and cannot be achieved quickly. The courts had been integral components of the authoritarian regime with the role of serving its needs. Among their main functions were the provision of a cover of legitimacy for political repression while ensuring that regime leaders and their supporters enjoyed a large degree of impunity from the working of the law. Political oversight of the courts was the norm and most judges absorbed the values of the system. In many countries, the "justice sector", including judges, prosecutors and police, was no different to the rest of the bureaucracy in that it was poorly paid and characterized by pervasive corruption.

Although the fall of the New Order opened the way to substantial democratic reforms, reform of the courts proved difficult, as indicated especially by their initial failure to tackle ubiquitous corruption that was increasingly exposed in the new democratic environment. In addition to the demand for democracy, one of the main slogans of the post-1998 reform movement called for the end of "KKN" (*Korupsi, Kolusi, Nepotisme*: Corruption, Collusion, Nepotism). As we shall see, very little was attempted during the early post-authoritarian years to curb corruption. Soeharto's centralized network was partly dismantled, but its fragmented remnants formed their own networks around sections of the bureaucracy, the newly liberated political parties and regional governments. Much of the post-1998 political and economic elite, therefore, had been deeply involved in the practices of the Soeharto regime and had no enthusiasm for a campaign against KKN.

It could hardly be expected, in these circumstances, that the courts would reform themselves. The courts during the New Order had never been insulated from the corruption of the regime and the majority of judges had been integrated quite comfortably into the system. Of course, some judges had preserved their integrity under authoritarian rule and others, even if they had succumbed to the pressures of the past, at least aspired to restore public respect for the judiciary in the new circumstances. The critical impetus for judicial reform, however, had to come from outside the judiciary itself from freely elected governments and legislatures, as well as the press and NGOs, backed by public opinion. Such pressures, however, were very uneven. Occasionally, former New Order officials were detained for interrogation, but the motivation often appeared to be political and indeed pecuniary as charges against wealthy officials of the old regime who had lost political protection were usually dropped after lengthy investigations. It was generally assumed that substantial payments were extracted by officials of the new regime.

The prospects for substantial judicial reform seemed bleak. A World Bank paper in 2003 reflected current expectations when it said: "The current environment is not one in which a comprehensive and broad-based strategy to strengthen accountability and reduce corruption is likely to work. The vested interests are too powerful, and the ability of the state to implement a broad based program of reforms is limited."[1] Robison and Hadiz asked, "How difficult would prosecution and confiscation be in the face of a civil bureaucracy, a judiciary and a state sector so embedded with the families and committed to the system of oligarchy?"[2] This chapter will examine steps taken to reform the legal system, focussing particularly on its performance in combating corruption. Prosecutions of high-level officials for corruption were rare during the terms of the first three post-Soeharto presidents but a more serious anti-corruption campaign was launched after the election of President Yudhoyono. Under the new president, senior officials became vulnerable to prosecution for corruption and many were convicted.

TOWARDS JUDICIAL INDEPENDENCE

The New Order judiciary was a caricature of the "integralist" concept that had provided much of the inspiration for the 1945 constitution. One of the main architects of that constitution, Raden Soepomo, rejected the concept of court oversight of the government and envisaged the function of the courts as serving the purposes of the corporatist state.[3] The restitution of the 1945 constitution in 1959 saw the flourishing of integralist ideas during the Guided Democracy period. The integration of the judiciary with the executive was such that the Chief Justice of the Supreme Court even sat in the cabinet and Law No. 19/1964 on Basic Judicial Powers explicitly empowered the president to intervene in court cases "(in) the interests of the revolution, the honour of the state and the nation, or the urgent interests of society at large".[4] Although the New Order replaced the 1964 law with Law No. 14/1970 on the Basic Principles of the Judiciary which explicitly upheld the principle of judicial independence, it was not uncommon for the president to convey instructions to judges in important cases.[5] The president's authority over the courts was reinforced in 1981 when a serving military officer was appointed as Chief Justice, a position that remained in military hands, except for three years, until the end of the New Order. Military officers also served as Attorney General for most of the New Order years.

Backed by a battery of repressive laws ranging from the colonial "hate-sowing edicts" to the Soekarno-era anti-subversion law, the courts performed the political function of "legitimately" repressing opposition to the regime. Not all judges were totally subservient to the regime, however, and a few brave maverick judges occasionally delivered "unwelcome" judgments.[6] In each of these cases, the president conveyed his displeasure to the Supreme Court and the judgments were soon reversed. The willingness of a handful of judges to resist the government's wishes, however, did not reflect the compliant attitudes of the overwhelming majority of judges. Despite massive corruption and human-rights abuse, the president's allies enjoyed virtual immunity from the law.

It was only when the entire New Order was discredited after the fall of Soeharto that the door to reform of the judicial system was opened. The public mood had been alienated by the abuses of the past which were now highlighted in the free media, while huge demonstrations were regularly blocking the boulevards of Jakarta, demanding the arrest and trial of the deposed president and his corrupt cronies. At the same time, the World Bank and the IMF were calling for judicial reform as a condition for renewed foreign investment. In contrast to the cases discussed in earlier chapters where key figures within institutions played important roles in initiating and supporting reform, the Supreme Court was identified by Pompe as "a striking laggard in the reform process". Pompe argued that "All court reforms undertaken in the turbulent early Reformasi period of 1998–2000 were initiated and pushed by Parliament or the Government, often in the face of Supreme Court opposition and obstruction."[7] Although judicial reform was never high on the list of priorities of the Habibie government and its immediate successors, it could not be ignored entirely. Judges had long resented political intervention and the control exercised over the administration of the courts by the Department of

Justice. With judicial backing, a broad coalition emerged to support measures to insulate the judiciary from direct executive interference.[8]

The public mood following the fall of Soeharto supported reforms to restore the integrity of the courts. President Soeharto's direct and indirect influence over court judgments had created much cynicism not only among the general public but also within the elite. Although most of the one thousand members of the MPR in 1998 were among the beneficiaries of Soeharto's patronage, they were anxious to distance themselves from him after his fall. At its Special Session in November 1998, the MPR attempted to respond to public expectations by adopting Decree No. X/MPR/1998 with an appendix setting out broad reform principles, including in the field of law. It noted that "Guidance of the courts by the executive provided an opportunity for the authorities to intervene in the judicial process and for the expansion of collusion and negative practices in the judicial process". It therefore called for "The strict separation of judicial and executive functions".[9]

In 1999, the Habibie government, with the support of the judiciary, took a relatively painless first step toward formally insulating the courts from direct political interference. Not only had judgments been vulnerable to executive pressure but the administration of the courts remained in the hands of the Department of Justice which determined appointments, promotions, transfers, dismissals and salaries — all of which could be used to reward cooperative, and punish uncooperative, judges.[10] The government proposed Law No. 15/1999 which provided for the eventual establishment — within five years — of a "one-roof" judiciary administered by the Supreme Court. This reform hurt the interests of bureaucrats in the Department of Justice whose control over the placement of judges provided opportunities for additional income but was welcomed by judges themselves who lobbied members of the DPR to support the bill.[11] The transfer met with initial bureaucratic resistance but was completed in mid-2004 when the general (consisting of criminal, civil and commercial), administrative, and religious courts were removed from the administrative and financial control of the Department of Justice (by then known as the Department of Justice and Human Rights) and placed directly under the Supreme Court.[12] Given the condition of the Supreme Court at that time, however, many observers believed that this "reform" only transferred control of the patronage network from the department to the court.

The Abdurrahman government took a more drastic step towards releasing the Supreme Court from executive domination. The opportunity arose in 2000 when the retirement of the chief justice and a substantial number of Supreme Court judges led to twenty vacancies. The law on the Supreme Court (Law No. 14/1985) required the DPR to submit a list of candidates from among whom the president would make the final selection. During the New Order, the process was smooth as the president's wishes were always conveyed to the DPR before it submitted its list. The president's unconstrained domination of the selection of judges, however, could no longer be sustained following the election of the far more assertive DPR in 1999. The DPR insisted on conducting what it called "fit and proper tests" in which each candidate was called before the DPR to explain his or her "mission" and "vision" and to answer questions. Of 46 candidates who were considered to meet the formal requirements, only 17 made the DPR's final list. Of these, President Abdurrahman selected 16, 9 of whom were "non-career" judges from mainly academic backgrounds.[13] Further rounds of "fit and proper tests" were conducted which resulted in the nomination in 2003 of 18 and in 2004 14 candidates, all of whom were appointed by President Megawati. The influx of "non-career" judges uncontaminated by long judicial careers was widely seen as a significant step forward although there were also concerns about the "politicization" of the selection process in the DPR.[14]

The selection of the new chief justice was even more politicized. The 1985 law provided for the DPR to nominate two candidates for the position of chief justice that fell vacant in August 2000. President Abdurrahman had much earlier made clear his preference for Benjamin Mangkoedilaga, currently a member of the National Human Rights Commission and the judge who had defied President Soeharto by lifting his ban on *Tempo* magazine in 1995.[15] Mangkoedilaga, however, had been a relatively junior judge and did not have much support in the DPR which eventually, in December 2000, nominated two "non-career" candidates, Muladi, a professor of law at the Diponegoro University in Semarang who had served as the justice minister in both Soeharto's last cabinet and the Habibie cabinet, and Bagir Manan, a law professor at Padjadjaran University in Bandung who had been a senior official in the Department of Justice during the 1990s. The president initially refused to accept either and requested that the DPR submit more names but the DPR refused.[16] Due to the stalemate, the leadership of the Supreme Court remained vacant until May 2001 when Abdurrahman, by then fighting off demands for his impeachment, finally gave way and appointed Bagir Manan.

The open process by which the judges of the Supreme Court were selected made it less susceptible to executive domination but opened the way to political pressures of a different sort. The selection of the chief justice was blatantly politicized as both Muladi and Bagir Manan had links with Golkar while their nominations were bitterly opposed by the president and the PDI- P whose members "walked out" of the DPR in protest. As the president's political position deteriorated towards the middle of 2001, his desperate search for political allies in the DPR and MPR forced him to back down. In the case of the nomination of judges by the DPR, the very transparency of the "fit and proper tests" tended to undermine public confidence in the process. Many of the questions put to candidates seemed irrelevant or even frivolous,[17] while it appeared that political considerations played a role and rumours spread about bribery.

The selection of the new chief justice and Supreme Court judges had unfortunately coincided with the political tensions leading to the impeachment of the president. Following Abdurrahman's dismissal, the MPR was able to reflect more calmly on recent experience and gave attention to proposals put by expert advisors. In response, the constitutional amendments adopted by the MPR in 2001 further insulated the selection process from political pressures — both from the executive and the legislature. One amendment required the judges themselves to elect the chief justice and his or her deputy.[18] Another provided for the establishment of a Judicial Commission to nominate Supreme Court judges for the DPR's consideration before it made its nominations to the president. This was to ensure that only legally qualified candidates could be proposed by the DPR. The Judicial Commission would also investigate accusations against judges and could propose sanctions, including possible dismissal.[19] Pointedly in view of opinions expressed by some of the members of the DPR during the earlier "fit and proper tests", one of the qualifications required of commission members was that they should "have knowledge and experience in the field of law".[20] The DPR's role in the selection of the members of the Judicial Commission was minimized. A selection committee of respected members of the legal profession was appointed by the president to nominate fourteen candidates who would then undergo "fit and proper tests" before the DPR's Commission III concerned with legal affairs which eventually voted to select the seven members of the Judicial Commission in June 2005.[21]

Under the leadership of Bagir Manan, the Supreme Court collaborated with several NGOs concerned with legal reform to prepare a series of "Blueprints" which aimed to address perceived weakenesses in the judicial system. Four main blueprints were produced between 2001 and 2003 dealing with reform of the Supreme Court itself, human resources in the subordinate courts, judicial education and training, and case management. The reform plans, however, do not appear to have been welcomed by many judges and court officials with the result that implementation was limited.[22]

Another major amendment to the constitution provided a further check on political intervention in the judicial process in the form of the Constitutional Court. The concept of judicial review of the constitutionality of laws was only introduced in a decree adopted by the MPR at its session in 2000.

That decree had given the MPR itself the authority to assess the consistency of laws with the constitution, while the authority of the Supreme Court to conduct judicial review was limited to assessing government regulations against laws.[23] The constitutional amendment in 2001 transferred the power of judicial review of laws from the MPR, which had in fact never exercised that power, to the new Constitutional Court, together with the authority to resolve disputes between state institutions, to dissolve political parties and settle disputes arising from general elections. The new court would also be involved in any potential impeachment of a president. Of the nine members of the Constitutional Court, three would be nominated by the Supreme Court, three by the DPR and three by the president. The members of the court would elect their own chief justice and deputy chief justice. The court was finally installed by President Megawati in August 2003, a few days before the deadline set by the amended constitution. The judges elected Professor Jimly Asshiddique as chief justice. Jimly was a professor of law at the University of Indonesia and had been a close advisor to President Habibie. In August 2008, the judges elected Mahfudz M.D., a law professor at the Indonesian Islamic University in Yogyakarta and President Abdurrahman Wahid's second defence minister.

These reforms meant that the executive's capacity to intervene in the courts was greatly diminished compared to the situation under the New Order. The president no longer exercised unilateral authority over the courts that had been, in effect, the prerogative of President Soeharto. The post-Soeharto presidents continued to make the final selection of Supreme Court judges but only from a list nominated by the DPR. And, after 2005, the DPR was restricted to nominating candidates from among those proposed by the new Judicial Commission. The president also lost the power to select the chief justice of the Supreme Court. Another major reform was the establishment of the Constitutional Court which prevented the president from ignoring constitutional provisions. Meanwhile, the independence of the judiciary at lower levels was enhanced by the transfer of the administration of the courts from the Department of Justice to the Supreme Court. However, as one observer pointed out, in the regions the independence of the courts could be compromised because of their dependence on regional governments for supplementary funding and facilities.[24]

COMBATING CORRUPTION

The Soeharto era left a legacy of ubiquitous corruption in the courts. In the post-Soeharto era, the enhanced independence of the judiciary was a substantial step forward but judicial independence only provided the framework. It did not address the most crucial issue: entrenched corruption within the judicial system itself.[25] Like everyone else employed by the state, judges and prosecutors received miniscule official salaries while corruption was the norm from the lowest district court to the Supreme Court in Jakarta. Major corruption cases often failed because of pervasive corruption involving judges, prosecutors and police.[26]

Despite their inadequate official remuneration, the lifestyles of most senior judges, prosecutors and police officers, like those of senior military officers and bureaucrats, did not accord with their low salaries.[27] Like the low salaries of senior military officers and bureaucrats, those of judges, prosecutors and police were also an instrument of political control. Judges, like other officials, were expected to use their positions to add to their incomes. By putting so many judges in positions that made them vulnerable to corruption charges, the regime was able to ensure that courts did not seriously limit the authority of the government. Judges, prosecutors and police joined military officers and bureaucrats in "living off the land". In the last years of the New Order, several Supreme Court judges themselves suggested that half of the judges were corrupt while other observers thought the number was higher.[28] Nevertheless, judges were expected to obey the "rules of the game" and could be transferred to outlying regions if they were "too greedy" and might even face the courts themselves in exceptional cases.[29]

That the judicial institutions were corrupt was of course well known during the New Order but it was only after Soeharto's fall that the extent of the degradation of the courts became a theme of public discussion in the press and other media. Civil cases were often described by lawyers as "auctions". One lawyer told a journalist that a judge would not even look at a supplicant for less than Rp 75 million (US$7,500). Another provided a general guide: for a civil case involving Rp 10 billion (US$1 million), nothing less than Rp 200 million (US$20,000) had to be paid, while a big case might need at least Rp 2 billion (US$200,000).[30] According to a survey conducted by Indonesia Corruption Watch (ICW), some big legal firms maintained special sections to "negotiate" with judges while others provided "friendly" judges with a monthly stipend. In Medan, the ICW reported, some judges preferred to conduct civil cases in their chambers rather than in open court. On the other hand, deals involving big Jakarta cases were sometimes negotiated in Singapore.[31]

In criminal cases, each stage of the process from the initial investigation by police to the framing of charges by prosecutors and the conduct of the trial itself involved negotiations. The ICW report on what it called the "Court Mafia" points out that the fall of the New Order brought about a "total change" for businesspeople for whom corruption had been normal in business. Wealthy businesspeople could no longer rely on their New Order patrons and "became a soft target for prosecutors". Those who failed to "buy" the dropping of charges were forced to bargain first with the police and then the prosecutors over the particular clauses of the criminal code they would face. The less severe the potential sentence, the more the accused had to pay. They would then have to bargain over whether the accused would be held in custody while awaiting trial or under house arrest or even "city arrest". Further bargaining was then needed with the judge in regard to the trial. At this stage, cooperation between the judge and the prosecutor could result in the prosecutor presenting such a weak indictment that it would be easy for the judge to decide that the accused was not guilty. After the fall of Soeharto, the new political atmosphere had introduced a new complication. It could be risky in high-profile cases attracting much public attention for judges to exonerate defendants completely so the bargaining is such cases tended to focus less on the verdict than the sentence. As ICW explained, judges often feel that "it is better to get less without endangering one's career than get a lot at the risk of losing one's career".[32] Even when found guilty, there remained the option of not ordering the newly convicted felon to be sent immediately to prison, thus providing the opportunity to abscond.[33]

In Indonesia's civil-law system, the judiciary is part of the civil service. Law graduates enter at the lowest level and gradually work their way through the judicial hierarchy to the higher courts. Corruption starts when the young law graduate applies to join the judicial service. One journalist interviewed an applicant who complained that she had been asked for Rp 15 million in 1999, Rp 20 million in 2000 and Rp 25 million (US$2,500) in 2001 but could not afford the payment. A successful applicant had told the same journalist that she had paid "much more than Rp 25 million". At that time the official salary of a new judge was Rp 1.35 million (US$135) per month plus allowances of up to Rp 800,000. The same journalist discovered that applicants for appointment as prosecutors were being asked for Rp 30 million (US$3,000).[34] Such payments did not end at recruitment but were needed for promotion throughout a judge's or prosecutor's career.

COURT FAILURE: BIG CORRUPTION CASES (1999–2004)

The fall of Soeharto in May 1998 had opened the way for demands for action against corruption, expressed most vociferously in huge student demonstrations in Jakarta and other cities. The Habibie government, which consisted largely of ministers and officials who had benefited from Soeharto's rule, was naturally reluctant to embark on a thorough campaign against corruption but at the same time was alert to the dangers of ignoring the issue. Responding to the mood of the times, the Golkar-dominated MPR was convened in a Special Session in November 1998 and, despite having unanimously re-elected Soeharto the previous March, adopted a decree (No. XI/MPR/1998) which called for "firm measures to eliminate corruption, collusion and nepotism carried out by anyone including state officials, former state officials, their families and cronies", specifically mentioning former President Soeharto by name.[35]

The inability of the courts to deal with corruption on a massive scale was demonstrated unambiguously in a number of high-profile cases during the Habibie, Abdurrahman and Megawati presidencies. The cases involved prominent political figures and bankers. Although prosecutions ensnared a few relatively minor players, the primary targets in one way or another almost always avoided retribution. In many cases they escaped prosecution altogether, while in others they were convicted but later won appeals. Among the bankers, a few were convicted but some managed to abscond before they could be taken to jail. The following pages will examine a few of the more egregious cases. While some of those accused relied on political backing, others sought to win their freedom by exploiting the entrenched corruption of the judiciary.

The Soeharto Family

The Habibie government resisted popular demands to initiate legal proceedings against the fallen president. Moments after President Habibie had taken the oath of office on 21 May 1998, General Wiranto, the Commander-in-Chief of the armed forces, stepped forward and declared that the armed forces "will continue to protect the honour and safety of former presidents/mandataries of the People's Consultative Assembly, including Bapak Soeharto and his family".[36] Habibie and Wiranto, in particular, owed huge personal debts of gratitude to Soeharto who had promoted them to high office and showered on them untold wealth. They also had another pressing reason for protecting him. If the demands of the students and their supporters were met and Soeharto put on trial, could they be sure that a betrayed Soeharto would not implicate his former lieutenants?[37] It was not just Habibie and Wiranto, of course, who had strong direct interests in protecting Soeharto's "honour and safety" but a large part of the entire New Order elite. The government faced a difficult dilemma and was fully aware of the potential costs of doing nothing. The spectre of the destruction wrought by rioting mobs in May still loomed large. Among those whose homes were destroyed were President

Soeharto's long-standing business partner, Liem Sioe Liong, in Jakarta and his until-recently-very-loyal official mouthpiece, the Golkar General Chairman and former Minister for Information, Harmoko, in Solo.[38]

Habibie's determination to protect Soeharto soon ran into difficulties involving successive attorneys general. Soedjono Chanafiah Atmonegoro, a career prosecutor who had served as attorney general in Soeharto's brief final cabinet and been re-appointed by Habibie, discovered that there was sufficient evidence of corruption to charge the former president. According to Soedjono, he presented his findings to the president at 10 am on 15 June 1998 and was informed of his dismissal at 3 p.m.[39] In need of a more accommodating replacement, Habibie turned to a military lawyer, Maj. Gen. Andi Muhamad Ghalib, whose real responsibility was to prevent, or at least delay, the prosecution of the former president — as dramatically revealed in a tape recording of a telephone conversation between Habibie and Ghalib that was leaked to the press.[40] Ghalib's tenure as attorney general ended suddenly in mid-1999 when Indonesia Corruption Watch, apparently on the basis of leaked information, accused him of receiving payments from two tycoons currently being investigated.[41] Although made "non-active" as attorney general, Ghalib was never charged over these allegations.

Despite continuing mass demonstrations, Habibie's new acting attorney general announced, just two days before a sharply divided Golkar confirmed Habibie as its candidate in the forthcoming presidential election, that the investigation had not produced sufficient evidence to charge Soeharto and would be halted.[42] Apart from his continuing respect for his benefactor, Habibie had apparently calculated that it was better to provoke the demonstrators in the streets than risk losing the support of Soeharto's sympathizers in the MPR, not only in Golkar but also in the military. As it happened, the gamble did not pay off and Habibie lost the presidency.

The new president, Abdurrahman Wahid, adopted a new approach but was also worried about Soeharto diehards. Riding a wave of public support, he quickly reopened the Soeharto case but, arguing that the institution of the presidency had to be respected, promised to pardon Soeharto after the trial on the condition that he returned corruptly acquired property.[43] After Soeharto failed to appear at his trial when it opened on 31 August 2000 and an "independent" medical team reported that the deterioration of his medical condition was "permanent", the judges declared that the court's proceedings would not continue.[44]

Meanwhile Soeharto's children, more vulnerable than their father, had also been called for interrogation. That Soeharto's sons, Bambang Trihatmodjo and Hutomo Mandala Putra (Tommy), were not taking these measures lying down was suggested by a series of bomb explosions in Jakarta that followed each interrogation.[45] In March 1999, the youngest son, Tommy, together with his business partner and Beddu Awang, the head of Bulog, were charged in relation to a deal involving Bulog and PT Goro Batara Sakti, a supermarket chain. The court, suspiciously, considered the deal in which Bulog lost Rp 95 billion (US$11 million) to be a civil rather than criminal matter and the defendants were acquitted a few days before Habibie lost what in effect was a vote of confidence in the MPR that ended his presidency.[46] The new Abdurrahman government, however, pursued the case and in September 2000 the Supreme Court sentenced Tommy to eighteen months' imprisonment.[47]

In a bizarre turn of events which raised big questions about the president's motives, Abdurrahman then had two private meetings with Tommy. When asked whether some kind of bargaining had taken place, one of the president's spokesmen replied that such bargaining was possible as "the country needs money".[48] During his later murder trial, Tommy claimed that he had given Rp 15 billion to two of the president's friends, Dodi Sumadi and Noer Iskandar.[49] Apparently no deal was reached because on 2 November Tommy's request for pardon was rejected by the president, but a delay in arresting him due to an intervening weekend allowed Tommy to "disappear" before he could be taken into custody on the following Monday.[50] Despite rumours of sightings in various places, it seems that Tommy in fact spent most of his time "on the run" in Jakarta.[51] When Judge M. Syafiuddin Kartasasmit, the chairman of the panel of judges that had convicted Tommy, was murdered by four men on 26 July 2001, Tommy immediately fell under suspicion. Ironically, a Supreme Court panel hearing Tommy's request for a review of his sentence on the grounds that new evidence was available, decided to exonerate Tommy on 1 October.[52] Tommy was eventually taken into police custody on 29 November. It was not entirely clear whether he was captured or had surrendered. Whether by coincidence or not, Tommy's capture occurred two days before the end of the term of General Surojo Bimantoro, the national chief of police. For months rumours had been circulating that some police officers had known all along where Tommy was hiding and had been amply rewarded for their cooperation.[53] Tommy's trial as the mastermind of the murder of Syafiuddin commenced in March 2002 and ended with his conviction and a jail term of fifteen years, later reduced to ten by the Supreme Court.[54] After generous remissions, he was eventually released from prison after serving slightly more than four years. Meanwhile the two men who fired the shots that killed Syafiuddin were sentenced to life imprisonment.[55]

The only member of the former president's family to be actually jailed for corruption was Soeharto's half-brother, Probosutedjo, who was sentenced to four years' imprisonment in 2003.[56] Other members of the family, particularly his daughter, Siti Hardijanti Rukmana and sons Sigit Hardjodjanto and Bambang Trihatmodjo, were subjected to interrogation. They remained in business but no longer won government contracts automatically as had been the practice under their father. Although none was actually charged with corruption, let alone convicted, it is highly likely that they, like their uncle Probosutedjo, had become soft targets for the extortion commonly practised by prosecutors and police. As Indonesia Corruption Watch pointed out, a long drawn-out process of investigation and interrogation was often an indication that expensive bargaining was taking place.[57]

The steps taken to prosecute members of the Soeharto family were not only ineffective but in most cases not even intended to succeed. The surviving members of the New Order elite opposed prosecution of Soeharto partly because of lingering loyalty to their former patron but also for fear of what a successful prosecution might mean for them personally. Despite the massive wealth that Soeharto and his family had acquired during the New Order, they nearly all escaped legal retribution although they suffered considerable public humiliation.

Banking and the BLBI Scandal

The Asian Financial Crisis, spreading from Thailand in mid-1997, brought about the collapse of the already-fragile Indonesian banking system. The penetration of key financial and commercial institutions by Soeharto's family and cronies meant that, as one observer put it, "there was a strong presumption that neither investors nor lenders would ever bear the full cost of any corporate or bank failure".[58] Within months, Indonesia's banks were overwhelmed by "non-performing loans" as public confidence collapsed, aggravated by the closure of sixteen insolvent banks as part of an IMF-supported "rescue" package launched on 31 October.[59] Depositors rushed to withdraw funds as the rupiah plunged from Rp 2,400 to the US dollar in July 1997 to its lowest point of Rp 17,000 in January 1998. Meanwhile the president had ordered the Bank of Indonesia to provide liquidity assistance to banks on the brink of default. Assistance under the Bank of Indonesia Liquidity Assistance (*Bantuan Likuiditas Bank Indonesia*: BLBI) and other schemes grew from Rp 11 trillion in July 1997 to Rp 178 trillion (about US$20 billion) in August 1998.[60]

The government established the Indonesian Bank Reconstruction Agency (IBRA) in January 1998 to take over the management and assets of weak and insolvent banks and attempt to recover some of the outstanding debt from bank owners and associated companies. The total cost of recapitalization, including BLBI support, was estimated at Rp 643 trillion (about US$89 billion) — around 60 per cent of GDP.[61] As Ross McLeod commented:

> It may be noted in passing that having the government 'contribute funds to recapitalise banks' is a euphemism for transferring accumulated bank losses (in excess of shareholders' funds) to the general public, rather than to the banks' depositors or other creditors. ... Since the amounts of these losses have turned out to be enormous, and since the vast bulk of Indonesia's poor do not own bank deposits, this has proved an extraordinarily inequitable policy choice.[62]

Although at the highest point over 160 banks were receiving some liquidity support, only about one third became "problematic".[63] However, it was clear that a substantial part of the assistance had been used illegally by recipients. In 2000, the State Audit Board (*Badan Pemeriksa Keuangan*: BPK) presented a report to the DPR on how BLBI funds of Rp 144.5 trillion (US$17 billion) had been used by 48 "problematic" banks.[64] The BPK was severely critical of the Bank of Indonesia (BI) for failing to apply prudential standards, permitting "sick" banks to continue to operate, accepting false reports from banks and failing to detect the common practice of excessive lending to affiliated companies.[65] The BPK found that due to "deviations, weaknesses in the system and neglect" potential losses for the state amounted to Rp 138.4 trillion or 95.78 per cent of the distributed funds. It also stated that assistance of Rp 84.8 trillion or 58.7 per cent had been provided in breach of regulations to banks with debit balances at BI.[66] It was obvious that criminal violations had taken place. Many banks had used BLBI assistance not to meet their obligations to depositors but to further their own commercial interests. Further, banks, especially those with political connections, had routinely lent a large part of their portfolios to related firms within their own commercial groups in violation of lending limits.

As popular anger rose against Soeharto, his family and his cronies, the Habibie government came under increasing pressure to investigate not only Soeharto but also the bankers who had benefited from the BLBI scandal. The political imperative to take action was reinforced by the experience of mass violence and anti-Chinese sentiment that had culminated in the May 1998 rioting and the fear that it could happen again, bearing in mind that nearly all the banks were owned or partly owned by Chinese. The government also wanted to recoup the massive losses incurred in trying to save the banks and decided to offer deals in November 1998 to bankers considered "cooperative".[67]

The assets handed over by the bankers to IBRA were evaluated in 1998–99 by international auditors but it soon became clear that they were grossly over-valued and sales fell well short of expectations.[68] As the four-year deadline for settling debts approached in 2002, the overall recovery rate was only 26 per cent, leaving the government to carry Rp 477 trillion of the Rp 650 trillion debt.[69] Rather than commence lengthy and uncertain prosecutions, the government opted to extend the period for repayment to ten years.[70] As a further incentive to debtors, President Megawati issued a presidential instruction providing "legal certainty" and "release and discharge". Debtors considered "cooperative" who had already paid, or who were genuinely attempting to pay, according to the terms of the 1998 agreements were formally released from criminal charges. On the other hand, those who had had not indicated willingness to repay their debts would face the full force of the law.[71]

By early 2004 most of the big debtors were deemed to have settled although their repayments fell far below the BLBI debts that they had incurred.[72] No distinction was made between debtors whose obligations had arisen largely from the adverse economic conditions created by the financial crisis and those who would otherwise be facing criminal charges for misusing BLBI assistance for private gain or violating legal lending limits. It is not impossible, of course, that the rush to resolve the BLBI debts on terms so favourable to the debtors during the early months of 2004 was related to the forthcoming general and presidential elections and the need of the government parties to raise funds for their electoral campaigns.

While the government was preparing the ground for the "release and discharge" of "cooperative" debtors in 2002, it had launched a series of prosecutions of debtors deemed "uncooperative". The performance of the government in prosecuting recalcitrant debtors, however, was not only almost completely unsuccessful but at times farcical. By the end of 2003 the attorney general revealed that his office had handled 52 cases.[73] But by 2008 only a few had been convicted. The 5 who received the heaviest penalties — 3 sentences of life imprisonment and 2 of 20 years — had been convicted in absentia as they had already fled overseas.[74] Two other bankers managed to abscond in bizarre circumstances despite their convictions. According to Indonesian judicial practice, the Supreme Court must send its judgments to the original lower court which then authorizes the Attorney General's Office to take the convict into custody. In the case of Samadikun Hartono, the President

Director of Bank Modern, the Supreme Court's judgment was issued on 23 May 2003 but the lower court only received a copy on 15 June and the Attorney General's Office finally issued a summons on 7 July. When a team of officials went to his house, they were apparently surprised to find that he was not at home.[75] It turned out that the Attorney General's Office itself had given him permission to seek medical treatment in Japan a month before the Supreme Court delivered its final judgment and he had not returned.[76] The story of David Nusa Widjaja (Ng Tjuen Wie), the Principal Director of Bank Umum Servitia, was similar. After a series of appeals he was eventually sentenced to eight years by the Supreme Court in July 2003. Like Samadikun, he had also left Indonesia before he could be arrested. "We haven't been able to do anything until now because we haven't got a copy of the verdict", the attorney general's spokesman told incredulous journalists.[77] David, however, was detained in the United States and brought back to Indonesia in early 2007 to begin his jail term. He was joined in prison by one of his bank's directors, Tarunodjojo Nusa.[78]

Another BLBI banker, Hendrawan Haryono, of Bank Aspac (Bank Asia Pacific) had also been a beneficiary of the slow transmission of the Supreme Court's judgments to the Attorney General's Office. His sentence had been finalized on 2 July 2003 but the original lower court only received it on 24 June 2004 — almost a year after the judgment had been decided. Unlike Samadikun and David Nusa Widjaya, however, Hendrawan did not flee.[79] Meanwhile the bank's President-Director, Setiawan Haryono (Hendrawan's brother), became the first BLBI banker to go prison after his orginal sentence was reduced on appeal to six months.[80]

The BLBI affair was estimated to have cost Bank Indonesia around US$20 billion yet by 2008 only four errant bankers had been jailed in Indonesia while another seven had fled abroad (although one was eventually returned). In addition, President Soeharto's close friend and golfing partner, Bob Hasan, who was designated a "cooperative" BLBI debtor, was sent to prison but not for a BLBI offence.[81] Three directors of Bank Indonesia were also convicted of violating banking regulations by approving BLBI loans for banks that did not meet the established criteria but later won appeals.[82] Rather than exacerbate economic conditions by attempting to prosecute bankers who had clearly misused BLBI liquidity support, successive governments preferred to designate most as "cooperative" and deemed them to have repaid their debts in full. The adoption of this lenient approach may, however, have allowed politicians and officials to extract substantial contributions from "cooperative" bankers.

Golkar and the 1999 Elections: The Bank Bali and Akbar Tandjung Cases

In the past President Soeharto had ensured that Golkar, as the party of the New Order regime, never had a problem in obtaining the funds necessary to win general elections with overwhelming majorities. Golkar was in essence a nationwide patronage network that rewarded a wide diversity of interests — regional, ethnic, religious and economic — in a single political movement that attracted support by offering material benefits — backed up of course by the security apparatus. As the first post-Soeharto legislative and presidential elections approached in 1999, however, it was obvious that Golkar would suffer a substantial loss of support, but the party still hoped to remain among the major political forces. This time, however, it faced a legislative election in which it would actually be challenged by other parties. And, after the general election President Habibie could expect a tough fight to retain his position when the members of the newly formed MPR convened in October. Both Golkar and President Habibie needed funds, but in the new democratic atmosphere resort to the old methods of raising them ran the risk of exposure by political rivals and the aggressive and newly freed media. Among many allegations, two major scandals damaged Golkar's electoral prospects not only in 1999 but also in 2004.

Bank Bali was a major private bank that had emerged from the financial crisis relatively unscathed and was even able to provide loans to vulnerable banks. For nine months it had been trying unsuccessfully to recover a debt from one of the largest failed banks taken over by IBRA. In January 1999, a company called PT Era Giat Prima (EGP) did a deal with Bank Bali's Indonesian-Chinese owner, Rudy Ramli, in which EGP would arrange for the release of the funds for a fee of 60 per cent (Rp 546 trillion or US$80 million). EGP was owned by another Indonesian-Chinese businessman, Djoko Soegiarto Tjandra, but its president-director was Setya Novanto, one of Golkar" deputy treasurers.[83] The chairman of IBRA, Glenn Yusuf, refused to release the money but on 1 June, while Glenn was overseas, one of his deputies, Pande Lubis, agreed to the payment. This was only a week before the legislative elections.

The case came to public notice inadvertently in July when the planned purchase of a 20-per cent stake in Bank Bali by the British Standard Chartered Bank was delayed due to the discovery during "due diligence" of the legally unnecessary US$80 million fee to recover the debt.[84] In response, both the World Bank and IMF suspended the disbursement of credit intended to help Indonesia recover from the financial crisis. As the October presidential election drew closer, President Habibie's rivals had an interest in exposing as much of the Bank Bali case as possible. They claimed that Golkar officials colluded with IBRA officials to force Rudy Ramli to pay the Golkar-linked EGP for its help in releasing funds the other parties owed to him and they raised questions about whether President Habibie himself knew of the scheme. The DPR commissioned an investigation by the international auditing firm, PricewaterhouseCoopers, which revealed that "a web of more than 150 sizeable transfers took place within days of EGP's receipt of funds from Bank Bali. Recipients included a host of politicians, parliamentarians and public officials."[85] In the ensuing scandal, much attention was focused on a meeting at the Hotel Mulya (close to the DPR building) on 11 February 1999. According to the indictment presented to the court trying Djoko Tjandra, among those who attended the meeting were Djoko Tjandra (Principal Director of EGP); Setya Novanto (President-Director of EGP and one of Golkar's deputy treasurers); Arnold Baramuli (Chairman of the Supreme Advisory Council and Golkar official); Tanri Abeng (the Minister of State for State Enterprises); Pande Lubis (deputy head of IBRA) and Syahril Sabarin (Governor of Bank Indonesia).[86] The public exposure of the involvement of Golkar officials in the Bank Bali scandal further dented the image of President Habibie's government, already battered by its prevarications over the prosecution of former President Soeharto.

Despite the involvement of many Golkar officials in this extortion project, only three people, none of whom were Golkar officials, eventually faced charges in court. The Principal Director of PT EGP, the Chinese Djoko Tjandra, was charged but the President-Director and Golkar official, Setya Novanto, was not. Djoko was successively acquitted in the district, high and supreme courts on the ground that the case was not one of corruption but merely a commercial dispute between EGP and Bank Bali.[87] One of the three Supreme Court judges assessing the case, the reform-minded Artidjo Alkoster, made a dissenting judgment and later told a friend that he had been visited by an unknown man who said that "We have already settled two judges. It only remains for us to give you the money".[88] The head of the National Ombudsman Commission, Antonius Sujata, provided the Chief Justice with reports claiming that bribes of Rp 20 billion (US$2 million) had been offered to the judges in the Djoko case.[89]

The second official charged was the Governor of the Bank Indonesia, Syahril Sabarin, who was arrested in June 2000 when President Habibie's successor, Abdurrahman Wahid, intervened in the case. Syahril had been appointed by Soeharto in 1998 for a five-year term but President Abdurrahman wanted to appoint his own nominee. Syahril's alleged participation in the

Hotel Mulya meeting with Djoko Tjandra and several Golkar officials gave the president the opportunity to put pressure on Syahril. "I was given a choice by the president", Syahril said, "resign and not be charged, or not resign and be charged". If he resigned, he could be appointed either to the Supreme Advisory Council or as ambassador to a Western country.[90] Syahril rejected the president's offer and was arrested in June 2000 although later allowed to resume his duties as governor of the Bank Indonesia while under house arrest. In March 2002, he was found guilty of corruption and sentenced to three years' imprisonment. Although not accused of personally benefiting from the release of funds to Bank Bali, he was held to have failed to act with proper caution.[91] However, in August 2002, a month after Abdurrahman's dismissal, the Jakarta High Court upheld Syahril's appeal and freed him.[92]

While the Bank Bali scheme was being implemented during the months before the 1999 election, another plot was hatched involving funds from the State Logistics Board (Bulog). During the New Order, Bulog had been a major source of "invisible" funding for President Soeharto's purposes and it continued in that role under President Habibie.[93] In February 1999, he instructed Rahardi Ramelan, the Minister of Trade and Industry who doubled as Head of Bulog, to provide "non-budgetary" funds of Rp 40 billion (US$4 million) to the State Secretary, Akbar Tandjung, Rp 10 billion to General Wiranto for a vigilante force to maintain security and Rp 4.6 billion as a loan to the troubled PT Goro Batara Sakti, which was partly owned by Tommy Soeharto.[94] The money given to Akbar Tandjung, who was also the chairman of Golkar, was purportedly to finance a social welfare scheme for those badly affected by the Asian Financial Crisis but, given the timing, many observers assumed it was intended to finance Golkar's election campaign. Although technically illegal, the use of Bulog funds for such purposes was normal presidential practice and later attempted also by Habibie's successor, Abdurrahman Wahid.[95]

Megawati, of course, had no reason to save Golkar from embarrassment and allowed her Attorney General, M. A. Rachman, to call back Rahardi Ramelan, who had been encouraged to go overseas by his Golkar colleagues after the fall of the Habibie government. During interrogation on 9 October 2001, Rahardi revealed that he had provided Rp 40 billion to Akbar Tandjung. Akbar claimed that the money had been channelled through a religious foundation which had distributed daily necessities in several regions badly affected by the economic collapse and El Nino weather conditions. Unfortunately, Akbar could not immediately remember the name of the foundation and it was soon discovered that its head, a businessman, Dadang Sukandar, had a close association with another of Golkar's deputy treasurers, M.S. Hidayat.[96] Investigations in areas where aid was said to have been distributed failed to find anyone who had received such aid and it was claimed that one of the members of the foundation, a taxi driver, had withdrawn Rp 20 billion from the foundation's bank account with a fake identity card but had since died.[97] The series of farcical explanations reached its climax when the man who claimed to be in charge of the distribution of the aid on the ground, Winfried Simatupang, admitted that he had been "negligent". He had distributed only Rp 7 billion and had kept the remaining Rp 33 billion for two years in a cupboard in his bedroom until he returned the full Rp 40 billion after his arrest.[98]

Although Akbar retained his post as Speaker of the DPR, he was arrested in March 2002 and put on trial, together with Dadang Sukandar and Winfried Simatupang. The long-running trial, from March to September, provided a continuous stream of embarrassing revelations. Despite prayers organized by Golkar, Akbar was convicted and sentenced to three years' jail. Nevertheless, he was released after a month in detention and resumed his duties as Speaker of the DPR while awaiting the hearing of his appeal to the Supreme Court.

The Golkar chairman's difficulties were a windfall for President Megawati's party, PDI-P. Megawati's husband, Taufiq Kiemas, saw advantage in allowing Akbar to "float" as head of Golkar. Reportedly, he told colleagues, "As long as Akbar is there, effigies will be burned by demonstrators — and they won't be effigies of Mega".[99] Fitting the strategic political needs of the PDI-P, the hearing of Akbar's final appeal to the Supreme Court did not take place until February 2004, just two months before the 2004 general election. By then Akbar was speculating openly about Golkar joining an alliance with the PDI-P in the presidential election and accepting the post of vice president under Megawati. In a 4-1 majority judgement, the court, presided over by Paulus Effendi Lotulung, exonerated Akbar. The judges concluded that Akbar could not be blamed for implementing a presidential instruction, nor for the failure of Danang and Winfried to carry out their obligation to distribute basic necessities to the poor. They also noted that Akbar had not benefited personally from the Bulog money.[100] The appeals of Danang and Winfried, however, were rejected.[101] Akbar's case, drawn out over two years, effectively destroyed his presidential or vice-presidential hopes. His party even opted to nominate General Wiranto as its presidential candidate in preference to its chairman.

Critics of the Akbar case pointed out that the initial charges laid by the prosecution made it easier for the Supreme Court ultimately to find Akbar not guilty. No one claimed that Akbar had siphoned off the Bulog money into his own pocket. The issue was whether the money was channelled to

Golkar's election campaign. The prosecution, however, only focussed on how the money was delivered to Akbar but, despite the incredible testimony of Danang and Winfried, did not trace its movement further. If that had been done, the critics claimed, the case against Akbar would have been much stronger.

Meanwhile, the hapless Rahardi Ramelan's trial and appeals continued. Rahardi was charged with misusing Bulog funds by diverting them not only to Akbar but also to Wiranto, Tommy's company, the presidential security force, several state construction projects and various other non-Bulog purposes.[102] Rahardi claimed that in October 2001 Akbar had tried to persuade him to say that Akbar had not received the money directly and that a report on its utilization had been provided. As a witness in Rahardi's trial, Akbar admitted meeting Rahardi at the Hotel Grand Mahakam but couldn't remember what had been discussed.[103] Although it appeared that Rahardi was implementing the president's instructions, he was found guilty and sentenced to two years' jail in December 2002. He lost his appeals.[104]

Dropped Cases

The cases actually brought to court made up only a small fraction of major cases investigated by prosecutors. Some were reported in the press but eventually just seemed to fade away. Others were brought to a conclusion through Orders to Stop Investigation (*Surat Perintah Penghentian Penyidikan*, SP3) issued by the Attorney General. SP3s were usually granted on very general grounds such as "insufficient evidence", "no loss suffered by the state", or the determination that the case was really civil, not criminal.[105] In many cases the decision to drop cases was taken after several years of investigation. Critics wondered how experienced prosecutors could have persisted with such cases for so long and questioned their bona fides. Such cases seemed to fit the explanations put forward in the ICW book on the "Court Mafia", summarized at the beginning of this chapter. The Deputy Attorney General for Special Crime, Sudhono Iswahyudi, announced that between 2001 and 2004 seventeen SP3s had been issued.[106] Many of these cases had not been announced immediately but only became known, often inadvertently, by the public several months later.[107] ICW claimed, on the basis of newspaper reports, that twenty-five individual SP3s had been issued between 1999 and 2004 although it identified only thirteen cases.[108] Among the recipients were several ministers in the Soeharto and Habibie cabinets including Ginanjar Kartasasmita, who somewhat suspiciously finally obtained his SP3 on 19 October 2004, one day before Megawati handed over the presidency to Susilo Bambang Yudhoyono.[109] Another was Soeharto's daughter and also Minister of Social Welfare in his last cabinet, Siti Hardijanti Rukmana.

Crony businessmen were also prominent among the SP3 recipients. Manimutu Sinivasan, the owner of the engineering conglomerate, Texmaco,[110] Prajogo Pangestu (Phang Djun Phen), whose timber interests were closely intertwined with those of Soeharto's children, and Syamsul Nursalim, whose bank was the biggest of the BLBI defaulters, received their SP3s during Megawati's presidency, but they had already obtained assurances of presidential protection from President Abdurrahman Wahid. In his usual informal way, at a meeting with Indonesian residents in South Korea in 2000 he had confided that he had decided to postpone cases against the three men because he considered them to be "the key to expanding exports".[111] Syamsul Nursalim eventually opted to live in Singapore which had no extradition treaty with Indonesia.

NEW ANTI-CORRUPTION AGENCIES

The performance of the courts in dealing with both the corruption of the Soeharto era as well as new cases involving post-New Order political leaders had been dismal. Despite the obvious crisis there were few signs of crisis-ridden reform in the courts and little indication of a sense of urgency in the government. The Habibie government had been driven less by commitment to tackling corruption than by the need to be seen to be doing something about it as the legislative and presidential elections approached. Given that the ordinary courts were universally regarded as corrupt, there was little public confidence in their capacity to deal with corruption cases. A more credible strategy required the establishment of new bodies to focus exclusively on the corruption issue.

Two new bodies were quickly foreshadowed. In response to public expectations, MPR Decree No. XI in 1998 had mandated the formation of a body that would require state officials "under oath according to their religion" to announce their wealth both on accepting and leaving public office.[112] For this purpose, Law No. 28/1999 to establish the Commission to Examine the Wealth of State Officials (*Komisi Pemeriksa Kekayaan Penyelenggara Negara*, KPKPN) was adopted by the DPR and signed by the president on 19 May 1999 — a fortnight before the legislative elections.[113] This was followed by Law No. 31/1999 on the Eradication of the Crime of Corruption which was signed by President Habibie on 16 August 1999 — two months before the presidential election. This law, apart from detailing crimes falling under the law and the procedures for dealing with them, required the formation within two years of a Commission to Eradicate the Crime of Corruption (*Komisi Pemberantasan Tindak Pidana Korupsi*, KPTPK but usually abbreviated to KPK) to co-ordinate, supervise and carry out the investigation and prosecution of corruption cases.[114]

The sense of urgency that had marked the passage of the two laws before the parliamentary and presidential elections soon faded after the elections had been held. No new measures were adopted during the remaining few months of the Habibie presidency and neither the Abdurrahman nor the Megawati governments gave high priority to establishing the bodies mandated by the Habibie laws. The KPKPN was only formed in January 2001, twenty months after the adoption of the law and, although the by-then-fatally-wounded Abdurrahman government submitted a bill on 5 June 2001 to establish the KPK,[115] the law was not passed by the DPR until November 2002 and only signed by President Megawati on 27 January 2003 — seventeen months after the expiry of the two-year deadline set in the original law.

The Abdurrahman government at least attempted to fill the gap before the formation of the KPK by issuing a government regulation to form the Joint Team to Eradicate the Crime of Corruption (*Tim Gabungan Pemberantasan Tindak Pidana Korupsi*, TGPTPK) on 23 May 2000.[116] The team was led by Adi Andojo Soetjipto, the dissident Supreme Court judge of the late Soeharto period, and was given authority, under the coordination of the attorney general, to investigate and prosecute. Far from inaugurating an effective campaign against corruption, however, the efforts of the team met with much resistance and only highlighted the entrenched nature of the problem.[117]

The team's initial focus on corruption in the judiciary naturally riled the judges. During the next ten months the team completed investigations of three cases, each of which involved judges. The most notorious case led to the trials of one retired judge of the Supreme Court, Yahya Harahap, and two current judges, Supratini Sutarto and Marnis Kahar. Acting on behalf of a party to a land dispute in Bandung, a broker named Endin Wahyudin claimed that he had paid bribes amounting to Rp 196 million (US$19,600) to the three judges who then ruled in favour of his client.[118] The case became public when complications arose that prevented his client occupying the land. Endin then complained to the TGPTPK which initiated the charges. Eventually, however, all three judges were exonerated by district courts on essentially technical grounds.[119] Meanwhile it was the "whistleblower", Endin, who was charged with criminal libel and received a suspended sentence of three months even before the trials of the three judges had been held.[120] The second case was similar. The Director of Administrative Law in the Supreme Court, Zainal Agus, was charged in a district court with demanding a bribe of

Rp 100 million but was acquitted. Like the Endin case, his accuser then faced a criminal libel charge.[121] The third case, however, brought a minor success for the TGPTPK. Fauzatulo Zendrato, a relatively junior "justicial judge" attached to the Supreme Court to assist Supreme Court judges, was found guilty of accepting a bribe of Rp 550 million (US$58,000) when previously serving as a High Court judge and sentenced to one year's imprisonment. Strangely, he was not required to repay the bribe because, as the judge in the case explained, "The prosecutor didn't mention it; we have no authority to rule on something that was not mentioned in the indictment".[122]

The "Endin case" sealed the fate of the TGPTPK. On 23 March 2001, several months before the trials of the three judges, a panel of Supreme Court judges chaired by one of the Assistant Chief Justices, Paulus Effendi Lotulung, annulled the government regulation establishing the TGPTPK on the grounds that it exceeded the authority provided by Law No. 31/1999 on the eradication of corruption. Clause 27 of the law read: "In the case of crimes which are difficult to prove, a joint team may be formed under the co-ordination of the Attorney General." The explanation attached to the law gave as examples crimes in banking, taxation, the capital market, trade and industry, but did not specifically mention the judiciary. The Supreme Court panel concluded that this clause could not be interpreted to cover the investigative activities of the TGPTPK.[123] The effect of the decision was to undermine the charges against the judges, but it also led to allegations that the Supreme Court judges were banding together in defence of their colleagues. Earlier Lotulung had accompanied two of the judges during their initial interrogation by the TGPTPK in August 2000 not, he insisted, as their legal advisor but only in his capacity as a chairman of the League of Indonesian Judges (*Ikatan Hakim Indonesia*, IKAHI).[124]

The KPKPN's legal foundation, a decree of the MPR, was much stronger than that of the TGPTPK but its life was not much longer. Although obliged by law to begin its work by May 2000, its formation was delayed by a quarrel between President Abdurrahman and the DPR ostensibly over the number of members of the commission. Eventually a compromise was reached and thirty-five members were installed in January 2001.[125] Headed by Jusuf Syakir, a politician from the Muslim PPP, the KPKPN began to collect data on the wealth of public officials from the president down, including not only government bureaucrats but also members of the central and regional legislatures, regional governors and bupati, judges, managers of state corporations and military and police officers. The fundamental weakness of the commission was that it had no authority to apply sanctions to officials who failed to provide the information it sought. During its first two years only 42.7 per cent of the 43,775 officials to whom the thirty-page forms were sent had responded.[126] One observer noted that "The KPKPN did not have the funds to hire the specialized legal, financial and investigative expertise that is essential to making sense of the mass of data flowing into its office."[127] The commission adopted the straight-forward strategy of simply feeding its data to the press with the hope that the public would draw attention to discrepancies. Over nearly four years it reported only eight officials to the police for suspected corruption, one of whom was President Megawati's attorney general, M.A. Rachman, who appeared to own a mansion in Cinere, South Jakarta, that had escaped his attention when completing the form.[128] A major obstacle in pursuing these cases was the legal requirement for the police to obtain the president's permission to interrogate senior officials and President Megawati's reluctance to grant such permission. Despite its lack of "bite" in carrying out its duties, the KPKPN had annoyed and embarrassed members of the political elite who claimed that it had gone beyond its initial mandate in Law No. 28/1999. A new law absorbed the KPKPN's functions and thus ended its existence as a separate entity.

The law on the Commission to Eradicate the Crime of Corruption (*Komisi Pemberantasan Tindak Pidana Korupsi*, KPK) was adopted by the DPR in November 2002 and signed by President Megawati on 27 December 2002 (Law No. 30/2002).[129] It established a five-member commission with authority to investigate and prosecute corruption cases of more than Rp 1 billion (US$100,000), involving members of law enforcement agencies or state officials as well as others linked to corruption committed by them, and giving rise to concern in society (Clause 11). The KPK was empowered to take over the investigation or prosecution of cases already begun by the police or prosecutors if complaints from society met with inadequate response (Clause 9). Its extensive powers included authority to tap telephones and record conversations, ban overseas travel, freeze bank accounts and obtain information from financial institutions. The KPK also had authority to appoint the prosecutors in the corruption cases it investigated. It did not require presidential permission to begin investigations. The KPK law further provided for the establishment of special Anti-Corruption Courts (*Pengadilan Tindak Pidana Korupsi*, Tipikor) to try cases investigated by the KPK.

The five members of the KPK were appointed through a two-stage process which, like the previous appointment of Supreme Court judges, involved "fit and proper" testing by the DPR. A selection committee, consisting of prosecutors, police and several prominent private lawyers and legal academics, proposed ten candidates to the president to be forwarded to the DPR's Commission II dealing with legal affairs. Of the 44 members of Commission II, 43 voted for Taufiequrahman Ruki, a retired police office who had sat previously in the military/police group in the DPR and then joined the staff of the Coordinating Minister for Political and Security Affairs, Susilo Bambang Yudhoyono. Taufiequrahman was appointed as chairman of the commission.[130] The other four successful candidates were well-known professionals with financial and legal skills.[131]

The next step was to form the new Anti-Corruption Court (*Tipikor*) at three levels corresponding to the District, High and Supreme Courts. The panel of judges hearing each case would consist of two "career" judges and three "ad hoc" judges. The ad hoc judges would be selected following "fit and proper tests", this time supervised by the Supreme Court rather than the DPR. One of the selection criteria listed in the law was that judges should already have experience in handling corruption cases.[132] It had been hoped to appoint 16 judges from 25 candidates, but the quality of the candidates was so poor that only 9 could be accepted during the first round of recruitment in 2004.[133] A second round of selection was held in 2005. Although the first group of judges had been appointed in the middle of 2004, they were complaining in early 2005, after the first cases had begun to be heard, that they had still not received any salary.[134] The Tipikor courts themselves were formally installed on 7 October 2004, only a fortnight before President Megawati left office.[135]

The attempts to create new agencies to by-pass the ordinary courts in dealing with corruption cases had met with substantial obstacles. The KPKPN had drawn public attention to the unexplained incomes of officials but it had no power to apply sanctions. The TGPTPK had more "teeth" but its focus on corruption in the courts upset the judges and it was quickly annulled by the Supreme Court. And the long delay in establishing the KPK eloquently indicated the lack of enthusiasm for such bodies in the Habibie, Abdurrahman and Megawati governments as well as among the political parties in the DPR. Nevertheless, public expectations could not be ignored entirely, especially as legislative and presidential elections drew closer. Towards the end of the Megawati presidency in 2004 the KPK and the new Tipikor courts were finally established and a law adopted to form the Judicial Commission envisaged in the third round of constitutional amendments in 2001.

YUDHOYONO'S ANTI-CORRUPTION DRIVE

The election of President Yudhoyono in 2004 opened the way to a more vigorous drive against high-level corruption. Despite its failings in the actual prosecution of corruption cases, Megawati's government had, by the end of its term, laid the institutional foundations which could be developed by her successor. In contrast to his predecessors, the new president promised personally to lead the anti-corruption campaign and, in December 2004, with considerable fanfare, issued a presidential instruction setting out the broad outlines of his proposed programme to "accelerate the eradication of corruption".[136] Having won the presidential election with a vote of 61 per cent, Yudhoyono had the political legitimacy to embark on a serious anti-corruption campaign. He had never been perceived by public opinion as a "corrupt general" with extensive connections to the business world and, although by no means a poor man, his personal wealth, as revealed during the 2004 election campaign, fell far below that of all the other presidential and vice-presidential candidates except the university professor and former Speaker of the MPR, Amien Rais.[137] As attorney general, he appointed the transparently "clean" Abdul Rahman Saleh, a former head of the Legal Aid Institute who as a Supreme Court judge had issued the lone dissenting opinion in the corruption trial that exonerated Akbar Tandjung.

Yudhoyono, however, lacked strong support in the DPR where his own Democrat Party held only 10 per cent of the seats. For that, as described in Chapter 3, he turned to his vice president, Jusuf Kalla, who won the leadership of Golkar two months after the presidential election and was thus able to bring the largest party in the DPR into the government's camp. Golkar's support came with a price. Kalla, a businessman who had prospered during the New Order, had already exercised substantial influence over the composition of the cabinet, including the appointment of another wealthy tycoon, Aburizal Bakrie, as Coordinating Minister for Economic Affairs. Bakrie, reputedly a major financial contributor to Yudhoyono's electoral campaign, had previously enjoyed close commercial ties with members of former President Soeharto's family and had not been the current president's first choice for the position.[138] Yudhoyono's dependence on Golkar support constrained the government's anti-corruption programme as he could hardly be expected to turn immediately on his new political allies, some of whom were vulnerable to corruption investigations. Moreover, questions were raised about some presumed contributors of funds to Yudhoyono's own electoral campaign, including commercial groups associated with the military. An important member of Yudhoyono's campaign "success team" was Lt. Gen. (ret.) T. B. Silalahi, the patron of the military-connected Artha Graha conglomerate that was run by the "controversial" tycoon, Tommy Winata.

In the early months of the Yudhoyono presidency, the attorney general gave consideration to re-opening about twenty cases which had been closed through the issuing of SP3 certificates by President Megawati's Attorney

General, M. A. Rahman, including the case involving Ginanjar Kartasasmita, whose SP3 had been suspiciously granted just before Megawati left office.[139] However, by early 2005 this plan had been abandoned and the president explained that "We would be better off preventing mega corruption cases from recurring in the future".[140] On another occasion he said that the main problem was "on-going corruption". He told officials, "I don't care about your past ... because if we continue to look to the past, we can't advance properly".[141] The cabinet secretary, Lt. Gen. Sudi Silalahi, announced that the government would not re-open SP3 cases except where new evidence was found.[142]

Under the law in force during most of the Megawati presidency, investigation of senior government officials could not commence without first obtaining written permission from the president or her representative. This requirement, however, was in effect abolished for heads of regional governments and their deputies in the new law on regional government adopted towards the end of Megawati's term, but remained partly in force for members of the DPR and regional DPRDs.[143] Megawati had been notorious for rarely providing such permission but Yudhoyono now gave it freely. During his first year in office, permission was granted to investigate 57 officials including 4 governors, 31 bupati, 7 deputy bupati, 6 mayors and 1 deputy mayor as well as 8 members of the DPR.[144] By the end of 2006 the number had risen to 92.[145]

The KPK took the lead in corruption prosecutions. In 2005, 9 cases were brought to trial, 10 in 2006 and 14 in 2007.[146] Many more cases were investigated by the KPK or by the police and prosecutors working under KPK supervision. The total number of completed dossiers ready for prosecution between 2004 and 2007 reached 59, many of whom had high public profiles. In sharp contrast to corruption cases heard by the ordinary courts, KPK had never lost a case prosecuted in a Tipikor court. Moreover, its appeals courts quickly acquired a reputation for increasing sentences with the result that potential appellants were tending to think twice about appealing.[147]

The first trial was that of the Golkar governor of Aceh, Abdullah Puteh, who was found guilty of corruptly gaining Rp 3.65 billion from the purchase of a Russian-manufactured helicopter and sentenced to ten years' imprisonment on 11 April 2005.[148] A fortnight later, two officials of the Department of Communications were convicted over a land case in Southeast Maluku involving Rp 10.3 billion and were sentenced respectively to terms that rose to eleven and eight years' imprisonment after appeals. The next high-profile case led to the convictions of members and employees of the national Elections Commission who were accused of accepting kickbacks from suppliers of equipment, materials and insurance related to the 2004 elections. Another prominent case resulted in the conviction in 2007 of Megawati's Minister of Maritime Affairs and Fisheries, Rokhmin Dahuri, for using "non-budgetary funds" collected by his department for a wide range of political and personal purposes. In 2008, the recently retired governor of the Bank Indonesia was convicted for approving payments to former bank officials facing prosecution as well as to members of the DPR.[149] In addition two senior officials of the bank were also convicted and in 2009 four former deputy governors were brought to court.[150] Other high-profile officials convicted in KPK cases included the governor of East Kalimantan, a former governor of Riau (and current member of the DPR), the chairman of the Investment Coordinating Board, a director-general in the Department of Law and Human Rights, and two former ambassadors to Malaysia (including one who had been Chief of National Police during Abdurrahman's presidency).

Initially the KPK and the special Tipikor courts, as newly established institutions, could not be expected to take all major corruption cases. President Yudhoyono therefore took steps to speed up investigations through "normal" channels by forming in May 2005 the Coordination Team for the Eradication of the Crime of Corruption (*Tim Koordinasi Pemberantasan Tindak Pidana Korupsi*: Tim Tastipikor) consisting of forty-eight members drawn from the Attorney-General's Office, the police and the Finance and Development Supervision Board (*Badan Pengawasan Keuangan dan Pembangunan*: BPKP).[151] Headed by the Assistant Attorney General for Special Crime, Hendarman Supandji, and directly responsible to the president, the team's priorities were to investigate sixteen state corporations (BUMN), four departments and the State Secretariat over a period of two years. In contrast to KPK, it had no special powers but was intended to reduce long-standing rivalry between the Attorney General's Office and the police by coordinating their investigations. It brought its cases to the ordinary courts instead of the Tipikor courts where all KPK cases were heard.[152]

Tim Tastipikor investigations also led to several high-profile prosecutions. In early 2006, President Megawati's Minister of Religion, Said Agil Husin Al Munawar, and one of his senior officials were convicted of corruption involving funds for the annual *haj* to Mecca. The investigation of the social security fund, PT Jamsostek, not only resulted in the conviction of the fund's principal director but also two prosecutors and a judge who had separately extorted substantial bribes from him.[153] In the case of the president-director of the state electricity company, PLN, however, cooperation between the police and prosecutors broke down and the suspect had to be released when the time limit for presenting his case expired.[154] Tim Tastipikor lost another major case involving the State Secretariat and the land on which the Hilton Hotel in Jakarta was built. In this case, the judgment, which was delivered one day after the team's two-year term expired, exonerated the two accused, one of whom was Ali Mazi, the lawyer who handled the original deal and now the governor of Southeast Sulawesi.[155] During its two years of existence, Tim Tastipikor completed 7 cases while 2 were being appealed, 11 currently prosecuted and a further 42 under investigation.[156] Following its dissolution in 2007, the remaining cases were distributed between the police and the Attorney General's Office while the head of Tim Tastipikor, Hendarman Supadji, was appointed as Attorney General.

The progress made by the KPK under Yudhoyono stood in sharp contrast to the entrenched corruption in the Attorney General's Office itself despite the relative success of the Tim Tastipikor. The depth and extent of the problem was dramatically exemplified in March 2008 when KPK agents arrested Urip Tri Gunawan, the head of the Attorney General's team investigating BLBI cases, outside the Jakarta home of Syamsul Nursalim, the largest BLBI debtor. Urip was found to be carrying US$660,000 (about Rp 6 billion) which he had just received from Artalyta Suryani, a businesswoman and close friend of Syamsul who prefers to stay in Singapore. Two days earlier, the Attorney General's Office had decided to stop further investigation of Syamsul in regard to his BLBI case. In September, Urip was found guilty of extortion and accepting a bribe for which he was sentenced to twenty years' imprisonment. During the course of the trial, a tapped telephone conversation between Urip and Artalyta indicated her familiarity with several other senior prosecutors, including the Junior Attorney General for Special Crimes. These officials were quickly dismissed from their positions by the Attorney General, Hendarman.[157]

The KPK and the Tim Tastipikor together contributed significantly to the government's anti-corruption programme. The number of corruption convictions obtained in the Tipikor and regular courts was still small but those convicted, although not usually among top-level officials of the government, were often part of the second-level elite who in the past would never have imagined that they could be brought to court, let alone imprisoned. At the very least, senior officials were now made aware of the risks of engaging in corrupt activity. However, the Urip case also demonstrated dramatically why little progress had been made in the BLBI and other cases during the previous decade. The presence of the KPK and other new institutions increasingly put established institutions on the defensive but corrupt practices remained widespread in institutions formally responsible for upholding the law.

CONFLICT BETWEEN AGENCIES

The KPK was, as already indicated, not the only new agency involved in anti-corruption activities. Apart from the temporary Tim Tastipikor, a Judicial Commission had also been formed to, among other duties, "uphold" the integrity of members of the judiciary. Given that these new agencies had been formed in response to the manifest inadequacy of the existing courts, including the Supreme Court, it was inevitable that tensions would emerge between agencies.

An open conflict between the KPK and the Supreme Court soon emerged in September 2005 when the KPK, apparently suspecting corruption, sought to question a Supreme Court judge and the head of the Central Jakarta District Court in relation to a case which had been decided in favour of Soeharto's half-brother, Probosutedjo. The Chief Justice of the Supreme Court, Bagir Manan, said he would have granted permission if there were indications of corruption but rejected the KPK's request because he found no grounds for suspicion in the case.[158] A week later the conflict moved to a higher level, again involving Probosutedjo.

On 30 September, the KPK arrested Probosutedjo's lawyer (and retired judge), Harini Wiyoso, and five administrative employees of the Supreme Court who were carrying US$400,000 and Rp 800 million in cash.[159] Probosutedjo was appealing to the Supreme Court in a separate case against a sentence of two years' imprisonment for corruption involving forestry. Two of those arrested said that the money was intended for Bagir Manan who chaired a panel of three judges hearing Probosutedjo's appeal but there was no concrete evidence implicating the Chief Justice. In his own later trial, one of them claimed that two of the judges were OK (*beres*) but not Bagir.[160] In late September, the KPK, with Bagir's permission, searched the offices of the three judges (including himself) and read preliminary drafts of their judgments which revealed that the views of the other two judges differed from those of Bagir. Although this discovery seemed to clear Bagir's name, he was outraged by the breach of the KPK's commitment to keep its findings confidential.[161] Following intervention by President Yudhoyono, Bagir formed a new panel of judges to hear the Probosutedjo appeal which resulted in the court enhancing Probosutedjo's sentence to four years.[162] At her own trial in the Tipikor court, Harini herself was also sentenced to four years.

Meanwhile the new Judicial Commission had only became operational after it elected its leadership at the end of August 2005 but it too soon entered the fray with the Supreme Court. The Commission's constitutional authority was limited to proposing the appointment of judges to the Supreme

Court and "protecting and upholding the honour, noble values (*keluhuran martabat*) and behaviour of judges" (Constitution, Article 24B.1). The Judicial Commission law empowered the Commission to "supervise" (*pengawasan*) judges by investigating their behaviour, demanding explanations of suspected violations of the code of ethics, and recommending sanctions to the Supreme Court (Law on Judicial Commission, Articles 21, 22). Its activities, however, soon encroached on spheres which the Supreme Court regarded as its own.

The Judicial Commission's first case concerned a dispute over the result of a mayoral election in Bogor, West Java. The West Java High Court had annulled the apparent victory of Nur Mahmudi Ismail, a former minister in Abdurrahman's government, and declared the Golkar candidate the winner, but this decision was overruled by the Supreme Court which described the judges' conduct as "unprofessional" and recommended their transfer although it did not find evidence of corruption.[163] Sensing corruption, the Judicial Commission carried out its own investigation and recommended to the Supreme Court that the chairman of the High Court be suspended for a year.[164] Then in December the Commission determined that the Banten High Court was mistaken when it imposed a sentence on a member of the local legislature that was less than the minimum provided by the law.[165] The Commission also intervened in the Supreme Court-KPK conflict by interrogating Harini and the five Supreme Court employees who had been arrested in the case.[166] It even requested that Bagir Manan himself appear for interrogation to which Bagir, apparently feeling the dignity of his office to be under challenge, indicated his willingness to receive the commission members if they came to his office but refused to be summoned to the Commission's office.[167] In May 2006, the Commission questioned a judgment of the Supreme Court in a case involving the arrest of a businessman and also recommended that the judges who had found the directors of Bank Mandiri not guilty of corruption should be suspended.[168] By early 2006, the Commission had made five recommendations to the Supreme Court that sanctions be imposed on errant judges but none were implemented and at least six judges had refused to appear before it. By mid-2006, the Supreme Court had failed to respond to eighteen recommendations.[169]

The Supreme Court judges, particularly the Chief Justice himself, were clearly offended by the Commission's approach which, in their view, had not been limited to the personal behaviour of judges but seemed to claim the right to review, and even reverse, their judgments. The "cold war" between the Supreme Court and the Judicial Commission had reached its peak in January 2006 when the Commission's chairman, Professor Muhammad Busyro Muquddas of the Yogyakarta-based Islamic University of Indonesia, proposed to President Yudhoyono that all current 49 Supreme Court judges undergo "re-selection".[170] Busyro declared that "corruption in the country has become chronic in the extreme".[171] Meanwhile the Commission provoked a new furore by revealing the names of 13 Supreme Court judges against whom complaints had been made.[172] In response, 31 of the 49 Supreme Court judges submitted a request for a judicial review by the Constitutional Court of the law on the Judicial Commission.[173]

The new Constitutional Court had the beneficial long-term function of providing authoritative resolutions to complex issues, but in the short term it was something of a "wild card" that could complicate the campaign against corruption. In its review of the Judicial Commission law it declared that sections relating to "supervision" had led to legal uncertainty and were in conflict with the constitution. It argued that the Commission's role was limited to examining the personal behaviour of judges and did not extend to assessing the content of Supreme Court judgments which were exclusively the province of the courts. The Judicial Commission's members, believing that the majority of judges were corrupt, had argued that it was necessary to assess judgments in order to demonstrate violations of the judges' codes of ethics and conduct. The Constitutional Court invalidated a key part of the commission's function and recommended that the government and DPR revise the Law on the Judicial Commission in conformity with the constitution.[174] The Constitutional Court's judgment in another case involving the KPK had less drastic implications. It found some of the Tipikor court's powers unconstitutional on the grounds that "legal dualism" was created by providing for the same crimes to be adjudicated in different courts using different procedures. The Constitutional Court did not require the immediate abolition of Tipikor but gave the DPR three years to adopt a new law. In the meantime, Tipikor would continue to hear cases brought by the KPK.[175]

The proliferation of new agencies concerned with fighting corruption had not been an unmixed blessing. Each in its own way had performed significant functions and important victories were achieved in the courts, but much effort had been expended on inter-agency rivalries. And then the constitutional "wild card" was played twice by the Constitutional Court in effect eliminating one of the assumed functions of the Judicial Commission although the Court gave time to the DPR to save the KPK and Tipikor.

ANTI-CORRUPTION POLITICS IN REGIONAL GOVERNMENT

While President Yudhoyono's anti-corruption drive was under way at the centre through the KPK and Tim Tastipikor, a surge in prosecutions was taking place in the regions. These prosecutions had their own dynamics independent of the centre, but they fed into the president's campaign and certainly boosted the national statistics in terms of trials, if not necessarily convictions. Corruption in regional government had, of course, been the norm during the Soeharto years with the result that governors, bupatis and mayors suddenly found themselves vulnerable during the early years of Reformasi but few prosecutions were launched.[176] It was only after the election of Yudhoyono when permission was freely given to begin investigations that the number of prosecutions rose sharply.

By early 2006 the list of approved investigations of regional officials included 7 (out of 33) governors, 45 (out of about 440) bupatis and mayors and 10 deputy bupatis and mayors.[177] The president also initiated the practice of giving permission for the arrest of bupatis and mayors to facilitate investigations.[178] In addition to the governors of Aceh (Abdullah Puteh) and Banten (Djoko Munandar), 6 bupatis, mayors or their deputies were convicted in 2005 and 4 in the first half of 2006.[179]

Although members of DPRDs had occasionally been investigated for corruption after 1998, most cases did not lead to charges in court and convictions. In a new development during the Megawati presidency but apparently not on her initiative, investigations targeted virtually the entire memberships of DPRDs in several regions.[180] In contrast to investigations which often appeared to have been motivated by political rivalries, an NGO, the Concerned Forum of West Sumatra (*Forum Peduli Sumatra Barat*) headed by a local historian, Mestika Zed, and a law lecturer in the Andalas University, Saldi Isra, took the initiative in West Sumatra.[181] The 1999 regional autonomy law had given full authority to DPRDs to determine their own budgets, including salaries, allowances and other perquisites for members. When DPRDs began to award themselves salaries and other benefits far higher than those enjoyed even by the national DPR in Jakarta, the Home Affairs Department issued Government Regulation No. 110 in November 2000 (PP 110/2000) setting guidelines for DPRD expenditure.[182] This gave the Concerned Forum the opportunity to propose that prosecutions of DPRD members could be launched on the basis of the new regulation. Aware that its budget violated these guidelines by a large margin, the DPRD challenged the regulations in the Supreme Court which reasserted the principle that a government regulation could not contradict a law, in this case Law No. 22/1999 on Regional Government, which authorized the DPRD to determine its own budget (Article 19). After the customary long delay, the Supreme Court, on 11 September 2002, declared PP 110/2000 invalid and issued a decision to that effect on 27 December 2002. The window of opportunity for prosecution appeared to have been closed.[183]

By then, however, the presidential election was only a year-and-a-half away. It has been suggested that the PDI-P-led government saw PP 110/2000 as an opportunity to convince voters of its anti-corruption credentials or at least to hit its political rivals.[184] On 12 March 2003, the Minister of Home Affairs, Hari Sabarno, issued a radiogram stating that PP 110/2000 was still valid until it was replaced by another PP.[185] Meanwhile the members of the DPRD in West Sumatra were already being interrogated as suspects. In contrast to West Java, for example, where the president had delayed permission to interrogate the speaker of the DPRD who represented the PDI-P and one of the deputy speakers who represented the PPP, there was no delay in providing such permission in West Sumatra where the PDI-P had only two representatives in the fifty-five-strong DPRD. The prosecutors argued that PP 110/2000 could still be applied in this case because the offence occurred before the Supreme Court declared it invalid.[186] In May, forty-three members of the DPRD were found guilty and received sentences ranging from two years to two years and three months.[187] In December, the month when the newly elected President Yudhoyono launched his anti-corruption campaign, the majority of the convicted legislators lost their appeal before the provincial High Court which enhanced their sentences to between four and five years, later confirmed in part by the Supreme Court.[188] The Supreme Court's judgment, however, was controversial. Facing an unusually large number of appellants in the original case, the court had divided them into two batches which were considered by two separate judicial panels. The first batch, consisting of thirty-three members, had their sentences confirmed by their Supreme Court panel in August 2005, while the second batch of ten, although previously convicted of the same offence, were freed by the second panel two years later in October 2007. The court explained that they should not have been prosecuted because the Supreme Court had already invalidated PP 110/2000 at the time of their trial.[189]

From late 2003, numerous prosecutions were launched against members of district DPRDs, some leading to convictions but others failing. Having won convictions in the West Sumatra provincial case in May 2003, prosecutors quickly moved on to the Padang municipality (the capital of West Sumatra) and were successful in convicting thirteen civilian members of the DPRD who were each sentenced to four-year terms in prison.[190] By June 2004, a spokesman for the attorney general said that about 300 legislators were under investigation in thirty provinces.[191] The rapid increase in investigations coincided with the national election timetable in 2004 — elections to the legislatures on 5 April, the first round of the presidential election on 5 July and the second round on 20 September. Yudhoyono's victory led to a further intensification of prosecutions as part of his anti-corruption campaign. In early 2006, the new Minister of Home Affairs told the DPR that permission to investigate 1,437 members of DPRDs had been given since 2004.[192] In 2005 at least 135 members of DPRDs were convicted and another 38 in the first half of 2006.[193]

As the leader of a new party which had no representatives in the DPRDs before 2004, Yudhoyono was not encumbered by the defeated president's problem. Megawati's PDI-P had been the leading party in the 1999 election and her party's representatives were strongly represented among those vulnerable to corruption charges. In February 2005, the PDI-P even held a meeting of 120 legislators facing charges to discuss ways of defending them.[194] Adeksi, the association of municipal parliaments, formed a legal team to defend its members and also pleaded for leniency on the grounds that many members were not well-informed on the details of both legislation and regulations, particularly PP 110/2000, and just voted along with their colleagues to adopt the budget. Erry Riyana Hardjapamekas, a deputy chairman of the KPK, also believed that some, although by no means all, were unaware of the details of the regulations. "Some clearly don't know and are unable to understand the regulations, but others are deliberate", he said.[195]

There were also suggestions that part of the anti-corruption campaign may have been driven by corrupt prosecutors and police who continued to conduct investigations based on PP 110/2000 three years after its invalidation by the Supreme Court. The chairman of Adeksi asked why PP 110/2000 continued to be used while a PDI-P leader, Dwi Ria, stated bluntly that many of her party members had been subjected to extortion by "upholders of the law" (*penegak hukum*) in the regions.[196] She was referring to the practice in some regions of police and prosecutors presenting legislators with charges based on PP 110/2000 and offering to drop them in exchange for "compensation". Such threats were apparently credible partly because judges continued to hear cases based on PP 110/2000 despite its invalidation by the Supreme Court. In 2006, a DPR committee claimed that PP 110/2000 had been used in at least nine municipality cases.[197] The previous year, the Attorney General, Abdul Rahman Saleh, had ordered prosecutors not to use PP 110/2000 because many judges were dismissing such cases.[198] In 2006, however, Rahman seemed to admit that his instruction was not always heeded. "Is this due to ignorance or are they deliberately not heeding my instruction?" he asked.[199]

Corruption remained deeply entrenched in regional government but investigations and prosecutions had created an atmosphere that forced officials and legislators to at least "think twice". Given President Megawati's obvious reluctance to authorize investigations involving regional officials, it is hard to conclude that the prosecutions were part of a planned government assault on corruption, although officials of the Department of Home Affairs had drafted the government regulation on which many of the prosecutions were based. In West Sumatra, an anti-corruption NGO had taken the initiative to exploit a little understood government regulation to launch a case that eventually saw almost all members of the provincial DPRD sentenced to long periods of imprisonment. The West Sumatra case sparked a chain of prosecutions in other parts of Indonesia in which local NGOs, however, played no significant role. Most of these prosecutions, it seems, cannot be separated from the rivalries associated with the coming election in 2004 and led to trials of members of virtually all parties.[200] The pre-election momentum was taken up enthusiastically by the newly elected president, whose own new party had no seats in DPRDs elected in 1999. Not only were more DPRD cases prosecuted, but numerous bupatis and mayors, as well as several governors found themselves in court. However, virtually all convictions were appealed, many of them successfully, and it is not clear that many offenders actually went to prison.

CONCLUSION

As this chapter has shown, reform of the judicial system moved very slowly compared to the areas discussed in previous chapters. Following the fall of President Soeharto, the public mood, as expressed by demonstrations in the streets as well as discussions in the media and other public fora, wanted reform in all fields. Responding to a severe sense of national crisis, the MPR and DPR adopted major constitutional changes, passed laws on democratic elections and laid the foundations for decentralized regional government. But, despite the public mood being no less supportive of reform in the judicial field, particularly in relation to corruption, the same national crisis did not have a substantial impact on the courts in which corruption was deeply entrenched.

The initial judicial reforms were aimed at making the courts more independent of government intervention. These reforms revived a long-standing call by the judges themselves and were supported by public opinion. Thus, the "one-roof" reform was adopted that freed the courts from the administrative control of the Department of Justice, and the dominant role of the president in the selection of Supreme Court judges and the appointment of the Chief Justice was drastically reduced. The creation of the new Constitutional Court, following constitutional amendments, provided a further institutional check on political meddling in judicial matters. But these reforms remained limited and did not confront directly the single most debilitating legacy of the New Order system of justice — endemic corruption.

Corruption in the courts, however, only reflected the entrenched nature of corruption in all state institutions. During the early Reformasi period, dozens of political figures, bureaucrats and businesspeople found themselves targets of corruption investigations by the police or prosecutors but few were eventually brought to court and even fewer convicted. In the case of former President Soeharto, the investigations were not only ineffective but not even intended to succeed. The massive diversion of public funds in the BLBI scandal led to the jailing of only four bankers. In other cases, investigations were aimed at cornering political opponents or extorting money as part of deals to avoid prosecution. Under strong public pressure to "do something about corruption", successive governments established a series of anti-corruption bodies but showed little determination to ensure that they worked effectively. The timing of laws adopted during the Habibie presidency strongly suggested that they were motivated by electoral considerations with the result that the actual establishment of new bodies was long delayed. The TGPTPK formed by President Abdurrahman looked more promising but was soon invalidated by the Supreme Court. The KPK, envisaged in a Habibie law, was only formed towards the end of Megawati's tenure and the new corruption court did not begin to hear cases until after she had been replaced by President Yudhoyono.

The long gestation of the KPK, however, was not entirely in vain as it provided a mechanism that was activated to implement President Yudhoyono's anti-corruption campaign. Yudhoyono freely gave the permission needed for the investigation of officials suspected of corruption — permission that Megawati had always been reluctant to grant. The KPK, together with the temporary Tim Tastipikor that Yudhoyono had established while the KPK was getting off the ground, soon began a series of prosecutions that, although limited in number, obtained signficant high-profile convictions. Meanwhile the statistics on prosecutions launched under Yudhoyono were boosted when a separate dynamic originating during Megawati's presidency resulted in large numbers of regional legislators being tried and often convicted but rarely actually jailed. That the anti-corruption campaign was having an impact in the bureaucracy was indicated by fears raised by critics that it might have a negative impact on development. Due to the chronic under-funding of developmental and other projects, it had become normal practice for bureaucrats to raise additional funds by, for example, extracting kickbacks from contractors. Such additional funding was used both to finance projects and to reward the members of the project team. Indeed, civil servants argued that most projects could not be completed without resort to these practices.[201] Ministers were now even complaining that it was difficult to persuade civil servants to accept appointments as "project leaders" — positions that had been much sought in the past.

Yudhoyono was less ensnared in the web of patronage arrangements on which previous presidents had depended and had gained strong political legitimacy through his convincing victory in Indonesia's first direct presidential election. Nevertheless, he was by no means completely free of political obligations, including to his vice president, Jusuf Kalla, and those who had helped finance his election campaign with the result that accusations of selective prosecution were often heard.

Although Yudhoyono had obtained important successes in his anti-corruption campaign, the judiciary to a considerable extent remained riddled with corruption and the number of corruption convictions was limited. In contrast to the reforms discussed in earlier chapters where members of legislatures and a section of the military had not only recognized the dangers of rejecting crisis-ridden reform but even saw advantage for themselves in accepting it and shaping its agenda, much of the political, bureaucratic and commercial elite realized that they could personally become victims of a thorough purge of corruption. It was mainly private legal practitioners, reformist NGOs and parts of the press that pressed for reform while judges and prosecutors, with notable exceptions, showed little enthusiasm. The dominant parties in the DPR shared that lack of enthusiasm. Money politics was rife in the DPR and many of those eventually tried and sometimes convicted in corruption cases had affiliations of one sort or another with those parties. In contrast to the structural reforms in the constitutional, legislative and even military fields discussed in earlier chapters which provided both benefits as well as costs to established elites, the campaign against corruption opened the prospect of very adverse personal consequences for many members of the elite. Nevertheless, the convictions obtained by the KPK brought about a dramatic change in the atmosphere and provided a deterrent that had been largely absent in the past. Significant progress was therefore made under President Yudhoyono.

Notes

1. But the paper hoped that local pressures might lead to some reform in the regions. World Bank (2003*b*), p. 17. For an earlier pessimistic assessment, see Lindsey (2000).
2. Robison and Hadiz (2004), p. 60.

3. The integralist concept was based on harmony between the components of the state. Just as the father leads the family and the family members respect his wise leadership, so society must follow the nation's leaders. The courts therefore do not challenge the nation's leaders but support the implementation of their policies. For a sample of Soepomo's ideas, see Soepomo (1970).
4. Cited in Lubis (1999), p. 176, footnote 16.
5. The dissident former Supreme Court judge, Adi Andojo Soetjipto, noted that "Soeharto, who was by law not allowed to intervene, did so frequently, although this was not done openly". He "never summoned a judge to give instructions himself. Rather he used subordinates in the ministries and military command to approach judges." Adi Andojo Soetjipto (2000), pp. 270–71. For numerous examples of government interference in the courts, see Pompe (2005), ch. 4.
6. For detailed discussion of such cases in the 1990s, see Pompe (2005), ch. 4. See also Bourchier (1999), pp. 240–41, 245–47. Even a military judge, Maj. Gen. Djaelani, at the time of his retirement in 1996 "painted a devastating picture of malaise, mismanagement, nepotism and deeply ingrained corruption in the Supreme Court". Bourchier (1999), p. 239.
7. Pompe (2005), p. 475.
8. Similar demands had been made by judges in the late 1960s following the fall of Soekarno's Guided Democracy but had been blocked by the new Soeharto regime. Pompe (2005), ch. 3.
9. Decree No. X/MPR/1998 on Basic Principles of Development Reform and the Normalization of National Life as the National Will. Ch. II.C; Ch. III. C.2a.
10. Lubis (1999), pp. 174–75. Pompe explains that "The vast archipelago with its wide variety of living conditions made transfers a highly effective instrument for dispensing or withholding favors. This subjective transfer system rendered judges vulnerable to political pressures in their decision making." Thus, "From the 1970s onwards, the judicial administration was marked by a spectacular rise of patronage systems, heavily influenced by financial considerations". Pompe (2005), pp. 124–25.
11. According to Rifqi, there was "intensive lobbying" by the judiciary "including the holding of a meeting in a hotel that was attended by members of the House of Representatives, which ended with the legislators being presented with 'attendance money'." Rifqi (2007), p. 16.
12. *Koran Tempo*, 9 December 2003; Rifqi (2007), pp. 13–14.
13. *Kompas*, 22 July 2000; *Kompas*, 5 September 2000.
14. Before 2000, almost all Supreme Court judges were "career" judges who had joined the judicial service as young law graduates and worked their way up through the system. The exceptions were military lawyers and the non-career chief justices, appointed by Soeharto (all but one with military backgrounds). On recruitment, see Pompe (2005), pp. 343–71.

15. In 1995 the Administrative Law Court (PTUN) ruled that the Minister of Information had exceeded his powers by effectively banning the popular weekly magazine, *Tempo*. See Millie (1999), ch. 19.
16. *Kompas*, 17 January 2001.
17. According to one newspaper report in 2004, "the questions were like weapons without bullets". *Kompas*, 16 June 2004.
18. Third Amendment of the 1945 Constitution, Clause 24A(4) and 24B.
19. Law No. 22/2004 on the Judicial Commission.
20. Third Amendment of the 1945 Constitution, Clause 24B.
21. *Kompas*, 9 June 2005.
22. Rifqi (2007), pp. 18–20; Butt (2007), p. 184.
23. Decree No. III/MPR/2000 on the Source of Law and the Precedence of Legislation, 5(1); Law No. 14/1985, on the Supreme Court, Clause 31.
24. According to Rifqi, "local governments also provide the courts within their regions with funding and other facilities as a result of the lack of funding provided by the state and the poor conditions (including pay) under which members of the judiciary are forced to work." Rifqi (2007), p. 29.
25. The last chief justice appointed by Soeharto, Air Marshal Sarwata, was openly accused in 2000 of using his son as a broker for clients involved in Supreme Court appeals. See "Sindikat 'Alap-Alap' Bertoga", *Tempo*, 27 March 2000.
26. However, as Adi Andojo pointed out, convictions for corruption were not uncommon during the New Order although they never involved politically important people. Interview with Adi Andojo Soetjipto, Jakarta, 13 September 2005.
27. It needs to be noted, however, that low "basic" salaries were often supplemented by substantial allowances.
28. Pompe (2005), p. 414.
29. For example, four judges were caught by the "Upholding Order Operation" (*Operasi Tertib*) in 1981. Two were convicted and imprisoned. Wasingatu Zakiyah et al. (2002), p. 4.
30. Fabiola Desy Unidjaja (2000).
31. Wasingatu Zakiyah et al. (2002), pp. 133–40. Indonesia Corruption Watch is an NGO that was founded during the month after Soeharto's fall. The survey was conducted in 2001 in Jakarta, Medan, Surabaya, Yogyakarta, Samarinda and Makassar.
32. Wasingatu Zakiyah et al. (2002), p. 108.
33. Wasingatu Zakiyah et al. (2002), ch. 4.
34. Muninggir Sri Saraswati (2002*a*); (2002*b*); (2002*c*). During this period the exchange rate fluctuated between Rp 7,000 and Rp 11,000 for the U.S. dollar.
35. Although Golkar was opposed to mentioning Soeharto by name in the decree, other parties reflected the public mood and even inserted "Soeharto's wealth" in the prospective decree's title. Eventually Golkar achieved a compromise whereby

Soeharto was not named in the title but only in the text of the decree. Interview with former Golkar Chairman, Akbar Tandjung, Jakarta, 19 April 2006.

36. Wiranto (2003), pp. 63–64. Apart from Soeharto himself, several members of his family were very vulnerable to corruption investigations, especially three of his six children — daughter, Siti Hardiyanti Rukmana (Mbak Tutut), and sons, Bambang Trihatmodjo and Hutomo Mandala Putra (Tommy) — all of whom had amassed huge fortunes from the favours that their father had bestowed on them. Another very vulnerable member of the family was Soeharto's half-brother, Probosutedjo.

37. Soeharto's unofficial legal advisor, Yohannes Yacob, later warned that "We need to point out that the probe (if) taken to court will also drag down government officials, ex-officials and all the cronies (who) are also suspected of improper gains through corruption, collusion and nepotism". *Van Zorge Report* I.5. 12 December 1999. See also O'Rourke (2002), p. 191.

38. As Speaker of the DPR on behalf of the DPR leadership Harmoko had publicly urged President Soeharto to resign a few days before 21 May 1998.

39. *Tempo*, 20 March 2000.

40. The leaked conversation was published in the Muslim magazine, *Panji Masyarakat*, in its issue of 24 February 1999.

41. Ghalib claimed that the tycoons, Prayogo Pangestu and The Nin King, had not made donations to him personally but to the Indonesian Wrestling Association of which he was chairman. An apparently outraged Ghalib reported the violation of bank secrecy to the police. *Kompas*, 15 June 1999. Ghalib later became a member of the DPR representing the Muslim PPP.

42. *Kompas*, 12 October 1999.

43. *Kompas*, 11 December 1999; *Kompas*, 2 March 2000. See also interview in Der Spiegel reported in *Sydney Morning Herald*, 23 January 2000.

44. In his usual casual style, President Abdurrahman, then travelling in Latin America, shifted the blame by claiming that he had asked the acting chief justice "to look for judges who are clean, strict and can't be bought" — implying that they had been bribed in the Soeharto case. *Jakarta Post*, 30 September 2000.

45. A bomb exploded in the Atrium shopping mall the day after Tommy was named as a "suspect". Three days after Bambang's interrogation a bomb exploded in a department store. The charging of Tommy was followed a fortnight later by another bomb in a shopping mall and his appearance in court was accompanied by yet another explosion. See O'Rourke (2002), pp. 233–34.

46. *Suara Merdeka*, 15 October 1999; *Tempo*, 18 October 1999.

47. *Kompas*, 27 September 2000. Beddu Awang was later sentenced to four years in prison.

48. *Kompas*, 18 October 2000.

49. *Jakarta Post*, 27 June 2002. As a witness in the trial of Abdullah Sidiq, Tommy said the amount of Rp 15 billion was agreed with Dodi Sumadi and Nur Iskandar. The money was handed over in the form of cash. Rp 5 billion was

intended for the judges and prosecutors, Rp 5 billion for a foundation headed by Abdurrahman's wife, and Rp 5 billion for Abdullah Sidiq, a *kyai* close to Abdurrahman. *Koran Tempo*, 17 February 2004.

50. The official entrusted with the responsibility to arrest Tommy was the head of the South Jakarta office of the attorney-general's department, Antasari Azhar, who was later elected as head of the KPK in 2007.

51. The Jakarta police chief, Inspector-General Sofyan Jacoeb, even claimed that Tommy was cooperating with the GAM separatist movement. *Koran Tempo*, 7 August 2001.

52. The Supreme Court panel, was chaired by the Deputy Chief Justice, M. Taufiq. The new evidence, that had somehow been overlooked in the original trial, was that Tommy, although owning 80 per cent of the shares in Goro and holding the position of principal commissioner of the company during the early stage of the negotiations, did not take part in day-to-day management and therefore could not be held responsible. *Kompas*, 2 October 2002; *Jakarta Post*, 2 October 2002. The implication was that the willingness of Bulog's head, Beddu Awang, to enter a highly disadvantageous deal had nothing to do with Tommy being the president's son.

53. During his trial, Tommy claimed that he had in fact spent a lot of time in his own home. He was able to do that because of "coordination with the police". *Kompas*, 27 June 2002. For doubts about the role of prominent police officers, see *Tempo*, 3 December 2001; "Pertanyaan yang Mengepung Empat Perwira Tinggi", *Tempo*, 29 July 2002.

54. *Kompas*, 27 July 2002. The sentence was reduced to ten years on the grounds that, according to the Supreme Court, avoiding arrest could not be considered as a crime. *Kompas*, 25 June 2005.

55. Tommy's case was treated with much scepticism by the public. A newspaper commented: "From the beginning the chain of events in the Tommy case was very strange. Full of coincidences that lead to doubts. Beginning with his secret meeting with Gus Dur, then the processing of the review of his case after his appeal for clemency was rejected. How could he escape so easily when the prosecutors came to arrest him? Then suddenly arrested one day before the retirement of the Chief of the National Police." *Koran Tempo*, 1 July 2002.

56. *Kompas*, 23 April 2003.

57. Wasingatu Zakiyah et al. (2002), p. 94.

58. Sharma (2001), p. 87. For an insightful picture of business conditions during the late New Order, see O'Rourke (2002), ch. 2–4.

59. As the governor of the Bank of Indonesia later noted, "It was ironic that a step designed to restore confidence resulted in the collapse of confidence and plunged the banking sector into chaos." Soedradjad (1999), p. 148. Three of the banks were closely associated with the Soeharto family — Bank Andromeda (partly owned by Bambang Trihatmojo and the tycoon Prajogo Pangestu), Bank Jakarta (owned by Probosutedjo) and Bank Industri (in which two of

Soeharto's daughters were shareholders). The president's good faith in closing these banks was immediately questioned by his son's transfer of all the assets of Bank Andromeda to another bank, Bank Alpha, which simply carried on Bank Andromeda's business under a new name.

60. Enoch et al. (2003), pp. 77–78; Soedradjad (2004), p. 70.
61. Sharma (2001), p. 106.
62. McLeod (2004), p. 103.
63. Soedradjad 2001), p. 68.
64. Although BLBI assistance was overtly intended to help banks remain viable and thus protect depositors' funds, in fact it was channelled to other purposes. Among such payments, the BPK report listed repayment of subordinate loans, undocumented repayments, payments to affiliates, purchase of monetary instruments (*surat berharga*), illegal payments to third parties, trading in derivatives, financing of placements, increasing credit, financing of general bank overhead and additional investment such as opening new branches, recruiting new staff, launching new products and replacing systems. The report noted that these activities could lead to suspicion of criminal violations.
65. The then governor of the BI, Soedradjad Djiwandono, later argued that BLBI had been necessary to prevent a total collapse of the banking system and the economy. While admitting that rules had been breached, he quoted a parliamentary report that argued that "Since this policy was intended to address the crisis it was not based on rules and regulations that apply under normal conditions". Soedradjad (2004), p. 72.
66. Badan Pemeriksa Keuangan (2000). *Siaran Pers BPK-RI tentang Hasil Audit Investigasi atas Penyaluran dan Penggunaan BLBI*. Jakarta, 4 August 2000.
67. The Master Settlement and Acquisition Agreement (MSAA) allowed debtors to settle their debts by surrendering to IBRA assets equivalent in value to the debt. In the case of debtors whose assets could not cover their debts, the Master Refinancing and Note Issuance Agreement (MFNIA) allowed them to cover the difference with personal guarantees. Smaller debtors were required to sign an Acknowledgement of Debt (*Akta Pengakuan Utang*, AKU).
68. *Kompas*, 10 August 2000. In August 2000 Kwik Kian Gie, the Coordinating Minister for Economic, Financial and Industrial Affairs, estimated that the assets of Rp 52.6 trillion pledged by the Salim Group in its MSAA had fallen in value to only Rp 20 trillion. Kwik also claimed that the Salim Group was trying surreptitiously to buy back its old properties at a cheap price.
69. *Koran Tempo*, 15 January 2002.
70. *Kompas*, 15 January 2002; *Tempo*, 4 March 2002. The then head of IBRA, I Putut Gede Ary Suta, pointed out that IBRA had already taken 2,400 cases to court but had lost most of the "hundred or so" (*seratusan*) already decided.
71. *Instruksi Presiden Republik Indonesia Nomor 8 Tahun 2002*, 30 December 2002.
72. For example, the repayments of Liem Sioe Liong's Salim Group, now represented

37 per cent. The performance of the Salim Group, however, was much better than those of the other four signatories of MSAAs — Syamsul Nursalim, Bob Hasan, Ibrahim Risjad (a close associate of Liem Sioe Liong) and Sudwikatmono (Soeharto's cousin) — but they too were freed from their debts and the prospect of criminal charges. Abdul Rahman Saleh (2008), p. 322. By October 2004, twenty-one "cooperative" big debtors had received their "release and discharge" while nine were classified as "uncooperative". *Koran Tempo*, 27 October 2004.

73. *Koran Tempo*, 9 January 2004.
74. The five were Hendra Rahardja (Tan Tjoe Hing), the owner of Bank Harapan Sentosa, and his son and daughter-in-law; and Bambang Sutrisno and Adrian Kiki Ariawan, both of Bank Surya. An attempt to extradite Hendra Rahardja from Australia failed when he died of cancer. Bambang Sutrisno, a business partner of Soeharto's cousin, Sudwikatmono, also claimed to be ill and was living in Singapore which had no extradition treaty with Indonesia.
75. The Supreme Court is located at Medan Merdeka Utara in the centre of Jakarta and the Attorney General's Office is in Jakarta's satellite town of Kebayoran Baru. As *Tempo* noted, "Even in the worst traffic jam in Jakarta, it does not make sense for a letter from Medan Merdeka Utara to take more than a month to reach Kebayoran Baru". *Tempo*, 21 July 2003.
76. *Kompas*, 15 July 2003; *Koran Tempo*, 18 July 2003; *Tempo*, 21 July 2003.
77. *Jakarta Post*, 25 June 2004.
78. Abdul Rahman Saleh (2008), p. 490.
79. *Koran Tempo*, 23, 30 July 2004.
80. *Kompas*, 14 January 2004.
81. In 2000, Hasan was convicted of defrauding the Department of Forestry and sentenced to two years' imprisonment which, surprisingly, the judge ordered him to serve in his own home. In the midst of public criticism, the prosecutor appealed to the Jakarta High Court which increased the sentence to six years and ordered that it be served in prison. At this point the new reforming Minister of Justice and Human Rights, Baharuddin Lopa, intervened and ordered that Hasan be moved from Jakarta to the old Dutch prison island of Nusakambangan — Indonesia's Alcatraz. There he was joined by Tommy Soeharto and together they financed the refurbishing of their living quarters in the prison and also funded sporting facilities and television for the other prisoners. *Tempo*, 25 August 2003. Meanwhile Baharuddin Lopa died suddenly during a visit to Saudi Arabia.
82. *Koran Tempo*, 23 June 2003; *Kompas*, 14 January 2004.
83. *Kompas*, 5 August 1999. The future minister in the Abdurrahman and Megawati governments, Kwik Kian Gie, asked "why did Rudy Ramli feel it necessary to use the services of PT EGP if it was his right to collect the debt from the government, and the regulations are very clear? And why was he willing to pay such a huge fee?" *Kompas*, 9 August 1999.

84. *Kompas*, 5, 6 August 1999.

85. O'Rourke (2002), p. 289.

86. *Jakarta Post*, 24 February 2000.

87. See *Jakarta Post*, 2 May 2000; *Asian Wall Street Journal*, 12 April 2000; *Jakarta Post*, 1 August 2000; *Kompas*, 29 August 2000; 29 June 2001.

88. *Koran Tempo*, 11 July 2001.

89. *Koran Tempo*, 31 July 2001.

90. *"Catatan Harian Lengkap Syahril Sabirin"*, *Kompas*, 14 June 2000.

91. *Kompas*, 14 March 2002.

92. The third man was Pande Lubis, the deputy head of IBRA who approved the release of the funds to Bank Bali. He was initially acquitted but eventually jailed for four years by the Supreme Court. Thus, the man who facilitated the release of the funds was convicted while those who benefited remained free. A separate case against Rudy Ramli and three Bank Bali directors was launched under the Habibie administration but all were quickly acquitted after the change in government. *Kompas*, 2 December 1999.

93. *Kompas*, 30 March 2002. An investigation by a DPR commission claimed that in the years 1994–99, Rp 2,007 trillion of "non-budgetary funds" from Bulog had been distributed. During this period the exchange rate for the US dollar ranged from about Rp 2,500 to Rp 800.

94. *Tempo*, 15 October 2001.

95. The process that led to President Abdurrahman's dismissal began with his attempts to get access to funds linked to Bulog.

96. *Tempo*, 5 November 2001.

97. *Tempo*, 21 February 2002.

98. *Kompas*, 8 May 2002.

99. *Koran Tempo*, 1 September 2002.

100. *Kompas*, 13 February 2004; *Tempo*, 16 February 2004. The dissenting judge was Abdul Rahman Saleh who concluded that Akbar had failed to prevent state losses. See Abdul Rahman (2008), pp. 36–69.

101. Following Golkar's expulsion of several leaders who had supported Susilo Bambang Yudhoyono in the presidential election, one of the dissidents, Anton Lesiangi, claimed that Dadang and Winfried had each been paid substantial sums to accept their sentences without implicating Akbar. *Koran Tempo*, 23 September 2004.

102. *Koran Tempo*, 6 April 2002; *Kompas*, 26 December 2002.

103. *Kompas*, 24 April 2002; *Koran Tempo*, 27 April 2002.

104. *Koran Tempo*, 6 August 2005. Rahardi was shocked by the discrepancy between the court's judgment in his case and in the Akbar Tandjung case.

105. *Tempo*, 1 September 2003.

106. *Koran Tempo*, 30 November 2004.

107. When questioned on this in the DPR in 2003, the deputy attorney general explained that there was no legal requirement to make such an announcement.

The head of information in the Attorney General's Office had a different explanation. We "were not yet ready from the point of view of administration". *Kompas*, 9 September 2005.

108. Emerson Yuntho (2004).

109. *Tempo*, 1 November 2004. The Ginanjar case was later reactivated but not prosecuted due to the expiry of time limitations in 2008.

110. Details of Manimutu Sinivasan's links with Soeharto and his business empire are provided in O'Rourke (2002), pp. 55–59.

111. The following day, the president added that the trials of the three businessmen would still go ahead although they would first be postponed. Akbar Tandjung, the Speaker of the DPR, said that the suspicion was unavoidable that the president was mobilizing funds for the 2004 election. *Kompas*, 20 October 2000.

112. MPR Decree No. XI/1998 on State Officials who are Clean and Free of Corruption, Collusion and Nepotism.

113. Law No. 28/1999 on State Officials who are Clean and Free of Corruption, Collusion and Nepotism.

114. Law No. 31/1999 on the Elimination of Corruption.

115. Romli Atmasasmita (2002), p. 10.

116. *Peraturan Pemerintah Nomor 19 Tahun 2000 tentang Tim Gabungan Pemberantasan Tindak Pidana Korupsi Presiden Republik Indonesia.*

117. According to Adi Andojo, some of the resistance came from within the team itself. Interview with Adi Andojo Soetjipto, Jakarta, 13 September 2005.

118. *Jakarta Post*, 24 April 2001.

119. *Kompas*, 23 August 2001. For example, Yahya Harahap's case was rejected by the judge on the ground that because the 1971 law on corruption had been replaced by the 1999 law, charges of corruption committed in 1998 could not be tried.

120. *Koran Tempo*, 25 October 2001.

121. *Kompas*, 23, 25 August 2001.

122. *Koran Tempo*, 5 February 2003; *Jakarta Post*, 24 April 2002. Indonesia Corruption Watch described Fauzatulo as only a "small fish" while the major players "were not touched". Wasingatu Zakiyah et al. (2002), p. 221.

123. *Kompas*, 2 April 2001.

124. *Kompas*, 6 April 2001.

125. *Kompas*, 12 January 2001.

126. Some respondents complained that the questionnaire was too complex and time-consuming for busy officials to complete quickly.

127. Sherlock (2002), p. 376.

128. *Koran Tempo*, 21 November 2003; *Kompas*, 15 March 2004. On the attorney general's house, see *Jakarta Post*, 4 December 2002.

129. Law No. 30/2002 on the Commission to Eradicate Corruption, 27 January 2003.

130. *Koran Tempo*, 17 December 2003.

131. They were Amien Sunaryadi, an accountant who had worked with the Body to Supervise Finance and Development (*Badan Pengawasan Keuangan dan Pembangunan*, BPKP), Sjahruddin Rasul, an auditor from the Department of Finance, Tumpak Hatorangan Panggabean from the Attorney General's Office, and Erry Riyana Hardjapamekas, the Principal Director of the state tin corporation, PT Timah from 1994 to 2002, who was also a recipient of the Bung Hatta Anti-Corruption Award. *Tempo*, 22 December 2003. The Bung Hatta award, in memory of Indonesia's first Vice President, was provided annually by a group of prominent citizens.

132. Professor Andi Hamzah wryly commented: "It should be judges without experience in handling corruption cases. The ones who usually handle corruption cases are usually also experienced in taking bribes." *Koran Tempo*, 24 December 2003.

133. *Tempo*, 28 June 2004. During the interviews, one candidate admitted to having never heard of a "dissenting opinion" while an academic candidate with a doctorate could not distinguish between "material offences" and "formal offences". *Kompas*, 20 June 2004.

134. *Koran Tempo*, 20 January 2005. They were, however, provided with simple accommodation and cars.

135. *Tempo*, 6 December 2004.

136. *Instruksi President Republik Indonesia No. 5 Tahun 2004 tentang Percepatan Pemberantasan Korupsi*, 9 December 2004.

137. Of ten presidential and vice-presidential candidates in 2004, the personal wealth of Yudhoyono (Rp 4.6 billion or US$563,000) was far below that of the other two retired military officers, presidential candidate Wiranto (Rp 46.2 billion or US$7.1 million) and vice-presidenntial candidate Agum Gumelar (Rp 8.8 billion). Yudhoyono's wealth was also far below that of the incumbent president, Megawati (Rp 58.9 billion or US$9.2 million) and her vice president, Hamzah Haz (Rp 17.3 billion). The only candidate less wealthy that Yudhoyono was Amien Rais (Rp 868 million or US$133,000). However, Yudhoyono's running mate, Jusuf Kalla, was the wealthiest of them all (Rp 123 billion). These figures were released by the KPK.

138. In December 2005, the president replaced Bakrie with the respected technocrat, Dr Boediono, and shifted him to the less vital post of Coordinating Minister for People's Welfare. Bakrie had been an unsuccessful candidate for Golkar's presidential nomination in 2004.

139. *Tempo*, 6 December 2004.

140. *Jakarta Post*, 26 February 2005.

141. *Kompas*, 28 July 2005.

142. *Kompas*, 11 May 2005.

143. In the case of regional heads and their deputies, presidential approval was deemed in the 2004 law to have been given if not received within sixty days. Law No. 32/2004 on Regional Government, Clause 36. In the case of members

of legislatures, the 1999 legislation required investigators of legislators to obtain the written approval of the president in the cases of members of the MPR and DPR; the Minister of Home Affairs in the cases of members of provincial DPRDs; and the governor in the cases of members of district DPRDs. Law No. 4/1999 on the Composition and Position of MPR, DPR and DPRD, Article 43. The 2003 revisions of that law contained similar provisions but specifically excluded investigations of corruption and terrorism as well as cases where a member is caught in the act of committing a crime. Such cases, however, must be reported to the relevant official so that permission can be obtained within forty-eight hours. Law No. 22/2003 on the Composition and Position of the MPR, DPR, DPD and DPRD, Article 106.

144. *Jakarta Post*, 4 August 2005.
145. *Kompas*, 2 January 2007.
146. *Kompas*, 28 February 2006; *Jakarta Post*, 28 May 2007; *Komisi Pemberantasan Korupsi* (2007), section 4.9; *Komisi Pemberantasan Korupsi* (2008), p. 48.
147. *Kompas*, 20 December 2005.
148. On Abdullah Puteh's government, see Isa Sulaiman and van Klinken (2007).
149. See Chapter 3 above.
150. The trial of the four former deputy governor's illustrated the president's determination to avoid allegations of favouritism. Among the four was Aulia Pohan who is indirectly related to Yudhoyono. The "*besan*" relationship is between parents whose children have married. Yudhoyono's son is married to Aulia's daughter.
151. *Keputusan President Republik Indonesia Nomor 11 Tahun 2005 tentang Tim Koordinasi Pemberantasan Tindak Pidana Korupsi.*
152. See Abdul Rahman Saleh (2008), pp. 122–35.
153. The judge in the South Jakarta district court, Herman Allositandi, was eventually sentenced to 4.5 years. *Kompas*, 22 June, 22 September 2006.
154. *Jakarta Post*, 18 June 2007 (Topo Santoso and Edi Suhardi of Partnership for Governance Reform in Indonesia).
155. *Kompas*, 20 June 2007.
156. Data from State Secretariat website.
157. *Tempo*, 23 June, 8 September 2008.
158. *Kompas*, 24 September 2005.
159. *Kompas*, 1 October 2005.
160. *Tempo*, 2 January 2006. One of the judges suffered a stroke at this time. His wife admitted to having five telephone conversations with Harini in August. *Kompas*, 14 December 2005.
161. *Kompas*, 28, 29 October 2005.
162. *Koran Tempo*, 6, 30 November 2005.
163. The chairman of the panel of judges was soon promoted to chairman of the Central Java High Court.
164. *Koran Tempo*, 16 September 2005; *Kompas*, 8 November 2005.

165. *Kompas*, 5 December 2005.

166. *Kompas*, 26 October 2005.

167. *Kompas*, 20, 23 December 2005.

168. *Constitutional Court: Putusan Nomor* 995/PUU-IV/2006.

169. *Kompas*, 8 March 2006; *Koran Tempo*, 29 May 2006; Butt (2007), p. 186.

170. *Kompas*, 5 January 2006.

171. *Jakarta Post*, 1 February 2006

172. *Koran Tempo*, 1 February 2006.

173. *Kompas*, 14 March 2006.

174. *Constitutional Court: Putusan Nomor* 995/PUU-IV/2006, 23 August 2006. See also Butt (2007), pp. 188–92. The reputation of the Judicial Commission suffered a further blow the following year when one of its seven members, who had been carefully selected after a "fit-and-proper" test by the DPR, was arrested in a case involving the purchase of land for the Commission's new building. The commissioner, Irawady Joenoes, was sentenced to eight years' imprisonment in 2008. *Koran Tempo*, 15 March 2008.

175. The judgment is contained in *Constitutional Court: Putusan No.* 012-016-019/ PUU-IV/2006. *Jakarta Post*, 11 January 2007.

176. Several governors appointed by Soeharto were investigated and two, the governor of Bali, Ida Bagus Oka, and the governor of Riau, Lt. Gen. (ret.) Soeripto, were eventually put on trial although ultimately exonerated, while investigation of the case against the governor of Central Java, Lt. Gen. Soewardi, continued until 2003 when it was formally dropped. *Kompas*, 5 November 2002, 16 January, 9 April 2004.

177. *Jakarta Post*, 15 February 2006.

178. *Kompas*, 11 November 2005.

179. Indonesia Corruption Watch (2006*a*). *"Pengadilan Masih Milik Koruptor"*; *"Pengadilan masih jauh dari Harapan"*. In the absence of official figures, ICW compiled lists of cases from newspaper reports.

180. For example, in West Java, all 100 members of the provincial DPRD received Rp 250 million (US$25,000) each from the provincial budget to purchase land for houses (*kaveling*). *Jakarta Post*, 22 July 2002; *Koran Tempo*, 8 July 2003; in this case, prosecutions were delayed by more than a year due again to the failure of the Minister of Home Affairs to permit their questioning and only began after President Yudhoyono replaced Megawati. *Kompas*, 26 August 2005.

181. See Davidson (2007), p. 81.

182. *Peraturan Pemerintah Nomor 110 Tahun 2000 tentang Kedudukan Keuangan Dewan Perwakilan Rakyat Daerah.*

183. Abdul Rahman Saleh (2008), pp. 305–06.

184. According to Davidson, "This high-profile success can be attributed largely to the politically motivated intervention of Hari Sabarno, the Interior Minister under the then President Megawati. Their party, the Indonesian Democratic Party of Struggle (PDI-P) saw the brewing scandal as an opportunity to take a

swipe at rival parties in a decidedly non-PDI-P bailiwick". Davidson (2007), p. 77. Retired General Hari Sabarno was not in fact a PDI-P official.

185. *Media Indonesia*, 21 March 2003. Interview with Gen. Hari Sabarno, Jakarta, 23 August 2006.
186. *Tempo*, 12 January 2004.
187. *Tempo*, 18, 24 May 2004. Of the original 55 members, 2 had died, 1 was ill and 3 became witnesses. The TNI members were to be tried separately.
188. *Kompas*, 27 December 2004; *Koran Tempo*, 29 September 2005.
189. *Kompas*, 23 October 2007. Even former attorney general, Abdul Rahman Saleh, had difficulty in understanding this outcome. "I don't understand why there are such differences between decisions." Abdul Rahman Saleh (2008), p. 318.
190. *Koran Tempo*, 15 June 2005. Eventually the number grew to forty but all won their appeals to the Supreme Court. *Tempo*, 10 August 2008.
191. *Jakarta Post*, 17 June 2004.
192. *Kompas*, 31 March 2006.
193. Calculated from Indonesia Corruption Watch (2006b). "*Daftar Kasus Korupsi Mantan dan Anggota DPRD yang telah Divonis Pengadilan Selama Tahun 2005–Semester I 2006*". Most of these cases, however, were still under appeal. It is not clear how many had actually been imprisoned. No information was available about the outcome of investigations of members of the TNI who were involved in seventeen cases and handed over to the military justice system.
194. *Kompas*, 16 February 2005.
195. *Kompas*, 5 February 2005.
196. *Kompas*, 11 December 2004; *Koran Tempo*, 16 February 2005.
197. Among these cases were those in Depok, Batam, Kendari, Manado, Bandung, Cirebon, Surakarta and Payakumbuh. *Kompas*, 31 March 2006.
198. *Koran Tempo*, 30 March 2006.
199. *Kompas*, 30 March 2006.
200. Referring to West Kalimantan, Davidson says that "the trials that did result but which produced no convictions were better explained by the fallout of local political struggles between rival factions within the executive and between the executive and the legislature". Davidson (2007), p. 77.
201. Deddy Supriady Bratakusumah of the National Administration Institute (*Lembaga Administrasi Negara*) explained that project leaders were obliged to find "tactical funds to meet unexpected needs". Among such "needs" were the unofficial requirement to contribute to regional officials ("menyetor ke pejabat daerah") and to make payments to speed up bureaucratic processes ("*melicinkan proyek*"). *Kompas*, 19 June 2006.

7

RESOLVING COMMUNAL
VIOLENCE IN MALUKU

The collapse of the New Order lifted the lid on simmering communal tensions in many regions of Indonesia. During the New Order violent conflicts between local ethnic and religious communities had broken out from time to time, but from 1998 to the early 2000s the extent and intensity of violence increased sharply.[1] Rioting in cities and towns caused many casualties and damage to property but usually lasted no more than a few days. In several regions, however, conflicts took the form of one-sided massacres while in others they were more akin to civil war. By the early 2000s, the number of lives lost in these conflicts had exceeded ten thousand and well over a million refugees had been forced to flee their homes to which many never returned. In East Timor, Aceh and Papua, the weakening of central authority provided the opportunity for the resurgence of existing separatist movements, one of which is discussed in the case study of the Aceh conflict in Chapter 8. In West and Central Kalimantan, Poso and Maluku, communal conflict intensified to a level that was beyond the capacity of the state to contain, as will be illustrated by the case of Maluku in this chapter.[2] These regions — whether afflicted by separatist or communal conflict — were overwhelmed by crises in which the state ceased to function effectively. If they had been independent countries, they would have been classified as "failed states" but in fact, of course, they — except East Timor — remained part of the Republic of Indonesia.[3] As we will see in the cases of both Aceh and Maluku, these regional conflicts had local origins but were also linked to political rivalries at the national level.

Maluku had been perceived as a peaceful region in which relations between Muslims and Christians were relatively harmonious. A complex combination of disparate factors, however, contributed to the breakdown of order in Maluku after the fall of the New Order regime. Demographic change had upset the balance between the two religious communities, the holding of free elections exacerbated uncertainty about the new constellation of power, national politics under Soeharto had encouraged increased Muslim assertiveness, divided religious loyalties immobilized local security forces, and radical Muslim groups outside Maluku sent militia forces to fight alongside their co-religionists. As the conflict in Maluku spread, the early Reformasi national governments were preoccupied with the economic crisis, growing separatist forces in East Timor, Aceh and Papua, and ever-present political challenges in Jakarta with the result that they seemed powerless to intervene in Maluku.

As serious as conditions might have been for the people of Maluku, the local crisis in this tiny and distant province was not of the same order as the national crises that had made imperative the "crisis-ridden" reforms discussed in earlier chapters. Successive governments in Jakarta had never given high priority to Maluku. It was only after a semi-stalemate had been reached on the ground that initiatives taken by national ministers gave momentum to a peace process that was already being explored by local moderates on both sides in Maluku. While Jakarta's apparent incapacity and indifference had allowed the conflict to grow, in the end it was Jakarta's intervention that proved crucial in restoring order. This chapter traces the unfolding of the Maluku crisis from its beginnings in a quarrel between a minibus driver and a passenger, through its spread and intensification, the tardy initial intervention of the national government, the eventual government-sponsored peace conference and a decisive change in local military command that led to the restoration of normalcy. Although the Maluku violence had its origins in Maluku itself, external forces of one sort or another played roles that both aggravated and eventually facilitated the restoration of order.

BACKGROUND

Writers on the Maluku conflict are divided between those who see the outbreak of the conflict on 19 January 1999 as the outcome of an accumulation of reinforcing social and political developments and those who believe that the conflict was deliberately instigated by elite interests to serve their own political ends. The first group saw the root cause of the post-1999 violence in the colonial legacy of Christian Ambonese dominance in local government being challenged by the growth of the Muslim community due to the influx of Muslim migrants. These communal tensions were aggravated by President

Soeharto's favourable approach to political Islam in the 1990s and, following his fall, the holding of free elections in mid-1999.[4] The alternative view focuses on the hidden manoeuvres of national or regional elites to provoke violence that could then be exploited to the political benefit of these elites.[5]

The changing population balance between the Christian and Muslim communities had fundamental implications for the distribution of political power in the new democratic context. Ambon, as part of the Spice Islands, had been the focus of early Dutch economic interest, accompanied by missionary activity leading to conversions to Christianity. It was from the Christian community that the Dutch colonial rulers recruited lower-level civil servants as well as soldiers for the colonial army. Even after independence, the Ambonese Christian elite continued to dominate the provincial civil service while Muslims were predominant in menial occupations. The city of Ambon was informally segregated between well-to-do Christian suburbs and poor Muslim areas. Although Christians — overwhelmingly Protestant — formed the largest community in the city, the island of Ambon was more evenly divided, while the islands of north Maluku were predominantly Muslim.

The ethnic and religious composition of the province, however, underwent steady change especially from the 1970s with the influx of "spontaneous" Muslim migrants from the southern part of Sulawesi in search of work and other economic opportunities. The Muslim proportion of the province's population had grown from 49.9 per cent in 1971 to 59 per cent in 1997. Of the population of 2.1 million in 1997 (before the province's bifurcation into Maluku and North Maluku in 1999), Protestants made up 34.3 per cent and Catholics 5.2 per cent. The Sulawesi migrants — Butonese, Bugis and Makassarese, the so-called BBM — need to be distinguished from "official" government-sponsored transmigrants, mainly from Java and Bali, who were settled on newly opened agricultural land. Between 1969 and 1999 the total number of official transmigrants was 97,422, only about 5 per cent of the provincial population. In contrast to the agricultural settlers from Java and Bali, "spontaneous" migrants tended to seek urban economic opportunities, especially in Ambon city, where the BBM ethnic groups were estimated to make up between a quarter and a third of the population by the late 1990s. In 1997, however, Christians still made up a clear majority in Ambon city where 51.92 per cent of the population was Protestant, 5.55 per cent Catholic and 42.38 per cent Muslim, in a total population of 312,000.[6]

The growing Muslim population, especially in the provincial capital, was seen as a challenge by the Christian elite. As in many other parts of Indonesia, enterprising migrants quickly gained a strong position in local markets, small-scale trade and public transportation, although larger enterprises usually remained in the hands of the tiny Chinese minority. As Indonesia's economy grew during the New Order era, many BBM migrants prospered and their children, together with those of indigenous Ambonese Muslims, took advantage of expanding educational opportunities. Although Maluku's main university, Pattimura University, was still a largely Christian institution and some 90 per cent of the employees of the Ambon city government were Christian,[7] Muslims with educational qualifications — both Ambonese and migrant — were increasingly recruited into the regional bureaucracy. As one Catholic priest put it, Muslims were "increasingly wearing coats and ties".[8]

The political consequences of social change accelerated in the 1990s due to developments at the national level. President Soeharto, increasingly concerned by signs of disaffection within some sections of the military, turned to the Muslim community for additional political support. In 1990, he endorsed the formation of the Indonesian Muslim Intellectuals' Association (*Ikatan Cendekiawan Muslimin Indonesia*: ICMI) headed by his protégé, B. J. Habibie, as a focus for the aspirations of the growing well-educated Muslim middle class. One of ICMI's goals was to achieve "proportionality" for Muslims in the bureaucracy, whereby the proportion of Muslims in senior government positions would roughly reflect their proportion in the community as a whole. During the New Order period before 1992, Maluku had never had a Muslim Ambonese governor,[9] but in that year Akib Latuconsina, the provincial head of ICMI and a professor of economics at Pattimura University, won the position. In 1997, Akib Latuconsina was succeeded by a distant relative, Saleh Latuconsina. Both Latuconsinas were prominent in Golkar while their main rival for the governorship in both 1992 and 1997 was Freddy Latumahina, a Christian Golkar leader. Both Muslim governors set about implementing the ICMI goal of increasing Muslim representation in the bureaucracy. Their policies were naturally disturbing for the Christian community whose fears were sometimes exacerbated by rumours of impending new pro-Muslim measures.[10]

Social tensions in the late 1990s had been aggravated by the economic collapse in 1997. Although the financial crisis had actually benefited some agricultural-exporting areas in the Outer Islands, its impact had been severe in Ambon city. The city's gross domestic regional product in constant prices had fallen from Rp 861,610 billion in 1997 to Rp 562,064 billion in 1999 leading to a sharp increase in unemployment.[11] Antagonism between Christian Ambonese and Muslim BBM had long been brewing and, combined with a high level of youth unemployment, often led to fights between youth gangs.[12] During the two months before the outbreak of massive violence on 19 January 1999, several clashes between Muslim and Christian villages took place in areas close to Ambon — especially involving Muslim migrants and Ambonese Christians. Far from Ambon, eight people were killed in several days of fighting that broke out on 14 January at Dobo, on the Aru islands of Southeast Maluku.[13]

These growing social, economic and political tensions were seen by some observers, however, as providing opportunities for threatened political forces to pursue their own interests by provoking wider conflict. A common perception among Muslims puts the blame for the violence on Christian leaders in Maluku who were feeling increasingly threatened by the strengthening political position of Muslims during the 1990s.[14] In this view, Christian politicians were particularly concerned about the likely outcome of the forthcoming June 1999 general elections, particularly in Ambon where the number of Muslim voters had increased substantially. It was therefore surmised that Christian politicians had instigated the violence with the intention of forcing migrant Muslim voters from South Sulawesi to flee from Ambon before the general election and thus reduce support for Muslim parties opposed to the PDI-P which, in Ambon, was the party of the Protestant community. It was further claimed that remnants of the largely Christian Republic of South Maluku (RMS) independence movement, which had been crushed half a century earlier in 1950, had also joined in the rioting.[15] Many Muslims believed that a series of minor clashes between Christians and BBM migrants in late 1998 in the Muslim villages of Wailete and Bak Air, across Ambon Bay from Ambon city, did not arise from the usual personal or inter-village disputes but were deliberate attacks by Christians and intended to provoke communal conflict. The violence in Southeast Maluku after 14 January, according to the conspiracy theory, was intended to draw security forces away from Ambon before the big clash on 19 January.[16] For many Muslims, the result of the election in June 1999 confirmed the theory. The PDI-P won 53 per cent of the votes in Ambon city, well ahead of the previously dominant Golkar with 19 per cent and the main Muslim party, PPP, with 14 per cent.

A quite different theory identifies "dark forces" from the displaced New Order regime in Jakarta as the conspirators behind the upheaval in Maluku. Former President Soeharto and members of his family were alleged to have financed "provocations", not only in Maluku but also in other parts of the country with the intention of undermining the new democracy. Elements within the military, keen to "teach the country a lesson" by showing what happens when the military is removed from power, were seen as playing a central role.[17]

The main evidence suggesting that the Maluku conflict was instigated by disaffected groups in Jakarta was the deportation of several hundred Ambonese gangsters from Jakarta following a gang fight in Ketapang, a district only a few hundred metres from the presidential palace in Jakarta. According to this account, Muslim Ambonese gang members were among the *Pam Swakarsa* mobilized by the military to support President Habibie at the Special Session of the MPR in November 1998. Four of the Ambonese were killed by an anti-Habibie mob. This led to the Ketapang clash on 22 November where Christian Ambonese guards at an illegal gambling casino fought with Muslim gangsters, resulting in fourteen deaths. At this point, the Jakarta government, headed by its governor, retired Lt. Gen. Sutiyoso, intervened and transported both Muslim and Christian gangsters back to Ambon where they resumed their fighting. Sutiyoso's expulsion of the Ambonese may have been motivated simply by the desire to preserve order in Jakarta, but others have suggested that military elements used the opportunity to spark the "religious" conflict in Ambon.[18]

Although the importance of social and political change in Ambon during the previous three decades in explaining the beginning of the conflict is accepted by all commentators, there is no consensus on the extent to which the conflict was spontaneous or manipulated. And among those who believe that it was manipulated, there is disagreement about who did the manipulating. The conspiracy theories cannot be dismissed out of hand although they suffer from a lack of hard supporting evidence. Once the conflict had begun, however, a more persuasive case could be mounted that some elements in the political elite — whether national or provincial — had both the motivation and capacity to keep it going.

THE BEGINNING OF THE CONFLICT

On the afternoon of 19 January 1999 — the date of Lebaran marking the end of *Ramadhan*, the Muslim fasting month — a quarrel between a Christian minibus driver and a Muslim Bugis youth at a bus terminal triggered fighting that quickly spread throughout Ambon city and then to other parts of the island of Ambon and beyond. It was not clear who started the conflict but soon both Muslims and Christians found themselves under attack. The initial fighting involved Christian Ambonese and Muslim BBM youths but its ethnic character became religious especially when mosques and churches began to be destroyed.[19] Although many Ambonese Muslims had shared some of the resentment felt by Ambonese Christians towards the BBM migrants, the battle lines were quickly drawn on the basis of religious affiliation. By February, clashes were taking place on the nearby islands of Haruku, Seram and Saparua and nearly two hundred people had been killed.[20]

The level of violence declined sharply during the next few months and the June general election was held peacefully. Although the Christian-based PDI-P was victorious in Ambon city, Muslims were well represented in the new provincial DPRD. In late July, however, fresh riots broke out in Ambon and other islands which continued intermittently during the rest of the year. Meanwhile, fighting started independently in North Maluku in August. The North Maluku fighting had a quite different dynamic and arose from a complicated local conflict between a Muslim ethnic group and a largely Christian indigenous community over the formation of a new sub-district in an area where a gold mine had been established. This fed into rivalry for the governorship of the recently formed province of North Maluku between the sultan of Ternate and candidates from Tidore. It was only later that the fighting took on the religious dimensions of the Ambon conflict.[21] By mid-December, official figures revealed that 775 people had been killed and 1,108 seriously wounded in the two provinces, while 8,665 homes, 115 churches and mosques and 942 shops had been destroyed.[22] The next few week then saw a sudden escalation in the ferocity of the conflict in both Ambon and North Maluku. During the three weeks after 26 December the number of deaths at least doubled and the number of recorded refugees reached 275,000, of whom as many as 100,000 migrants had fled back to South and Southeast Sulawesi.[23]

THE GOVERNMENT'S WEAK RESPONSE AND THE POOR PERFORMANCE OF THE MILITARY

Meanwhile the national government's attention was by no means focused on the two Maluku provinces whose combined population amounted to about 1 per cent of the nation as a whole. The Habibie government was under constant challenge as it prepared to face the June 1999 election with the economy in massive decline and growing popular discontent. From the perspective of Jakarta, rising violence in East Timor, Aceh and Papua was higher on its list of priorities than in places such as Maluku, West Kalimantan or Poso. Following his election as president, Abdurrahman Wahid assigned responsibility for Maluku to Vice President Megawati but her involvement was perhaps symbolized by the shopping trip she made to Hong Kong during the last week of December when violence in Maluku was reaching its peak. Both the president and vice president made a brief visit to Ambon on 12 December where Abdurrahman dismayed local leaders by telling them that "The government can only encourage a settlement" and that they should resolve the problem themselves.[24]

The government's capacity to curb the spreading violence in Maluku was limited by the availability of security forces. Despite the crisis, the number of military and police (*Brimob*) troops in Maluku in March 1999, following the arrival of limited reinforcements, was only 5,300.[25] By November the number had risen slightly to 6,000.[26] The major reason why more troops could not be sent to Maluku was that East Timor was seen at that time as the nation's greatest regional challenge. At least 18,000 security personnel were deployed in East Timor during 1999 in the lead-up to the referendum on 30 August and reserves were not available for other duties. It was only after the humiliating withdrawal from East Timor in September that preparations could be made to deploy these troops elsewhere. By January 2000, the number of battalions had increased to 15 or about 11,250 men,[27] and by June 19 (17 army and 2 Brimob) with a total strength of about 14,000.[28] The build-up of forces from Kostrad and other regional commands, however, was too late. If reserves had been available in January 1999 it might have been possible to nip the fighting in the bud, but by the end of the year the "war" had become entrenched.

The problem, however, was not just the number of troops but what came to be called "contamination". The core security forces in the region were three local army battalions, the so-called "organic" territorial troops forming part of the regional military command, and the local police. But being largely recruited from the region, they were divided between Muslims and Christians. It is difficult to obtain a breakdown of religious affiliation within the security forces but it was commonly estimated that the local army troops were more or less evenly divided between Muslims and Christians while about 70 per cent of the police were Christian. As professional security forces, they were expected to deal even-handedly with rioters but as the conflict progressed this became more difficult. Many soldiers and police lived with their families in communities that had come under attack. When security personnel returned to their homes and found houses burnt down and family members or neighbours dead or wounded, it became impossible to maintain their professional discipline. Early in the conflict in March 1999, the military Commander-in-Chief, General Wiranto, told cabinet that "some individual soldiers from the region were apparently influenced by the conflict and supported one side because of family connections".[29] Later, Maj. Gen. Suaidi Marasabessy, a Muslim Ambonese who had headed a team of Ambonese officers sent to Maluku to oversee operations, stated bluntly that some military personnel had joined the conflict because family members had been killed.[30]

Troops were deployed in small squads to areas of potential conflict where they were stationed between Christian and Muslim villages. Their presence was intended to deter or prevent attacks and both Muslim and Christian marauders were sometimes arrested. From the beginning, however, there were many reports of military units failing to take action to protect threatened communities.[31] Sometimes this may have been because soldiers or police were from the same religious community as the mob doing the attacking. Occasionally officers defended the reluctance of troops to engage in action by claiming that in the new democratic era soldiers feared that they might be accused of human rights abuse if firm action resulted in deaths. The commander of the Pattimura army regional command, Brig. Gen. Max Tamaela, said that his troops feared that "legal charges may be brought against them in the future if they open fire on mobs".[32] Later, after the Laskar Jihad had reached Maluku, the provincial police chief, Colonel I Dewa Astika, pointed out that sometimes "rioters outnumber the troops and are armed with standard military weapons".[33] A dozen or so soldiers would be reluctant to intervene in an assault launched by a large band of well-armed assailants. Another explanation was suggested by a Muslim member of the DPR who had heard of cases where under-paid and under-supplied troops had requested money before they would protect a village or housing area from attack.[34]

Increasingly reports indicated deeper active involvement of soldiers and police. Muslim troops were often deployed to protect Muslim villages and Christian troops to protect Christian villages. This increased the risk that troops would no longer stand between the two hostile communities but take up the cause of one of them. Thus when Christian gangs attacked a Muslim village they were often confronted by Muslim troops while Muslim militias faced Christian troops. Troops naturally identified with the villagers they defended and were often given food, drink and cigarettes by them. Sometimes soldiers or police would even participate in revenge attacks on "enemy" villages. Aware of this, Brig. Gen. Tamaela claimed that military units were deliberately mixed and were regularly rotated so that they did not become too close to the villagers they were protecting in order to avoid "contamination".[35] However, in practice a degree of such "contamination" could not be avoided.

The military leadership in Jakarta was concerned about the "contamination" problem among local troops. As early as March, Maj. Gen. Suaidi said that local troops would be returned to their barracks and that outside troops would take over operations.[36] But as the conflict expanded it seems that "organic" troops continued to be used. In December 1999, when it became possible to deploy outside troops in larger numbers, the TNI Commander-in-Chief, Admiral Widodo, reiterated that "it would be better if local troops are not directly involved in handling clashes".[37] However, it seemed that outside troops, too, were not immune from "contamination", especially when the level of fighting escalated after the arrival of the Laskar Jihad in May 2000.

There is also evidence that military and police personnel supplied combatants with arms and ammunition. According to Maj. Gen. Suaidi, combatants in the first five months of the conflict had used home-made firearms and "traditional" weapons such as machetes, spears and knives, but by the second half of 1999 standard military weapons were becoming more common.[38] In February 2000, the national chief of police, Gen. Rusdihardjo, estimated that 80 per cent of bullets used in the conflict originated from the security forces.[39] In many cases military personnel sympathized with the struggle of their co-religionists and helped them with weapons and bullets. However, such sympathy was not the only motive. It was reported that soldiers and police sometimes rented out weapons and sold bullets to combatants. Even weapons were sometimes sold. As discussed in Chapter 5, military and police personnel were extremely poorly paid and were expected to supplement their meagre official incomes by other means in the field. In Maluku during the early stage of the conflict, ordinary soldiers received daily allowances of around Rp 7,000–10,000 (about US$1) which was barely sufficient for daily needs. As one member of the national DPR claimed, "The ammunition and guns are sold by soldiers who need money to live".[40]

The poor performance of the military in Maluku was frankly acknowledged by the army chief of staff, Gen. Tyasno Sudarto, who apologized for the failure of his troops to stop the fighting. He admitted that "the TNI itself does not have the capacity and is not trained to face (communal) conflict and to disperse (religious militias). Frankly, until now we don't have this capacity and at this moment are still learning".[41] This did not mean, however, that troops never intervened to prevent attacks or to arrest offenders. Following the deployment of additional forces from outside Maluku the level of violence declined considerably after the upsurge in December 1999 and January 2000.

THE LASKAR JIHAD AND THE CIVIL EMERGENCY

The last week of 1999 had seen a sudden escalation of the conflict in both Ambon and in North Maluku. In one of the worst incidents, following the influx of thousands of Christian refugees from other parts of North Maluku, Christian militias had attacked several Muslim villages near Tobelo city on the island of Halmahera, North Maluku. At least six hundred people were killed and thousands forced to flee.[42] Reports of the massacre in Jakarta, particularly in the ICMI newspaper, *Republika*, inflamed Muslim emotions throughout Indonesia and led to a mass rally on 7 January 2000 in the *Lapangan Merdeka*

(Merdeka Square) in central Jakarta addressed by Muslim leaders, including Amien Rais, the recently elected chairman of the MPR, Hamzah Haz, the leader of the Muslim PPP and Ahmad Sumargono of the radical Islamic group, KISDI. Following the rally, various Muslim organizations pledged to send members to Maluku to carry out *jihad* in defence of the beleaguered Muslim community. The most prominent of these groups was the Laskar Jihad, the militia wing of a Salafi Islamist organization, *Forum Komunikas Ahlus Sunnah wal-Jama'ah*, that had been formed in Yogyakarta the previous year.[43] In accordance with Salafi practice, the Forum had first obtained the approval of six leading Salafi *ulama* in Saudi Arabia and Yemen.[44]

Led by Ja'far Umar Thalib, aged in his late thirties and a veteran of the Afghanistan resistance to the Soviet Union, several thousand youths received rudimentary military-style training at a camp set up outside Bogor, an hour's drive from Jakarta. The training was conducted, according to one of the organization's leaders, by members of the military "in their private capacity, not on behalf of the institution".[45] After several hundred sword-wielding, white-robed trainees had descended on the presidential palace in Jakarta on 6 April, the government ordered the closure of the camp. Despite President Abdurrahman's oral instruction that they not be permitted to go to Maluku, about three thousand fighters made their way unimpeded to Surabaya where they boarded ships that took them to Ambon at the end of April. Neither the military nor the police in Surabaya took any measures to prevent their departure. Noorhaidi Hasan describes the Laskar Jihad members being welcomed by military officers at Ambon's port and supplied with standard military weapons.[46] Nevertheless, the Acting Coordinating Minister for Political and Security Affairs, Lt. Gen. (ret.) Surjadi Surdirdja, claimed that "Actually, the government has done everything to prevent them from entering the area of conflict, through containment by the police and military as well as through surveillance by the communication ministry".[47] Later the dismayed Defence Minister, Juwono Sudarsono, complained about "a container loaded with firearms entering the area. They (i.e. the military) did nothing about it, they let it enter".[48]

There can be little doubt that the entry of the Laskar Jihad to Maluku was facilitated by elements within the military. It is impossible that several hundreds, let alone thousands, of Laskar Jihad members could gather near Bogor for military-style training without at least the tacit permission of the military. Nor could they have then made their way across Java to Surabaya and then embark for Maluku if the military and police had wished to prevent them. And who arranged for a container of arms to be waiting for them on their arrival in Ambon? Military and police officers said that they had no grounds for intervening because Indonesian citizens are free to travel anywhere in the country and the Laskar Jihad members did not carry arms. In Maluku, the governor and the regional military commander expressed the opposite view. The governor said "I am really disappointed with and concerned about the way they entered Maluku, despite an order from the President to deny them entry. They should have been banned from embarking for this province."[49] The regional military commander, Brig. Gen. Max Tamaela, asked "Why didn't the officials at Tanjung Perak Port (in Surabaya) stop them ... and what happened to the other military commanders?"[50]

Why did military officers allow the Laskar Jihad to go to Maluku? First, like much of the Muslim community, many Muslim officers were genuinely outraged by the casualties suffered by Muslims in Maluku at the hands of Christian gangs and the inability of the military to protect them. For these officers, the dispatch of the Laskar Jihad would help the military to protect the Muslim community.[51] Second, there was concern that an attempt to prevent the Laskar Jihad from leaving Java could lead to a clash that would further destabilize an already vulnerable political situation. One of the Laskar Jihad leaders, Ayip Syafruddin Soeratman, had warned that "If we cannot go, then we will conduct our jihad on Java ... We will attack Christians who are most responsible for what is happening in Ambon".[52] And third, although military officers in general had no ideological sympathy for fundamentalist Islamic movements, military intelligence officers had a record of using Muslim radicals in pursuit of other political purposes. The apparent military backing for the Laskar Jihad, therefore, was consistent with the view that the intensification of the Maluku conflict was intended to serve the military's aspiration to regain some of its lost influence. At that time, the mood in the military was strongly opposed to the president's steps to hold negotiations with the Free Aceh Movement and his friendly overtures to advocates of independence in Papua. More specifically, the Laskar Jihad had emerged less than a month after President Abdurrahman's dismissal of General Wiranto from his cabinet after an Indonesian commission of enquiry held him responsible for military behaviour in East Timor.[53] The exacerbation of the conflict in Maluku could therefore both undermine the president's credibility and underline the need to restore some of the military's previous powers. It was also seen by some as serving the Soeharto family's interest in discrediting the new government. The apparent cooperation between Kostrad troops in Maluku with the Laskar Jihad supported this hypothesis as Lt. Gen. Djadja Suparman, who had been Kostrad commander until replaced by the president at the end of March, was a Wiranto ally.[54] It is, however, far from clear whether these strategies were formulated by a discontented military clique or represented the policy of the military institution itself.

By the middle of May, the level of violence was escalating sharply in Ambon as Laskar Jihad fighters joined local Muslim militias in launching attacks on Christian targets. Even more serious were reports indicating that soldiers from army battalions, both local and those brought in from outside, were giving open support to the Muslim fighters.[55] Increasingly the police were seen as siding with the Christians while army units were favouring the Muslims. The rising conflict culminated on 21 June in an attack on the police Brimob headquarters and armoury in which the Brimob deputy commander was killed. Local sources claimed that the attack involved personnel from Kostrad and Maluku-based battalions. Without army support it is hard to believe that the Laskar Jihad forces with their minimal training could have overcome police resistance.[56] As a result of the attack on the armoury, 800 rifles and thousands of bullets fell into the hands of the combatants while cooperation between the army and the police effectively ended. The chaotic situation was exacerbated by an increase in military and police deserters, often called *Pasukan Siluman* (Invisible Forces). Numbering in their dozens, they included both Christian and Muslim Ambonese, many of whom had lost family members during the fighting. Mainly NCOs rather than officers, they often provided leadership to local youths engaged in the fighting.[57]

On the Christian side, the combatants were largely drawn from youth gangs that often had a background in criminal activities.[58] The main Christian gang leader in the early part of the conflict was Agus Wattimena, a man aged in his fifties, who called his force *Laskar Kristus*, and seems to have had good links with the Protestant church.[59] In December 2000, a Christian group headed by a physician, Alex Manuputy, proclaimed the formation of the Maluku Sovereignty Front (*Front Kedaulatan Maluku*: FKM) to revive the RMS goal of independence for Maluku. The FKM never became a large mass movement but it looked to Wattimena to provide some grassroots support.[60] Wattimena, however, was challenged by a younger rival, Berthy Loupatty, whose gang was known as *Coker*, originally from *Cowok Keren* (slang term meaning "Handsome Boys") but later turned into *Cowok Keristen* (Christian boys). In March 2001, Wattimena was murdered in unexplained circumstances in his home, leaving Berthy as the pre-eminent gang leader in the Christian sector.[61]

President Abdurrahman, like President Habibie, had resisted calls to declare an emergency in Maluku, presumably to block avenues for the reassertion of military power. But by the end of June 2000, the death toll throughout

Maluku had risen to about 3,000 and the local government had lost control as army and police forces confronted each other.[62] In these circumstances, on 26 June the national government declared the introduction of a "civil emergency", the lowest of three levels of emergency provided under the 1959 State of Emergency Law. In contrast to a "military emergency", under which power was vested in the military commander, the governors of Maluku and North Maluku headed separate civil emergency administrations in the two provinces. The introduction of the emergency, however, had no immediate impact in Ambon where fighting continued as before. The two sides had seemed to have been relatively evenly matched until the entry of the Laskar Jihad undoubtedly tipped the balance in favour of the Muslim side.

Despite government orders under its emergency powers to expel the Laskar Jihad, prevent the entry of outsiders into Maluku and close the Laskar Jihad's radio station, the Laskar Jihad continued its campaign with the backing of army troops. Christian residential areas close to the Pattimura University were occupied and the university virtually destroyed on 4 July. Widespread fighting continued during July in Ambon city and other areas. Between Laskar Jihad's arrival in May 2000 and February 2001, eight Christian villages on Ambon island were occupied by Muslim forces,[63] although two Muslim and one mixed village were taken over by Christians.[64] Nevertheless the intensity of the fighting declined during the latter part of 2000. In October, the head of an investigating team from the Indonesian National Commission on Human Rights said that mass conflicts involving thousands were no longer taking place although people were still being killed in inter-village clashes.[65] In March 2001, the TNI spokesman noted that by then "there were only minor, sporadic conflicts in the island and the situation has been relatively calm over the last couple of months due to fast and effective movement of crack troops".[66]

THE NEW MILITARY STRATEGY

In January 2000, the TNI Commander-in-Chief, Admiral Widodo had stressed that "One of the keys to the successful prevention of the conflict is the neutrality of our personnel in the sense of impartiality in their actions. In the past there have been individuals who, due to family ties, place of residence and other factors, have been involved in the conflict. This is true of both sides in some of the areas of conflict."[67] Following the introduction of the civil emergency, a new regional military commander, Brig. Gen. I Made Yasa, and a new regional chief of police, Brig. Gen. Firman Gani, were appointed. Yasa, who had served as a Korem commander in Maluku in the late 1980s, had the advantage of being a Balinese Hindu and therefore, it was hoped, would not be identified with either the Muslim or Christian side. Both gave high priority to the removal of "contaminated" troops. Shortly after his appointment, convinced that his forces were unreliable, Yasa ordered the precipitate withdrawal of troops guarding several Christian residential areas which were then immediately subjected to Muslim attack, including the sacking of Pattimura University.[68] Despite this setback, Yasa continued his "decontamination" strategy by rotating two battalions (about 1,400 men) out of Maluku while his police counterpart eventually transferred 600 police personnel.[69] The division in the police force was so severe that Christian police were concentrated in the provincial police headquarters while Muslims were placed in the Ambon city headquarters.[70] A major problem, however, was the desertion of a substantial number of soldiers and police who had either joined militias or taken their families out of the province. In August, Firman Gani admitted that 10 per cent of his force was missing. "I don't know their location, whether they have deserted or joined the rioters", he said.[71]

To deal with the high level of "contamination", the military adopted a new approach. A Joint Battalion (*Batalyon Gabungan* — Yon Gab) was formed consisting of 450 personnel drawn from the elite forces of the three military services — the army's Kopassus, the navy's Marines and the air force's Paskhas. The Yon Gab arrived in Maluku on 9 August 2000. In contrast to the previous practice of dispersing forces in small units which tended to side with communities where they were placed, the Yon Gab was kept together as a centralized unit insulated from the community.[72] Its role, according to Yasa, was to "function as a tactical command unit and only to be used in certain emergency situations".[73] The original Yon Gab stayed in Maluku until May 2001 while an additional battalion was in Maluku from November 2000 to August 2001.[74]

The Yon Gab arrived in Maluku at a time when the Muslim side, backed up by the Laskar Jihad, was on the offensive, which meant that its operations were primarily directed against Muslims and it quickly acquired a reputation among Muslims as being anti-Muslim. This reputation was enhanced by two incidents in January and June 2001.[75] In the January incident, Yon Gab troops carried out a "sweeping" operation in a Muslim part of Ambon city in which several Muslims were killed and others arrested and, as was the custom with elite forces, physically beaten. In a follow-up "sweep", a fire-fight broke out early in the morning which led to the capture of fourteen Muslim men in a hotel who turned out to be police officers and a lone military officer. They were apparently engaged in drug trafficking. The captured officers were badly beaten by the Yon Gab men. Not only did this incident aggravate the Yon Gab's relations with the Muslim community but it dealt another heavy blow to police-military cooperation.

In the second incident in June, Yon Gab troops directly confronted the Laskar Jihad near its headquarters in the Ambon district of Kebon Cengkeh. The Yon Gab was conducting a "sweeping" operation in the area when it clashed with Laskar Jihad forces and one of its soldiers was killed. The Yon Gab troops then attacked a building used by the Laskar Jihad as a medical centre and a radio station. Versions of exactly what happened are inconsistent but the outcome was that twenty-three Muslims were killed. Allegedly, a dozen Laskar Jihad members were put onto a military truck and executed on the way back to the Yon Gab's base.[76] Commenting on the clash, the TNI spokesman pointed out that "The Yon Gab consists of Kopassus, the Marines and Paskhas which are highly trained for combat. The battle was therefore unequal. We were more expert and better armed so there were casualties."[77] In response, the Laskar Jihad leader, Ja'far Umar Thalib, issued a statement declaring that it was obligatory for Muslims to kill I Made Yasa.[78]

Yasa, who had initially been criticized by Christians, now received much praise in the Christian community but he was reviled by Muslims. Muslims claimed that ever since his arrival in Maluku he had made little effort to establish personal contact with Muslim leaders and had rarely ventured into the Muslim sector of Ambon city. The brutality of his troops in dealing with their Laskar Jihad captives threatened to turn Muslims against the military not only in Ambon but in other parts of Indonesia as well.[79] In dealing with the "contamination" problem, Yasa had thus created a new problem by alienating much of the Muslim population. The national government, aware that a long-term settlement could not be achieved without the participation of the Muslim community, now concluded that the presence of the Yon Gab had become an obstacle to future progress. Four days after the Kebon Cengkeh clash, I Made Yasa's name appeared on a national list of 111 officers to be moved to new positions in what was described as a "routine" transfer and the next month the Yon Gab was disbanded.

The presence of the Yon Gab under Yasa, despite its brutality, had been accompanied by a marked decline in communal violence. Open clashes between Muslim and Christian forces were not taking place, the Laskar Jihad was no longer mobilizing Muslim villagers to launch attacks on Christian neighbours and, after the June clash, Ambon experienced a period of relative calm. It appeared that the Laskar Jihad was re-assessing its strategy following its losses at the hands of the Yon Gab and was reluctant to risk another open confrontation.

THE MALINO PEACE AGREEMENT

By the end of 2001 fighting had long ended in North Maluku partly because minorities had fled to areas where their community was the majority. Ambon, too, had experienced several months of calm, despite the outbreak of isolated bomb explosions and shootings during the last two months of the year. Although Ambon remained divided between Christian and Muslim sectors, Christians and Muslims were visiting street markets in several narrow "neutral" zones and both Christian and Muslim students were attending classes at the Pattimura University's temporary campus and at a few high schools in "neutral" areas. The conflict had reached a stalemate that was increasingly seen as providing a window of opportunity to search for a more permanent solution.

During 2000, the national government made several attempts to encourage dialogue between the communities but little progress was made.[80] On one occasion, the National Human Rights Commission sponsored a course on mediation in Bali with thirty participants from each side, but tensions between them led to the course being conducted separately for the two groups at different hotels.[81] As fighting continued in Maluku, the atmosphere was hardly conducive even for talks outside the region. By late 2001, however, as the fighting was subsiding, the governor, Saleh Latuconsina, encouraged informal contacts between "moderates" in the two communities and in late November he sponsored a series of secret meetings held late at night at his home.[82] In order to preserve secrecy, the four participants on each side even walked home separately in the dark after the meetings. The Muslim participants said it would have been dangerous for the Muslims if their participation had been known by the Muslim hardliners.[83]

The tentative moves in Maluku were reinforced by international developments following Al Qaeda's attacks on Washington and New York in September 2001 and pressure from the United States for governments in Muslim countries to crack down on Islamic militants. Articles soon began to appear in leading Western newspapers linking Laskar Jihad to Osama bin Laden (although in fact there was no such linkage).[84] Faced with increased international pressure, the Indonesian government was encouraged to intervene more seriously in Maluku.

In late December, Jusuf Kalla, the Coordinating Minister for People's Welfare, and Susilo Bambang Yudhoyono, the Coordinating Minister for Political and Security Affairs in the national government, mediated an agreement between warring Muslims and Christians in Poso, Central Sulawesi. This prompted the Maluku governor and the moderates to suggest to Kalla that he embark on a similar mission in Maluku. The governor held separate meetings with leaders of both sides and Kalla and Yudhoyono visited Maluku for further discussions in late January. This led to a joint meeting on 11–12 February 2002 in Malino, South Sulawesi, attended by thirty-five participants from each camp, including several referred to as "field commanders" who had been physically involved in the fighting. The preparatory meetings on the Muslim side had been attended by both moderates and radical hardliners but several of the radicals later withdrew, including representatives of the Laskar Jihad and their Maluku allies such as Ustaz Muhammad Attamimi, a lecturer at the Islamic College (*Sekolah Tinggi Agama Islam Negeri*: STAIN) who led the Promote Good and Reject Evil taskforce (*Satgas Amar Ma"ruf Nahi Munkar*) and Husni Putuhena of the Maluku Defenders of Islam Front.[85] Attamimi regarded the delegation which had been selected by the governor as unrepresentative.[86] It appears that the dissidents were particularly unhappy with the appointment of the moderate Thamrin Ely, the leader of PAN in the provincial DPRD, as the team's leader.

Jusuf Kalla, assisted by Farid Husain and Hamid Awaluddin, played the major mediating role at Malino.[87] Kalla's approach was informal and pragmatic, and apparently included offers of financial incentives. He later said that he had asked both sides whether they preferred peace or wanted to continue the fighting. If they had chosen the latter, he told them that he was ready to supply them with weapons so that they could finish the conflict more quickly.[88] On the first day of the meeting, the mediators met the two teams separately in preparation for the second day when they faced each other in the same room. In the end an eleven-point peace agreement was accepted by both sides. While the Christian side, led by Tonny Pariela, a sociology lecturer at Pattimura University, gave top priority to ending the fighting as a pre-condition for further progress, the Muslims, led by Thamrin Ely, insisted that justice was a pre-condition to peace and demanded a full investigation into how the conflict had started in January 1999.[89] The Muslim side called for the prosecution of Christian leaders whom they accused of starting the conflict and rejected terms such as "reconciliation" and "peace". They also demanded a statement rejecting separatism, specifically mentioning the RMS which had become a kind of Muslim code for "the Christian side", while the Christians denied that they supported RMS or separatism.[90] For their part, the Christians demanded the expulsion of the Laskar Jihad, while the Muslims defended the right of all citizens to live and work in Maluku.

The final agreement called for the ending of "all forms of conflict" and the upholding of the supremacy of law. A crucial clause declared that "All forms of organizations, community squads (*satuan kelompok*) or armed bands (*laskar*) without permission in Maluku are banned and must surrender their arms or be disarmed and face the law. Those from outside who cause trouble in Maluku must leave Maluku". At the same time, the statement accepted the right of all citizens to live in Maluku "while observing local custom". Another key clause called for an independent national investigation of "the 19 January 1999 incident", the FKM, the "Christian RMS", the Laskar Jihad, the Laskar Kristus and forced religious conversion. Other clauses called for the rejection of the RMS and separatism, the return of refugees to their home areas, government support for rebuilding the economic infrastructure and social facilities and the observation of the law in the practice of religion "without compulsion". The statement also hoped for "unity and firmness" from the security forces. Finally, a special paragraph supported the rehabilitation of the Pattimura University on the basis of "common progress" with recruitment and other policies determined transparently and with justice.[91] The government's willingness to provide financial support for reconstruction may have been an important consideration for both sides.

The agreement, however, was quite ambiguous in some of its key provisions. The Christians had hoped that the Laskar Jihad would be expelled from Maluku, but the agreement only called for the banning of "armed bands" and the expulsion of those "who cause trouble" without identifying the Laskar Jihad by name. On the Muslim side, the promised investigation of the causes of the conflict was established but its findings were never made public. The report was eventually presented to President Megawati but it was feared that its publication could provoke renewed conflict.[92] One of the most important contributions of the Malino meeting was simply that it had indeed been held and allowed personal contacts to develop between the adversaries. In the new atmosphere, the failure of the government to ensure the full implementation of some of the key points of the agreement did not lead to its breakdown.

While the agreement received widespread support from the Christian community — despite reservations about the reference to the "Christian RMS" with its suggestion that Christians supported separatism — a section of the Muslim community, led by a group calling itself the "Team of Eleven", refused to accept it.[93] Some among them had participated in the preliminary meetings in Ambon, but had not been invited to the final conference because of their hostile attitudes. Their approach was expressed by Djamu Tuani, the secretary of the Maluku Indonesian Ulamas' Council (*Majelis Ulama Indonesia*: MUI), who declared that the conflict could be resolved with just one word, "Forgive". "The Christians", he asserted, "must confess that the

19 January 1999 tragedy was begun by them".[94] This statement reiterated a deeply felt conviction on the Muslim side that was naturally rejected by the Christians.

News of the agreement was warmly received in Ambon, although a small group of Muslim protesters threw stones at the Muslim delegation as they were driven into the city. On 27 February, a mass rally was held by Muslims at the Al Fatah mosque to welcome the peace and on the following day they marched into the Christian sector where they were enthusiastically welcomed. Muslims and Christians began to cross the informal boundaries between the sectors, public transport returned to old routes that served both Christian and Muslim areas, and it became possible to travel by road to the airport.[95] The euphoria that followed the agreement, however, was soon interrupted by a series of incidents. On 2 March, a motorcycle convoy of Muslim and Christian youths was pelted with stones near the Al Fatah mosque and police were called on to protect Christians who were visiting Ambon's main shopping mall on the Muslim side of the city.[96] Although the Malino agreement was followed by a marked downturn in violence, clashes continued on a reduced scale.

KOPASSUS AND SPORADIC VIOLENCE

Brig. Gen. I Made Yasa and the Yon Gab had become so unpopular with Muslims after the June 2001 clash with the Laskar Jihad that the military leadership in Jakarta decided that a change in direction was needed. Yasa was suddenly replaced by Brig. Gen. Mustopo, a Kopassus officer, and the Yon Gab disbanded and replaced by a Kopassus unit. According to a Kopassus officer in Ambon, the Yon Gab had been formed to confront the large-scale clashes taking place in the middle of 2000. It had performed its mission well but now the challenge came from sporadic bombings and shootings. This officer claimed that Kopassus had the skills needed to deal with these disturbances.[97] The Kopassus contingent consisted of an intelligence attachment of 150 men and a covert operations unit (*Sandhi Yudha*) of 75.[98] Meanwhile, Brig. Gen. Mustopo had concluded that the local "organic" battalion 733 based in the centre of Ambon was so hopelessly "contaminated" that he had it transferred to Papua.

The arrival of the Kopassus force coincided — suspiciously in the opinion of some — with the renewal of sporadic shooting and bombing incidents at a time when quiet "peace" feelers were being put out between Muslim and Christian "moderates". The incidents occurred mainly in the Christian sector. On 9 November 2001, two men were killed when the bomb they were carrying on a motorcycle exploded prematurely in front of Ambon's main Protestant church.[99] A few days later on 12 November a bomb was thrown into a shop in the centre of the Christian sector. On 11 December an explosion on a Christian passenger ship, the Kalifornia, killed 10 and and injured 46 passengers. In response to this explosion, a mob burnt down the building of the Ambon city legislative assembly — only about a hundred metres from the regional police headquarters. On 19 December nine people were killed when another Christian boat was fired on in Ambon Bay. On 27 December, yet another Christian ship was fired on but this may have been related to a battle involving Brimob, an army unit and the marines following the wounding of several policemen in shootings earlier in the day.[100] On 8 January, masked men with military weapons destroyed two small cafés in the Muslim sector, killing a waiter. During November and December around fifty people were killed in bombings and shooting in Ambon city.[101]

As the International Crisis Group reported at the time,

> The attacks were not directed against strategic targets and did not bring significant benefits to either the Muslim or Christian sides. The victims and potential victims were usually not involved in the main struggle — women taking goods to the market on a Christian boat, a waiter in a Muslim café, and passers-by in bomb explosions. The purpose seemed less to impose losses (except perhaps in the conflict between the police and the marines) than to maintain a general level of tension that would prevent progress towards a lasting peace. It is possible that the perpetrators hope the attacks on one community or the other will provoke the victims' side to retaliate.[102]

Following the Malino accord, this pattern resumed on a more destructive level. On 3 April, a bomb was thrown from a passing car into a crowd of people in Jalan Jan Pays in the centre of the Christian sector, killing 4 and wounding 58. A Christian mob then moved on to the nearby governor's office and started a fire that destroyed the building.[103] Police then released the Muslim-sounding names of two men identified as suspects in the initial bombing.[104] Later in the month, on 26 April, Ja'far Umar Thalib preached a fiery sermon in which he called on the congregation to "use bombs and fire them at the enemy".[105] Whether in response to this sermon or not, the Christian village of Soya was attacked early in the morning of 28 April, killing 12 residents and burning down 30 houses and a famous old church. Witnesses claimed that there were about one hundred masked attackers and that mortars were used. While some blamed the Laskar Jihad for the attack, others expressed doubts that Muslims could have entered the exclusively

Christian area undetected.[106] During the next few days, snipers fired on boats in Ambon Bay and several clashes took place near the borders between the Christian and Muslim sectors. And then, on 12 May, the home of Thamrin Ely, the leader of the Muslim delegation at Malino, in a Muslim residential area not far from the Laskar Jihad headquarters, was burnt down by unidentified assailants. Just as it would have been difficult for Muslims to carry out the attack on Soya village, it seemed unlikely that Christians could have been responsible for the attack of Thamrin's home.[107]

Two days after the attack on Thamrin's house, a revealing incident occurred in Kudamati, a Christian area in Ambon city.[108] Police were searching for the prominent Christian gang leader, Berthy Loupatty, in relation to claims that he had been involved in fighting between two Christian villages on the island of Saparua. The police eventually found Berthy in the company of two men who resisted arrest. After a fire-fight in which men on both sides were wounded, the police succeeded in arresting Berthy and his friends who were taken to the police headquarters and, in accordance with the custom, subjected to a beating. It turned out, however, that the two men were undercover members of Kopassus's covert operations unit, Sandhi Yudha, who were said to be on an "intelligence mission" monitoring the nearby home of the separatist FKM leader, Alexander Manuputty.[109] It was revealed that Berthy had been working for some time with Kopassus, reporting directly to First Lieutenant Rory Sitorus, one of the men found with him in the police raid. At this point it seemed that open conflict between the police Brimob and Kopassus was about to break out.[110]

In the raid on the house in Kudamati the police had arrested another member of Berthy's gang who claimed that he had been ordered by Berthy to place a bomb in a church and that Berthy had received his order from Kopassus.[111] The military police quickly took over the investigation from the police but soon released Berthy "into the care of Kopassus".[112] Six months later in November the police requested the assistance of the new Pattimura commander, Maj. Gen. Djoko Santoso, to ensure that Kopassus handed Berthy back to the police[113] and, on 18 November Berthy reported to a police station — surprisingly in Solo, Central Java.[114] The Maluku police chief, Brig. Gen. Sunarko, revealed a long list of incidents allegedly organized by Berthy and his gang including a bomb at the temporary campus of the Pattimura University in August 2001, a bomb on a minibus in September, the bomb on the Kalifornia ship in December, the bomb thrown on 3 April 2002, fighting between Christian villages in Saparua, the attack on Soya, and a bomb which killed two schoolgirls in September.[115] Berthy and nineteen members of his gang were put on trial in Jakarta in June–July 2003 and sentenced to various terms of imprisonment. Berthy himself was accused of killing 84 people and destroying 461 buildings and a passenger ship for which he was sentenced to twelve years in jail.[116]

Why had Kopassus been protecting a Christian gang leader who carried out attacks that seemed designed to keep tensions high and undermine the Malino peace agreement? The bombings and shootings were mainly in the Christian area and seemed intended to create the impression that Muslims were responsible and perhaps to provoke Christian retaliation. In retrospect, puzzling aspects of the attacks became clear after Berthy's capture. It had been possible to accept that a Muslim on a motorbike might be able to bring a bomb into the Christian area unnoticed at night, but how could Muslims have managed to plant a bomb on the Kalifornia or to attack Soya village? And why was it so easy to burn down the Ambon city Legislative Assembly building only a short distance from the police headquarters and then the governor's office protected by Kopassus troops? The problem disappears if the perpetrators were not in fact Muslims but members of a Christian gang enjoying the backing of Kopassus.

What was the motive? One likely purpose was to ensure that conditions did not improve to the point where the civil emergency was lifted. Indeed, it might have been hoped to lift the level of the emergency from civil to military. And the higher the level of tension, the easier it was to persuade commercial enterprises to pay troops to protect them. As the national police spokesman in Jakarta, Saleh Saaf, commented on Berthy's arrest, "The more rioting, the more people request security. And then money can be requested from them."[117] Several senior police officers claimed that military personnel were becoming very wealthy in Maluku.[118]

The revelations in May 2002 had been embarrassing for the Pattimura commander, Brig. Gen. Mustopo, himself a Kopassus officer. Following the clash between the police and the undercover Kopassus men, Mustopo was quoted as saying that it was "just a misunderstanding". In Jakarta, however, the Coordinating Minister for Political and Security Affairs, Yudhoyono, expressed his impatience: "I greatly regret yet another shameful incident."[119] He called on the commander-in-chief of the TNI and the chief of police to explain what had happened "to the public in a transparent way" and told them to replace commanders who were incapable of maintaining the peace in Maluku.[120] Two new Kostrad battalions were sent to Maluku and a Brimob force was replaced.[121] On 30 May, Mustopo was replaced by Maj. Gen. Djoko Santoso, a Kostrad officer personally close to Yudhoyono, who was placed at the head of a new command structure with authority over the police.[122] It was not until November, however, that Berthy was handed over by Kopassus to the police in Central Java. In August 2003, after Djoko's promotion to the position of deputy chief of staff of the army, his successor, Maj. Gen. Agustadi Sasongko Purnomo, announced that Kopassus troops would be withdrawn from Ambon "because these troops would be better serving in Aceh, not in Ambon".[123] No information was revealed to the public, however, about whether the commander of the Sandhi Yudha unit, Major Imam Santosa Ramadhani, or Berthy's "controller", Lt. Rory Sitorus, were held responsible for the offences committed by Berthy and his gang. Nor was information divulged about the extent to which Brig. Gen. Mustopo endorsed their strategy.

THE DEPARTURE OF THE LASKAR JIHAD

Brig. Gen. Mustopo, who had replaced Brig. Jen. I Made Yasa in June 2001, had attempted to win back the support of the Muslim community which had been alienated by his predecessor's approach. As part of his new approach, Mustopo established contact with the Laskar Jihad and even persuaded them to hand over home-made weapons and bombs in a ceremony that he attended.[124] The Laskar Jihad's cooperation with Mustopo may have been in part a response to his accommodating policy, but it was also probably due to the growing weakness of its position in Ambon, especially after the Malino agreement.

Since its arrival in Ambon, the Laskar Jihad had been seen by many Muslims as their ultimate protector against a resurgence of Christian militancy. As the level of fighting declined, however, there were signs that some Muslims were uncomfortable with the Laskar Jihad's prominence, particularly its aim of imposing a more fundamentalist approach on the relatively relaxed traditionalist Islam of the Ambonese Muslim community which was closer to the flexible and pragmatic Nahdatul Ulama in Java than to the more orthodox Muhammadiyah.[125] Many Muslims continued to appreciate the contribution of the Laskar Jihad in the form of medical services, education and even the collection of garbage, but resented what they saw as its attempts to dominate the Muslim community. In these circumstances, while Yasa was still the military commander, the police decided to take the risk of arresting Ja'far Umar Thalib at the Surabaya airport in May 2001 after he had presided over the stoning to death of an adulterer in Ambon. In an effort to appear even-handed, the way was prepared on 30 April by arresting Alexander Manuputty, the leader of the FKM. Ja'far's arrest on a charge of, in effect, implementing syariah law, however, led to protests by Muslim leaders throughout Indonesia although it did not provoke violence in Maluku. Apparently in response to Muslim political pressure, Ja'far was soon released and indeed warmly welcomed at the vice-presidential office by the newly elected vice president, the PPP leader, Hamzah Haz.[126]

From the latter part of 2001, the Laskar Jihad maintained a relatively low profile and focused more on its religious, educational and social-welfare activities. According to military sources, the number of Laskar Jihad forces in Maluku was declining[127] and there were also indications that the organization was not as well funded as previously.[128] One possible explanation for the Laskar Jihad's financial difficulties relates to earlier speculation about the initial military backing for the Laskar Jihad. In July 2001, the drawn-out proceedings leading to the impeachment of President Abdurrahman Wahid were finally completed and he was succeeded by his vice president, Megawati Soekarnoputri. In contrast to their fractured relations with the erratic Abdurrahman, military officers had little to fear from Megawati who shared their deep commitment to the unity of Indonesia and was content to leave it to them to decide how this was to be preserved. If earlier speculation was correct that a group of military officers had backed the Laskar Jihad's venture in Maluku for the purpose of undermining Abdurrahman, the Laskar Jihad's utility for the military was now in sharp decline. The apparent serious shortfall in funds experienced by the Laskar Jihad from the second half of 2001 suggests that its previous supply could well have been from military officers and perhaps members of the Soeharto family who no longer had a reason to finance them once Abdurrahman was no longer in office.

The Laskar Jihad's weakened position was indicated in May 2002 when Ja'far was again arrested at Surabaya airport on his return from Ambon where he had delivered the provocative sermon which had preceded the attack on the Soya village discussed above. This time he was put on trial but eventually found not guilty in January 2003 amidst speculation about a possible deal with the authorities. Meanwhile the *Ahlus Sunnah wal Jama'ah* movement had become increasingly divided on whether the Laskar Jihad's campaign in Maluku still met the religious criteria required for jihad. The issue was resolved by a communication from a revered ulama in Saudi Arabia who believed that the Laskar Jihad had deviated from these requirements and on 3 October 2003 the council of the *Forum Ahlus Sunnah wal-Jama'ah* decided to dissolve both itself and the Laskar Jihad.[129] On 14 October 2003, Ja'far announced the dissolution and one day later, 700 members left Ambon by ship, reportedly leaving 400 behind in Maluku.[130] It appears that Jusuf Kalla helped to finance their departure.[131] Another Laskar Jihad leader added that "Financially, the Laskar Jihad can no longer afford to continue as an organization".[132] The timing of Ja'far's announcement, only two days after the Bali bombing, led to some speculation that the real reason for the dissolution may have been to distance themselves from those involved in that attack.[133] It appears that the decision had in fact been taken by the Forum before the bombing but a reluctant Ja'far had only accepted it afterwards.[134]

The Laskar Jihad had not been the only irregular Muslim force in Maluku. In December 1999, a group called Laskar Mujahidin had come to Ambon. Consisting mainly of non-Ambonese, it was considered by Muslims as more aggressive than the Laskar Jihad.[135] It seems, however, that Laskar Mujahidin members had come from Sulawesi to Buru Island, close to Ambon, where they received military training from the middle of 1999 and originally used the name Laskar Jundullah.[136] Unlike the Laskar Jihad, the Laskar Mujahidin was an "underground" group. Estimates of its strength ranged from "dozens" to five hundred.[137] Later it was revealed that the Laskar Mujahidin was part of the Jemaah Islamiyah network and linked to Al Qaeda through an Al Qaeda agent, Omar al-Farouk, who had married the daughter of the Laskar Mujahidin commander, Abu Dzar, who had been killed in battle in Maluku.[138] Laskar Jihad and Laskar Mujahidin had important ideological differences despite their common Christian enemy in Maluku. Ja'far Umar Thalib was particularly dismissive of Osama bin Laden whom he regarded as a rebel against Saudi Arabia, a state that implemented syariah.[139] The Laskar Mujahidin virtually disappeared from Maluku after the government crackdown on Jemaah Islamiyah in the wake of the Bali bombing.

As the influence of the Laskar Jihad declined, so did that of its allies in Maluku. The government, both in Jakarta and Maluku, continued to work to win over the Muslim radicals who had opposed the Malino agreement. Instead of isolating them, they were cultivated. Yudhoyono and Kalla maintained contact with Ustaz Attamimi and brought him to Jakarta several times. Later, after the appointment of the Christian bureaucrat, Sinyo Harry Sarundajang as acting governor of Maluku in December 2002, Attamimi was appointed to head the Islamic College (STAIN) which was provided with additional facilities and funding. Attamimi was not the only beneficiary, however. Sinyo Harry, who had previously been acting governor of North Maluku and presided over the restoration of calm in that province, was described by several sources as very adept at dealing with the Muslim radicals, particularly by understanding their economic requirements and providing them with appropriate assistance.[140]

THE LIFTING OF THE EMERGENCY

Conditions improved steadily in Ambon following the exposure of Kopassus's links with Berthy Loupatty and the departure of the Laskar Jihad. Although

Ambon's population remained largely segregated into Christian and Muslim residential areas, residents had begun to move between the two sectors and mix in markets and shopping centres. Occasional shootings and bomb explosions took place but they were not necessarily all connected with intercommunal conflict and did not provoke mass mobilizations like those during the conflict.

In August 2003, conditions were sufficiently stable to elect a new governor of the province. Under the regional government law at that time, governors were still elected by the local DPRD. In contrast to the PDI- P-dominated Ambon city legislature, Golkar was the largest party in the provincial assembly with 12 of the 45 seats, followed by the PDI-P with 10 and PPP with 8. In a closely fought election, retired Colonel Karel Ralahalu, backed by the PDI-P, defeated Zeth Sahubarua, the Golkar speaker of the assembly, 20 votes to 18 in the second round of the voting after 6 votes were disqualified.[141] Both Ralahalu and Sahubarua are Christians but both had Muslim running mates for the deputy governorship. The two other candidates were also members of mixed Christian-Muslim teams.[142] Following the peaceful election of the new governor, the central government lifted the civil emergency that had been in effect for more than three years.

Communal harmony, however, faced a serious challenge when clashes over a few days in April 2004 killed thirty-eight people and forced thousands to flee their homes but the incident did not spark a downward spiral into widespread violence.[143] Although Ambon continued to witness isolated shootings and bombings, many of which were later revealed to have been perpetrated by men linked in one way or another to radical Muslim groups from both Maluku and Poso,[144] the Maluku population seemed no longer interested in returning to the destructive violence that had almost destroyed their society in the years after 1999.

CONCLUSION

As this chapter has shown, the roots of the communal conflict lay within Maluku itself where, in contrast to most regions of Indonesia, Dutch colonial rule had created a Christian political and social elite that dominated a large Muslim minority in Ambon and a Muslim majority in the rest of the province. Demographic change over several decades had gradually shifted the balance between the communities due largely to the influx of Muslim migrants from Sulawesi with the result that Christian political dominance was increasingly under challenge. The breakdown of state authority in Maluku, however, was not purely a regional phenomenon but was directly related to the collapse of the New Order regime in Jakarta and the diminution of the centre's authority not only in Maluku but throughout the country. By the 1990s, Muslim politicians in Maluku had strengthened their influence in the regional government and were displacing Christian patronage networks in favour of their own Muslim networks. In van Klinken's view "the unstable nature of these networks in a moment of regime transition provides ... the key to understanding Maluku's war".[145]

The turning point followed the fall of the New Order in Jakarta in the context of economic collapse and the weakened authority of the succeeding regime which faced similar breakdowns of law and order in other parts of the country, including in Jakarta itself. In these circumstances the transition from authoritarianism to democracy with its promise of regional elections in a society more or less evenly divided along religious lines created new uncertainties for local politicians.[146] The initial conflagration in Ambon pitted Christian Ambonese against Muslim migrants but quickly spread to engulf Muslims regardless of ethnic origin. The conflict soon exceeded the capacity of local security forces, but reinforcements in sufficient numbers were not immediately available because of Jakarta's need to cope with breakdowns in order elsewhere, including the growing challenge in East Timor. As the violence in Maluku spread, that province was by no means at the top of the list of the central government's priorities. In the absence of firm external intervention, the Maluku conflict was in effect left to run its course.

Ineffective national governments, under both Habibie and Abdurrahman, lacked common purpose and were preoccupied with threats to their own survival, while regional government in Maluku virtually disintegrated and "contaminated" military and police forces were immobilized by competing religious loyalties. As sporadic fighting continued in Maluku, interspersed with major outbreaks, a new conflict in North Maluku seven months after the first clash in Ambon had its own causes and added to the sense of powerlessness felt by both the provincial and national governments. A well-publicized massacre of Muslim villagers in North Maluku enraged Muslims throughout Indonesia and led to the formation of the Laskar Jihad which defied the president's orders that it not travel to Maluku where its arrival initiated a new phase in the conflict which put the Christian side on the defensive. The entry of the Laskar Jihad had been facilitated by military personnel who provided training and weapons. In Maluku itself, some military units sided with the Laskar Jihad while elements of the police backed the Christian side.

The Maluku conflict had been raging for more than a year but it was only in mid-2000 that the government recognized it as a full-blown regional crisis and responded with "crisis-ridden" measures equivalent to those taken at the national level described in earlier chapters. President Abdurrahman declared an emergency in Maluku and a new military strategy was adopted in which elite troops confronted the Laskar Jihad in an often brutal way. By mid-2001, the "amateur" fighters of the Laskar Jihad had found that they were no match for the professional forces of the TNI. However, the decline of the Laskar Jihad appeared to be related to another factor. Many TNI officers had lost confidence in the president due to his intervention in TNI affairs, his dismissal of General Wiranto from his cabinet, his peace gestures toward separatists in Aceh and Papua, and his general unpredictability. When Abdurrahman was replaced by Megawati, the financial support and protection that the Laskar Jihad had been receiving from some military officers gradually dried up and it adopted a lower profile.

Although President Megawati did not appear to play a major role in promoting the return to order in Maluku (and Poso), two of her coordinating ministers, Yudhoyono and Kalla, took the initiative to promote peace talks between the warring parties. Although the agreement reached by the government-sponsored meeting at Malino in February 2002 was not fully implemented, it marked a sharp reduction in inter-communal tension which received open public support as barriers between Muslims and Christian districts were dismantled and residents once again mingled together in shopping centres. Nevertheless, occasional shootings, bombings and arson attacks continued which seemed designed to prevent a return to normalcy. These "provocations", however, suddenly stopped when a notorious Christian gang leader with close Kopassus connections was arrested and the regional military commander, a senior Kopassus officer, was prematurely replaced. The conclusion was inescapable that elements in the military had been trying to keep tensions at a high level for their own purposes, most likely to facilitate extortion from commercial enterprises and perhaps to ensure that emergency rule would continue in Maluku.

The replacement of the regional military commander by Yudhoyono's protégé, Djoko Santoso, marked the end of the Maluku crisis and was followed by the lifting of the emergency, the departure of the Laskar Jihad, and in 2003 a new governor — a Christian with a Muslim deputy — was elected. Although large numbers of refugees were living in refugee centres and residential areas had become segregated, life had more or less returned to normal in a province that had not long before been a regional "failed state".

The regional crisis in Maluku had its roots in Maluku itself but it had been aggravated by the failure of the national government to guarantee conditions that would facilitate the maintenance of order. The fall of the authoritarian regime and the sudden holding of democratic elections in a communally divided society contributed to the tensions that led to the violence, but government failure allowed the violence to continue for more than three years. The inability of the national government to reinforce security forces in the early stages of the conflict, its failure to prevent the intervention of the Laskar Jihad, its inability to assure both communities of adequate protection, and its tolerance of the involvement of military personnel in provoking further conflict all contributed to the long delay in restoring order. It was only when two of Megawati's leading ministers took the initiative to hold the Malino peace conference and eventually ensured the removal of the Maluku military commander and later the departure of the Laskar Jihad that the people of Maluku were able to return to normal life. In contrast to the democratic election of 1999 which aggravated communal rivalries, the election of a new governor in 2003 and the second national democratic elections in 2004 further consolidated the return to normalcy in Maluku.

Notes

1. For overviews of this violence, see van Klinken (2007); Sidel (2006).
2. On West Kalimantan, see Human Rights Watch (1997); Edi Peterbang and Eri Sutrisno (2000). On Central Kalimantan, see International Crisis Group (2001*g*); van Klinken (2002); van Klinken (2007), ch. 8. On Poso, see Rohde (2001); Aragon (2002); Human Rights Watch (2002*a*); Aditjondro (2004). In contrast to the violence in Poso and Maluku, the period of extreme violence in Kalimantan was relatively brief and the combatants were not primarily disinguished by religion. In both Kalimantan provinces, the victims were Muslim Madurese, but in West Kalimantan both non-Muslim Dayaks and Muslim Malays were the perpetrators while in Central Kalimantan, many Dayaks are Muslim.
3. This devastating violence, however, should be seen in perspective. The populations of affected provisions amounted to about 5 per cent of the total Indonesian population.
4. van Klinken (2001) and Bertrand (2004), in different ways, represent this approach. Sidel adds that "Against this backdrop, the dominant structures of power associated with Protestantism and Islam in Maluku, much like their counterparts in Poso, were haunted by rising doubts and fears as to their authority, identity and coherence". Sidel (2006), p. 174.
5. See Aditjondro (2001); O'Rourke 2002, p. 348. Variations on these themes were publicly supported from time to time by President Abdurrahman Wahid and his Defence Minister, Juwono Sudarsono. *Jakarta Post*, 15 July 2000.
6. The 1997 population statistics are taken from the Ambon Information Website, <http://websitesrcg.com.ambon> (consulted in 2001). The 1971 figure is from the calculations of Lance Castles cited in van Klinken (2001), p. 12.

7. Bertrand (2004), ch. 7. Sinansari Ecip provides statistics showing that 25 of 29 senior posts in the city bureaucracy were held by Christians. Sinansari Ecip (1999), pp. 69–70.
8. Conversation with Father Cornelis Boehm, Ambon, 6 November 2001.
9. The acting governor in 1965–68 was an Ambonese Christian, G.J. Latumahina. The next three governors were non-Ambonese military officers, Sumitro (1968–75), Hasan Slamet (1975–87), and Sebastian Sukoso (1987–92). The only Ambonese Muslim governor had been Muhammad Padang (1960–65) who, although born in Ambon, was of West Sumatran descent.
10. In October 1998, an anonymous pamphlet appeared which claimed that the new governor, Saleh Latuconsina, was planning to fill the thirty-eight top positions in the civil service with Muslims — an allegation that was so widely believed by Christians that the governor later identified it as one of the main triggers for the rioting that began in January 1999. At that time, 74 per cent of the top positions in the provincial bureaucracy were already held by Muslims. There is no evidence that the governor really had such a plan. Van Klinken (2001), pp. 18–19; Sinansari Ecip (1999), pp. 69–70.
11. Najib Azca (2000), p. 30.
12. Bertrand, who had visited Ambon in 1993 and 1996, recorded that "tensions in Ambon city were mainly between Christian Ambonese and Muslim migrants. Frequent fights had occurred between youths in the predominantly Christian neighborhoods of Mardika and the neighboring one of Batu Merah, with a high concentration of Butonese and Bugis migrants". Bertrand (2004), p. 123. Thamrin Ely, who later led the Muslim side in the Malino peace negotiations, noted that such fights occurred almost every month. Ahmad Suaedy (2000), p. 28.
13. Ahmad Suaedy (2000), pp. 61–65; Erwin H. Al-Jakartaty (2000), pp. 36–37; S. Sinansari Ecip (1999), pp. 48–51; Rustam Kastor (2000) Part 1/ch. 3, Najib Azca (2003), pp. 78–82.
14. Schulze (2002), p. 63.
15. On the original RMS, see Richard Chauvel (1990). In reality, the RMS was not a significant political force in 1999.
16. The writings of Rustam Kastor are representative of this approach. Brig. Gen. (ret.) Rustam previously served as commander of the Pattimura Korem (sub-regional military command) in Maluku. Rustam Kastor (2000).
17. See note 5 above.
18. For one version of this story, see Aditjondro (2001). For a sceptical assessment, see van Klinken (2001), p. 9. Various rumours are summarised in Najib Azca (2003), pp. 73–78.
19. Interview with Rev. P. Titaley, moderator of the Protestant Church of Maluku at the time of the outbreak of the conflict. Ambon, November 2001.
20. A chronology of the first two months of fighting is provided in Human Rights Watch (March 1999). See also van Klinken (2007), ch. 6.

21. For a full account of the conflict in North Maluku, see Christopher Wilson (2008). See also van Klinken (2007), ch. 7; International Crisis Group (2000), pp. 6–7; Tamrin Amal Tomagola (2000).
22. *Kompas*, 13 December 1999.
23. *Kompas*, 14 January 2000.
24. *Kompas*, 13 December 1999.
25. *Republika*, 19 March 1999. The Brimob is the police's paramilitary force. Unfortunately the reinforcements included a Kostrad battalion from South Sulawesi, the home territory of many of the BBM migrants, creating the erroneous impression that the Kostrad force consisted of Muslims from Sulawesi.
26. *Kompas*, 6 December 1999.
27. *Gatra*, 22 January 2000.
28. According to the Minister of Defence, *Jakarta Post*, 15 July 2000.
29. *Republika*, 4 March 1999.
30. *Kompas*, 1 December 1999.
31. For examples, see Human Rights Watch (1999), p. IV; Najib Azca (2000), pp. 87–88; Ahmad Suaedy (2000), pp. 79–101.
32. *Jakarta Post*, 26 June 2000.
33. *Jakarta Post*, 26 June 2000.
34. *Republika*, 3 March 1999.
35. Interview with Maj. Gen. Max Tamaela, Jakarta, 11 September 2001.
36. *Republika*, 12 March 1999, cited in Human Rights Watch (1999).
37. *Kompas*, 10 December 1999.
38. *Kompas*, 20 October 1999.
39. *Kompas*, 17 February 2000.
40. *Jakarta Post*, 10 December 1999.
41. *Kompas*, 18 April 2000.
42. Wilson (2008), ch. 5; International Crisis Group (2000c), p. 8.
43. *Ahlus Sunnah wal-Jama'ah* is not the name of a Yemeni "preacher of *khwarji*" (sic) whom Zachary Abuza claims influenced Ja'far Umar Thalib, but a common term for members of the Sunni community and the name of the Laskar Jihad's sponsoring organization. See Zachary Abuza (2003), p. 69. Abuza's claim that Laskar Jihad was affiliated with Al Qaeda is also wrong. The most comprehensive study of Laskar Jihad is by Noorhaidi Hasan (2006). See also Schulze (2002).
44. Noorhaidi Hasan (2006), pp. 116–21.
45. *Gatra*, 25 March 2000. Noorhaidi adds that the trainers included former members of university student regiments as well as veterans of Islamic campaigns in Afghanistan, Mindanao and Kashmir. Noorhaidi Hasan (2006), p. 17.
46. Noorhaidi Hasan (2006), pp. 186, 190.
47. *Jakarta Post*, 10 May 2000.
48. *Jakarta Post*, 15 July 2000.

49. *Jakarta Post*, 12 May 2000.

50. *Jakarta Post*, 16 May 2000.

51. The author heard a very senior TNI officer assess the Laskar Jihad's initial entry into Maluku as "positive" although by September 2000, when this conversation took place, he felt that it had become "negative".

52. *Jakarta Post*, 12 April 2000. The author was told by a former very senior minister in Abdurrahman's cabinet that the president himself had eventually acquiesced in the Laskar Jihad's involvement in Maluku because he feared the troubles it could cause in Java and elsewhere if it were prevented. See also International Crisis Group (2000), pp. 17–18; Davis (2002), p. 19.

53. See Chapter 2 above.

54. In a conversation with the author, President Abdurrahman identified Djadja Suparman as a pro-Laskar Jihad officer. July 2000. Djadja, however, was not an ideological sympathizer.

55. The moderator of the Protestant Church, Rev. Sammy Titaley, told the American journalist, Dan Murphy, that "The military is the whole problem in the Moluccas — if the military can do its job properly, as a referee, then we could end this conflict". See International Crisis Group (2000), p. 19.

56. Noorhaidi describes most of the Laskar Jihad force as "unskilled combatants" and says that most went as preachers while "no more than one hundred" were "intended to become combatants". Noorhaidi Hasan (2006), p. 193.

57. See Najib Azca (2003), p. 102.

58. Schulze (2002), p. 63.

59. On Wattimena, see International Crisis Group (2000), p. 15; van Klinken (2007), p. 99. One Christian journalist said Laskar Kristus was "just a gang" that lacked Laskar Jihad's structure. "If they heard that a Christian community was facing a threat, they would just go there and help defend them", he said. Interview, Ambon, December 2005.

60. Schulze (2002), p. 64.

61. Details on gang rivalries among Christians are provided in George Aditjondro (2001).

62. Human Rights Watch Backgrounder (29 June 2000).

63. This data is taken from maps on the Laskar Jihad's website. The website was closed when the Laskar Jihad dissolved itself in 2002.

64. Najib Azca (2003), p. 21. Altogether there are about seventy villages on Ambon Island.

65. Bambang W. Soeharto in *Kompas*, 4 October 2000.

66. *Jakarta Post*, 1 March 2001.

67. *Gatra*, 22 January 2000.

68. Najib Azca (2000), p. 105. As a result of this incident, Yasa's reputation was initially very poor among Christians.

69. International Crisis Group (2000a), p. 10; *Jakarta Post*, 3 March 2001.

70. A senior military officer told the author that the military faced a dilemma

whenever they made an arrest. If they handed over a Christian to the city police, it was likely that he would be "finished off" but if he were handed over to the provincial police he would probably be released. The reverse applied when they detained a Muslim. Interview, Jakarta, October 2001.

71. *Jakarta Post*, 7 August 2000.
72. According to one officer, soldiers were not even permitted to accept cigarettes from local people.
73. *Jakarta Post*, 14 August 2000.
74. Najib Azca (2000), p. 107.
75. These incidents are described in more detail in International Crisis Group (2002*a*), pp. 12–13.
76. As a very senior Maluku official said, "the number on the truck when it arrived was less than the number when it left". Interview, Ambon, November 2001.
77. *Kompas*, 23 June 2001.
78. The statement appeared on the Laskar Jihad website.
79. In response to demands from Muslim organizations, the National Commission on Human Rights established a team to investigate the Kebon Cengkeh killings and reportedly recommended that charges be laid either in civil or military courts. However, its report was never made public and no trials were held. *Koran Tempo*, 24 November 2001.
80. International Crisis Group (2002*a*), pp. 22–23.
81. Interview with Maj. Gen. Samsuddin (ret.), a member of the Human Rights Commission, Jakarta, September 2001.
82. Interview with Saleh Latuconsina, Jakarta, 30 August 2004.
83. Interviews with several participants, Ambon, December 2005.
84. A report in the *New York Times* cited a U.S. official as claiming that "armed Islamic fundamentalist groups have received money, men and arms from the bin Laden group and its allies". The report mentioned the Laskar Jihad in this context. Weiner (2001). See also Aglionby (2001). For a sceptical assessment, see International Crisis Group (2002*a*), pp. 18–19.
85. Interview with Thamrin Ely, the leader of the Muslim delegation, Jakarta, 30 November 2005. Attamimi's taskforce carried out vigilante raids on bars and brothels.
86. Interview with Ustaz Attamimi, Ambon, 8 December 2005.
87. Farid and Hamid are both from Kalla's home province, South Sulawesi. Both were also deeply involved in the Aceh settlement, discussed in Chapter 8.
88. *Jakarta Post*, 25 August 2005.
89. See interviews with the two leaders in *Koran Tempo*, 15 February 2002.
90. One of the Muslim moderates said that, unlike the hardliners, the moderates realised that nothing could be achieved unless the fighting stopped, but in the end they decided not to object to hardline points in the agreement because this made it easier for the hardliners to accept the agreement. In any case, they

reasoned, the hardline points were not likely to be implemented. Interview, Ambon, 10 December 2005.

91. The full agreement appeared in *Kompas*, 13 February 2002.
92. Interview with a member of the investigation team, Jakarta, 1 December 2005.
93. The "Team of Eleven" included Ustaz Attamimi, Luqman Ba'abduh of the Laskar Jihad, and retired Brig. Gen Rustam Kastor.
94. *Koran Tempo*, 18 February 2002.
95. During the conflict, the airport could only be reached from Ambon city by speedboat from two boarding points, one in the Muslim sector and the other in the Christian sector.
96. *Jakarta Post*, 3 March 2002, *Kompas*, 4 March 2002.
97. Interview with Kopassus officer in Ambon, November 2001.
98. Najib Azca (2003), p. 45.
99. The author happened to be talking with a group of Christian leaders in a hotel facing the church when the explosion occurred.
100. A comment by the Coordinating Minister for Political and Security Affairs suggested that the conflict between the marines and Brimob was over possession of petroleum, the price of which was about to rise. *Koran Tempo*, 22 January 2002.
101. *Jakarta Post*, 26 January 2002.
102. International Crisis Group (2002*a*), p. 20.
103. *Kompas*, 4 April 2002.
104. *Kompas*, 9 April 2002. One of these men, known as "Idi Amin" Thabrani Pattimura alias Ongen Pattimura, was later convicted for his involvement in 2005 in a shooting at a karaoke bar at Hative Besar, on the north side of Ambon Bay.
105. *Jakarta Post*, 5 May 2002.
106. *Kompas*, 29 April 2002, *Koran Tempo*, 30 April 2002.
107. Thamrin Ely was convinced that the Laskar Jihad had attacked his house but he also suspected Kopassus involvement. Interview, Jakarta, 27 May 2002.
108. This account is based on reports in *Kompas*, *Koran Tempo* and *Jakarta Post*, 15–17 May 2002.
109. According to the regional police commander, Brig. Gen. Sunarko, "as soon as we realized they were from Kopassus", they were handed over to the army. Interview, Jakarta, 13 September 2005.
110. According to the governor at that time, Saleh Latuconsina. Interview, Jakarta, 30 August 2004.
111. *Koran Tempo*, 17 May 2002.
112. *Koran Tempo*, 21 May 2002.
113. *Jakarta Post*, 16 November 2002.
114. *Koran Tempo*, 22 November 2002. A major Kopassus base is located at Kartasura, not far from Solo.

115. *Sinar Harapan*, 22 October 2002; interview with Brig. Gen. Sunarko, Jakarta, 13 September 2005.
116. *Koran Tempo*, 16 July 2003; *Kompas*, 24 July 2003.
117. *Kompas*, 22 October 2002.
118. Separate interviews with senior police officers in 2002 and 2005. One added, "there are also plenty of opportunities for police officers". See also Najib Azca (2003), p. 38.
119. *Kompas*, 16 May 2002.
120. *Jakarta Post*, 16 May 2002.
121. Crisis Centre Diocese of Ambon (2002).
122. *Koran Tempo*, 1 June 2002.
123. *Kompas*, 13 August 2003.
124. *Kompas*, 20 May 2002.
125. One prominent Ambonese Muslim leader told the author of his annoyance when a Laskar Jihad member travelling in his car had told him to turn off music being played on his radio.
126. On these developments, see International Crisis Group (2002*a*), pp. 15–16. The vice president himself, however, was not a fundamentalist militant but a wily Muslim politician who was willing to cultivate Muslim support from any quarter.
127. One military source estimated that the number had fallen to 1,300–1,500 by early 2001 and another estimated 800 in October 2001.
128. A conversation with two Laskar Jihad "foot-soldiers" in Jakarta in early 2002 indicated that their daily living allowances when in Maluku had declined sharply during the previous year.
129. *Detik*, 15 October 2003. The ulama was Syekh Rabi' bin Hadi al Madkhali in Medina. The debate is summarized in International Crisis Group (2004*b*), pp. 12–18.
130. *Detik*, 15 October 2003, *Koran Tempo*, 17 October 2003. Those who remained in Maluku included Ambonese members and those who had married Ambonese women.
131. Interview with Jusuf Kalla's advisor, Hamid Awaluddin. Jakarta, 11 September 2005.
132. *Koran Tempo*, 16 October 2003.
133. Indonesia's first large-scale terrorist attack took place in Bali on 12 October 2002. 202 people were killed.
134. Noorhaidi Hasan (2006), pp. 211–13.
135. Interview with Ustaz Ali Fauzy, an early "field commander" and leader of the Maluku branch of PBB. Ambon, 4 January 2002.
136. International Crisis Group (2002*c*), pp. 22–23.
137. Noorhaidi says that "their actual number did not exceed three hundred, including a dozen foreigners from France, Pakistan, Afghanistan, Saudi Arabia, and Algeria". Noorhaidi Hasan (2006), p. 196.

138. International Crisis Group (2003c), pp. 24–25.
139. International Crisis Group (2001b), p. 13; International Crisis Group (2002), p. 19. Although both Ja'far Umar Thalib and the Jemaah Islamiyah members had joined the *mujahidin* fighting against the Soviet occupation of Afghanistan, they had joined rival guerilla forces.
140. Several confidential interviews, Ambon, December 2005.
141. Col. Ralahalu had been appointed to the command of the Maluku Korem in March 1999, two months after the outbreak of the conflict.
142. Similar mixed teams contested direct district elections in 2005 and later.
143. International Crisis Group (2004a).
144. International Crisis Group (2005).
145. Van Klinken (2001), p. 2. See also van Klinken (2007).
146. On the dangers of post-authoritarian free elections in communally divided societies, see Snyder (2000).

8

RESOLVING THE SEPARATIST CHALLENGE IN ACEH

As discussed in Chapter 4, the fall of the Soeharto regime was followed by rising assertiveness in the regions outside Java that resented what they saw as excessive central domination while the weak Habibie government, challenged on all sides, was aware of its limited capacity to repress outbreaks of resistance to central rule. Indonesian leaders, including senior military officers, were alarmed by what seemed to be parallels with the break-up of the Soviet Union and Yugoslavia while public debate began to touch on what had previously been "unimaginable" — the disintegration of the republic. The leading candidate for secession was, of course, East Timor, where Indonesia's occupation since 1975 continued to meet with armed resistance within the territory and widespread condemnation among the international community. In a dramatic effort to settle the East Timor problem once and for all, President Habibie proposed the holding of a referendum in East Timor which led, in 1999, to an overwhelming vote in favour of independence, a massacre of supporters of independence by pro-Indonesia militias and the withdrawal in chaotic circumstances of the Indonesian administration and military. The referendum resolved the East Timor issue but it stimulated further demands in Papua and Aceh — the next two most probable candidates for secession — for their own referenda.

In fact, there was no realistic prospect that the Indonesian government would agree to release Aceh from the republic. Indonesia's national ideology, *Panca Sila* (Five Principles), formulated by Soekarno and upheld by Soeharto, portrayed Indonesia as a multi-ethnic, multi-religious and multi-cultural nation in which all ethnic and religious communities have a recognized place.

The government saw itself as the successor of the Netherlands East Indies and therefore the inheritor of all its territory, including Aceh (but not East Timor). It argued further that the people of Aceh had identified with the nationalist struggle against Dutch colonialism and were an integral part of the Indonesian nation.[1] In the wake of the collapse of the New Order, this vision was challenged by ethnic and religious violence leading to heightened fears of national disintegration, especially after the secession of East Timor. Indonesia's self-image, encapsulated in the national motto *Bhinekka Tunggal Ika* (Unity in Diversity), would be further devastated if one of its original regions were to follow East Timor's example. Even worse was the prospect that, if Aceh somehow won its freedom, a process of national unravelling like that of the old Soviet Union could begin.

Political, ideological and emotional ties with Aceh were reinforced by material interests. Unlike East Timor, Aceh is a resource-rich province that contributed disproportionately to both central government revenues and exports. Its major resource, the huge offshore Arun gas field, supplied a petrochemical complex in Lhokseumawe that included a natural gas plant, two major fertilizer plants and a pulp paper plant.[2] In 1999, Aceh, with only 2 per cent of the total Indonesian population, was the source of about 30 per cent of Indonesia's total oil and gas exports, amounting to 11 per cent of total exports.[3] Moreover, before the implementation of decentralization laws, all oil and gas revenues flowed directly to the central government. Aceh was also a significant source of timber both for domestic use and export. In short, Indonesia felt it could not afford to lose Aceh.

No major political group in Indonesia — outside Aceh itself — favoured the granting of independence to Aceh. Not only did they oppose independence but many objected to the government negotiating with rebels whom they considered to be "criminals" and "traitors". They believed that the government, by talking with the Free Aceh Movement, GAM (*Gerakan Aceh Merdeka*), had allowed itself to be humiliated by effectively according GAM international status. Even those who accepted the holding of negotiations complained about the presence of international mediators, the holding of talks outside Indonesia, and talking to GAM as if its status were equal to that of the government.[4] And when negotiated cease-fires broke down, the DPR strongly endorsed the launching of renewed military offensives.

In particular, military officers opposed negotiations with GAM. Most military officers believed that the way to deal with rebels who refused to surrender was to hunt them down and kill them. During the first decade of independence, the military had engaged in a series of operations to defend the state against regional rebellion and acquired a perception of itself as the indispensable "glue" that held Indonesia together. Military ideology stresses its duty to defend national unity in the form of the Unitary State of the Republic of Indonesia (*Negara Kesatuan Republik Indonesia*: NKRI). Fresh from its humiliating withdrawal from East Timor, the TNI was in no mood to compromise on Aceh. Far from wanting to negotiate with GAM, prominent officers called for the implementation of a military emergency in the province.

Apart from its nationalist fervour, the TNI also had significant economic stakes in Aceh. As described in Chapter 5, the TNI has never been able to cover its financial needs from formal budget allocations. It therefore required that its troops rely on their own initiative to supplement meagre salaries and raise funds to cover operating expenses. Fund-raising opportunities were particularly bountiful in resource-rich Aceh which hosted major economic projects, such as the petrochemical industrial complex in Lhokseumawe.[5] Like in other regions of Indonesia, the military in Aceh was also deeply involved in illegal logging, smuggling, the marijuana trade and routine extortion from commercial enterprises.[6] Even Maj. Gen. Endang Suwarya, the martial law commander after the declaration of the emergency in 2003, admitted that "I know about indications of the involvement of members of the security forces in a mafia" engaged in smuggling luxury cars and refined sugar from the Sabang free trade zone. He also mentioned the smuggling of timber and marijuana.[7]

The outlook for a peaceful settlement in Aceh at the end of Megawati's presidency in 2004 was therefore very bleak. In Grindle and Thomas's terms, continuous fighting between GAM and government forces had made the province "crisis-ridden" not only since 1998 but throughout the 1990s. Aceh's crisis, however, did not constitute a national crisis equivalent to that of the years immediately after Soeharto's fall. Aceh was certainly a serious problem but was not perceived widely as a national disaster that would compel the government to change course in order to achieve a settlement. Neither GAM nor the Indonesian government was willing to make significant concessions in order to lay the foundations for peace and there was no strong organized political pressure within Indonesia in support of a settlement.

Yet, within two years of his election in 2004, President Yudhoyono, who had been in charge of the failed negotiations in 2003, not only succeeded in re-opening negotiations with GAM but was able to offer sufficient concessions to convince it to abandon its goal of independence in exchange for broader rights of participation in regional government. The agreement was reached and a new law on governance in Aceh adopted despite military dissatisfaction, significant opposition in the DPR and the initial absence of strong public support. This chapter will examine the failure of earlier attempts to seek a resolution and will then trace the developments that led to the end of three decades of separatist rebellion in Aceh.

BACKGROUND

The Roots of Separatism

Aceh's sense of distinct identity goes back to the sixteenth and seventeenth centuries when the Acehnese sultanate was a major regional power.[8] Although the sultanate declined in later centuries, Aceh was one of the last regions to come under Dutch colonial rule and was only subjugated in the first decade of the twentieth century following a thirty-year military campaign. Dutch control, however, was short-lived and ended with the Japanese occupation of the Netherlands Indies during the Second World War. During the Indonesian revolution from 1945 to 1949, Acehnese identified with Indonesian nationalism and the Dutch did not even attempt to re-establish themselves in the province.

Aceh's population is virtually 100 per cent Muslim and Muslim scholars (ulama) have always exercised much influence. Their political dominance, however, was soon challenged as the new national government gradually extended its authority to Aceh in the early 1950s. Many ulama were disappointed by the government's refusal to declare Indonesia as an Islamic state but the final straw was the denial of separate provincial status to Aceh and its inclusion in the province of North Sumatra governed from Medan. An ulama-led rebellion was launched in 1953 and allied itself with Darul Islam rebellions in West Java and South Sulawesi. The Darul Islam movement was not separatist but aimed to establish Islamic law throughout Indonesia.[9] In Aceh, the rebellion was contained in Aceh by military repression combined with political concessions.[10] Support for the movement declined after 1957 when Aceh obtained provincial status and 1959 when the province was granted special autonomy in the fields of religion, *adat* (custom) and education. Finally, in 1962, the last remnants of the movement abandoned their struggle and by 1965 the ulama were cooperating with the military in its campaign of extermination against the small provincial PKI which was based on migrant Javanese plantation workers. That old aspirations were not entirely forgotten, however, was indicated when the provincial DPRD adopted a regulation providing for the partial implementation of Islamic law in 1968. Despite the "special autonomy" granted to Aceh in the field of religion, Soeharto's new government immediately blocked this move.

Aceh was largely quiescent for the next decade until a new rebellion broke out in 1977. By then the Arun natural gas fields had been discovered and international corporations were establishing petrochemical industries around Lhokseumawe on the north coast of Aceh — the area where the Darul Islam had strong support in the 1950s. The new industries gave Aceh one of the highest per capita incomes in Indonesia but it also had one of the highest poverty rates. Timothy Kell presents a picture of growing Acehnese resentment against wealthy non-Acehnese enclave communities and the failure of the central government to ensure that Aceh received a "fair" share of the new prosperity. He also describes how industrialization and "modernization" disrupted rural Acehnese society.[11] In contrast to the Islamic goals of the Darul Islam in the 1950s, the new movement aimed to "restore" the national sovereignty that Aceh had lost to the Dutch. The new petrochemical industries, they believed, would ensure the economic viability of an independent Aceh.

The rebellion was led by Teungku Hasan Muhammed di Tiro, whose grandfather, Teungku Cik di Tiro, had been one of the leaders of resistance to the Dutch in the 1890s.[12] Hasan Tiro had gone to the United States as a student in 1950 and remained there as a businessman until 1976 when he returned to found the Acheh-Sumatra National Liberation Front (ASNLF), also known as GAM, on 4 December of that year. Hasan was not an ulama and his movement gave only limited attention to Islam. GAM's tiny military force of a few hundred launched its first uprising in 1977 but was no match for the Indonesian military which crushed it over the next two years.[13] Several surviving leaders eventually obtained refuge in Sweden from where they continued to direct GAM's operations. In 1986, Hasan managed to interest Libya in his struggle and obtained military training for several hundred supporters who returned to Aceh where they launched the next phase of their rebellion in 1989 with a force of about 750 men.[14] Once again the Indonesian government responded with military force, treating the province as a "Military Operations Area" (*Daerah Operasi Militer*: DOM) in which de facto martial law was applied.[15] The Special Forces (*Komando Pasukan Khusus*: Kopassus) played a leading role in the counter-insurgency operations that broke the back of the movement within a few years. The methods used by the military were particularly brutal and involved summary executions, hundreds of arrests, "disappearances", burning of villages and the placing of corpses in prominent places in townships and villages. Human rights organizations estimated that about 2,000 were killed in military operations in the two years after mid-1989.[16]

Although GAM was effectively defeated by 1991, so-called "non-organic" troops brought in from outside Aceh remained in the province where they became deeply entrenched in military "fund-raising". In a very frank book, Brig. Gen. Syarifudin Tippe, who was appointed to command the Korem based in Banda Aceh in 1999, points to the lack of professionalism of army troops in Aceh.

> During the DOM period elite soldiers with professional capacity in fact besmirched the good name of the TNI through their behaviour that violated human rights and contradicted the ethics and identity of soldiers of the TNI. And then in the post-DOM period, the professional capacity of soldiers sent to the region was extremely doubtful. ... Even worse, they were caught up in and unable to free themselves from undisciplined behaviour, arrogance, illegal extractions and even extortion.

Syarifudin refers to "the reality of the weak capacity of the security forces to carry out security operations to resolve the Aceh conflict".[17] The brutal and exploitative behaviour of the military in the 1990s was a major factor explaining the widespread support for GAM after the fall of Soeharto in 1998.[18]

As in the case of the Darul Islam in the 1950s, GAM's influence in the 1990s was largely limited to the northern and eastern coast of Aceh — the districts of Aceh Besar, Pidie, North Aceh and East Aceh — which are peopled by the Acehnese ethnic community. The movement had some influence among the Acehnese along the west coast but its support in the 1990s was insignificant among other ethnic communities such as the highland Gayo in Central Aceh, the Alas and Singkil in the south and Javanese transmigrants.[19] It is commonly estimated that the ethnic Acehnese make up more than 70 per cent of the province's population.[20]

Based on an ethnic community widely perceived as "fanatical" in their commitment to Islam, GAM was often portrayed as a "fundamentalist" Islamic movement but its goals were essentially nationalist. GAM argued that the Acehnese sultanate was an internationally recognized state when it was invaded by the Dutch in 1873 and that sovereignty should have been returned to the sultanate instead of the "Javanese colonialists" of the Republic of Indonesia when the Dutch withdrew in 1949. Referring to the pre-colonial sultanate, GAM claimed in the 1980s that it was fighting to "re-establish(ing) the historic Islamic State" in Aceh. Given that virtually all Acehnese are Muslims and the province is often known as the "Verandah of Mecca", it is not surprising that GAM's rhetoric had an Islamic flavour but, as Schulze points out, this is "mainly ... a reflection of Acehnese identity and culture rather than Islamist political aspirations".[21] An Islamic splinter group led by Fauzi Hasbi, the brother of GAM's first vice president, never became a significant force.[22] GAM was hostile to fundamentalist Islamic organizations that attempted to gain influence in Aceh. Visits to Aceh by an Al Qaeda agent, Omar al-Faruq, in December 1999 and Al Qaeda's deputy leader, Ayman al-Zawaheri, in June 2000 were apparently fruitless,[23] while the Java-based Laskar Jihad failed to establish itself in Aceh in 2002.[24]

The Post-Soeharto Revival of GAM

The fall of President Soeharto in May 1998 and the discrediting of his regime led to a loosening of authoritarian controls throughout the nation. The emboldened press publicized cases of military abuse and revealed the existence of mass graves in Aceh. In response, the military Commander-in-Chief, General Wiranto, made an unprecedented apology to the people of Aceh in August 1998 although he stressed that it had been "individual soldiers" (*oknum*) and not the military institution as such that had been responsible.[25] This was followed by an apology from President Habibie in March 1999 "for what has been done by the security forces, by accident or deliberately".[26] Wiranto also ordered the removal from Aceh of "non-organic" troops, that is troops not belonging to the North Sumatra regional army command of which Aceh was part. Among the troops ordered to leave were those from Kopassus which was believed to have been responsible for many of the human rights abuses.

Acehnese aspirations for independence received an inadvertent boost on 27 January 1999 when President Habibie offered to hold a referendum on independence in East Timor. Within days, students in Aceh formed the Aceh Referendum Information Centre (*Sentral Informasi Referendum Aceh*: SIRA) to demand a similar referendum in Aceh. Meanwhile, since late 1998 GAM was increasingly engaged in skirmishes with the security forces and carrying out revenge assassinations of suspected government informers. GAM's strength was replenished when, as part of post-Soeharto liberalization, Habibie ordered the release of political prisoners, including many GAM fighters, while GAM members who had sought refuge in Malaysia began to return. Anti-Jakarta sentiment was further aggravated by a series of military atrocities in which over one hundred people were killed.[27] In the latter half of 1999, popular support for a referendum was expressed in a two-day strike on 4–5 August and a massive rally in Banda Aceh on 8 November. As the twenty-third anniversary of the proclamation of GAM (on 4 December 1976) approached, the local authorities made no attempt to prevent the celebration. They allowed GAM flags to be flown and permitted the GAM military commander, Abdullah Syafi'ie, to appear three times on government television to appeal for calm.[28] Even the provincial governor and DPRD issued a statement favouring a referendum.[29] The Korem commander at that time explained that he did not have enough troops to deal with the situation in any other way.[30]

By the end of 1999, local and village government had virtually ceased to operate in many areas along the north and east coasts. Local government functions were increasingly taken over by GAM-backed "shadow" governments. One indication of the decline of government authority was the turnout for the national general election in June 1999 which was only 1.4 per cent in North Aceh, 11 per cent in Pidie and 50 per cent in East Aceh.[31] Following East Timor's vote in favour of independence in August, the prospect of the "loss" of Aceh seemed real. The North Sumatra regional army commander, Maj. Gen. Abdul Rahman Gaffar, was sure that a referendum in Aceh would support independence. "How could a referendum be held without losing?" he asked reporters.[32]

Jakarta's Response: Contacts with GAM

During a visit to Aceh in March 1999, President Habibie promised a series of measures that he hoped would win back the loyalty of the Acehnese people. He promised that the military would "no longer act violently and cause bloodshed", military personnel who broke the law and abused human rights would be investigated, and political prisoners would be released. The government would open the mass graves of the "victims of military operations" and pay for re-burial according to Islamic rites. Funds were also to be made available for religious schools, the re-opening of a railway line and expansion of the Banda Aceh airport.[33] In September, the national DPR adopted a law acknowledging the formal role of the ulama in government in Aceh and providing for autonomy in the fields of religion, custom and education — in effect repeating the weakly implemented concessions given by President Soekarno in 1959.[34] Then in October, the MPR explicitly called for "special autonomy" in Aceh (and Papua). However, these concessions had little impact against a background, despite the president's promises, of continuing military operations, rising casualties and the unwillingness of the government to prosecute human-rights offenders. On the other hand, the military and other nationalist forces were in no mood to agree to major concessions to separatists in the wake of the East Timorese decision to opt for independence.

The MPR special session in October 1999 saw the replacement of Habibie with Abdurrahman Wahid. In contrast to Habibie who had shown little interest in the grievances of the Acehnese in the past and gave the impression of a leader desperately offering concessions in a vain attempt to win political support, Abdurrahman, or Gus Dur as he was usually known, had long been concerned about developments in Aceh and indicated that his government would adopt a conciliatory approach. Abdurrahman, however, often made contradictory off-the-cuff comments to journalists without first consulting officials. Even before his election as president, he claimed during a visit to Aceh that "For a long time I have said that I agree with a referendum in Aceh".[35] After his election, he asked foreign journalists:"If we can do that in East Timor, why can't we do that in Aceh?"[36] These comments raised hopes in Aceh while at the same time outraging the military and nationalist groups whose support — or at least acquiescence — would be needed for implementation. During a tour of Southeast Asian countries over the next few weeks, the president continued to make confusing comments as he attempted to draw back from his apparent support for a referendum before finally telling the DPR leadership that he would not tolerate the separation of Aceh from Indonesia.[37]

Gus Dur, however, continued to believe that a negotiated settlement could be achieved with GAM. He accepted an offer from the Geneva-based and Red Cross-linked Henri Dunant Centre (HDC)[38] to mediate talks with the Stockholm-based GAM leadership-in-exile and on 27 January 2000, Hassan Wirayuda, Indonesia's ambassador to the UN in Geneva, met the GAM leader, Hasan Tiro. Both acknowledged the existence of a stalemate where the government could not eliminate GAM while GAM did not have the military capacity to drive Indonesian forces out of Aceh.[39] Further meetings led to what was in effect a cease-fire agreement on 12 May. Called the "Humanitarian Pause", it established mechanisms to allow for the delivery of humanitarian assistance and the promotion of "confidence-building measures towards a peaceful solution to the conflict situation in Aceh".[40] The agreement required the government not to carry out offensive operations, but specifically allowed "normal police functions for the enforcement of law and the maintenance of public order" — a provision that could be interpreted to cover action against GAM. It appears that GAM used the lull in fighting to recruit and train more fighters and to take over more local government functions in rural areas, including the intensified collection of "taxes". Clashes between the security forces and GAM continued despite the "pause" although the numbers killed dropped sharply.[41] During the latter part of 2000 and early 2001, however, clashes became more frequent and the number of casualties increased. Reports of military and police (especially the paramilitary Brimob) abuses also became more common, including summary executions, "disappearances", torture, extortion, rapes and burning of villages.[42]

Most military officers had been dismayed by President Abdurrahman's willingness to talk with "bandits" and "traitors" and there were signs that troops on the ground in Aceh were deliberately attempting to sabotage his efforts to begin talks. In January 2000, Abdurrahman had invited the GAM military commander, Abdullah Syafi'ie, to join a discussion with other Acehnese leaders but Syafi'ie pulled out when troops carried out operations in an area where he was staying in an apparent attempt to capture him before the meeting.[43] Two months later, the president sent the acting state secretary, Bondan Gunawan, to meet Syafi'ie at his headquarters in a GAM-controlled region, but any goodwill arising from the visit was lost that evening when troops conducted raids in search of Syafi'ie in nearby villages.[44] Syafi'ie was finally killed in January 2002, ten days before new talks were due to begin, after an emissary from the Aceh governor had delivered a note proposing province-level talks. GAM believed that the emissary's real purpose was to ascertain Syafi'ie's whereabouts.

The deterioration of conditions in Aceh coincided with the weakening of the political position of President Abdurrahman. As described in Chapter 2, impeachment proceedings against the president began in January 2001 and from then on Abdurrahman's genuine desire to reach a settlement with GAM was increasingly subordinated to political moves designed to defend his presidency. During 2000, as shown in Chapter 5, he had already alienated most of his generals and in 2001 he felt compelled to make an ultimately unsuccessful bid for their support. As GAM gained ground in Aceh, military officers pressed for the formal resumption of military operations, especially after increased GAM activity forced the closure in March of the ExxonMobil natural-gas plant. In April the president finally succumbed and signed a presidential instruction ordering the military to resume offensive operations in Aceh, formalizing what had long been a reality on the ground. The instruction was drawn up by General Yudhoyono, who had been appointed as Coordinating Minister for Political, Social and Security Affairs the previous August. In contrast to the military hardliners who were calling for the "extermination" of GAM, Yudhoyono argued that "it is dangerous to give priority to military methods" and stressed the need for a "comprehensive" approach including political, economic, social and legal measures.[45] The order was accompanied by the deployment of more troops who, in practice, paid little regard to "political, economic, social and legal measures" and were mainly concerned with hunting down GAM fighters. The number of reported casualties rose sharply. According to the NGO, Kontras, 539 people were killed between April and August, compared to 256 between January and April.[46] In November, Yudhoyono, who had been re-appointed to the same position by the new president, Megawati, bowed to the wishes of the majority in the government by declaring that there would be "no more compromise with separatism" and no more dialogue with GAM.[47]

The government's approach now centred on a new law providing for the "special autonomy" proposed by the MPR in 1999. Instead of seeking further talks with GAM, the government unilaterally offered special autonomy in the hope that this would win such wide public support in Aceh that GAM would have to accept it. Draft legislation drawn up by the conservative Department of Home Affairs was superseded by a draft prepared by provincial politicians, Acehnese members of the DPR and prominent Acehnese in Jakarta that promised far wider autonomy.[48] In contrast to the national law of 1999 on regional autonomy that devolved power to districts, the new special autonomy law on *Nanggroe Aceh Darussalam* (NAD) — the Acehnese term for the state of Aceh — preserved the authority of the provincial government. Key features of the law were generous provisions allowing the province to retain a much larger share of oil and natural-gas revenues, as well as other resource revenues, compared to the other provinces. The law also permitted the Aceh government to implement syariah (Islamic law), a concession that did not apply to any other province, and provided for the direct election of the governor and district heads instead of indirect election through the DPRD. The law was finally adopted by the DPR a few days before the fall of Gus Dur in July and was signed by President Megawati on 9 August 2001.

The Cease-fire Agreement and its Collapse

Military operations continued after the adoption of the NAD law but the moderate Yudhoyono continued to keep open the prospect of renewed talks.[49] After several months the military offensive had put GAM on the defensive and forced it to withdraw from some of its stronghold areas. The tireless HDC, despite protests in the DPR against "foreign interference", had continued to keep in contact with both sides and, on the behind-the-scenes initiative of the United States, had recruited a small international team of respected "wise men" to give additional weight to the pressure for agreement.[50] New talks began in Geneva in February 2002, the Indonesian delegation now headed by retired ambassador, Wiryono Sastrohandoyo, in place of Hassan Wirajuda whom President Megawati had appointed as Foreign Minister. Guided by Yudhoyono, the government's strategy was to force GAM to accept that future talks could only be conducted on the basis of the NAD law which implied GAM's recognition of Indonesian sovereignty over Aceh. Under heavy pressure from continuing military operations, GAM eventually "accepted" the NAD law but only as "a starting point" for negotiations.[51]

The ambiguity of "acceptance as a starting point" was to bedevil future talks but it did not prevent the achievement on 9 December 2002 of a "cessation of hostilities framework agreement" (COHA) which provided for gradual disarmament of GAM and disengagement of the security forces over a period of seven months. A major concession from the government was its agreement to permit the monitoring of the implementation of the agreement by international observers from Thailand and the Philippines in joint teams with Indonesian and GAM representatives. This would be accompanied by an "All-Inclusive Dialogue" involving all sections of Acehnese society and ultimately "the election of a democratic government".[52] Clashes between GAM and government forces did not stop completely but the number of casualties dropped sharply. Initial public elation in Aceh, however, did not last long. The two sides were soon arguing over the interpretation of the agreement. The government accused GAM of using the period of relative peace to consolidate and expand its forces and to set up its own shadow government structure while GAM was reluctant to disarm.[53] Meanwhile military hardliners, most notably the army chief of staff, General Ryamizard Ryacudu, and the Kostrad commander, Lt. Gen. Bibit Waluyo, issued bellicose warnings to GAM and casualties began to creep upwards. During March 2003, a series of "spontaneous" demonstrations in various towns protested against GAM and the peace process. These demonstrations — some of which were violent — were transparently "engineered" by local military units and presaged the final collapse of the agreement. The number of clashes and casualties increased sharply during April and new troops were brought into the province.

The military hardliners in effect took charge on the ground and were determined to renew their offensive to "finish off" GAM. General Ryamizard, whose views seemed to reflect those of most officers, made it clear that the military did not want further negotiations. Earlier, while still Kostrad commander, he complained that "For two years we (the TNI) have been pushed around all the time and have not been able to move. It is as if our feet are tied but GAM's are not and our men are slaughtered and killed ... In any country those who are terrorists or armed insurgents will be eliminated. How can we make peace with them? ... How can we negotiate a thousand times".[54] Later, as army chief of staff, he declared that "Dialogue for a thousand years won't bring any results".[55] For Ryamizard, the TNI "is ready to carry out its task of annihilating (*menumpas*) GAM for as long as it takes. The TNI does not want to set targets for the final annihilation of GAM. We are ready to continue annihilating them for 1,000 years".[56] It is unlikely that soldiers who violated the cease-fire were worried about being disciplined by General Ryamizard.

The moderates around Yudhoyono were losing the struggle and were receiving no support from the president and little from the DPR. Moreover, they themselves felt "betrayed" by GAM which had used the peace to consolidate its forces and extend its influence. Backed by international pressure, especially from Japan, the United States and the European Union, Yudhoyono made a last-ditch effort to save the peace by holding a further meeting with GAM's Stockholm-based leaders in Tokyo. He laid down two conditions for GAM: an explicit statement accepting special autonomy within Indonesia, and the effective disarmament of GAM. When GAM failed to meet these conditions, which in effect amounted to a demand to surrender, President Megawati declared a military emergency (martial law) in Aceh from midnight on 18 May 2003. The security forces, which had increased to more than 30,000 military personnel and 12,000 police during the previous few weeks, went into action immediately.[57]

The Military Emergency

The Indonesian military operation in Aceh was launched two months after the American invasion of Iraq and was apparently inspired in part by the American "shock and awe" approach. GAM strongholds were initially strafed from the air and bombarded from land and sea. The military's immediate objective was to "separate" GAM fighters from their rural support base, particularly along the north and east coasts of the province, by forcing villagers to move to temporary refugee camps. This would give the military a free hand for "sweeping" operations against GAM members left in the villages. Village people were taken by trucks to government refugee camps where they were kept from several days to nearly a month until the "sweep" was completed. The government anticipated a total of 100,000 refugees, although not all at the same time.[58] The highest number reported at any one time was less than 50,000.[59]

Planned initially for six months, the military emergency was extended to a year and then downgraded to a "civil" emergency, but in practice the difference was hardly noticeable.[60] The military hardliners' goal of "exterminating" GAM, however, was not achieved. Just before the launching of the emergency, the army chief of staff had estimated that GAM's strength had risen to 5,000 men with 2,100 weapons.[61] After eighteen months of emergency rule, the military claimed that it had killed 2,879 GAM members while 1,954 had surrendered and 1,798 were detained — a total of 6,631 which was more than the estimated original number.[62] However, the new Coordinating Minister for Political and Security Affairs, Admiral Widodo, told the DPR that GAM still had 2,423 personnel with 866 weapons, while the Aceh Regional Military Commander, Maj. Gen. Endang Suwarya, estimated that 30 per cent of the original GAM force was still active.[63] These figures were open to several interpretations. First, they suggested that despite its losses, GAM was still recruiting new fighters. Suwarya, however, provided a different explanation. He claimed that the number of GAM at the start of the emergency had been under-estimated and that the true figure had been 8,000.[64] Another suggestion came from the TNI spokesman, Maj. Gen. Syafrie Syamsuddin, who admitted that the military's initial estimates of GAM's losses exaggerated the number as "many of the people who have been arrested or surrendered are GAM sympathizers, and not armed rebels".[65] The same logic could also be applied to the number killed. Human-rights NGOs claimed that many of those counted as "GAM casualties" were in fact ordinary people caught in cross-fire or killed as "suspected GAM". A statistic supporting that interpretation was the small number of GAM weapons recovered. Thus, at the end of the first year of the emergency, General Endriartono announced that 3,061 GAM fighters had been killed or surrendered but the number of weapons recovered was only 1,012.[66] It appeared that many of the GAM "fighters" had been unarmed. The security forces also suffered casualties. During the first year of the military emergency, military statistics recorded the loss of 159 members of the TNI and police.[67] Another 46 members of the TNI were killed during the first five months of the civil emergency, but, according to the TNI commander, 31 of these were not killed by GAM but died in accidents or other non-combat activities.[68]

The Indonesian government probably calculated that, following the United States' bombing of Iraq, the Americans would hardly be in a position to condemn Indonesia for launching a full-scale military operation and would be inclined to overlook human-rights violations. Not surprisingly, stories soon emerged of serious abuses of local people believed to be sympathetic towards GAM. On the second day of the emergency soldiers, following a clash with GAM in Bireuen, entered a village and killed seven villagers, including a thirteen-year-old boy. The military claimed that all seven were GAM members although it appeared that none carried arms. The incident became widely known when several foreign journalists interviewed villagers who claimed that the seven were not killed in combat but lined up and summarily executed.[69] In another widely reported case, also in a GAM-dominated village in Bireuen, soldiers severely beat villagers who did not provide information about GAM, including the elderly village head and a woman who both had to be hospitalized. In this village one man was summarily executed after trying to escape.[70] The military was further embarrassed during the first few weeks of the campaign by several rape cases and one involving robbery. In an effort to save the military's image, trials were held with lightning speed in the next few weeks. The soldiers who had beaten the villagers were found guilty and sentenced to imprisonment of four months and twenty days.[71] In another case, however, a military judge found that twelve Kostrad soldiers had indeed beaten villagers but, as victims and witnesses had failed to identify the perpetrators, he found the soldiers not guilty.[72] Of the rapists, the heaviest sentence was three years and six months while the robber got four months. Those responsible for summary executions, however, were not charged as their victims were said to be GAM members.

Despite rhetoric about winning hearts and minds, the earliest military operations often had the opposite effect. Villagers who had been forcibly evacuated from their homes not only complained about poor conditions in camps but were dismayed on their return to find that livestock such as chickens and goats as well as other property, such as television sets, radios, bicycles and jewellery, were missing. Even the commander-in-chief of the TNI, General Endriartono, had to apologize and admit that "Even if the refugees stayed in the camps for three or four days only, they found their homes looted when they moved back to their homes". Endriartono acknowledged that soldiers might have been responsible and promised to bring them to court.[73]

One immediate consequence of the exposure of these cases was a tightening of controls on the media and NGOs. Indonesian journalists were already restricted by the adoption of the American practice in Iraq of "embedding" journalists in military units where they were expected to "write within the framework of NKRI", as Maj. Gen. Suwarya put it.[74] The Indonesian press was also asked to no longer publish statements from GAM sources. Regulations issued at the start of the military emergency required foreign journalists to obtain the permission of the Department of Foreign Affairs to visit Aceh and to report to the military authorities, but by early June their applications were being rejected and three journalists already in Aceh had been expelled. Similar requirements were also imposed on foreigners working for NGOs.[75] The Indonesian authorities remembered how the presence of foreigners in East Timor in 1991 had exposed the Dili massacre that turned the tide of world opinion against Indonesia and led to the 1999 referendum. On the other hand, as the Acehnese observer, Rizal Sukma, pointed out, "These restrictions clearly raise suspicions about what is really happening in Aceh".[76]

At the end of the first six months of the military emergency, the martial law commander, Maj. Gen. Suwarya, admitted that "we found the Achenese people's resistance (against GAM) remained weak, efforts toward improving the people's welfare did not work and law enforcement authorities failed to capture as many rebels as we had expected". He added, "Perhaps our soldiers in the field used an inappropriate approach to win the people's trust".[77] The TNI, however, continued to make progress. Military operations forced GAM to move into the hills away from centres of population and paved the way for the government to regain control of local institutions. At the beginning of the emergency the government admitted that of 223 sub-districts in Aceh, 25 had ceased to function and another 54 were not functioning well (*kurang berfungsi*). The non-functioning villages were in Pidie, Bireuen, North Aceh and West Aceh. In 13 of the non-functioning sub-districts junior military officers were appointed as *camat* (sub-district head) after a one-week training course and another 12 assisted previously ineffective *camat*.[78] Of 5,862 villages, 1,034 were not functioning at all at the beginning of the emergency and 1,615 were not functioning well. In many of these areas officials were afraid to live in their villages or to go to their offices because of threats from GAM.[79] By early 2004 the number of non-functioning villages had dropped to 153 and those not working well had fallen to 875.[80] A more cautious assessment was provided by the military commander, speaking of preparations for the coming general election, who said that of 2,440 *rayon*, 1,365 were under control (*aman*), 622 were "grey" while 453 were still "black".[81] A further indication of the restoration of government control was the estimate of the Rectors' Forum, an election observer group, that 93 per cent of enrolled voters had cast their ballots in the general election in April 2004.[82]

GAM

GAM was under no illusion that its meagre military forces could drive the TNI out of Aceh. Nor did it believe that the Indonesian government would withdraw from Aceh as a result of negotiations.[83] Its long-term strategy was based on the belief that "Indonesia-Java" was not a viable entity and sooner or later would disintegrate.[84] As one GAM negotiator put it, "Indonesia's cancer has already spread too far for it to recover".[85] GAM could have easily recruited a force much larger than the several thousand counted by the TNI but this was not required to serve its main purpose which was to keep alive the spirit of resistance. GAM's goal was to survive so that it could take over when the inevitable day of Indonesia's collapse finally arrived. Meanwhile, it continued its low-level insurgency designed to keep the costs of counter-insurgency high.[86]

The Indonesian government's complaint that GAM was "not sincere" in negotiating was therefore not without some foundation. GAM at that time could not give the crucial concession demanded by Indonesia, namely abandonment of its goal of independence, without risking its own credibility in the eyes of its supporters. Nevertheless, participation in negotiations promised some benefits for GAM. By agreeing to negotiate, the Indonesian government allowed GAM to enhance its prestige by presenting itself as representing the people of Aceh. Negotiations also facilitated the "internationalization" of the conflict through the HDC, the international "wise men", and Thai and Philippine cease-fire monitors. As Schulze points out, "for GAM the negotiations were not a way to find common ground with Jakarta but a means to compel the international community to pressure Jakarta into ceding independence".[87] Although no major foreign government ever endorsed GAM's goal of independence, the United States, Japan and the European Community actively supported the negotiation process.[88] With the East Timor precedent in mind, GAM leaders could hope that by associating the international community with the negotiations, major nations might be persuaded at some point in the future to support a referendum and eventual independence for Aceh.

The successive military offensives launched by the TNI undoubtedly damaged GAM but were still far from destroying the organization. Although many GAM "foot soldiers" were killed or captured during the post-2003 emergency, no top leaders of GAM were captured and only one, the East Aceh leader, Daud Ishak, was killed. There is also much doubt, as discussed above, about the real number of GAM casualties due to the difficulty in distinguishing between GAM fighters and sympathisers or even mere passers-by.

The central question is whether military operations reduced support for GAM or, as is sometimes claimed, actually increased it. As Rizal Sukma wrote, "A prolonged military campaign, while it might deal a further blow to GAM's military strength, might also prolong resentment toward central rule from Jakarta".[89] High "body counts" do not necessarily mean reduced support, especially if as suspected, a significant number of those counted as GAM fighters were not actively engaged in the fighting. As the Aceh chief of police replied when asked about GAM recruitment, "if someone's relative is shot, they then join GAM".[90] The presence of up to 50,000 under-paid and poorly disciplined troops entrusted with the task of "exterminating" GAM made it virtually inevitable that the abusive practices of the past would continue and further alienate the people whose hearts and minds had to be won.[91] The military had quickly clamped down on the media after reports of killings and abuse had appeared in both the domestic and international press. However, a report by Human Rights Watch, based on interviews with eighty-five recent Acehnese refugees in Malaysia, suggested that abusive behaviour continued to be routine among members of the security forces in the form of summary executions, beatings, disappearances and so on. Extortion of money was also reported.[92] Although the interviewees were refugees who appeared to be sympathetic to GAM, the consistency of their detailed claims supported their credibility.[93] Ten months later similar allegations were documented in a report by Amnesty International.[94] Certainly, the rhetoric and attitudes of some senior TNI officers would not have deterred abuses.[95]

It should not be assumed, however, that all Acehnese supported GAM and its demand for independence. While much of GAM's popularity stemmed from its resistance to the security forces and a provincial government that was seen as no more than an extension of rule by Jakarta, it had not been reluctant to resort to force and intimidation to strengthen its influence. GAM regarded itself as the legitimate government of Aceh and therefore collected "taxes" to finance its own activities.[96] Like the military, GAM sent its "tax collectors" to plantations and business enterprises (including major corporations such as ExxonMobil) and threatened them with violence if they refused to pay. GAM also demanded a percentage of funds made available for development projects, including projects financed by foreign donors. "Taxes" were also imposed on civil servants, school teachers and other employees who were expected to pay about one month's salary per year.[97] Those who refused to pay faced the prospect of retribution. The rectors of Aceh's two main universities, Professor Safwan Idris of the Islamic institute, IAIN Ar-Raniry, and Professor Dayan Dawood, of Syiah Kuala University, were both assassinated, apparently by GAM agents for refusing to divert funds from campus development projects.[98] GAM was also accused of assassinating members of local DPRDs and senior officials although in most cases no arrests were made. People often found themselves in an invidious position. If they rejected GAM's demands they risked assassination but if they made a contribution they could be accused by the military of supporting GAM. For example, a Golkar member of the Aceh Besar DPRD was sentenced to three years jail for giving Rp 300,000 each to three GAM leaders.[99]

RESOLVING THE CONFLICT

By 2004 the long-running war in Aceh had reached a stalemate. The experience of the military emergency had demonstrated decisively that the TNI could inflict substantial damage on GAM but the military campaign had not been able to eliminate it. On the other hand, the earlier peace initiatives of the Abdurrahman and Megawati governments had provided brief periods of respite but failed to achieve a long-term resolution. The conflict in Aceh no doubt constituted a severe crisis for the 2 per cent of the population that lived in that province but public opinion elsewhere in the country was not unduly agitated. Public support for continuing military operations was high and national politics were focused on other matters. The outlook for the future was therefore not promising and no one could have expected that a peace agreement would be achieved the following year and that at the end of 2006 a GAM leader would be elected as governor of Aceh. In retrospect, the election of the Yudhoyono-Kalla ticket in the 2004 presidential election proved to be a crucial turning point. The new government quickly began to send out secret peace feelers to GAM while taking steps to neutralize potential opposition in the military and the DPR. The prospects of achieving a settlement, however, received enormous impetus from the tragic intervention of a natural disaster.

The Indonesian political elite was by no means fully in favour of peace talks with GAM. Many political leaders supported the military view that military operations should continue until GAM surrendered. In essence, the eventual peace agreement required GAM to abandon its goal of independence, to dissolve its military force and surrender its arms to the government in exchange for recognition of its right to participate in the democratic political process. Even though GAM had made fundamental concessions, retired military officers and many politicians continued to criticize the agreement, and substantial opposition remained in the DPR when the government introduced a bill to implement it. Although GAM did not participate directly in the discussion of the bill, the eventual Law on the Governance of Aceh reflected further compromises on the part of both the government and GAM. Despite the concessions that it made, GAM achieved its bottom-line goal of participating in the forthcoming elections of the provincial governor and districts heads.

Towards Negotiations

Even after the launching of military operations under the military emergency in 2003, Yudhoyono, as Megawati's Coordinating Minister for Political and Security Affairs, had continued to hope that military pressure on GAM fighters in Aceh would induce at least some of them to reconsider their loyalty to the GAM leadership in exile in Sweden.[100] Meanwhile, Jusuf Kalla, the Coordinating Minister for People's Welfare and Yudhoyono's partner in the earlier peace negotiations that opened the way to resolving conflict in Maluku and Poso, had obtained President Megawati's approval to look for other means of reaching a resolution in Aceh.[101] However, as Michael Morfit explained, "Megawati did not oppose, neither did she enthusiastically embrace it or make it part of a coherent overall government strategy".[102] In February 2004, Kalla, with the approval of the president, had asked his deputy at the coordinating ministry, Dr Farid Husain, to explore possible contacts with the GAM leadership in Sweden but the GAM leaders refused to meet him.[103] At that stage, as Indonesia's military campaign was in full swing, the top Stockholm-based leaders could hardly have expected significant concessions from Jakarta and therefore had virtually no incentive to give up the goal to which they had devoted their lives. At the same time GAM commanders on the ground in Aceh continued to proclaim their loyalty to Hasan Tiro and refused to comment on political issues which they regarded as the prerogative of the leaders in Stockholm. Nevertheless, there had been speculation that some Aceh-based commanders might begin to see their struggle as increasingly futile as the long-awaited disintegration of Indonesia failed to happen and ordinary people continued to suffer from the consequences of the war.[104] Moreover, it could be anticipated that the emotional grip of the Stockholm leaders could become less firm when Hasan Tiro, who was born in 1925 and partly disabled by a stroke, eventually left the scene.

The prospect that the Megawati government would return to serious negotiations seemed slight. During the last days of her presidency she had even nominated the hard-line army chief of staff, Gen. Ryamizard, to be the next Commander-in-Chief of the TNI — a nomination soon withdrawn by the new President Yudhoyono. While Yudhoyono continued to endorse the military operations in Aceh, he allowed his vice president to quietly send out feelers to local GAM leaders in Malaysia and Indonesia, including some who were in prison. It seems that Kalla's approach to GAM members may have been accompanied by financial or other economic incentives.[105] These efforts met with rejection from Stockholm where a statement in the name of Hasan Tiro on 4 December warned "all groups to guard against the Indonesian government's exploiting or making fools of them" and not to "become known as traitors to the nation". Imprisoned GAM members told Kalla's intermediaries that they should approach the GAM leadership in Sweden, not those in Aceh.[106]

Previously, during his unsuccessful attempt to meet GAM leaders in February 2004, Kalla's emissary, Farid Husain, had met an old friend, a Finnish businessman, Juha Christensen, who put him into contact with the Crisis Management Initiative (CMI), a Helsinki-based NGO headed by a former president of Finland, Martti Ahtisaari, who had previously played peace-making roles in Namibia, Kosovo and Northern Ireland. Following Indonesia's presidential election and with Ahtisaari's encouragement, Farid and Christensen acted as informal intermediaries between the new Indonesian vice president and the Stockholm-based GAM leadership who showed interest in what the new government might have in mind. The GAM leaders, however, were still unsure about the extent of Christensen's access to the Indonesian government but were eventually convinced when he was allowed to visit detained GAM leaders in prison.[107] Christensen's efforts to persuade the GAM leaders bore fruit and he informed Ahtisaari "about two days before Christmas" that the two sides were willing to renew talks.[108] Ahtisaari responded immediately and formal invitations were issued in January 2005.

Circumstances were transformed, however, on the day after Christmas when a disaster, far more destructive than the decades of fighting between GAM and the government's forces, struck Aceh. On 26 December 2004 Aceh was hit by an earthquake followed by a huge tsunami that devastated the province's west coast, and much of the north coast including about half of Banda Aceh, and left 166,000 people dead or missing. In the midst of national and international emergency efforts, President Yudhoyono recognized that the tragedy of the tsunami could make GAM more amenable to abandoning its armed struggle. "I spoke directly with GAM leaders in Aceh", he said later. "Their response was encouraging. However they always said that they were ready but wondered about GAM in Sweden. So I asked the Secretary General of the United Nations to appeal to the GAM leadership in Sweden not to obstruct the process in Indonesia leading towards the ending of the conflict in Aceh. The response was positive."[109] As massive international assistance — both material and personnel — flowed into Aceh, the government could not afford to be seen by the international community as more interested in pursuing its campaign against GAM than in facilitating emergency assistance, while GAM's credibility in the eyes of the people of Aceh would have been damaged if it had rejected peace talks. Although both sides had already indicated willingness to participate in talks before the tsunami, the disaster gave a powerful impetus to their ultimate conclusion.

The Indonesian government hoped that in the new circumstances GAM could be pressed to drop its demand for independence and disband its military force. Military operations since 2003 had badly damaged GAM's infrastructure on the ground in Aceh and their forces had suffered substantial casualties. One of GAM's negotiators later admitted that "the truth of the matter was that logistically GAM was not in a position to continue the armed struggle".[110] On the other hand, the TNI was still far from "eliminating" GAM.[111] GAM knew that Indonesia was not about to give concessions that could open the way to independence but, on the other, engaging in talks would again allow

GAM to raise its international profile and draw attention to its cause. The GAM leaders also calculated that pressure on their forces in the field would be eased if talks began and, encouraged by the initiatives taken by the new government in Jakarta to contact GAM, were interested in seeing what Jakarta had to offer. The Indonesian government, however, refused to implement a cease-fire and its negotiating position remained essentially the same as at the failed 2003 talks. Any agreement would have to be on the basis of GAM's abandonment of its goal of independence and explicit acceptance of "special autonomy". Although GAM had agreed to participate in new talks before the tsunami, it was only after the tsunami that senior GAM leaders began seriously to reconsider its goal of independence.[112]

The Helsinki Talks and the Peace Agreement

Despite continuing reservations, both sides accepted CMI's invitation to meet in Helsinki on 27 January 2006. The GAM delegation was led by its "prime minister", Malik Mahmud, and "foreign minister", Zaini Abdullah, but was disadvantaged by the government's refusal to release the members of its earlier negotiation team who had been detained following the collapse of the 2003 negotiations.[113] The Indonesian team was "supervised" by the Coordinating Minister for Political, Legal and Security Affairs, Admiral Widodo Adi Sucipto, and included two other cabinet ministers, Kalla's protégé, Hamid Awaluddin, as chief negotiator and the Acehnese Sofyan Djalil.[114] In practice, the Indonesian negotiators were in regular contact with Kalla in Jakarta. As Morfit explains, "While SBY (Yudhoyono) had his eye on this larger strategic picture, he delegated to Kalla the responsibility for overseeing and managing the Helsinki negotiations on a day-to-day basis".[115]

The GAM delegates were unhappy from the beginning of the talks because of Indonesia's refusal to implement a military cease-fire in Aceh. The atmosphere deteriorated further when the CMI mediator, Ahtisaari, stated that the talks were based on the condition that GAM accept "special autonomy" — the Indonesian term for Aceh's current relationship with Jakarta. "Thus", wrote GAM's Australian "advisor", Dr Damien Kingsbury, "the first day of the talks ended in crisis, with an apparent impasse having developed which appeared would preclude any further progress".[116] The prospects at the second round on 21–23 February were therefore grim. At this point, however, GAM proposed "self-government" as a means of avoiding the deadlock to which the talks seemed to be heading. Although GAM's spokesman, Bakhtiar Abdullah, denied that GAM had abandoned its goal of independence, this proposal gave new life to the talks.[117] An indication of the direction of GAM's thinking had appeared in an article in the *Jakarta Post* on 24 January, just before the opening of the first round. Written by Kingsbury, the article called for "genuine autonomy" in which "Acehnese aspirations for self-determination would be functionally met" but also acknowledged that an agreement would need "to accommodate the bottom line" for Indonesia "which is the physical integrity of the state".[118] GAM negotiator, Nur Djuli, later mentioned the case of the self-governing Aland Islands in Finland as an example of what GAM had in mind.[119]

GAM's willingness to consider an outcome short of independence allowed the talks to continue but was met by increased Indonesian pressure from both outside and inside the talks. President Yudhoyono re-affirmed that "special autonomy" was the "final solution",[120] GAM negotiators who had been imprisoned after the failure of the 2003 negotiations were not released, and the "supervisor" of the Indonesian team, Admiral Widodo, did not attend the third round that began on 12 April. The Aceh regional army commander, Maj. Gen. Endang Suwarya, said that whatever happened in Helsinki, military operations would continue against GAM in Aceh, and added that "if you ask my opinion, a ceasefire is useless".[121] The TNI Commander-in-Chief, Gen. Endriartono Sutarto, said that the TNI had abandoned its defensive posture and would not withdraw until GAM surrendered all its weapons.[122] Strong opposition was expressed in the DPR to giving concessions to GAM and also to the talks themselves. It was not only PDI-P politicians but also members of Jusuf Kalla's own party, Golkar, who criticized the talks.[123] From the beginning, prominent politicians had opposed holding talks outside Indonesia and the involvement of a foreign mediator.[124] Others were more sweeping. Djoko Susilo of PAN said there was no benefit in talking with GAM, Yuddy Chrisnandy of Golkar dismissed the talks as "stupid", Effendi MS Simbolon of PDI-P called on the government "to stop these shameful negotiations" and Effendy Choirie of PKB said that what was done by Jusuf Kalla "makes no sense" (*tidak masuk akal*).[125] The speaker of the DPR and Golkar deputy chairman, Agung Laksono, even wrote to the president proposing that the talks be abandoned.[126]

It is, of course, possible that some, but by no means all, of the attacks on the peace process were not intended to end the peace talks but designed to put more pressure on GAM. In addition to such negative pressure, it appears that positive initiatives were also taken in the form of financial incentives offered by a member of the Indonesian delegation to members of the GAM team.[127] An attempt was also made to "soften" the approach of the GAM advisor, Damien Kingsbury, who despite a current ban on his entering Indonesia, was invited "secretly" to Jakarta where he had a meeting on 24 March with Jusuf

Kalla.[128] That both sides were still serious about the talks was indicated by progress in Helsinki on less controversial issues relating to natural resources, trade, tourism, harbours, education and village government.

By the fourth round, beginning on 26 May, considerable agreement had been reached but fundamental unresolved issues remained. The first was the status of political parties in Aceh — a crucial issue for both sides. The Indonesian government was willing to allow GAM to participate in elections but only in ways consistent with current Indonesian electoral law which limited candidates to those nominated by recognized national parties, defined as parties with significant representation in at least half of Indonesia's thirty-three provinces. The Indonesian law was in fact intended to deal with cases like Aceh where a "separatist" party might win a provincial election and then demand independence. More broadly, it also arose from a concern that parties representing regional ethnic or religious groups could provoke inter-communal violence — not only in Aceh but anywhere in Indonesia. The government's position enjoyed considerable support among the parties in the DPR. Ferry Mursyidan Baldan of Golkar believed that "local parties are the entry point for the destruction of NKRI,"[129] while the PDI-P leader in the DPR, Soetjipto, and his party colleague, Permadi, both considered the formation of local parties as a step toward separatism.[130] Speaking for the PKB, former president Abdurrahman Wahid said "in the world of democracy it is extremely improper to form local parties,"[131] while former army deputy chief of staff, Lt. Gen. (ret.) Kiki Syahnakri, regarded local parties as a "Pandora's box".[132]

Reflecting the concerns expressed in the DPR, the Indonesian team at the fifth round, beginning on 12 July, came up with a bizarre proposal that existing parties "donate" members to GAM in other parts of Indonesia so that GAM could meet the requirements for recognition as a "national" party. GAM, however, argued that it was not seeking a special "sweetheart" deal for itself but the right of any group of Acehnese to set up their own party in Aceh. Agreement had still not been achieved on this issue on the last day of the meeting but negotiations continued informally outside the negotiation room and, following a telephone call to the vice president in Jakarta, finally resulted in a somewhat ambiguous provision which committed the Indonesian government to "facilitate the establishment of Aceh-based political parties that meet national criteria" but also required the government "within one year or at the latest eighteen months" of the signing of the agreement to create "the political and legal conditions for the establishment of local political parties in Aceh in consultation with Parliament". It was also agreed, in contrast to other regions which required candidates for executive positions such as governor, bupati or mayor to be nominated by political parties, that non-party candidates could contest such elections in Aceh, thus clearing the way for GAM candidates to contest as independents if elections were held before the necessary new legislation was adopted.[133] These last-minute concessions from the government allowed GAM to sign the final agreement.

The government, however, had its way on a second vital issue. GAM was required to disband its military force and surrender a substantial number of its arms for destruction by international monitors while the number of Indonesian forces deployed in Aceh would be reduced drastically. The numbers of TNI and police permitted to remain in Aceh, however, had been left blank in the agreement until 15 August, the day of the signing. In the fourth round, the GAM "prime minister" Malik Mahmud had proposed that GAM's forces should be integrated in the TNI but most of the GAM delegation believed that the best that could be achieved was the placement of GAM units within the Aceh police.[134] The head of the European Union Assessment Mission, Pieter Feith, had earlier provided a briefing to GAM that suggested that the combined TNI and police manpower in Aceh would be reduced to 4,800.[135] The agreement provided for the withdrawal of all "non-organic" military and police personnel (i.e. troops not permanently part of the local territorial command), but on the day of the signing the CMI-approved agreement contained a figure of 14,700 for TNI and another 9,100 for the police — a total of 23,800.[136] It was obvious that the TNI had simply re-defined the term "organic" in order to retain troops that had previously been considered as "non-organic". The GAM delegates were shocked and felt betrayed but acknowledged that they had not followed the issue closely and accepted the fait accompli.[137] The GAM leaders apparently calculated that the government's concession on local parties more than compensated for the increased number of troops based in Aceh.

The Memorandum of Understanding (MoU) signed by the two parties on 15 August 2005 was concerned with two broad areas: the future government of Aceh and the immediate requirements of ensuring the peace. In regard to the political future, the agreement committed the government to adopt by the end of March 2006 a new Law on the Governance of Aceh and contained detailed provisions concerning relations with the central government, political participation, the economy, the rule of law and human rights (including a Human Rights Court and a Truth and Reconciliation Commission). Many — although not all — of the details were in principle not very different to the existing law on Special Autonomy which GAM had so vigorously rejected at the beginning of the negotiations. As Aspinall notes, "Overall, setting aside the question of local political parties, the MoU does not seem to suggest a radical extension of the existing Special Autonomy Law."[138]

In regard to immediate measures to support the peace, the MoU provided amnesties for GAM members, the release of political detainees, and reintegration assistance to GAM combatants and detainees in the form of suitable agricultural land or employment, while at the same time offering similar assistance to "all civilians who have suffered a demonstrable loss due to the conflict". Security arrangements provided for the demobilization of 3,000 GAM combatants and their surrender of 840 weapons while the government would, as discussed above, "withdraw all elements of non-organic military and non-organic police" and decommission weapons in the hands of "any possible illegal groups and parties" — a euphemism for military-backed civilian militias. The implementation of the MoU would be the responsibility of an Aceh Monitoring Mission (AMM) staffed by personnel from the European Union and ASEAN countries. Finally, the Indonesian government promised "to allow full access for the representatives of national and international media to Aceh".

On the fundamental issue of the talks, GAM's abandonment of its original raison d'etre and its dissolution of its military force were far greater than any concessions given by the Indonesian government. Naturally this resulted in some resistance to the agreement among GAM commanders on the ground who felt that they had survived the Indonesian military's onslaught and therefore had no pressing need to abandon their struggle. Ultimately it seems that GAM commanders were persuaded by the fact that although GAM had survived relatively unscathed, many ordinary Acehnese had suffered terribly.[139] The massive destruction brought by the tsunami had persuaded GAM that they could not just reject the talks without risking the loss of sympathy among ordinary Acehnese. Moreover continuing Indonesian military operations would have led to further casualties among GAM's own forces in the field without improving ultimate prospects of success, while GAM's earlier hopes that Indonesia would simply implode had become even more fanciful. But the agreement also provided GAM with a significant opportunity. The key issue was the forthcoming elections of the regional governor and district heads. The talks happened to coincide with the months leading up to the next gubernatorial election in Aceh and a series of elections of district heads due later in the year. The NAD law of 2001 applying just to Aceh and the Law on Regional Autonomy of 2004 applying to the entire nation had already provided for direct elections of regional heads but candidates still had to be nominated by political parties that had contested the previous general elections in which only "national" parties had been allowed to participate.

Despite protests from nationalist parties and military officers in Jakarta, the government had agreed to "facilitate the establishment of Aceh-based political parties that meet national criteria" within 12–18 months, thus providing GAM with an opportunity to form its own party. As the necessary regulations were unlikely to be ready in time for GAM to form its own party before the coming elections, the government made a further "one-off" concession that enabled the nomination of independent candidates for the next, although not later, elections. Still confident that it retained much popular support, GAM saw itself as abandoning independence in exchange for victory at the polls. Having won that concession, GAM was even willing to accept a vastly larger military and police presence than had been initially envisaged.

Implementing the MoU

News of the peace agreement was greeted with celebrations in Aceh but opponents of the Yudhoyono government in Jakarta were quick to protest.[140] Even before the MoU was signed in Helsinki, former president Abdurrahman had gathered opponents of the MoU at his home, including Megawati and her husband, Taufiq Kiemas, former vice president General Try Sutrisno, unsuccessful Golkar presidential candidate General Wiranto, former Golkar chairman Akbar Tandjung and several PDI-P politicians.[141] Megawati claimed that the MoU "threatens the existence of the nation" and protested by refusing to attend Independence Day celebrations on 17 August, two days after the signing of the MoU in Helsinki. Her party, the PDI-P, regretted that the agreement contained no clause requiring the dissolution of GAM and called for a judicial review on the grounds that the MoU implied unconstitutional federalism. The party Secretary-General, Pramono Anung, said that the MoU "clearly contains the substance of giving independence to Aceh" and that all that Aceh needs to do "to achieve independence is to issue a proclamation and wait for international recognition.[142] Pramono's words were echoed ten days later by former army chief of staff, Ryamizard Ryacudu, who added that not only Aceh, but Papua also, now only needed "a declaration and international recognition".[143] Akbar Tandjung, who had lost the leadership of Golkar to Jusuf Kalla, added his voice to the protest by claiming that the MoU "is in conflict with the spirit of the NKRI".[144] Lemhannas, the former military think-tank, discovered sixteen points in the MoU that contradicted the constitution while former army deputy chief of staff, Lt. Gen. (ret.) Kiki Syahnakri, said that the "MoU amputates Indonesian sovereignty".[145] A statement issued by the association of retired army officers declared that "the MoU is the next stage in the grand scheme of foreign forces to break up the sovereignty" of

Indonesia.[146] On 2 September dissidents, including Megawati, Abdurrahman, General Try Sutrisno, Akbar Tandjung, PKB leader Muhaimin Iskandar, and perennial oppositionist, Hariman Siregar, formed what they called the United Rise of Nusantara Movement (*Gerakan Nusantara Bangkit Bersatu*).[147] These leaders, however, were mainly disappointed politicians who felt bitter about the election in 2004 of Yudhoyono as president and Jusuf Kalla as chairman of Golkar. For them, the Aceh agreement offered a welcome opportunity to undermine the government.

Meanwhile Yudhoyono and Kalla worked to persuade critics at least to "accept" the MoU. A week before the signing in Helsinki, the president called a "consultation meeting" with the DPR leadership, the leaders of the ten party groupings and the leaders of Commission I (foreign affairs and defence) and Commission II (government). After what was described as a "marathon consultation", they agreed to "give the opportunity" to the government to sign the MoU,[148] and, despite their earlier reservations, both the current Speaker of the DPR and Golkar Deputy Chairman, Agung Laksono, and the Speaker of the MPR and former PKS leader, Hidayat Nurwahid, indicated their support.[149] Military officers in general had remained suspicious of the agreement but by mid-2005 the president had gradually placed his own supporters in senior positions. In particular, the replacement of General Ryamizard as chief of staff of the army by Yudhoyono's protégé, General Djoko Santoso, had been a crucial pre-condition for the Aceh settlement.

In Aceh itself the Aceh Monitoring Mission (AMM), headed by the Dutch diplomat, Pieter Feith, quickly prepared for the implementation of the agreement.[150] The government assigned Sofyan Djalil as its "special representative" to AMM while GAM was represented by Tengku Irwandi Yusuf. International monitors, numbering 226 from the European Union and ASEAN countries, supervised the parallel disarmament of GAM and withdrawal of non-organic TNI and police forces which began in September and was completed in December.[151] Several minor military clashes took place in late August and early September but were quickly resolved and the destruction of GAM weapons proceeded smoothly.[152] In Jakarta, Commission III of the DPR attempted to play a spoiling role by proposing that in order to gain amnesties, GAM members would have to sign humiliating loyalty oaths to "NKRI, the Constitution and Pancasila"[153] but the government ignored the proposal and 1,424 GAM detainees were released on 31 August (although another 91 continued to be held on ordinary criminal charges).[154]

Having abandoned its dream of independence for which it had fought for more than three decades, GAM accepted the implementation of the agreement. In addition to providing GAM the opportunity to fully participate in future elections, the government's strategy was also directed toward the material welfare of GAM's fighters in the field.[155] The MoU provided for "re-integration" assistance to 3,000 GAM combatants. Initial payments of Rp 1 million (US$100) were followed by the establishment by the provincial government of the Aceh Reintegration Agency (*Badan Reintegrasi Aceh*: BRA) which provided additional funds of Rp 25 million each over a year for specific projects. Aid was also provided for other residents of Aceh who had suffered losses due to the fighting.[156] Of the total of Rp 450 billion required, Rp 200 billion (US$20 million) came from the Indonesian budget and Rp 250 billion from international donors.[157]

The Law on the Governance of Aceh

As implementation of the MoU's immediate measures to support the peace proceeded more or less smoothly in Aceh, the next crucial step would be taken in Jakarta where the MoU required that the DPR adopt a Law on the Governance of Aceh by 31 March 2006.[158] Opponents of the MoU were already beginning to mobilize against it. Towards the end of August, the PDI-P and PKB together with the small Bintang Pelopor Demokrasi (BPD) group were demanding a formal government explanation (*interpelasi*) to the DPR, but it soon became clear that the majority of the DPR had no intention of blocking the agreement. By then, Jusuf Kalla had brought pressure to bear on Golkar members who had initially criticized the MoU. That the majority opposed the interpelasi proposal, however, did not mean that the entire MoU would be accepted. Initially, leading members of the main parties in the DPR adopted a "minimalist" position. Ferry Mursyidan Baldan of Golkar and Alex Litaay of PDI-P favoured the simple amendment of the Special Autonomy Law of 2001 to accommodate the MoU, particularly by allowing GAM members to contest elections. In similar vein, Saifullah Ma'shum of PKB proposed that the 2004 regional autonomy law should also be amended.[159]

At the other extreme, outside the DPR was GAM which prepared its own draft that basically called for the full implementation of the MoU. GAM's draft referred to the "region" (*wilayah*) rather than "province" of Aceh, suggesting that Aceh was not a mere province with the same status as the other Indonesian provinces. GAM also proposed that the octogenarian Hasan Tiro be appointed as the first *Wali Nanggroe* (head of state) for life with successors selected by the DPRD.[160]

In Aceh, a Joint Forum (*Forum Bersama*), led by the PAN politician, Ahmad Farhan Hamid, and consisting of Acehnese members of the DPR and DPD from all parties, held a "Grand Seminar" (*Seminar Raya*) at the

Syiah Kuala University in Banda Aceh on 11–12 October to discuss the preparation of the Aceh bill. Aceh's three main universities, Syiah Kuala, Malikussaleh, and the Islamic institute Ar-Raniry, submitted drafts while one of the GAM negotiators, Nur Djuli, represented GAM. Immediately after this seminar, the regional DPRD established a Special Committee (Pansus), headed by Ashari Basar of Golkar, to prepare a draft bill, drawing on the discussions at the seminar.[161] Elected in 2004, the Aceh DPRD consisted of representatives of the "national" parties but their sense of Acehnese identity, their appreciation of the new peace, and their awareness of GAM's potential electoral influence, led them to adopt a draft that largely incorporated the provisions of the Helsinki MoU.[162] The draft needed to take account of two audiences. First, it had to meet the expectations of GAM. The whole purpose of the exercise would have been lost if it left a substantial part of GAM alienated and ready to return to armed resistance. But, on the other hand, it needed to avoid unduly upsetting the representatives of the rest of Indonesia in the DPR, particularly the nationalist group led by the PDI-P, and both active and retired military officers.

In Jakarta, the Minister of Home Affairs accepted the Aceh DPRD's draft as the basis of the government bill.[163] After "synchronization" with the Department of Home Affairs, the bill was sent by the president to the DPR on 26 January 2006. The Department of Home Affairs, as we saw in Chapter 4, was deeply committed to the idea of the unitary state and was ultra-suspicious of suggestions of "federalism".[164] Much of the new bill followed the lines of the Aceh draft but, reflecting the concerns of the Department of Home Affairs and in anticipation of DPR objections, some potentially controversial clauses were dropped or qualified. Vice President Kalla, however, declared that the government would be ready to accept amendments. He said that the government had been careful to include only matters related to the MoU but left it to the DPR to decide what changes were necessary.[165] There was little doubt that the bill would eventually be adopted but the government would have to make concessions in view of continuing opposition, particularly but not only from nationalist quarters. As the bill was about to be sent to the DPR, Megawati Soekarnoputri bluntly told a visiting delegation from Aceh headed by the Acting Governor, Mustafa Abubakar, that she thought the MoU was "absurd".[166] Ir. Soetjipto, in his opening statement on behalf of the PDI-P in the DPR, declared that the party "cannot accept the Helsinki MoU"[167] and unsuccessfully proposed that the title of the bill be changed to "Governing the Province of the Special Region of Aceh",[168] to emphasize that Aceh was still part of Indonesia. During the discussions in the DPR significant clauses in the MoU were also rejected by prominent members representing

PKB, PAN, PKS and others. Retired military officers also testified at the DPR against the bill which they regarded as inconsistent with the constitution and "a betrayal of Indonesia".[169]

The most pressing issue that needed to be resolved concerned GAM's expectation that it would be able to contest the forthcoming elections of the governor, bupatis and mayors originally due in October 2005 but, after several postponements, eventually held in December 2006.[170] The government bill, in accordance with the MoU, permitted the formation of "local parties" which, together with existing "national" parties, would be entitled to nominate candidates for executive positions but it removed the MoU's provision permitting the nomination of non-party independent candidates. In the absence of such a provision, GAM may not have had sufficient time to form its own party before the elections and would therefore be prevented from nominating its own candidates, thus nullifying GAM's most important reason for accepting the peace agreement. The PDI-P, supported by the small Christian PDS, opposed not only local parties but also provision for independents to run for executive posts.[171] On the other hand, the two main government parties, Golkar and PD, were concerned about the implications on the peace process if GAM were in effect excluded. They therefore wanted a temporary provision for independent candidates to apply only to the forthcoming regional elections in Aceh that were already overdue.[172] The government, therefore, changed its position during the DPR's consideration of the bill and the Minister of Home Affairs accepted an amendment that did not require candidates to be nominated by parties as was required in all other provinces. Moreover the law did not describe this as a temporary provision.[173]

The opponents of the participation of GAM in local elections, however, continued their efforts to put obstacles in the path of non-party GAM candidates. The ultra-nationalist PDI-P legislator, Permadi, proposed unsuccessfully that one of the requirements of candidates should be that they had "never voluntarily been a citizen of another country"[174] — no doubt with exiled GAM leaders in mind who had become citizens of Sweden or, in the case of Malik Mahmud, had been born a Singaporean. The government, however, not only rejected this proposal but facilitated GAM participation by explicitly exempting those who had received amnesties for treason or political crimes from a provision disqualifying those who had served prison sentences for serious crimes.

In the discussions in the DPR, the opponents of the MoU realized that they could not defeat the entire bill but concentrated on blocking some of its provisions. In the case of the bill's security provisions, the dissidents had the powerful backing of the military. The MoU had stated that the military would be restricted to the "external defence of Aceh" while "in normal peacetime circumstances, only organic military forces would be present in Aceh". As we have seen the TNI had already undermined this provision in practice by redefining "organic military forces" to cover a far larger number of troops than was normal. The MoU's limitation to "external defence" was removed in the government's bill and, in the law as eventually adopted, the TNI's role in Aceh was in effect no different to its position in other parts of Indonesia. The law provided that the TNI "implement national defence and other functions in Aceh", among which were to "defend, protect and maintain the integrity and sovereignty of NKRI" while there was no requirement to restrict troops to "organic" units. The MoU had also required that the appointment of the chief of police in Aceh be approved by the head of the Aceh government. To implement this, the Aceh DPRD's draft bill had proposed that the national chief of police submit three names from among whom the governor would select one after consulting the legislature but the DPR rejected this provision although the national chief of police still needed to obtain the governor's agreement to the appointment of the provincial police chief.

The MoU's provisions on human rights were virtually abandoned by the DPR. Based on the MoU, the Aceh draft included a chapter on human rights requiring the formation of a Human Rights Court in Aceh and a Truth and Reconciliation Commission. In the event that the investigation of "gross human rights abuses" in Aceh cannot "guarantee" a just outcome, the Aceh draft even allowed the government to permit a special rapporteur or other UN official to visit Aceh. The provisions for the formation of the Human Rights Court and the Truth and Reconciliation Commission remained in the government draft but the article envisaging investigation of human rights abuses by the UN special rapporteur had provoked outrage in the DPR and was excised. The Aceh draft had called for the formation of a Human Rights Court within twelve months but the government bill imposed no timetable. In the DPR the PDI-P proposed that members of the military and police should be pardoned for any human rights violations committed in Aceh. Sidharto Danusubroto, a former police general now representing the PDI-P in the DPR, argued that "If GAM is given an amnesty, then TNI and the Police must be given pardons". Golkar members also supported this view but Farhan Hamid of PAN and leader of the Aceh "Joint Forum", pointed out that GAM's amnesty applied to treason while they could still be prosecuted for human rights violations.[175] Provision for pardons, however, was not needed as both PDI-P and Golkar opposed retrospective prosecution.[176] The final version of the law restricted cases in the Human Rights Court to violations that occurred after the adoption of the law which meant that the massive violations during the previous three decades were beyond the court's scope.[177] The MoU had also required that crimes committed by military personnel should be tried in civil courts rather than in military courts that were notorious for their lack of transparency and extraordinary leniency. In the end, the law only required that criminal cases involving members of the TNI would be tried according to "existing regulations".[178]

Several controversial clauses from the MoU and the Aceh draft that emphasized Aceh's special status had survived "synchronization" in the Department of Home Affairs and remained in the government bill brought to the DPR. Among these clauses were those that in effect gave Aceh a veto on central government policies affecting Aceh by requiring that international agreements and decisions of the national parliament that affected Aceh could only be adopted with the agreement of the Aceh legislature in Aceh and requiring that administrative policies involving Aceh could only be adopted with the agreement of the governor. These provisions, regarded as fundamental principles in the MoU and strongly supported by most Acehnese, were seen as blatant "federalism" by many members of the DPR. In his opening speech, Soetjipto of the PDI-P had declared that the adoption of such provisions would mean that Indonesia was no longer a unitary state.[179] Heeding these objections, the DPR replaced "agreement" with the requirement that such policies could only be adopted after "consideration" (*pertimbangan*) by the Aceh legislature or the governor. The DPR also amended wording in earlier drafts that could be interpreted as strengthening Aceh's special status. Thus, while the Aceh draft described the government of Aceh as "self-governing" within the Unitary State of the Republic of Indonesia, the government bill, as revised by the Department of Home Affairs, removed all references to "self-government" (*pemerintahan sendiri*). The DPR cancelled another clause derived from the Aceh draft that permitted Aceh to cooperate with other "countries" and international agencies, including "direct" cooperation with UN agencies, while institutions in Aceh were permitted to become members of UN agencies and other international organizations.[180] Such language suggesting that Aceh aspired to "national status" met with strong opposition. As amended by the DPR, the clause allowed cooperation except in fields that fall within "the authority of the (national) government" and excluded cooperation with "countries" and the reference to individual institutions in Aceh joining UN agencies.[181]

The government bill also contained a potentially significant, but ambiguous, provision that seemed to provide an opportunity to expand the authority of the central government. Where the MoU provided Aceh with "authority within all sectors of public affairs" except six fields reserved for the central government,[182] the government bill added a clause (Clause 7.3) that explicitly opened the way for the central government to exercise its authority over "other activities of government determined by legislative regulations (*peraturan perundang-undangan*) as authorities of government". This clause was subjected to strong criticism in the DPR because of its open-ended nature and was eventually removed.[183] However a new Clause 7.3 allowing the government "to set norms, standards and procedures as well as conduct supervision of implementation" led to new suspicions, including within GAM which saw them as reducing "the absolute and complete authority of the Government of Aceh in regard to public matters". A GAM delegation headed by Malik Mahmud raised this issue with Acehnese members of the DPR but seemed satisfied by Ahmad Farhan Hamid's explanation that the norms and standards were intended only to ensure "quality control" of the provision of public services.[184] This provision in fact conformed to a similar provision in the Law on Regional Government (No. 34/2004) applying to all the provinces of Indonesia.[185]

The law also regulated economic and revenue issues. The Aceh draft laid claim to Acehnese control over all natural resources in the province but the DPR excluded oil and natural gas which were to be managed jointly by the government of Aceh and the central government. The government argued that oil and natural gas were national resources that should not be monopolized by producing regions but contribute to national development throughout the country. Regarding the distribution of revenue between the centre and the province, initial claims in the Aceh draft were rejected by the DPR which reaffirmed Aceh's shares in national taxes and natural resource revenues at the levels established in the 2001 special autonomy law — except that the oil and natural gas share of 70 per cent was made permanent instead of declining after eight years as provided in the 2001 law.[186] In the final stages of the bargaining, the government made a significant concession which provided Aceh with substantially increased allocations of "special" revenue from the central government.[187] Although the Aceh legislature's initial proposals were rejected, the final outcome was an improvement for Aceh compared with the already generous special autonomy law.

A final controversial issue involved the role of syariah. The 2001 special autonomy law had already ceded authority to Aceh to implement syariah, in contrast to all other provinces in Indonesia. The debate in the DPR on this issue, however, was not so much between the government and the region as between parties in the DPR itself. The Aceh DPRD took the view that it would be unfair if people committing the same crime, such as gambling, were tried in different courts so it allowed non-Muslims to be brought before syariah courts in such cases.[188] On the other hand, the government's bill required Muslims in Aceh to observe syariah and other Indonesian citizens and non-citizens living in, or visiting, Aceh to "respect" the practice of syariah. The Islamist PKS, however, wanted syariah to be applied fully to everyone, including non-Muslim visitors to Aceh. PPP also wanted to apply syariah to all, only excluding non-Muslims from family law. PKB believed that syariah should apply in all criminal cases but only to Muslims in civil disputes. Golkar and BPD proposed that syariah could only be applied to non-Muslims if they voluntarily agreed. On the other hand, PDI-P, PDS and the Democrat Party wanted syariah to be restricted to Muslims in all cases.[189] The government's version was finally adopted.[190]

The Law on the Governance of Aceh failed to meet the deadline of 31 March 2006 set for its adoption in the MoU but was eventually passed, by consensus as usual, on 11 July after undergoing significant amendments. The main opposition had come from the PDI-P but in the end, realizing that it could not block the law, it concentrated on blocking particular clauses which it saw as undermining Indonesia's unitary state. On the other hand, the president's PD and the vice-president's Golkar provided consistent support, while the medium-sized Muslim-based parties generally accepted the bill while sometimes objecting to specific clauses. Throughout, Acehnese members of the DPR, regardless of party, gave full support. Although assented to by the government and largely incorporated in the Aceh draft bill, the principles of the MoU were eroded in important ways but not entirely abandoned as the bill moved through the Department of Home Affairs and the DPR. Language that implied that Aceh was more than a mere province of Indonesia was quickly removed but its special character was ultimately recognized. Initial attempts by Acehnese politicians to place special conditions on the military and police different to those obtaining in other regions were blocked in the DPR, and the guidelines for Aceh's Human Rights Court and Truth and Reconciliation Commission were in practice barely different to their national equivalents.[191] In particular, the DPR insisted that the Human Rights Court would not be retroactive. Indeed it is unlikely that the peace settlement would have been possible if military and police personnel were not protected from retrospective prosecution of crimes committed in Aceh. On the other hand, additional economic benefits flowing to Aceh as a result of the law were very attractive to the Acehnese. But the key provisions related to elections. The law paved the way for the eventual formation of a GAM-based political party and made it possible for GAM candidates to contest the forthcoming elections of heads of provincial and district governments.

Initially, however, the law met with much anger in Aceh. Lhokseumawe was reported to be "paralysed" on 11 July while other groups called for mass strikes.[192] A month later, on 15 August, around 50,000 people protested against the law at the Baiturrahman mosque in Banda Aceh and listened to speeches by SIRA leaders including Muhammad Nazar and Dawan Gayo.[193] But the GAM leaders quickly accepted the reality of the law and focussed on the opportunity it offered. Malik Mahmud had initially expressed GAM's disappointment and accused the government of "greatly distorting the subjects in the MoU"[194] but later said that GAM did not "question most of the material of the law".[195] Zaini Abdullah called for amendments but assured that GAM did not want to disturb the peace.[196] Another GAM leader, Irwandi Yusuf, complained about the law but said that GAM wanted the election, now delayed until December, to go ahead.[197]

Local Elections

The delayed passage of the Aceh law forced the date of the elections to be further delayed from 26 April until 11 December 2006. The elections were for governor and 19 of 21 district heads.[198] Following the completion of the hand-over of GAM's arms as required in the MoU, GAM formally dissolved the Aceh National Army (*Tentera Neugara Aceh*) on 27 December 2005 although GAM itself was not dissolved. Former GAM fighters then formed the Aceh Transition Committee (*Komite Peralihan Aceh*: KPA) headed by former GAM commander, Tgk Muzakkir Manaf.[199] A major function of the KPA was to look after the interests of former GAM fighters, including the distribution of "re-integration" payments, but it also became a political base for GAM in the coming elections. It also continued to extort funds from contractors involved in infrastructure and other projects and was therefore able to provide financial support for GAM candidates.

During the decades of military struggle in Aceh, GAM fighters on the ground had maintained an extraordinary level of loyalty to the GAM leadership in exile in Sweden. Indeed, overt factionalism was more common between groups in GAM overseas than between GAM in Aceh and the leadership in Sweden. Ironically, tensions between the two groups only became obvious after the achievement of the peace as GAM was transforming itself into an electoral organization. The final straw was Malik's endorsement of an alliance between GAM and the "national" Muslim party, PPP, to contest the gubernatorial election. The GAM candidate would be Hasbi Abdullah, the younger brother of Zaini.[200] Malik and Zaini returned to Aceh on 19 April, a month before GAM leaders in Aceh held a meeting on 22–24 May to plan its electoral strategy. Asked by journalists whether he would be standing for governor, Malik replied that he was ineligible as a non-citizen and planned to spend his time between Aceh, Europe and the United States.[201] However, by then Malik was losing the confidence of GAM members in Aceh who decided to reject a coalition with another party and to nominate their own candidate as an independent.[202] The meeting then voted to nominate a GAM field commander and peace negotiator in 2002–03, Tgk Nashruddin Ahmad, for governor with the SIRA leader, Muhammad Nazar as his deputy.[203] Nashruddin received 39 votes while Hasbi won 34 and Irwandi Yusuf 9. However, Nashruddin, who had not attended the meeting, was apparently persuaded by members of the GAM "old guard" not to accept the nomination. In the face of this division, Malik Mahmud decided that GAM would not nominate a candidate but leave members free to stand as independents.[204]

The failure of GAM to agree on its own candidate allowed the revival of the previous idea of a GAM-PPP coalition. The veteran Aceh-based GAM leader, Tgk Muhammad Usman Lampoh Awe, and the head of the KPA, Muzakkir Manaf, with the backing of Malik Mahmud, gave their support to a ticket headed by a well-known intellectual and civil society activist, Humam Hamid, representing PPP, with Hasbi Abdullah as deputy.[205] The coalition looked promising. PPP had always had a strong base in Aceh, even occasionally outpolling Golkar during the New Order, while GAM could also mobilize substantial support in rural Aceh. Hasbi, however, had not been a GAM guerilla although he spent fourteen years in jail until Habibie's release of GAM prisoners in 1999 but had spent most of the time since then studying for his Ph.D. in economics in Bandung. Younger-generation GAM supporters, however, felt that GAM should stand alone and not rely on an alliance with a "national" party. They therefore turned to a new team consisting of Irwandi Yusuf and Muhammad Nazar. Irwandi had joined GAM in 1990 and, after studying veterinary science at Oregon State University in the United States, returned to Aceh where he assisted GAM's military leadership. Nazar had been SIRA's main leader since its foundation in 1999. Both had been detained in the 2000s.[206] As support for the Irwandi-Nazar team seemed to be rising in late November, Muzakkir announced that KPA had decided to take a neutral stand between the two GAM-linked teams.

The gubernatorial election on 11 December was contested by eight pairs of candidates. The Irwandi-Nazar team, formally independent but actually representing a wing of GAM, was overwhelmingly successful with 38.2 per cent of the votes. They won majorities in fifteen of the 21 districts.[207] The Humam-Hasbi partnership between PPP and the other wing of GAM ran second with 16.6 per cent, followed by Malek Raden (Golkar, backed by

PDI-P, PD and PKPI) with 14.0 per cent and former acting governor, Azwar Abubakar (PAN) with 10.6 per cent. Four candidates received less than 10 per cent, including the two candidates with military backgrounds, Lt. Gen. Tamlicha Ali, who came second last and former Aceh regional army commander, Maj. Gen. Djali Yusuf, last. In the district elections, GAM candidates from one or other of the two factions won in six in December and another three in 2007 and January 2008.[208]

CONCLUSION

Aceh had a long history of resistance to rule by outsiders since the thirty-year war that ended with Dutch occupation in the early twentieth century. In the early years of Indonesian independence a new Islamic rebellion was launched against Jakarta followed by a series of uprisings under the leadership of GAM in 1976–77, then again in 1989–91, and for a third time following Soeharto's fall. In each case the rebels were suppressed by brutal means that resulted in deep resentment within the Acehnese community and laid the foundation for the next rebellion. In the post-New Order era, successive governments combined military repression with peace initiatives but it was only the Yudhoyono government that was able to achieve an effective peace settlement.

The collapse of the New Order resulted in a drastic weakening of the authority of the central government not only in Aceh but throughout the nation. In this context the third GAM rebellion broke out during the short Habibie presidency and, inspired by Indonesia's withdrawal from East Timor, grew rapidly in strength. Habibie's successor, Abdurrahman Wahid, was ideologically sympathetic to the grievances raised by supporters of independence in Papua and Aceh but hoped to implement reforms that would persuade them to accept their status within Indonesia. His efforts to start negotiations with pro-separatist groups in both territories, however, dismayed the military and political groups that had been outraged by the exit of East Timor. Abdurrahman's successor, Megawati, represented nationalist forces opposed to giving concessions to rebellious regions and she promoted hardline nationalist officers to high positions in the TNI. Nevertheless, she agreed to continue the negotiations with GAM started by Abdurrahman but eventually sided with her generals in mid-2003 by declaring the introduction of martial law and launching a huge military campaign designed to "eradicate" the separatists.[209]

Not all elements in the government and military, however, adopted an unqualified hardline stance. While none favoured withdrawal from Aceh, some were willing to consider substantial concessions to GAM in the hope that a negotiated settlement could be reached. For successive post-Soeharto governments, the question was not whether to grant independence to Aceh but whether negotiations should be held and what concessions could be offered to persuade GAM to abandon its armed struggle. The fundamental obstacle to a negotiated settlement was the incompatibility between the "bottom line" positions of the two main protagonists. So long as the Indonesian government insisted that Aceh was a province of Indonesia while GAM could accept nothing less than independence, a final resolution was impossible. By 2004, when Susilo Bambang Yudhoyono won the presidency, GAM had been subdued but not defeated. The prospects of a negotiated settlement, however, had become bleaker than ever during the last year of the Megawati presidency.

The military campaign under the military emergency declared in May 2003 did substantial damage to GAM's forces on the ground in Aceh but was still far from eliminating the rebel movement. Indeed the behaviour of Indonesian troops seems to have deepened the antagonism felt by many Acehnese, especially in the villages, toward Jakarta. But, at the same time, GAM was still far from achieving its own objectives. There were no signs of the long-awaited disintegration of Indonesia, nor of any indication that the international community was likely to abandon its unwillingness to support Aceh's independence. The GAM leadership in exile in Sweden initially rejected feelers from the new government in Jakarta but, just before the tsunami in late 2004, had taken a more flexible stance and, during the Helsinki talks, downgraded its goal to "self-government", which implied that it no longer sought full independence. This new approach made it possible for the two sides to reach agreement in Helsinki.

The Helsinki MoU, however, was only the first step. The implementation of the MoU required legislation in Jakarta in the form of a comprehensive law on the governing of Aceh. GAM had made concessions to achieve the Helsinki agreement but was then confronted with the need for further compromise when the legislation went to the national parliament in which it had no representation and 537 of its 550 members did not represent Acehnese constituencies. Within the DPR, the PDI-P (20 per cent of seats) and PKB (9 per cent) formed the core of the parties rejecting the MoU together with several small parties and individuals in other parties. On the other hand, Jusuf Kalla's Golkar (23 per cent) and Yudhoyono's PD (10 per cent) were committed to adopting the law and could expect support from PPP (11 per cent) which had a foothold in Aceh. Although criticism from the DPR was strong, the critics did not in fact expect to defeat the bill but aimed to remove particular clauses which they saw as giving excessive authority to the province. Initially Golkar members were among the strong critics of the concessions given to GAM but it seems that Jusuf Kalla exerted his authority over them with the result that their comments were toned down. It is widely believed that financial inducements are often provided to secure the support of members of the DPR and it is not impossible that some members were influenced in this way. Although GAM was not represented in the DPR, the government was aware that the peace settlement could only last if it contained sufficient benefits for GAM to accept the result. The DPR removed or amended significant concessions that GAM had won in Helsinki but left enough for GAM to feel that the benefits provided by the law still outweighed the drawbacks. In particular, the law provided the opportunity for GAM candidates to contest elections for the governorship of Aceh and district headships — elections in which GAM eventually won the governorship and nearly half the district headships. Moreover, the financial provisions of the law promised substantial increases in national allocations to the provincial budget.

The benefits that top GAM leaders in Aceh expected from the law were clear enough but what did the settlement provide for ordinary GAM guerillas? The Helsinki MoU provided for the "re-integration" of GAM fighters into society, including land and employment opportunities. With funds supplied by the central government and foreign donors, GAM fighters were given at least some assistance to re-establish themselves.[210] It also appears that Vice President Jusuf Kalla had made arrangements that enabled some GAM leaders to gain assistance and facilities to establish themselves in business.[211] Although many military officers continued to believe that GAM's acceptance of the peace was just a ruse and that they planned to return to their armed struggle, GAM's willingness to hand over arms and the ease with which guerillas returning to their homes could be identified made it a very risky strategy if in fact they had a secret plan to continue the rebellion.[212] Moreover, it appeared that many ex-guerillas were reluctant to go back to the privations of guerilla life in the jungles. GAM supporters could also expect that GAM-dominated regional executives, supported by increased allocations of funds from the central government, would take measures to take care of its own base of support.

Concern that the military would not accept the election of GAM leaders to senior positions in the provincial and district governments was also misplaced. Many observers had believed that the military's presence in Aceh gave it, as an institution, and its personnel access to numerous ways to supplement income, both legally and illegally. During previous pauses in the conflict, the military had undermined peace agreements that threatened its sources of finance. During the peace process in 2005, like previous attempts by governments to negotiate peace in 2000 and 2002–03, many military officers made it clear that they did not trust GAM and continued military operations. Yet this time, after the signing of the Helsinki MoU, the peace was observed almost without violent incidents. Why did the military accept the 2005 peace after undermining previous endeavours?[213]

In 2005 the government in Jakarta, following the convincing victory of President Yudhoyono in the direct election of 2004, enjoyed much more legitimacy than the Abdurrahman and Megawati governments and was more capable of implementing its goals in a coherent way. Yudhoyono had been deeply involved in the failed efforts of the previous governments that had been undermined by military groups. That he would not tolerate a repeat of such military sabotage was shown from the beginning of his government when he rejected Megawati's attempt to have the hard-line Ryamizard appointed as commander-in-chief of the TNI. As a senior military officer himself, Yudhoyono not only understood the politicking that was occurring within TNI but also had sufficient authority to control it. Officers hoping for promotions to senior positions quickly drew their own conclusions. While his vice president, Jusuf Kalla, was making secret contact with GAM, Yudhoyono was cementing his own base of support within the TNI that would enable him to curb attempts to disrupt the Helsinki negotiations.

As the process moved from negotiations with GAM in Helsinki to the national parliament in Jakarta, "federal" aspects of the new law were removed and the threat posed by Human Rights Courts to military officers was neutralized. But why was it so easy to persuade the military to forsake the economic opportunities offered by postings in Aceh? First, the withdrawal of military forces from Aceh only affected combat troops who had been brought in from other parts of Indonesia. Organic units, which had been based in Aceh before the emergency, not only remained but their numbers were substantially increased under the MoU. Unofficial military fund-raising, therefore, continued as before. Moreover, the large increase in revenues provided by the Law on the Governance of Aceh meant that there would be opportunities for the military to demand its share in the good fortune. The military may not have liked the electoral provisions that led to the election of a GAM governor and nine GAM district heads but it was not likely to suffer financially. And, following the embarrassing performance of the two retired generals who contested the race for the governorship, the military was hardly in a position to complain.

Notes

1. In contrast to East Timor, Acehnese had always been well represented in the Jakarta elite — as cabinet ministers, military officers, diplomats, senior bureaucrats and so on.

2. The gas fields and the natural gas plant are operated by the American corporation, ExxonMobil. ExxonMobil has a 30 per cent stake in the Arun LNG Company which owns the gas plant. The majority stake is held by the Indonesian national oil corporation, Pertamina.

3. Virtual Information Centre (VIC). 20 December 1999. "Mobil Oil Indonesia, Aceh Province." The VIC was issued by USCINCPAC (U.S. Commander-in-Chief Pacific).

4. See comments by Akbar Tandjung (Speaker of the DPR and General Chairman of Golkar), *Jakarta Post*, 16 May 2000; Muhaimin Iskandar (one of the Deputy Speakers of DPR representing the president's party, PKB), *Kompas*, 16 May 2000; and a group of scholars (including President Habibie's foreign policy advisor, Dewi Fortuna Anwar) from the Indonesian Institute of Sciences (*Lembaga Ilmu Pengetahuan Indonesia*: LIPI), *Kompas*, 12 May 2000.

5. International Crisis Group (2001*e*), pp. 12–14.

6. On drug running by the military, see Lesley McCulloch, Australian Broadcasting Commission, Asia Pacific, 9 September 2002.

7. *Kompas*, 2 October 2003.

8. The name of Sultan Iskandar Muda (1606–36) continues to be bestowed on many institutions in Aceh, including the regional military command, Banda Aceh's airport, a fertilizer plant and a military hospital. Sultan Iskandar Muda roads can be found in many of Aceh's towns.

9. On Darul Islam, see van Dijk (1981). On the revolt in Aceh, see Nazaruddin Syamsuddin (1965).

10. As Aspinall points out, the brutality of military repression of the Darul Islam in the 1950s had much in common with later military repression of GAM. Aspinall (2006*a*).

11. Kell (1995), pp. 13–28; See also Robinson (2000), pp. 220–25.

12. On Hasan di Tiro, see Isa Sulaiman (2006). Isa Sulaiman died in the 2004 tsunami.

13. The revolt was launched prematurely after GAM's plans were leaked to the authorities in Jakarta. Nazaruddin Syamsuddin (1984), p. 113.

14. Kell (1995), p. 72.

15. Sukma (2004), pp. 3–11.

16. Amnesty International (1993). Throughout the DOM period from 1990 to 1998, no member of the security forces was ever charged with a human-rights offence. Amnesty International (2004), section 9.

17. Syarifudin Tippe (2000), pp. 94–95.

18. Robinson (2000); Sukma (2004).

19. Schulze (2004), pp. 14–16.

20. Reid (2006), p. 5. A study based on the 2000 census suggested that the Acehnese ethnic group made up only 50.32 per cent of the population. Suryadinata et al. (2003), pp. 15, 158. However, military operations at that time meant that less than half the population was surveyed. As much of the conflict occurred

in the densely populated Acehnese districts along the northern coast where GAM had its strongholds, it can be assumed that it was mainly these areas that were excluded with the result that the Acehnese ethnic group was greatly under-estimated. In the half of the population covered by the census survey, Javanese transmigrants and their descendants made up 16 per cent. The largest non-Acehnese indigenous community covered in the survey was the Gayo, consisting of Gayo Lut and Gayo Lues, who together made up 11 per cent.

21. Schulze (2004), pp. 7–8.
22. Schulze (2004), pp. 22–23. It later became known that Fauzi Hasbi had become an agent of the Indonesian intelligence agency, BIN.
23. International Crisis Group (2002*c*), p. 9.
24. Sofyan Dawood, GAM's military spokesman, called on the Laskar Jihad to cancel its planned visit to Aceh in February 2002. Press Statement, 14 February 2002. Referring to the Laskar Jihad in an interview with CNN, GAM spokesman, Teuku Kamaruzzaman, warned that "if we see them, we will chase them out because we do not want Aceh to become the base of a group which stirs up racial and religious sentiment". *CNN.com*, 14 July 2002.
25. *Kompas*, 8 August 1998.
26. *Reuters*, 26 March 1999.
27. In February 1999, troops killed 7 people who were intending to listen to a pro-GAM sermon at a mosque, in May 39 were killed when troops fired on a demonstration, and in July 65 were killed at a religious school. *Laporan Komisi Independen Pengusutan Tindak Kekerasan di Aceh, Ringkasan Eksekutif* (Report of the Independent Investigation of Violence in Aceh, Executive Summary) (1999), pp. 16–17. The credibility of the military was badly damaged by absurd explanations given by army spokesmen. In one case, the local military commander claimed that villagers were aiming to gain control of surface-to-air missiles held at a military base. At the religious school what was described by the military as an "armed clash" resulted in 65 deaths among pro-independence Acehnese but no military casualties at all.
28. *Serambi Indonesia*, 2 December 1999; *Kompas*, 3 December 1999.
29. *Kompas*, 9 December 1999; *Serambi Indonesia*, 9 December 1999. The Governor, Syamsuddin Mahmud, said he signed the statement at the request of the local military in order to calm the situation. Interview with Syamsuddin Mahmud, Jakarta, March 2003.
30. Interview with Brig. Gen. Syarifudin Tippe, Banda Aceh, March 2003.
31. *Kompas*, 14 July 1999.
32. *Kompas*, 12 November 1999.
33. *Kompas*, 27 March 1999.
34. Law No. 44/1999 *tentang Penyelenggaraan Keistimewaan Propinsi Daerah Istimewa Aceh*.
35. *Serambi Indonesia*, 16 September 1999.
36. *Straits Times*, 5 November 1999.

37. *Kompas*, 9 December 1999. For examples of some of his statements, see Aspinall and Crouch (2003), p. 9.
38. The HDC later changed its name to the Humanitarian Dialogue Centre. See Huber (2004).
39. Conversation with Hassan Wirayuda, Jakarta, May 2000.
40. Joint Understanding on Humanitarian Pause for Aceh, 12 May 2000, Geneva.
41. The NGO, Forum Peduli HAM, estimated that 69 civilians and 14 security personnel were killed during the first three months of the "pause". *Kompas*, 5 September 2000. This compares with more than 300 during the first four months of the year. *Media Indonesia*, 30 August 2000.
42. See Human Rights Watch reports (March 2001 and August 2001).
43. *Suara Pembaruan*, 9 January 2000; *Jakarta Post*, 18 January 2000.
44. *Kompas*, 18 March 2000. In an interview, Bondan Gunawan, generously suggested that the troops may have been engaged in a routine operation coincidentally in that area. Interview with Bondan Gunawan, Jakarta, 24 August 2000.
45. Yudhoyono (2001).
46. *Kompas*, 23 August 2001.
47. *Media Indonesia*, 30 November 2001.
48. McGibbon (2004), pp. 15–17. The gap between the Home Affairs draft and the original Acehnese draft is shown in Appendix A of International Crisis Group (2001*f*).
49. For a detailed account of the peace process, see Aspinall and Crouch (2003).
50. International Crisis Group (2003*a*), p. 6. Among the "wise men" were retired General Anthony Zinni from the United States, former Thai Foreign Minister, Surin Pitsuan, and former Yugoslav Foreign Minister, Budimir Loncar. General Yudhoyono played a key role in persuading reluctant elements in the government to accept the "wise men".
51. For details, see International Crisis Group (2003), pp. 8–11; Aspinall and Crouch (2003), pp. 26–34.
52. "Cessation of Hostilities Framework Agreement Between Government of the Republic of Indonesia and the Free Aceh Movement", Geneva, 9 December 2002.
53. The provincial police chief estimated that GAM controlled at least 40 per cent of the province's villages and sub-districts. *Kompas*, 16 April 2003. Schulze suggests that GAM controlled 70–80 per cent of the province at that time. Schulze (2004), p. 2.
54. *Kompas*, 25 August 2001.
55. *Koran Tempo*, 12 July 2002.
56. *Kompas*, 13 June 2003.
57. *Kompas*, 8, 10 May 2003. By September, troop numbers had risen to about

35,000 from TNI and 14,000 from the police. *Jakarta Post*, 8 September 2003.

58. *Kompas*, 9 May 2003.

59. In early July it was reported that the number of refugees was 48,282. *Koran Tempo*, 4 July 2003.

60. The main difference is that under a military emergency, emergency operations are under the authority of the military commander while under a civil emergency the governor, at least nominally, is in charge.

61. *Kompas*, 29 March 2003.

62. *Kompas*, 18 November 2004.

63. *Kompas*, 18 and 19 November 2004.

64. *Kompas*, 18 November 2004.

65. *Jakarta Post*, 22 May 2004.

66. *Kompas*, 19 May 2004.

67. Teuku Kemal Fasya, in *Kompas*, 18 November 2004. This article also notes that four of the military were killed in a quarrel between military personnel.

68. *Kompas*, 27 October 2004.

69. *Tempo*, 2 June 2003, *Kompas*, 23 June 2003. *Tempo* adopted an even-handed approach by pointing out that the foreign journalists' sources were probably GAM supporters. Komnas HAM claimed that two of the seven were young boys. *Koran Tempo*, 14 June 2003.

70. *Jakarta Post*, 2 June 2003; *Tempo*, 9 June 2003. Soldiers admitted that they had become "emotional" when the villagers claimed not to know about GAM in the village. In the case of the summary execution, Indonesian reporters, together with a television crew from the Australian SBS, happened to be in the area and filmed the newly executed man tied to a stake.

71. *Tempo*, 9 June 2003.

72. *Jakarta Post*, 11 October 2003.

73. *Jakarta Post*, 30 July 2003.

74. *Kompas*, 23 June 2003.

75. *Jakarta Post*, 26 June 2003.

76. Sukma (2004), p. 27.

77. *Jakarta Post*, 22 November 2003.

78. *Kompas*, 15 July 2003.

79. *Kompas*, 6 June 2003.

80. *Koran Tempo*, 1 March 2004.

81. *Koran Tempo*, 1 March 2004.

82. *Koran Tempo*, 12 April 2004.

83. Interview with GAM negotiator, Teuku Kamaruzzaman, Banda Aceh, March 2003. See also Schulze (2006), p. 243.

84. Edward Aspinall's interviews with GAM leaders, Malik Mahmud and Zaini Abdullah, in Stockholm, July 2002. See Aspinall and Crouch (2003), p. 4.

85. Interview with GAM negotiator, Sofyan Ibrahim Tiba, Banda Aceh, March

2003. Sofyan was arrested after the collapse of COHA and died when his prison in Banda Aceh was hit by the tsunami.
86. See Schulze (2006), pp. 226–36.
87. Schulze (2004), p. 3. From the beginning, Hasan Tiro had realized the necessity of foreign support if Aceh were to achieve independence. Nazaruddin Syamsuddin (1984), p. 116.
88. The belief of some foreign observers (and the Singapore government) that GAM was somehow associated with Al Qaeda was contradicted by GAM's interest in winning support from the United States and the international community.
89. Sukma (2004), pp. 36–37.
90. *Koran Tempo*, 22 November 2004.
91. A random survey of adults in sub-districts in three conflict-affected kabupaten (Pidie, Bireuen, North Aceh) in December 2005 and January 2006 revealed "remarkably high levels of terrible and accumulated traumatic events as a result of violence". Thirty-eight per cent of respondents had experienced fleeing from burning buildings, the husbands of 8 per cent of women had been killed in the conflict, and 5 per cent had lost children killed in the conflict. Forty-one per cent had a family member or friend killed while 33 per cent said that a family friend had been kidnapped or disappeared. Seven per cent had been forced to betray family or friends and 6 per cent had been forced to harm or injure a family member. Seventeen per cent had been publicly humiliated and 8 per cent had been forced to humiliate another person. Forty-five per cent claimed that their property had been confiscated or destroyed while 33 per cent experienced extortion or robbery. The survey was conducted by researchers from the International Organization for Migration (OIM) and the Harvard Medical School, assisted by staff of the Syiah Kuala University in Banda Aceh. International Organization for Migration, Universitas Syiah Kuala, Harvard Medical School (2006), pp. 2, 14.
92. Human Rights Watch (2003).
93. The Indonesian Foreign Affairs Department, however, issued a press release that declared that "The report lacks credibility". The release notes that Human Rights Watch claimed that most of the eighty-five interviewees had arrived in Malaysia after the introduction of martial law. "This claim is baseless", it says, because "there has not been any report on a new wave of refugees from Aceh to Malaysia" since the beginning of martial law. Department of Foreign Affairs Republic of Indonesia, Press Release, No. 072/PR/X11/2003, 18 December 2003. The Department seemed to assume that all refugees dutifully report to the Indonesian embassy in Kuala Lumpur on their arrival. By August 2004, the number of Acehnese registering with the UNHCR in Kuala Lumpur since the introduction of martial law was 7,115. Amnesty International (2004), Part 2, section 12.
94. Amnesty International (2004).
95. In a conversation with the author at the Kodam headquarters in Banda Aceh

in March 2003, a middle-level officer explained that the TNI had not been able to finish off GAM quickly because of pressure from Western countries on human rights.

96. Schulze (2004), pp. 24–29.
97. As the late Kontras journalist, Muharram, pointed out, most Acehnese were not alienated by GAM's tax collecting because they were too poor to be subjected to it. Interview, Banda Aceh, March 2003. Muharram died in the tsunami of 2004.
98. Safwan Idris was killed in September 2000 and Dayan Dawood in September 2001. One of Dayan's killers was tried and convicted in 2004. *Jakarta Post*, 14 January, 25 March 2004.
99. *Koran Tempo*, 29 February 2004.
100. At a meeting with members of the East-West Center's Aceh Study Group (including the author), General Yudhoyono said that he did not expect that the Stockholm-based leaders would ever give up their aspiration for independence but he saw some indications of willingness to compromise among Aceh-based commanders. Jakarta, June 2003. Later Jusuf Kalla said that "our theory was that there must be a disconnect between the GAM leadership in Sweden and the field commanders". In reality, however, the commanders remained remarkably loyal to their leaders in exile and it was the GAM leadership in Sweden that was ready to compromise. Morfit (2007), p. 122.
101. Farid (2007), p. 22. See also Kingsbury (2006), p. 69. Even before the government's declaration of a military emergency in Aceh, rumours had circulated about Kalla's involvement. By coincidence, the author happened to meet one of Kalla's emissaries in the room of one of the GAM negotiators at the Kuala Tripa Hotel in Banda Aceh in March 2003. Farhan mentions "economic compensation" offered by Kalla at this time. Farhan (2006), p. 167.
102. Morfit (2007), p. 120.
103. Farid (2007), pp. 48–52. Kingsbury (2006), p. 18. Farid, a medical doctor, had known Kalla's family in Makassar since his schooldays. He had already played a significant role in the peace processes in Maluku and Poso. Interview with Farid Husain, Jakarta, 12 April 2006.
104. On signs of disaffection, see International Crisis Group (2005a), p. 5.
105. Aspinall describes Kalla's approach as "basically one of co-optation". Aspinall (2006b), p. 17. See also Farhan (2006), pp. 170–71.
106. International Crisis Group (2005a), pp. 1–3. Hasan Tiro's statement was dated 4 December, the anniversary of GAM's foundation.
107. Farid (2007), pp. 72–74; 87–88.
108. Marthi Ahtisaari in interview in *Tempo*, 22 August 2005.
109. *Tempo*, 31 January 2005.
110. Interview with Nur Djuli, Banda Aceh, 1 June 2007.
111. Interview with former GAM negotiator, Teuku Kamaruzzaman, Banda Aceh, 5 June 2007.

112. Interview with Teuku Kamaruzzaman, Banda Aceh, 5 June 2007.
113. The other members of the GAM team were Bakhtiar Abdullah (who, like Malik and Zaini, was based in Sweden), Nur Djuli (based in Malaysia), and Nordin Abdul Rahman (a former political detainee currently studying at the University of Wollongong in Australia). An Australian advisor, Dr Damien Kingsbury, of Deakin University in Australia, also participated in the talks. Later they were joined by an informal advisor, Irwandi Jusuf, who had escaped from prison after the tsunami.
114. Hamid Awaluddin was the Minister of Justice and Human Rights; Sofyan Djalil was Minister of State for Information and Communication. The other members of the Indonesian negotiating team were Farid Husain, I Gusti Agung Pudja (Department of Foreign Affairs), and Usman Basyah (Deputy in the Coordinating Ministry of Political and Security Affairs), and temporarily Maj. Gen. Syarifuddin Tippe, the head of the army staff and command college and former chief of staff of the Aceh regional military command. The "supervisor", Widodo, did not take part directly in the negotiations but seems to have had the role of making sure that concessions were limited.
115. Morfit (2007), p. 129
116. Kingsbury (2006), p. 27.
117. Aspinall (2006*b*), pp. 27–29.
118. *Jakarta Post*, 24 January 2006. The article was entitled "Aceh's disaster could herald political change".
119. Interview with Nur Djuli, Banda Aceh, 1 June 2007.
120. *Kompas*, 25 February 2005.
121. *Jakarta Post*, 18 April 2005.
122. *Kompas*, 24 April 2005; *Jakarta Post*, 28 June 2005.
123. Interviews with Hamid Awaluddin, Jakarta, 11 September 2005; Ferry Mursyidan Baldan, Jakarta, 4 September 2006.
124. For example MPR speaker Hidayat Nur Wahid (PKS), DPR Speaker Agung Laksono (Golkar), Chairman of DPR Commission I Theo Sambuaga (Golkar).
125. *Koran Tempo*, 13 February 2005 (Djoko Susilo); *Kompas*, 25 February 2005 (Yuddy Chrisnandy); *Kompas*, 19 April 2005 (Effendi M.S. Simbolon), *Detikcom*, 13 July 2005 (Effendy Choirie).
126. Aspinall (2006b), p. 34.
127. Confidential interview with GAM source who described a specific incident.
128. Kingsbury (2006), pp. 68–72; Farid (2007), pp. 114–17.
129. *Kompas*, 27 July 2005.
130. *Kompas*, 17 February 2006.
131. *Koran Tempo*, 25 July 2005.
132. *Kompas*, 28 July 2005.
133. Memorandum of Understanding, 1.2. See also Kingsbury (2006), ch. 10; Aspinall (2006*b*), pp. 42–43.

134. Kingsbury (2006), pp. 125–26.
135. Kingsbury (2006), p. 137.
136. Memorandum of Understanding, 4.5 and 4.7. In his speech at the signing of the MoU, Malik Mahmud complained that "there will be around twice as many troops to be stationed in Acheh (sic) as any other areas in Indonesia. This outcome cannot be explained by a focus on external defense, and it does not create confidence in TNI's intentions". Kingsbury (2006), p. 176.
137. Kingsbury (2006), pp. 156–57.
138. Aspinall (2006*b*), p. 44.
139. Interview with Nordin Abdul Rahman, one of the GAM negotiators in Helsinki. Bireuen, Aceh, 11 May 2008.
140. For a summary of negative assessments, see Farhan (2006), pp. 245–53.
141. *Kompas*, 13 August 2006.
142. *Kompas*, 18 August 2005; *Koran Tempo*, 18 August 2005.
143. *Koran Tempo*, 29 August 2005.
144. *Kompas*, 18 August 2005.
145. *Koran Tempo*, 20 August 2005.
146. Farhan (2006), p. 260. The association was the *Persatuan Purnawirawan TNI-Angkatan Darat*.
147. *Koran Tempo*, 3 September 2005. This movement never became an actual organization.
148. *Kompas*, 10 August 2005; *Jakarta Post*, 10 August 2005.
149. *Koran Tempo*, 18 August 2005.
150. For a brief assessment of the AMM, see Adam Burke (2008).
151. International Crisis Group (2005*c*), pp. 1–2.
152. *Kompas*, 27, 29 August 2005, 15 September 2005.
153. PKS representatives were prominent in this attempt, including the MPR chairman, Hidayat Nur Wahid. Farhan (2006), pp. 269–71.
154. *Kompas*, 1, 7 September 2005. By 2008, the number of GAM detainees had been reduced to eleven. Kontras (Aceh) (21–27 August 2008).
155. See Farhan (2006), pp. 291–93.
156. International Crisis Group (2006*a*), pp. 6–8.
157. *Koran Tempo*, 31 October 2005; *Kompas*, 30 November 2006.
158. A valuable source on the debate on this law is Farhan (2006). Ahmad Farhan Hamid is a leading Acehnese member of the DPR representing PAN.
159. *Kompas*, 29 August 2005.
160. *Kompas*, 18 November 2005.
161. *Koran Tempo*, 9 December 2005.
162. Of the DPRD's 69 members, Golkar and PPP each had 12, PAN 9, PBB, PKS and PBR 8 each, PD 6 and smaller parties 6, among which were the parties most critical of the MOU in Jakarta — PDI-P and PKB — which had 2 and 1 respectively. *Kompas*, 17 February 2006.
163. *Koran Tempo*, 19 November 2005.

164. See International Crisis Group (2006*a*), p. 2.
165. *Kompas*, 6 February 2006.
166. *Koran Tempo*, 24 January 2006.
167. "Pendapat PDI-P" delivered to the DPR on 15 March 2006.
168. *Kompas*, 12 April 2006.
169. Farhan (2006), pp. 347–48.
170. *Kompas*, 19 August 2005.
171. Farhan (2006), p. 378. Later, after conceding that local parties would be formed, it proposed unsuccessfully that local parties be obliged to "affiliate" with national parties. Farhan (2006), p. 420.
172. *Kompas*, 21 April 2006.
173. Clause 68, Law on Governance of Aceh.
174. *Kompas*, 25 April 2006.
175. *Koran Tempo*, 8 May 2006. Farhan (2006), p. 407.
176. *Jakarta*, 18 May 2006.
177. It should be noted that the law did not actually establish a Human Rights Court which required a separate law.
178. At the time, soldiers charged with ordinary crimes faced military courts but it was anticipated that in the future their cases would be heard by civil courts.
179. Sutjipto in speech to DPR on 15 March 2006.
180. There was no provision for Aceh itself to join the United Nations, as sometimes misreported in the press. *Kompas*, 3 December 2005.
181. The DPR also removed an odd provision, taken over from the MoU, that allowed the government of Aceh to determine interest rates different to those determined by the Bank of Indonesia. Questioned about how the provision got into the MoU, the government's Helsinki negotiator, Sofyan Djalil, was forced to admit that "the Indonesian government negotiators were not on top of the details of banking". Earlier the practical-minded Jusuf Kalla had explained that it didn't matter anyway. "Interest rates are determined by the market, not the government. If the rate in Jakarta is 14 per cent and Aceh wants 10 per cent, just go ahead. But the government of Aceh will have to provide a subsidy." *Kompas*, 18 August 2005.
182. The six fields are foreign affairs; external defence; national security; monetary and fiscal matters; justice, and religion. These fields are also identified in Law No. 34/2004 on Regional Government.
183. Farhan (2006), pp. 417–19. Many Acehnese had understood the clause as providing exclusive authority outside the six areas reserved for the central government.
184. Farhan (2006), pp. 429–31, 454.
185. Clause 7.3 later became Clause 11.1 of the law as finally adopted.
186. Oil production, however, was expected to decline considerably during the next eight years.

187. World Bank/Decentralization Support Facility, *Laporan Hasil Pemantauan Konflik di Aceh*, 1–31 December 2006.

188. *Kompas*, 23 March 2006.

189. *Kompas*, 26 April 2006.

190. On the implementation of syariah law in Aceh, see International Crisis Group (2006*b*).

191. On the theme of "peace without justice" see Aspinall (2008).

192. *Kompas*, 14 July 2006.

193. *Kompas*, 16 August 2006.

194. *Koran Tempo*, 10 July 2006.

195. *Kompas*, 16 August 2006.

196. *Jakarta Post*, 16 August 2006.

197. *Kompas*, 3 August 2006.

198. The terms of two district heads had not expired.

199. *Koran Tempo*, 26 December 2005.

200. Zaini and Hasbi are nephews of Tgk Hasan di Tiro.

201. *Kompas*, 28 April 2006; *Jakarta Post*, 29 April 2006.

202. *Kompas*, 22 May 2006.

203. *Jakarta Post*, 30 June 2006.

204. International Crisis Group (2006*c*), pp. 5–6.

205. Kontras (Banda Aceh) (24–30 August 2006). Humam is the younger brother of the PAN politician, Ahmad Farhan Hamid.

206. *Koran Tempo*, 28 November 2006. Irwandi escaped when his prison in Aceh was destroyed by the tsunami. Nazar had been imprisoned in East Java.

207. *Kompas*, 30 December 2006. They failed to gain majorities in Banda Aceh, Pidie, Aceh Tengah, Bener Meriah, Singkil and Aceh Tamiang. Of these districts, only Banda Aceh and Pidie are dominated by the Acehnese ethnic group. Support for the Humam-Hasbi team was strong in Pidie. See International Crisis Group (2006*c* and 2007).

208. GAM-supported candidates won more than 25 per cent of the votes and therefore first-round victories in Aceh Utara, Aceh Timur, Pidie, Sabang, Aceh Jaya and Lhokseumawe. *Jakarta Post*, 18 December 2006. The following year a GAM candidate won a run-off vote in West Aceh with 76 per cent of the votes. GAM also won two later elections in South Aceh and Bireuen where one of the GAM negotiators in Helsinki, Nordin Abdul Rahman, was successful.

209. Megawati's grasp of realities in Aceh often seemed tenuous. After the collapse of the May 2003 talks she wondered why the GAM leaders still wanted independence: "Haven't they ever breathed the free air of their homeland?" she asked. "Such people should get out of Indonesia." *Kompas*, 19 May 2003. When asked during the 2004 election campaign about cultural decline in Aceh — implicitly referring to the consequences of military operations — she responded by talking about the high quality of Acehnese handicrafts. The author was present during this question-and-answer session.

210. On problems in allocating this assistance, see International Crisis Group (2005c), pp. 4–6.
211. Confidential interview, April 2006.
212. In mid-2007, the Aceh regional army commander, Maj. Gen. Supiadin, was confident that GAM would observe the agreement. He said that single weapons in the hands of individuals had been found but there was no indication that GAM had a store of weapons. Interview with Maj. Gen. Supiadin, Banda Aceh, 4 June 2007.
213. The author and his colleague, Ed Aspinall, were among those who had doubted that the TNI would accept a peace agreement. Aspinall and Crouch (2003).

9

REFORM IN UNPROMISING CIRCUMSTANCES

The collapse of an authoritarian regime opens wide the prospect of political reform. As Grindle and Thomas point out, "many reforms emerge and are considered in which policy elites believe that a crisis exists and that they must 'do something' about the situation or they will face grave consequences".[1] But "doing something" does not guarantee that political reforms will be implemented. A crisis can force elites to take action but it doesn't determine the exact nature of that action. Even when the fall of an authoritarian regime leads to a "democratic transition", new or revived democratic institutions are not necessarily able to implement effective reforms. This study has focused on six institutional areas where reform has been attempted with varying degrees of success or failure. The starting point for Indonesia's crisis was the Asian Monetary Crisis that originated in Thailand in mid-1997 and quickly spread to several other Asian countries. Although five countries suffered severely, none was hurt as badly as Indonesia. Several Asian heads of government lost office in the wake of the crisis, but it was only in Indonesia that the political system itself was fundamentally changed. Many civil society organizations and even members of the Soeharto regime had been pressing for gradual political change before the upheaval in May 1998 but it was only after the lifting of New Order political controls following the demise of the regime that far-reaching political reform suddenly appeared possible.

Circumstances, however, were not especially propitious. The massive economic collapse that precipitated the fall of Soeharto's authoritarian regime led to a breakdown in order through much of the country. Huge anti-government protests continued in Jakarta and many regional capitals, rioting and ethnic violence became common, and the economic decline continued as investors and businesspeople withdrew capital from Indonesia. But there was no cohesive alternative elite ready to take over power. Although the fallen president and his hard-core supporters were removed, the initial post-authoritarian government was headed by Soeharto's hand-picked vice president and consisted largely of Golkar hold-overs from the previous cabinet while the bureaucracy and the military remained intact. The free 1999 election brought new parties into the government and the legislature but ministers associated with the New Order continued to sit in the Abdurrahman and Megawati cabinets alongside representatives of new political forces, many of whom were either drawn into existing patronage networks or quickly established their own. While a handful of reformers won seats in the legislature and a few were appointed to these cabinets, especially by Abdurrahman, they were never dominant forces within these governments.

The central question asked in this book is how political reform could take place in such unpromising circumstances. Many of the New Order's political and patronage structures that had upheld the authoritarian order survived the fall of Soeharto and gave scope to the remaining elements of the old elite to protect their vital interests while new elements were divided and unable to form a coordinated force pressing for a common reform agenda. Nevertheless, despite the absence of a strong and coherent movement leading the struggle for reform, significant political reforms were in fact carried out during the presidencies of Habibie, Abdurrahman and Megawati and the basis laid for further reform under Yudhoyono.

Political reform was undoubtedly driven initially by the threat posed by the economic and political collapse in 1998–99. As long as the New Order regime remained in power, serious reform had remained off the agenda, but its fall in the wake of the economic collapse lifted the lid on previously repressed political opposition while providing scope for gradual, as well as reluctant, reformers within the regime to find ways to accommodate opposition demands. The New Order elite had been held together by Soeharto who relied on patronage distribution backed by repression but without him the ties between the components of the regime began to unravel. The key condition for the achievement of reform, therefore, was the collapse of the old regime and the inability of its remnants to reconstitute themselves as a unified elite. The long-repressed opposition groups, however, were even less united than the New Order remnants. As long as Soeharto was still in power, the various opposition groups had at least agreed on the goal of bringing him down. But even then they differed over tactics, timing and ideology while there was little consensus on the shape of the successor government.

The fragmentation of political forces, therefore, meant that no powerful and organized reform movement emerged to fight for a common reform agenda. Instead the supporters of reform consisted of disparate groups — both within and outside government — which each had their own expectations of what reform would bring. The inability of any group to establish its leadership of the reform movement, however, facilitated broad acceptance of a democratic framework that would permit the representation of all major groups — including those who had worked to overthrow the Soeharto regime as well as those who had defended it. As it happened, the New Order had preserved formal structures of democracy even though its spirit had been thoroughly ignored. Formally democratic institutions, such as legislatures and elections, provided the foundation for an institutional framework that more or less met the needs of all the major contending forces, including both survivors from the chaotic collapse of the old regime as well as the smorgasbord of political forces that emerged in its wake.

Democratic reform had been foreshadowed during the last phase of the New Order in the 1990s when some components of the ruling elite, including President Soeharto himself, had shown signs of awareness that steps toward political reform might be necessary provided they were implemented very gradually. Compared to earlier decades, military predominance in the government was gradually declining and civilian politicians played a more prominent role. A new government-backed Muslim organization headed by B. J. Habibie was founded and Golkar elected one of the president's civilian cronies as its first civilian general chairman although retired officers headed most of its provincial branches. Meanwhile an experimental pilot programme of limited decentralization was launched in selected districts. These mild measures, however, hardly hinted at the flurry of substantial reforms that would soon be implemented after the fall of the regime.

It was the unanticipated economic collapse sparked by the Asian Monetary Crisis and the Soeharto government's incapacity to cope with it that opened the way to substantial political reform in Indonesia. The political crisis arising from the economic crisis set the stage for what Grindle and Thomas called "crisis-ridden" reform. Crisis-ridden or crisis-driven reform provided the necessary breakthrough but more extensive reforms could only continue in circumstances that Grindle and Thomas called "politics-as-usual". Unlike crisis-ridden reform which is impelled by an immediate threat to the existing social and political order and thus affects institutions in a wide range of areas more or less simultaneously, the nature of politics-as-usual reform depends very much on particular circumstances that vary from case to case.

REFORM IN RESPONSE TO CRISIS

Earlier chapters have described how the national crisis of the late 1990s drove drastic policy reversals during the Habibie presidency in three key areas of Indonesia's "architecture" of governance.[2] Authoritarian controls were quickly dismantled and democratic procedures introduced that transformed the New Order's central governing institutions; the New Order's extraordinarily centralized system of regional government was abandoned and replaced with a system that was no less extraordinarily decentralised; and the long-entrenched military began to step back from its deep direct involvement in government.

Drastic reforms driven by the crisis threatened to impose heavy costs on the New Order elite and their supporters who faced the prospect of being cut off from the benefits that flowed their way during the Soeharto era. Democratization would deprive Golkar of its guaranteed electoral victories, decentralization would transfer resources from the national elite to the regions and the reduction of the political involvement of the military could deprive it of the sustenance that it derived from its territorial network. Many beneficiaries of the old regime therefore resisted change. Others, on the other hand, understood that drastic changes were needed if further breakdowns in public order with potentially disastrous long-term consequences were to be avoided. In these circumstances, these segments of the New Order elite calculated that their long-run interests would be better protected by accepting the inevitability of reform. Their initial focus was on damage control but some among them also looked for opportunities to advance their institutional interests in the new environment. Among those segments were sections of the Golkar party and a group of reform-minded military officers who in different ways adapted themselves to the new political landscape. In so doing they also indirectly facilitated the reform process.

President Habibie was an unlikely democratic reformer. The initial impetus to democratic reform did not emanate from a sudden change of heart on the part of the new president and his Golkar and military colleagues who had never previously indicated strong dissatisfaction with Soeharto's authoritarian rule. The reforms were in response to the new circumstances that threatened not only the political stability of the nation but also its leaders' grip on power. While Habibie was convinced that his embrace of "democratization" was necessary to bring an end to the anarchy that had preceded, and continued after, his ascension to the presidency, he was no less aware that his own tenure was also at stake. Lacking the Soeharto regime's repressive capacity and faced with massive student demonstrations and a general breakdown in order, he quickly drew the conclusion that his only hope of gaining the legitimacy that would enable him to remain in office was by turning toward democratization, including the holding of democratic elections. His first weeks in office were marked by the lifting of many of the New Order's repressive controls. Restrictions on the mass media were withdrawn, new political parties and trade unions were allowed to form themselves, political prisoners were released, and preparations started for the holding of Indonesia's first free election since the 1950s. Instead of the manipulated polls that guaranteed overwhelming Golkar victories, the 1999 election was vigorously contested by dozens of political parties and produced results that were widely accepted. That support for Golkar fell from almost 75 per cent in 1997 to 22 per cent in 1999 and President Habibie failed to win re-election in the MPR a few months later were convincing evidence that the institutional architecture really was changing although not exactly in the way that Habibe had anticipated.

Habibie's democratization programme was accompanied by drastic decentralization. The combined effects of the economic collapse, the breakdown in public order and the fall of the New Order government were making it difficult and sometimes impossible for Jakarta to maintain its authority in regions outside Java. Reinvigorated separatist movements emerged in East Timor, Aceh and Papua, while federalist aspirations that had been repressed by the Soeharto regime were boldly expressed in some regions outside Java. Suddenly the possibility of national disintegration no longer seemed "unthinkable" — a prospect that would soon move closer to reality when the referendum offered by Habibie in East Timor resulted in that territory's separation from Indonesia. As it seemed that the nation might be approaching the brink of a downward spiral into national disintegration, Indonesia's first non-Javanese president drastically reversed his predecessor's approach to the regions by embarking on a radical programme of decentralization that transferred substantial powers and resources from the centre to the regions.

These reforms of the political architecture required the adoption of new laws on elections and regional government by the DPR which had been elected in the last New Order election in 1997 and remained overwhelmingly dominated by Golkar and its military ally. Golkar was not enthusiastic about holding early elections that would most likely result in a massive loss of seats for the party but it also feared the unpopularity that would follow if it rejected its leader's proposal. So necessary was the holding of elections for the government's legitimacy that Golkar's leaders, especially President Habibie, refrained from using the party's numerical dominance in the legislature to pass electoral laws in its own favour. If it had ridden roughshod over the other two parties, Golkar would have risked provoking further rounds of demonstrations and even rioting, while an election seen as designed to ensure a Golkar victory, like those of the New Order, would have failed to give the Habibie government the legitimacy that it lacked. Golkar gave way, as we saw in Chapter 3, on several key issues in the electoral laws although it was still able to secure the adoption of provisions that enabled it to gain a strong position among regional representatives in the MPR, the body empowered at that time to elect the president. In contrast to the "sacrifice" it made in order to safeguard the passage of the electoral laws, Golkar found it easier to back the new laws on decentralization, as discussed in Chapter 4, which gave it the opportunity to retain much of its grip on regional government despite anticipated losses due to the holding of competitive local elections. Although Habibie in the end failed in his bid for re-election by the MPR, Golkar managed to emerge in the 1999 general election as the second largest party in the DPR and a major force in many regional DPRDs, especially outside Java.

The national crisis also set in motion a parallel reversal in the armed forces, as explained in Chapter 5. Torn between loyalty to their patron and their realization that his leadership might not be sufficient to save the regime, military officers found themselves confused and divided when they were unable to prevent the massive rioting that brought down the New Order in May 1998. By then public demands that the military withdraw from its political role were no longer limited to demonstrating students but were winning support from the wider community, especially among the urban middle class. President Habibie had little personal influence within the military so left military affairs largely to the military itself under it recently appointed Commander-in-Chief, General Wiranto. Wiranto was a Soeharto loyalist but he understood — in contrast to many officers who would have preferred to re-assert military authority — that any attempt to re-establish Soeharto-like rule could easily ignite an even greater conflagration.

Parallel to Golkar's accommodation of reform in the DPR but through a quite different process, reform-minded officers responded to the crisis by initiating a drastic reversal of military perceptions of its proper role. Advised by a small group of reform-minded staff officers, Wiranto was convinced that the military's own interests would be endangered if it did not reduce its direct political involvement. Despite the deep reservations of most officers, Wiranto's reformist advisors drew up what they called the "New Paradigm" as a temporary manifesto that led eventually to the abandonment by the military leadership of the *Dwi Fungsi* doctrine that had provided the ideological foundation for military domination of civilian affairs under the New Order.

Like Golkar which had grasped the opportunity to ensure its own political future by endorsing new political trends following the downfall of the New Order, Wiranto's advisors provided a broad initial roadmap for the military's post-authoritarian future.

The capacity of central institutions of the New Order — the Golkar-dominated DPR and the military — to adapt to the New Order's demise not only allowed them to continue to play major roles in national politics but also facilitated what, in retrospect, was a relatively steady, although sometimes tumultuous, transition towards a more or less democratic political order. Golkar did not initially welcome democratization but as a pragmatic patronage organization *par excellence*, it was quick to appreciate that its future depended on its continuing participation in government no matter what form it took. The military, too, provided its basic interests were respected — particularly its access to self-funding resources and the impunity of its officers from legal proceedings — soon worked out a *modus vivendi* with the post-authoritarian governments. The voluntary incorporation of two major New Order forces in the post-New Order polity provided a foundation for the transition from crisis-ridden reform to politics-as-usual.

It needs to be noted at this point, however, that the impact of the national crisis was not spread evenly across institutional areas. The exception among the four major areas discussed in this book was the judiciary, examined in Chapter 6, where reform was barely noticeable before the election of President Yudhoyono in 2004. The demands of public opinion, as expressed by demonstrators in the streets and opinion-leaders in the press, were no less directed at the courts than at other major institutions. In particular, the failure of the judiciary to deal effectively with corruption and indeed its ubiquitous presence in the courts themselves was a major focus of popular anger, exemplified by a series of corruption scandals involving the Soeharto family and other senior government leaders. We will return below to the questions of reform of the judiciary and corruption in the post-crisis period.

POST-CRISIS REFORM

The deep sense of political crisis that forced the Habibie government to turn towards democratization was eased when free elections produced a DPR and MPR in which all major political forces were represented and a new president was elected in a process that was broadly accepted as fair despite its obvious shortcomings. The election of Abdurrahman marked a decline of the tumultuous political struggles and uncertainties of the Habibie presidency. The crisis was by no means over but was increasingly perceived as merely "chronic but not acute".[3] The economy remained stagnant, inter-communal and inter-religious conflict spread and the challenge from revitalized separatist movements in Aceh and Papua grew following the exit of East Timor, but the sense that the nation was on the brink of total disaster gradually subsided. There was little confidence, however, that the new leadership would find solutions to the nation's challenges. Indeed, President Abdurrahman's erratic behaviour and policy pronouncements themselves contributed to the regular mini-crises that eventually overwhelmed his brief presidency.

Although the Abdurrahman presidency was in some ways more a case of "crisis-as-usual" than "politics-as-usual", the formation of the freely elected DPR and MPR provided the major political forces with fora to consider further institutional changes. In contrast to the DPR during the Habibie presidency in which four-fifths of the seats were occupied by Golkar and the military, no party held anything close to a majority of seats after the elections of 1999 and 2004. The main parties ranged from Golkar to the nationalist PDI-P and several Muslim groups representing rival traditionalist and modernist variants of Islam while the military retained a reduced quota of appointed seats until 2004. Due to the peculiarity of Indonesia's presidential system under the original 1945 constitution, the president was not elected directly by the people in a national election but indirectly by the MPR which also had constitutional authority to dismiss the president. Presidents Abdurrahman and Megawati therefore felt they had no choice but to seek parliamentary support by including virtually all major political forces in their cabinets. Even after the introduction of the direct election of the president, President Yudhoyono also believed it was necessary to include representatives of most parties in his cabinet. As a result governments lacked political coherence and reflected rivalries between the parties represented in the DPR.

Numerous studies by political scientists stress the dangers of excessive party fragmentation in legislatures which, in the absence of stable coalitions, can prevent the formation of effective governments and obstruct the passage of legislation. Indonesia's own experience in the 1950s provides an example of a fragmented legislature in which multi-party cabinets rose and fell in quick succession leading eventually to the abandonment of constitutional democracy. The prospects of serious reform in such circumstances are therefore questionable. Andrew MacIntyre summarizes a common view among political scientists who have argued that "fragmentation and dispersal of power stemming from the interplay of constitutional structure and the character of the party system leads to policy delay, gridlock, and immobilism". Thus, "Countries in which ... the electoral system produces weak or incoherent parties and multiparty coalitions or in which the structure of government produces fragmented authority among multiple decision-making bodies are likely to be slow to reform and have difficulty responding to policy challenges that demand prompt focused action."[4] Many scholars have warned that presidential democracies are particularly vulnerable when combined with fragmented multiparty legislatures.[5]

It might be expected that as the impetus provided by an ongoing system-threatening crisis abates, political reform would face severe, even insuperable, obstacles when a multiparty government co-exists with a multiparty legislature. In the Indonesian case, such obstacles were present and post-crisis reform was undoubtedly slow and piecemeal as compromises had to be reached between self-interested politicians in both the executive and the legislature. At the same time, the interests of other political forces such as the military and surviving elements of the New Order elite had to be taken into account. Contrary to the expectations of many observers, however, important reforms were in fact carried out in "politics-as-usual" circumstances despite party fragmentation in both government and legislature. The process and outcomes of "politics-as-usual" reform, however, differed markedly between institutions. The most extensive reforms were those concerning governing institutions themselves — the constitution, legislatures, elections and regional government. On the other hand, reforms that had to be imposed on institutions by the government or legislature proceeded less smoothly as in the cases of military and judicial reform. While fragmentation could be a positive factor in facilitating reform of the "architecture of governance", it undermined efforts to impose civilian control over the military and to reform the courts.

REFORM OF GOVERNING INSTITUTIONS

The Habibie government and the DPR adopted radical reforms of the electoral system and regional government in response to the national crisis. The "crisis-ridden" 1999 electoral laws, however, were only the first legislative step toward a post-crisis overhaul of the 1945 Constitution and further revision of the electoral laws in preparation for the 2004 elections. The drastic decentralization of regional government was also followed by post-crisis legislation that, in this case, responded to "excesses" of the 1999 legislation and sought to achieve a revised balance between central, provincial and district authority. Driven by the crisis, the legislation needed for the Habibie reforms of the political architecture was completed in each case within months by the Golkar-dominated DPR. In contrast, the deliberation of post-crisis legislation by the new politically fragmented DPR under "politics-as-usual" circumstances required years. The amendments of the constitution were spread over three years from 1999 to 2002 and the related electoral law revisions were only completed the following year. The reconsideration of the regional government laws took from 2001 to 2004.

Observers were initially pessimistic about the prospects of a substantial overhaul of the constitution.[6] Since its reintroduction in 1959, the 1945 Constitution had acquired virtually "sacred" status under Presidents Soekarno and Soeharto. As a sacred document, it was considered by many — especially within the military and among nationalist circles — as beyond amendment. On the other hand, it had provided the constitutional foundation for two successive authoritarian regimes and was widely considered a major obstacle to the democracy demanded by the forces of reform. In the case of constitutional reform and ensuing electoral changes, the Megawati government — itself an uneasy multiparty coalition — allowed much of the initiative to be taken by the MPR and DPR. The prospects of major reform seemed unpromising in view of the rivalries in these politically fragmented institutions.

Nevertheless, major reforms were adopted. As MacIntyre points out, "politicians are the primary actors in the redesign of rules that are to govern their own behavior" and therefore have a direct interest in outcomes.[7] The initial electoral and regional government laws were adopted by the DPR that had been elected in 1997 and was completely dominated by Golkar and its military ally. In crisis-ridden conditions both calculated that it would be wiser to go along with these reforms. But the most important reforms were adopted in post-crisis conditions by legislatures that did not conform to the conditions that MacIntyre and others regarded as facilitating reform. The MPR that transformed the 1945 Constitution and the DPR that adopted the laws regulating the 2004 elections were both severely fragmented bodies and therefore, according to the common perception, more likely to be bogged down in stalemate and deadlock than to agree on significant democratic reforms. But, precisely because of the absence of a single dominant party or stable coalition in these legislatures, conditions were suitable for the standard Indonesian legislative style of taking decisions through *musyawarah* (deliberation) and *mufakat* (consensus).[8]

In the absence of a single dominant party or stable coalition, the process of amending the constitution and revising the electoral laws was based on bargaining and compromise with decisions taken by consensus in accordance with long-established tradition (except in one minor case). As was shown in Chapter 3, the positions of the main parties diverged substantially on many key issues and at times deliberations seemed to be on the verge of breakdown, particularly on the question of how the president should be elected. Party positions were often transparently based on calculations about what would serve each party's electoral interests but, because no party could impose its will unilaterally, compromises were eventually reached which left all sides at least partially satisfied. The achievement of compromises on major issues like constitutional reform and electoral laws was also facilitated by concerns about loss of legitimacy if they were not adopted in time to hold the 2004 presidential and legislative elections. The final outcome was the establishment of institutions of government more or less in conformity with internationally accepted standards of formal democracy. On this basis, the legitimacy of the president and parliament elected in 2004 faced no serious challenges.

The amended constitution had established legitimate institutions of government but the adoption of reforms does not, of course, guarantee that institutions will always work in ways that meet democratic expectations. At the very beginning of the Yudhoyono presidency, the president faced what Juan Linz called one of the "perils of presidentialism".[9] Although Yudhoyono had won the presidential election with an impressive majority, his party and its allies constituted a minority group in the legislature. The potential threat that the president faced from the legislature, however, was overcome within a few months when his vice president won the leadership of Golkar and brought that party into the ruling coalition. True to form as a party of patronage *par excellence*, Golkar provided the new president with the legislative backing that the president's own party could not provide and was therefore suitably rewarded. Of course, potential deadlock between president and legislature does not always end with such a favourable outcome for democratic stability.

Like the electoral laws and the constitutional amendments, the revision of the regional government laws directly affected the interests of the political parties whose representatives in the fragmented DPR were determining the content of a law that would have substantial implications for party interests in the regions. The hasty crisis-driven adoption of very radical laws in 1999 had led to much confusion in implementation and exacerbated rivalries between national government departments and regional governments as powers and access to material benefits were transferred from the centre to the regions. The revised laws adopted in 2004 were the result of a complex series of compromises involving not only the government and the political parties in the DPR but also bureaucrats at the national and regional levels. The Department of Home Affairs' original draft of the new law was soon withdrawn when it met with much opposition from regional interests which objected to its "recentralizing" character. The much delayed new bill was eventually amalgamated with a separate bill providing for the direct election of provincial and district heads, a provision strongly supported by the main political parties which were preparing themselves to contest these positions in regional elections to be held after the national elections. While the national government — through the Department of Home Affairs — succeeded in restoring some of its earlier authority, the introduction of the direct election of regional heads reinforced decentralization. In the absence of a dominant party or coalition, the drawn-out deliberations in the fragmented DPR achieved a balance that was broadly accepted by all major groups and provided the basis for direct elections of nearly 500 heads of regional governments — both provincial and district — during the following five years. Fears that regional elections might unleash ethnic and religious conflict proved unfounded as political leaders from rival communities calculated that their prospects of success would be enhanced by forming inter-communal coalitions, the composition of which differed drastically from region to region according to local constellations of power.

REFORM OF THE MILITARY

In contrast to reform of governing institutions in which politicians were the ultimate arbiters in reforming their own institutions, fragmented legislatures and governments were less successful in imposing reforms on other institutions. Military reform involved an institution that had been directly controlled by President Soeharto during the New Order and had never been subjected to independent civilian control through the DPR. The initial limited reforms of the military had been introduced on the initiative of a small group of reform-minded military officers in the wake of the national crisis. The early burst of reform within the military, however, soon lost its momentum as the crisis itself abated and mainstream military officers, who had been deeply demoralized at the height of the crisis, began to re-assert themselves.

Civil-military relations were in a state of confusion during the Habibie and Abdurrahman presidencies. Both presidents relied on ad hoc responses to immediate challenges without a systematic reform programme. On one hand, President Habibie exercised civilian supremacy by holding a referendum on East Timor's future and, under heavy international pressure, ordered the withdrawal of the military from East Timor when a large majority of East Timorese opted for independence. On the other hand, although the military had not openly opposed the president's policy, officers were able to mobilize East Timorese civilian militias to undermine its implementation. Similarly, when President Abdurrahman sponsored negotiations with GAM in Aceh, troops on the ground blatantly sabotaged a series of ceasefire agreements. But these were not simply conflicts between civilians and the military as most of the DPR opposed concessions to separatist rebels in East Timor and Aceh as well as in Papua.

The military's enduring political influence was derived from its territorial network stretching throughout the entire country. Through this network, military personnel supplemented their own incomes and operating funds, most of which were not met by the state budget. This enabled the military institution to sustain a force far larger than was possible if it had relied on the state budget alone for its funding. Military officers were thus in positions where they could exert indirect political influence, especially on regional governments, as well as potentially "cause trouble" if deemed necessary in the interests of the military institution or even individual officers. Politicians, learning from their experiences under the New Order, were habituated to be wary of antagonizing the military.

During the Habibie, Abdurrahman and Megawati presidencies, military (and police) officers continued to be represented in the DPR and MPR, as well as the regional DPRDs, where their numbers gave them influence equivalent to a medium-sized party, while the commander-in-chief remained a member of the cabinet. In the fragmented legislatures, the military was often wooed by parties seeking support on particular issues. As a consequence, legislation that threatened military interests was normally "watered down" or delayed. Thus, even in the wake of the New Order's fall in 1998, reformist party leaders refrained from demanding the immediate removal of the military from the DPR, later legislation on human rights courts was softened, the drafting of laws concerning the military was largely left to the military itself, illegal military fund-raising activities continued to be tolerated and the military's claim to determine security policies was largely respected. Even after the removal of military representation from the legislatures, parties often looked for military and police backing in elections.

Government measures to establish civilian control over the military therefore proceeded very slowly. Although Abdurrahman had begun his presidency with rhetoric about placing the military under civilian control, he himself appreciated the value of military backing after the DPR initiated proceedings aimed at his dismissal when he attempted in vain to draw the military into the political battle on his own side. Megawati understood this lesson and showed little interest in initiating further reforms. On the contrary, she appointed some of the most unyielding "hard-line" officers to senior positions and the laws that regulated the military during her presidency fell far short of establishing full civilian control.

Yudhoyono's victory in the presidential election promised further reform but he preferred to move very cautiously. At the beginning of his presidency, he successfully foiled his predecessor's attempt to foist on him an arch-conservative commander-in-chief and then proceeded gradually to promote "professional-oriented" officers to top positions. Despite widespread military opposition to negotiations with GAM, the president — through his vice president — initiated secret contacts which led to the Helsinki peace agreement and the adoption of the Law on the Governance of Aceh that eventually allowed a GAM leader to win the governorship of the province in a direct election. The resolution of the thirty-year conflict in Aceh was not only a major achievement in itself but was also a huge step toward strengthening civilian control over the military. Nevertheless, fundamental issues seemed unlikely to be resolved as long as the national government was unable to fund the military from the government budget.

REFORM OF THE COURTS

Despite heavy pressures emanating from the national crisis that forced at least some Golkar politicians and military officers to conclude that survival required the quick acceptance of "crisis-ridden" reforms, the atmosphere in the courts continued to be one of "business-as-usual" as entrenched corruption persisted regardless of the crisis. The small number of reform-oriented judges and other legal officials was overwhelmed by colleagues who had willingly — or perhaps in some cases reluctantly — accepted the values and practices of the Soeharto era. Following Soeharto's fall, the tolerance of corruption in the courts was reinforced by the self-interest of many members of the Habibie government who themselves had been beneficiaries of New Order patrimonialism. It soon became clear that one of President Habibie's main goals was to save his patron, Soeharto, from prosecution for corruption. In so doing, the president and other members of the New Order regime had their own interests in protecting the fallen president. If Soeharto could be convicted of corruption, who among his underlings would not be vulnerable?

Public pressure, ranging from massive demonstrations to newspaper editorials, continued to demand action but during the first three post-1998 presidencies neither government nor legislatures showed serious interest in combating corruption. Many party politicians, whether in the cabinet or the legislature, were themselves involved in raising funds on behalf of their parties or for more personal purposes and were vulnerable to corruption charges. During the Abdurrahman and Megawati presidencies, it was not unusual for high-profile political, bureaucratic and business figures to face corruption charges and some were even brought to court but the motivation often seemed to be political or simply pecuniary as corrupt judges and prosecutors secured the dropping of charges or release from prison of wealthy detainees. The DPR's lack of enthusiasm for anti-corruption legislation was indicated by long delays in the actual establishment of new anti-corruption institutions.

Although the first three post-Soeharto presidents made little headway in combating corruption, they at least laid the legislative framework that could be used by the fourth president. Bypassing the regular courts in which corruption was endemic, Yudhoyono activated the new anti-corruption institutions to bring a series of high-level officials — including several former cabinet ministers, senior officials and former governors as well as lower officials — to court where most were found guilty and sentenced to substantial terms in prison. In contrast to the previous post-1998 presidents who were vulnerable to parliamentary-style dismissal and therefore inhibited in pursuing genuine anti-corruption measures against officials with political connections, Yudhoyono enjoyed the legitimacy of a convincing victory in Indonesia's first direct presidential election and was less vulnerable to impeachment under an amended constitution that was now more truly presidential. Indeed, his anti-corruption campaign enhanced his political legitimacy.

Yudhoyono's anti-corruption campaign, however, was often described as selective. Although less dependent on patronage ties than previous presidents, he faced the political reality that his party commanded only a small share of the seats in the DPR and that the longevity of his government required additional support in the legislature which was forthcoming when Vice President Kalla won the leadership of Golkar. Limits were thus imposed on the anti-corruption campaign which did not extend to the highest levels of the government although it ensnared important officials just below the top level as well as a few of Megawati's ministers. The president did not have a completely free hand but his anti-corruption campaign seemed to have a deterrent effect although some of the most influential seemed exempt.

Unlike reform of political institutions which offered part of the existing elite — in government, legislatures and the military — opportunities not only to survive the national crisis and even advance their interests, the potential implications of thorough judicial reform were disturbing for many politicians, judges and bureaucrats as well as tycoons in the private sector. Reform of the legislature might lead a politician to lose his seat or access to patronage benefits while military reform could obstruct an officer's prospects of promotion but strict implementation of anti-corruption measures could have direct personal consequences: offenders could be put behind bars. Given the ubiquity of bureaucratic and political corruption during the New Order and the extent of post-Soeharto money politics in the national and regional legislatures, it was hardly surprising that reform of the judiciary moved slowly.

RESTORATION OF REGIONAL "FAILED STATES"

In contrast to the issues examined in Chapters 3 to 6, the most basic reform needed in the cases discussed in Chapters 7 and 8 was to achieve the capacity to restore law and order. During the New Order, the Soeharto government clamped down severely on manifestations of what it called SARA (*suku, agama, ras, antar-golongan*: ethnic, religious, racial, inter-group) conflict. These conflicts challenged the fundamental premise of Indonesian nationalism which proclaimed the unity of a nation in which all its citizens, despite their ethnic, religious and regional affiliations, shared a common Indonesian identity. From time to time, however, local ethnic groups fought each other, anti-Chinese rioting broke out, radical Muslims attacked Christian churches, or workers and peasants launched violent protests, but the New Order's security apparatus was usually able to limit such actions to only a few days. The Soeharto regime was also challenged by long-running armed separatist movements in Aceh, Papua and East Timor but none was close to achieving its goals before May 1998.

The collapse of the New Order, however, lifted the lid on protest which in some regions opened the way to the spread of violent conflict beyond the capacity of security forces to control. SARA conflict was most devastating in Maluku, Poso, and West and Central Kalimantan while reinvigorated separatist movements intensified resistance in East Timor, Aceh and Papua. Following the exit of East Timor in 1999, the most destructive separatist war was taking place in Aceh, while the most devastating SARA conflict was between Muslims and Christians in Maluku. If either of these provinces had been an independent state, it would have been classified as "failed". But these conflicts were largely contained within their own regions with populations constituting respectively only 2 and 1 per cent of the national population. Continuing conflict in Aceh and Maluku was undoubtedly of great concern but still far from constituting top-priority challenges for the Habibie and Abdurrahman governments although they received more attention under Megawati.

Although isolated, these conflicts were not insulated from national developments. Maluku's troubles did not arise purely from quarrels between indigenous Malukan Muslims and Christians. The influx of Muslim transmigrants from Sulawesi over several decades was changing the demographic balance when the fall of the New Order opened the way to national democratic elections of 1999 and the prospect of unsettled regional politics. Whatever its exact origins, the fighting spread throughout the Maluku islands and could not be stopped by security forces which were themselves divided between Muslims and Christians. Meanwhile political rivalries in Jakarta prevented the Abdurrahman government from taking decisive action and provided the opportunity for a military-supported Java-based Islamic militia to journey to Maluku where its presence intensified the conflict. In reaction, the Abdurrahman government finally abandoned its hands-off approach, introduced emergency rule in the province and sent more non-Malukan troops. But by late 2001 sporadic peace initiatives sponsored both locally and in Jakarta had made little headway.

In these unpromising circumstances, the national government finally took the initiative. Although President Megawati's role seemed marginal, two of her coordinating ministers, Yudhoyono and Kalla, sponsored peace conferences first in Poso and then in Maluku. Although the Maluku peace agreement was broadly welcomed by residents, violence in the form of bombings, arson and murder continued on a reduced scale. A fortuitous clash between the police and the army revealed the involvement of military officers in provoking the violence and provided the opportunity for the Jakarta government to intervene decisively. The dismissal of the army regional commander at the behest of Yudhoyono in 2002 was followed by a sudden decline in violence while Kalla arranged for cooperative Muslim and Christian leaders to gain access to material opportunities and provided funding to transport the radical-Muslim militia out of Maluku. Although a form of "ethnic cleansing" resulted in the residential segregation of the two communities and left many in refugee camps, the restoration of order paved the way for the return to normality when peaceful regional elections were held in which Muslim and Christian candidates ran on joint tickets.

The conflict in Aceh also had deep local roots but could not be separated from national politics. The rise of a movement fighting for independence was inherently linked to the province's status as part of Indonesia. Armed resistance to Jakarta had already started in the 1950s and the wounds of that war were still being felt when armed conflict was renewed in the 1970s and continued on-and-off until the peace agreement of 2005. Acehnese also resented economic exploitation which made a major contribution to the nation's oil and natural gas exports but left Aceh as one of Indonesia's poorest regions, while the influx of Javanese transmigrants was seen as threatening Acehnese identity. But not all Acehnese supported GAM's struggle for independence.

Many Acehnese benefited from the opportunities arising from being part of a larger nation. In contrast to Papuans and East Timorese, for example, many Acehnese were engaged in national activities and were well represented in the national elite in Jakarta.

Even more than the case of Maluku, Jakarta was divided on how to deal with Aceh. President Abdurrahman's attempts to seek a negotiated settlement were undermined by the military that would accept nothing short of GAM's surrender. Nevertheless Megawati's coordinating minister for security affairs, Yudhoyono, revived talks with GAM which led to a short-lived "cessation of hostilities" that ended in 2003 with the launching of a military campaign that imposed heavy casualties on GAM. It was only after the replacement of Megawati by Yudhoyono that serious steps to revive talks with GAM could begin, reinforced fortuitously by the devastating tsunami that struck Aceh at the end of 2004. A greatly weakened GAM agreed to abandon its struggle for independence in exchange for participation in elections of the governor and district heads, as well as the right to form local political parties. Yudhoyono's authority secured military acceptance of the agreement while Kalla's agents ensured that funds were available to win over those who were reluctant to drop the struggle for independence. The agreement was later watered down by the DPR but the elections resulted in victories of GAM candidates as governor and in almost half of the districts.

In both Maluku and Aceh, regional conflicts could only be resolved when the national government took advantage of opportunities to intervene effectively. The policies that brought peace to Maluku and Aceh were implemented in conditions that were "crisis-ridden" from the point of view of the two regions but "politics-as-usual" for the national government. In Maluku, the government facilitated compromises between the rival camps, supplied funds for those who cooperated, replaced the military commander and eventually held elections. In Aceh, peace was achieved after a new national government had paved the way to negotiations with GAM by vetoing the appointment of Megawati's proposed hard-line candidate for command of the TNI. The final resolution took the form of a new law on Aceh negotiated in the national parliament in which GAM was not represented. Although GAM's concessions went deeper than those of the government, it still achieved its "bottom-line" objective of participation in elections. In both cases, conflicts that had arisen in part from the interaction of distant provinces with the rest of the country could only be resolved when the national government achieved sufficient consensus at the national level to negotiate compromises that ultimately led to the democratic election of new regional leadership.

UNEVEN REFORM

The prospects for political reform in Indonesia seemed bleak in the years immediately after the fall of the New Order in 1998 as the Habibie government struggled to establish its authority. Pessimism was widespread and some Indonesians were even envisaging the break-up of their nation. In place of the centralized New Order that was dominated by a long-established president backed by the military and Golkar, power shifted to weak coalition governments consisting of rival political parties and lacking in cohesion. Fragmented cabinets facing fragmented legislatures, in the view of many, did not augur well for the future of reform. But, as the chapters in this book have shown, successive governments were able to initiate and oversee significant reform of the major political institutions during the next decade.

Reform, however, did not proceed evenly across different fields. The most thorough reforms were in governing institutions — the architecture of governance. The constitution had been thoroughly amended and now approximated to formal international democratic standards, while elections, at both national and regional levels, produced results that broadly reflected the preferences of voters, although the performance of elected politicians generally fell far short of public expectations. Centre-region relations had also been drastically overhauled and, despite limited restoration of central authority in 2004, regional governments had much more control over their own affairs than during the New Order, although their performance often failed to meet the standards of "good governance". The previously dominant military had stepped back from direct political participation although it continued to exercise informal political influence and full civilian control had not been achieved. The least progress was made in the judicial sector where corrupt courts could not deter the corruption that remained rampant in government and business until new anti-corruption institutions began to impose heavy penalties on a relatively small number of officials with the result that the risks of corruption rose sharply. Meanwhile, central government intervention had restored order and brought an end to mass violence in two provinces where regional institutions had most seriously "failed" while violence was curbed in other regions.

This book has shown how political reform was initiated and proceeded in key political institutions. But it has also highlighted the limits of the reforms achieved and has only touched lightly on reform in economic institutions. In virtually all institutions, reforms were introduced in an atmosphere where "money politics" was a normal aspect of government activities. The stability of Soeharto's New Order was due in part to the regime's capacity to suppress dissent but no less important was its patronage network that tied various layers of diverse beneficiaries to the hierarchy that Soeharto headed. The collapse of his regime led to the fragmentation of the unified New Order patronage structure and the emergence of new networks around both surviving segments of the New Order and political forces that had previously been suppressed. Money politics remained prevalent at all levels of the governing institutions and, despite significant progress, major obstacles continued to hinder further reform. Not the least was the dependence of many politicians and officials on the circulation of irregular funds as has been noted throughout this book.

Notes

1. Grindle and Thomas (1991), p. 14.
2. On the "architecture" of governance, see Reynolds (2002); MacIntyre (2003).
3. For a contemporary analysis, see the report of the International Crisis Group (2000) entitled "Indonesia's Crisis: Chronic but not Acute".
4. MacIntyre (2003), pp. 25, 27.
5. See Linz (1993); Mainwaring (1993).
6. See contemporary comments by observers quoted in Chapter 3.
7. MacIntyre (2003), p. 107.
8. Decision-making by consensus was always the practice in Indonesian legislatures not only during the New Order but also Soekarno's Guided Democracy. The "consensus" during those eras, however, was always pre-ordained by the regime and accepted without question by the legislators. As David Reeve once put it, in those days, regime-imposed *mufakat* (consensus) preceded the *musyawarah* (discussion).
9. Linz (1993).

BIBLIOGRAPHY

Books, Monographs, Articles, Reports etc.

Abdul Rahman Saleh. *Bukan Kampung Maling, Bukan Desa Ustadz: Memoar 930 Hari di Puncak Gedung Bundar* [Neither Village of Thieves nor Shire of Preachers: A Memoir of 930 Days at the Top of the Round Building]. Jakarta: *Kompas*, 2008.

Abuza, Zachary. *Militant Islam in Southeast Asia: Crucible of Terror*. Boulder, London: Lynne Rienner, 2003.

Adi Andojo Soetjipto. "Legal Reform and Challenges in Indonesia". In *Indonesia in Transition: Social Aspects of Reformasi and Crisis*, edited by Chris Manning and Peter van Dierman. Singapore: Institute of Southeast Asian Studies, 2000.

Aditjondro, George J. "Guns, Pamphlets and Handie-Talkies: How the Military Exploited Local Ethno-religious Tensions in Maluku to Preserve Their Political and Economic Privileges". In *Violence in Indonesia*, edited by Ingrid Wessel and Georgia Winhoefer. Hamburg: Abera Verlag Markus Voss, 2001.

Aditjondro, George J. "Kerusuhan Poso dan Morowali, Akar Permasalahan dan Jalan Keluarnya" [Rioting in Poso and Morowali, the Root of the Problem and the Way Out]. Unpublished paper presented at Propatria seminar at Hotel Santika, Jakarta, 7 January 2004.

Aglionby, John. "Islamists in SE Asia Linked to Bin Laden", *Guardian*, 11 October 2001.

Ahmad Suaedy et al. *Luka Maluku: Militer Terlibat* [Maluku's Wounds: Military Involvement]. Jakarta: Institut Studi Arus Informasi, 2000.

Alagappa, Muthiah, ed. *Coercion and Governance: The Declining Political Role of the Military in Asia*. Stanford, California: Stanford University Press, 2001.

Ali Alatas. *The Pebble in the Shoe: The Diplomatic Struggle for East Timor*. Jakarta: Aksa Karunia, 2006.

Alm, James, Jorge Martinez-Vazquez, and Sri Mulyani Indrawati, eds. *Reforming Intergovernmental Fiscal Relations and the Rebuilding of Indonesia*. Cheltenham, UK and Northampton, MA, USA: Edward Elgar, 2004.

Amnesty International. "'Shock Therapy': Restoring Order in Aceh, 1989–1993". London: Amnesty International, 2 August 1993.

————. *Power and Impunity: Human Rights Under the New Order*. London: Amnesty International, 1994.

————. "Indonesia: New military operations, old patterns of human rights abuses in Aceh (Nanggroe Aceh Darussalam)". London: Amnesty International. 6 October 2004.

Anderson, Benedict R.O'G., ed. *Violence and the State in Suharto's Indonesia*. Ithaca, New York: Southeast Asia Program, Cornell University, 2001.

Arief Budiman, Barbara Hatley, and Damien Kingsbury, eds. *Reformasi: Crisis and Change in Indonesia*. Clayton: Monash Asia Institute, 1999.

Aragon, Lorraine V. "Communal Violence in Poso, Central Sulawesi: Where People Eat Fish and Fish East People". *Indonesia* 72 (October 2001).

Asia Foundation. *Indonesia Rapid Decentralization Appraisal* (IRDA), Third Report. Jakarta: Asia Foundation, 2003.

Aspinall, Edward. "The Downfall of President Abdurrahman Wahid: A Return to Authoritarianism?". In *Women in Indonesia: Gender, Equity and Development*, edited by Kathryn Robinson and Sharon Bessell. Singapore: Institute of Southeast Asian Studies, 2002.

————. *Opposing Suharto: Compromise, Resistance, and Regime Change in Indonesia*. Stanford: Stanford University Press, 2005*a*.

————. "Elections and the normalization of politics in Indonesia". *South East Asia Research* 12, no. 2 (July 2005*b*).

————. *The Helsinki Agreement: A More Promising Basis for Peace in Aceh?* Washington: East-West Center, 2006*a*.

————. "Violence and Identity Formation in Aceh under Indonesian Rule". In *Verandah of Violence: The Background of the Aceh Problem*, edited by Anthony Reid. Singapore: Singapore University Press, 2006*b*.

————. "Peace without Justice? The Helsinki Peace Process in Aceh". HD Report. Geneva: Henry Dunant Centre for Humanitarian Dialogue, 2008.

Aspinall, Edward and Harold Crouch. *The Aceh Peace Process: Why It Failed*. Washington: East-West Center, 2003.

Aspinall, Edward and Greg Fealy, eds. *Local Power and Politics in Indonesia: Decentralisation and Democratisation*. Indonesia Update Series, Research School of Pacific and Asian Studies, Australian National University. Singapore: Institute of Southeast Asian Studies, 2003.

Barton, Greg. *Gus Dur: The Authorised Biography of Abdurrahman Wahid*. Jakarta, Singapore: Equinox Publishing, 2002.

Bertrand, Jacques. *Nationalism and Ethnic Conflict in Indonesia*. Cambridge: Cambridge University Press, 2004.

Bresnan, John. "The United States, the IMF, and the Indonesian Financial Crisis". In *The Politics of Post-Suharto Indonesia*, edited by Adam Schwarz and Jonathan Paris. New York: The Council of Foreign Relations, 1999.

Bourchier, David. "Magic Memos, Collusion and Judges with Attitude: Notes on the Politics of Law in Contemporary Indonesia". In *Law, Capitalism and Power in Asia*, edited by Kanishka Jayasuriya. London and New York: Routledge, 1999.

Burke, Adam. "Peacebuilding and Rebuilding at Ground Level: Practical Constraints and Policy Objectives in Aceh". *Conflict, Security and Development* 8, no. 1 (2008).

Butt, Simon. "The Constitutional Court's Decision in the Dispute between the Supreme Court and the Judicial Commission: Banishing Judicial Accountability?". In *Indonesia: Democracy and the Promise of Good Governance*, edited by Ross H. McLeod and Andrew MacIntyre. Singapore: Institute of Southeast Asian Studies, 2007.

Campos, Jose Edgar and Joel S. Hellman. "Governance Gone Local: Does Decentralization Improve Accountability?" In *East Asia Decentralizes*, by World Bank. Washington, D.C.: The World Bank, 2005.

Chauvel, Richard. *Nationalists, Soldiers and Separatist*. Leiden: KITLV Press, 1990.

Crisis Centre Diocese of Ambon. "The Situation in Ambon/Moluccas". Report 790–91. Ambon, Maluku, 2002.

Crouch, Harold. *The Army and Politics in Indonesia*. Ithaca: Cornell University Press, 1978.

———. "Patrimonialism and Military Rule in Indonesia". *World Politics* 31, no. 4 (July 1979).

———. "Indonesia: An Uncertain Outlook". *Southeast Asian Affairs* (1994*a*).

———. "Democratic Prospects in Indonesia". In *Democracy in Indonesia, 1950s and 1990s*, edited by David Bourchier and John D. Legge. Clayton, Victoria: Centre of Southeast Asian Studies, Monash University, 1994*b*.

———. "Indonesia's 'Strong' State". In *Weak and Strong States in Asia-Pacific Societies*, edited by Peter Dauvergne. Sydney: Allen & Unwin, 1998.

———. "Wiranto and Habibie: Military-Civilian Relations Since May 1998". In *Reformasi: Crisis and Change in Indonesia*, edited by Arief Budiman, Barbara Hatley, and Damien Kingsbury. Clayton: Monash Asia Institute, 1999.

———. "Political Update 2002: Megawati's Holding Operation". In *Local Power and Politics in Indonesia: Decentralisation and Democratisation*, edited by Edward Aspinall and Greg Fealy. Singapore: Institute of Southeast Asian Studies, 2003.

Daughters, Robert and Leslie Harper. "Fiscal and Political Decentralization Reforms". In *The State and State Reform in Latin America*, edited by Eduardo Lora. Washington: The Inter-American Development Bank, 2007.

Davidson, Jamie S. "Politics-as-usual on Trial: Regional Anti-corruption Campaigns in Indonesia". *The Pacific Review* 20, no. 1 (March 2007): 75–99.

Davis, Michael. "Laskar Jihad and the Political Position of Conservative Islam in Indonesia". *Contemporary Southeast Asia* 24, no. 1 (April 2002): 12–32.

Dewi Fortuna Anwar. "The Habibie Presidency". In *Post-Soeharto Indonesia: Renewal or Chaos?*, edited by Geoff Forrester. Netherlands: KITLV Press/Singapore: Institute of Southeast Asian Studies, 1999.

Dewi Fortuna Anwar dkk. *Gus Dur versus Militer: Studi tentang Hubungan Sipil-Militer di Era Transisi* [Gus Dur versus the Military: A Study of Civil-Military Relations in an Era of Transition]. Jakarta: Grasindo, 2002.

Diamond, Larry and Marc F. Plattner, eds. *The Global Resurgence of Democracy.* Baltimore and London: The Johns Hopkins University Press, 1993.

Diamond, Larry, Marc F. Plattner, Yun-han Chu, and Hung-Mao Tien, eds. *Consolidating the Third Wave Democracies: Themes and Perspectives.* Baltimore and London: The Johns Hopkins University Press, 1997.

Eaton, Kent. "Political Obstacles to Decentralization: Evidence from Argentina and the Philippines". *Development and Change* 32, no. 1 (2001).

Edi Peterbang and Eri Sutrisno. *Konflik Etnik di Sambas* [Ethnic Conflict in Sambas]. Jakarta: Institut Studi Arus Informasi, 2000.

Ellis, Andrew. "The Indonesian Constitutional Transition: Conservatism or Fundamental Change?". *Singapore Journal of International and Comparative Law* 6 (2002): 116–53.

————. "Indonesia's Constitutional Change Reviewed". In *Indonesia: Democracy and the Promise of Good Governance*, edited by Ross H. McLeod and Andrew MacIntyre. Singapore: Institute of Southeast Asian Studies, 2007.

Emerson Yuntho. "Mencermati Pemberian SP3 Kasus Korupsi". *Hukum Online*, 25 November 2004. <www.antikorupsi.org/docs/cermatis3kasuskorupsi.pdf> (last accessed 19 June 2009).

Enoch, Charles, Olivier Frecaut, and Arto Kovanen. "Indonesia's Banking Crisis: What Happened and What Did We Learn?". *Bulletin of Indonesian Economic Studies* 39, no. 1 (2003).

Erwin H. Al-Jakartaty. *Tragedi Bumi Seribu Pulau* [Tragedy in the Land of One Thousand Islands]. Jakarta: BukKMaNs, 2000.

Erwiza Erman. "Illegal Coalmining in West Sumatra: Access and Actors in the Post-Soeharto Era". In *The Politics and Economics of Indonesia's Natural Resources*, edited by Budy P. Resosudarmo. Singapore: Institute of Southeast Asian Studies, 2005.

————. "Deregulation of the Tin Trade and Creation of a Local Shadow State: A Bangka Case Study". In *Renegotiating Boundaries: Local Politics in Post-Suharto Indonesia*, edited by Henk Schulte Nordholt and Gerry van Klinken. Leiden: KITLV Press, 2007.

Fabiola Desy Unidjaja. "Payoffs Prominent in Court System". *Jakarta Post*, 22 March 2000.

Fadli Zon. *Politik Huru-Hara Mei 1998* [Politics of Upheaval in May 1998]. Jakarta: Institute of Policy Studies, 2004.

Fane, George. "Change and Continuity in Indonesia's New Fiscal Decentralisation Arrangements". *Bulletin of Indonesian Economic Studies* 39, no. 1 (2003).

Farid Husain. *To See the Unseen: Kisah di Balik Damai di Aceh* [The Story Behind Peace in Aceh]. South Jakarta: Health & Hospital, 2007.

Farhan Hamid, Ahmad. *Jalan Damai Nanggroe Endatu: Catatan Seorang Wakil Rakyat*

Aceh [The Road to Peace in the Land of Our Ancestors: Notes of an Acehneses People's Representative]. Jakarta: Suara Bebas, 2006.

Feith, Herbert. *The Decline of Constitutional Democracy in Indonesia*. Ithaca, NY: Cornell University Press, 1962.

Ford, Michele Ford. "Who Are the *Orang Riau*? Negotiating Identity across Geographic and Ethnic Divides". In *Local Power and Politics in Indonesia: Decentralisation and Democratisation*, edited by Aspinall, Edward and Greg Fealy. Singapore: Institute of Southeast Asian Studies, 2003.

Forrester, Geoff, ed. *Post-Soeharto Indonesia: Renewal or Chaos?* Netherlands: KITLV Press/Singapore: Institute of Southeast Asian Studies, 1999.

Geddes, Barbara. "A Comparative Perspective on the Leninist Legacy in Eastern Europe". *Comparative Political Studies* 28, no. 2 (July 1995).

Geertz, Clifford. *The Religion of Java*. New York: Free Press of Glencoe, 1960.

Global Witness. *Paying for Protection: The Freeport Mine and the Indonesian Security Forces*. Washington: Global Witness Publishing Inc., 2005.

Greenlees, Don and Robert Garran. *Deliverance: The Inside Story of East Timor's Fight for Freedom*. Crows Nest, NSW: Allen and Unwin, 2002.

Grindle, Merilee S. and John W. Thomas. *Public Choices and Policy Change: The Political Economy of Reform in Developing Countries*. Baltimore and London: The Johns Hopkins University Press, 1991.

Habeahan, B.P. dkk. *Sidang Istimewa MPR dan Semanggi Berdarah* [The Special Session of the MPR and Bloody Semanggi]. Depok: Permata AD, 1999.

Habibie, Bacharuddin Jusuf. *Detik-Detik yang Menentukan: Jalan Panjang Indonesia Menuju Demokrasi* [Decisive Momenets: Indonesia's Long Road to Democracy]. Jakarta: THC Mandiri, 2006.

Hadiz, Vedi. "Power and Politics in North Sumatra: The Uncompleted *Reformasi*". In *Local Power and Politics in Indonesia: Decentralisation and Democratisation*, edited by Aspinall, Edward and Greg Fealy. Singapore: Institute of Southeast Asian Studies, 2003.

―――. "Decentralization and Democracy in Indonesia: A Critique of Neo-Institutionalist Perspectives". *Development and Change* 35, no. 4 (2004).

Hafidz, Tatik S. *Fading Away? The Political Role of the Army in Indonesia's Transition to Democracy 1998–2001*. Singapore: Institute of Defence and Strategic Studies, 2006.

Hefner, Robert. *Civil Islam: Muslims and Democratization in Indonesia*. Princeton NJ: Princeton University Press, 2000.

Hery Susanto dkk. *Otonomi Daerah dan Kompetensi Lokal: Pikiran serta Konsepsi Syaukani HR* [Regional Autonomy and Local Competence: The Thoughts and Concepts of H.R. Syaukani]. Jakarta: Millenium Publisher, 2003.

Hill, Hal, ed. *Indonesia's New Order: The Dynamics of Socio-Economic Transformation*. St. Leonards: Allen and Unwin, 1994.

―――. *The Indonesian Economy*. 2nd ed. Cambridge: Cambridge University Press, 2000.

Hofman, Bert and Kai Kaiser. "The Making of the 'Big Bang' and Its Aftermath: A Political Economy Perspective". In *Reforming Intergovernmental Fiscal Relations and the Rebuilding of Indonesia*, edited by James Alm, Jorge Martinez-Vazquez, and Sri Mulyani Indrawati. Cheltenham UK/Northampton MA, USA: Edward Elgar, 2004.

Honna, Jun. "Military Ideology in Response to Democratic Pressure during the Late Suharto Era: Political and Institutional Contexts". In *Violence and the State in Suharto's Indonesia*, edited by Benedict R.O'G. Anderson. Ithaca, New York: Southeast Asia Program, Cornell University, 2001.

————. *Military Politics and Democratization in Indonesia*. London: Routledge-Curzon, 2003.

————. "Local Civil-Military Relations During the First Phase of Democratic Transition: A Comparison of West, Central and East Java". *Indonesia* 82 (October 2006): 75–96.

Huber, Konrad. *The HDC in Aceh: Promises and Pitfalls of NGO Mediation and Implementation*. Washington: East-West Center, 2004.

Human Rights Watch/Asia. *The Limits of Openness: Human Rights in Indonesia and East Timor*. New York: Human Rights Watch, 1994.

————. "Indonesia: Communal Violence in West Kalimantan". Vol. 9, No. 10 (C). New York: Human Rights Watch, 1997.

————. "Indonesia: The Violence in Ambon". New York: Human Rights Watch, March 1999.

————. "Indonesia: The War in Aceh". Vol. 13, No. 4 (C). New York: Human Rights Watch, August 2001.

————. "Breakdown: Four Years of Communal Violence in Central Sulawesi". Vol. 14, No. 9 (C). New York: Human Rights Watch, December 2002*a*.

————. "Indonesia: Accountability for Human Rights Violations in Aceh". Vol. 14, No. 1 (C). New York: Human Rights Watch, March 2002*b*.

————. "Aceh Under Martial Law: Inside the Secret War". Vol. 15, No. 10 (C). New York: Human Rights Watch, December 2003.

————. "Too High a Price: The Human Rights Cost of the Indonesian Military's Economic Activities". Vol. 18, No. 5 (C). New York: Human Rights Watch, 2006.

Ikrar Nusa Bhakti et al. *Tentara yang Gelisah* [An Uneasy Army]. Bandung: Mizan, 1999.

Indonesia Corruption Watch. "Pengadilan Masih Milik Koruptor" [The Courts are still the Property of Corruptors]; "Pengadilan masih jauh dari Harapan" [The Courts are still far from Expectations]. Jakarta: ICW, 2006*a*.

————. "Daftar Kasus Korupsi Mantan dan Anggota DPRD yang telah Divonis Pengadilan Selama Tahun 2005–Semester I 2006" [List of Corruption Cases of Former and Present Members of DPRDs who were Sentenced by Courts during 2005 and the First Half of 2006]. Jakarta: ICW, 2006*b*.

————. "Evaluasi Kinerja Pemberantasan Korupsi Komisi Pemberantasan

Korupsi (KPK), 2004–2007" [Evaluation of Repression of Corruption by the Commission to Eradicate Corruption (KPK) 2004–2007]. Jakarta: ICW, 2007.

Indria Samego et al. *"...Bila ABRI Menghendaki"* [...When ABRI Wants...]. Bandung: Mizan, 1998.

Huntington, Samuel P. *Political Order in Changing Societies*. New Haven and London: Yale University Press, 1968.

————. *The Third Wave: Democratization in the Late Twentieth Century*. Norman and London: The University of Oklahoma Press, 1991.

International Crisis Group. "Indonesia's Crisis: Chronic but not Acute". ICG Report. Jakarta/Brussels: 31 May 2000*a*.

————. "Indonesia: Keeping the Military Under Control". Asia Report No. 9. Jakarta/Brussels: 5 September 2000*b*.

————. "Indonesia: Overcoming Murder and Chaos in Maluku". Asia Report No. 10. Jakarta/Brussels: 19 December 2000*c*.

————. "Indonesia: Impunity Versus Accountability for Gross Human Rights Violations". Asia Report No. 12. Jakarta/Brussels: 2 February 2001*a*.

————. "Indonesia: National Police Reform". Asia Report No. 13. Jakarta/Brussels: 20 February, 2001*b*.

————. "Indonesia's Presidential Crisis". Asia Briefing. Jakarta/Brussels: 21 February 2001*c*.

————. "Indonesia's Presidential Crisis: The Second Round". Asia Briefing. Jakarta/Brussels: 21 May 2001*d*.

————. "Aceh: Why Military Force Won't Bring Lasting Peace". Asia Report No. 17. Jakarta/Brussels: 13 June 2001*e*.

————. "Aceh: Can Autonomy Stem the Conflict". Asia Report No. 18. Jakarta/Brussels: 27 June 2001*f*.

————. "Communal Violence in Indonesia: Lessons from Kalimantan". Asia Report No. 19. Jakarta/Brussels: 27 June 2001*g*.

————. "Indonesia: Violence and Radical Muslims". Asia Briefing No. 10. Jakarta/Brussels: 10 October 2001*h*.

————. "Indonesia: Next Steps in Military Reform". Asia Report No. 24. Jakarta/Brussels: 11 October 2001*i*.

————. "Indonesia: Natural Resources and Law Enforcement". Asia Report No. 29. Jakarta/Brussels: 20 December 2001*j*.

————. "Indonesia: The Search for Peace in Maluku". Asia Report No. 31. Jakarta/Brussels: 8 February 2002*a*.

————. "Indonesia: The Implications of the Timor Trials". Indonesia Briefing No. 16. Jakarta/Brussels: 8 May 2002*b*.

————. "Indonesian Backgrounder: How the Jemaah Islamiyah Terrorist Network Operates". Asia Report No. 43. Jakarta/Brussels: 11 December 2002*c*.

————. "Aceh: A Fragile Peace". Asia Report No. 47. Jakarta/Brussels: 27 February 2003*a*.

————. "Aceh: How Not to Win Hearts and Minds". Asia Briefing, No 27. Jakarta/
        Brussels: 23 July 2003*b*.

————. "Jemaah Islamiyah in Southeast Asia: Damaged but still Dangerous". Asia
        Report No. 63. Jakarta/Brussels: 26 August 2003*c*.

————. "Indonesia Backgrounder: A Guide to the 2004 Eletions". Asia Report
        No. 71. Jakarta/Brussels: 18 December 2003*d*.

————. "Indonesia: Violence Erupts Again in Ambon". Asia Briefing No. 32.
        Jakarta/Brussels: 17 May 2004*a*.

————. "Indonesia Backgrounder: Why Salafism and Terrorism Mostly Don't Mix".
        Asia Report No. 83. Jakarta/Brussels: 13 September 2004*b*.

————. "Indonesia: Rethinking Internal Security Strategy". Asia Report No. 90.
        Jakarta/Brussels: 20 December 2004*c*.

————. "Aceh: A New Chance for Peace". Asia Briefing No. 40. Jakarta/Brussels:
        15 August 2005*a*.

————. "Weakening Indonesia's Mujahidin Networks: Lessons from Maluku and
        Poso". Asia Report No 103. Jakarta/Brussels: 13 October 2005*b*.

————. "Aceh: So Far, So Good". Asia Briefing No. 44. Jakarta/Brussels: 13 December
        2005*c*.

————. "Aceh: Now for the Hard Part". Asia Briefing No. 48. Jakarta/Brussels:
        29 March 2006*a*.

————. "Islamic Law and Criminal Justice in Aceh". Asia Report No. 117. Jakarta/
        Brussels: 31 July 2006*b*.

————. "Aceh's Local Elections: The Role of the Free Aceh Movement (GAM)".
        Asia Briefing No. 57. Jakarta/Brussels: 29 November 2006*c*.

————. "How GAM Won in Aceh". Asia Briefing No. 61. Jakarta/Brussels: 22 March
        2007.

International Institute of Strategic Studies. *The Military Balance 2007*. London:
        Routledge, 2007.

International Organization for Migration, Universitas Syiah Kuala, Harvard Medical
        School. "Psychosocial Needs Assessment of Communities affected by the Conflict
        in the Districts of Pidie, Bireuen and Aceh Utara". <www.iom.or.id> 2006.

Isa Sulaiman, M. "From Autonomy to Periphery: A Critical Evaluation of the
        Acehnese Nationalist Movement". In *Verandah of Violence: The Background of
        the Aceh Problem*, edited by Anthony Reid. Singapore: Singapore University
        Press, 2006.

Isa Sulaiman, M. and Gerry van Klinken. "The Rise and Fall of Governor Puteh".
        In *Renegotiating Boundaries: Local Politics in Post-Suharto Indonesia*, edited
        by Henk Schulte Nordholt and Gerry van Klinken. Leiden: KITLV Press,
        2007.

Jomo K.S., ed. *Tigers in Trouble: Financial Governance, Liberalisation and Crises in
        East Asia*. London and New York: Zed Books, 1998.

Kahin, George McTurnan. *Nationalism and Revolution in Indonesia*. Ithaca: Cornell
        University Press, 1952.

Kell, Tim. *The Roots of Acehnese Rebellion, 1989–1992*. Ithaca: Cornell University, Cornell Modern Indonesia Project, 1995.

King, Blair Andrew. "Empowering the Presidency: Interests and Perceptions in Indonesia's Constitutional Reforms, 1999–2002". Ph.D. dissertation, Ohio University, 2004.

King, Dwight Y. *Half-Hearted Reform: Electoral Institutions and the Struggle for Democracy in Indonesia*. Westport/Connecticut/London: Praeger, 2003.

Kingsbury, Damien. *Peace in Aceh: A Personal Account of the Helsinki Peace Process*. Jakarta/Singapore: Equinox Publishing, 2006.

Kivlan Zen. *Konflik dan Integrasi TNI-AD* [Conflict and Integration of the Indonesian Military]. Jakarta: Institute for Policy Studies, 2004.

Komisi Pemberantasan Korupsi. *Laporan Tahunan* [Annual Report] *2006*. Jakarta: Komisi Pemberantasan Korupsi, 2007.

————. *Laporan Tahunan* [Annual Report] *2007*. Jakarta: Komisi Pemberantasan Korupsi, 2008.

Lela E. Madjiah. "Myriad Problems Mar TNI Relations with the Police". *Jakarta Post*, 5 October 2002.

Liddle, R. William. "The Islamic Turn in Indonesia: A Political Explanation". *Journal of Asian Studies* 55, no. 3 (1996).

————. "Indonesia: Soeharto's Tightening Grip". *Journal of Democracy* 7, no. 4 (October 1996).

Liddle, R. William and Saiful Mujani. "Indonesia in 2005: A New Multiparty Presidential Democracy". *Asian Survey* 46, no. 1 (January 2006).

Lijphart, Arend. "Constitutional Choices in New Democracies". In *The Global Resurgence of Democracy*, edited by Larry Diamond and Marc F. Plattner. Baltimore and London: The Johns Hopkins University Press, 1993.

Lindsey, Timothy. *Indonesia: Law and Society*. Leichhardt, New South Wales: The Federation Press, 1999.

————. "Black Letter, Black Market and Bad Faith: Corruption and the Failure of Law Reform". In *Indonesia in Transition: Social Aspects of Reformasi and Crisis*, edited by Chris Manning and Peter van Dierman. Singapore: Institute of Southeast Asian Studies, 2000.

————. "The Criminal State: *Premanisme* and the New Indonesia". In *Indonesia Today: Challenges of History*, edited by Grayson Lloyd and Shannon Smith. Singapore: Institute of Southeast Asian Studies, 2001.

————. "Indonesian Constitutional Reform: Muddling Towards Democracy". *Singapore Journal of International and Comparative Law*, no. 6 (2002): 244–301.

Linz, Juan J. 1993. "The Perils of Presidentialism". In *The Global Resurgence of Democracy*, edited by Larry Diamond and Marc F. Plattner. Baltimore and London: The Johns Hopkins University Press, 1993.

Linz, Juan J. and Alfred Stepan. "Toward Consolidated Democracies". In *Consolidating the Third Wave Democracies: Themes and Perspectives*, edited by Diamond, Larry,

Marc F. Plattner, Yun-han Chu, and Hung-Mao Tien. Baltimore and London: The Johns Hopkins University Press, 1997.

Lloyd, Grayson and Shannon Smith, eds. *Indonesia Today: Challenges of History*. Singapore: Institute of Southeast Asian Studies, 2001.

Lowry, Robert. *The Armed Forces of Indonesia*. St. Leonards, NSW: Allen & Unwin, 1996.

Lubis, Todung Mulya. "The Rechtsstaat and Human Rights". In *Indonesia: Law and Society*, edited by Timothy Lindsey. Leichhardt, New South Wales: The Federation Press, 1999.

MacIntyre, Andrew. "Political Institutions and the Economic Crisis in Thailand and Indonesia". In *Politics of the Asian Economic Crisis*, edited by T.J. Pempel. Ithaca: Cornell University Press, 1999.

———. *The Power of Institutions: Political Architecture and Governance*. Ithaca and London: Cornell University Press, 2003.

Mackie, Jamie and Andrew MacIntyre. "Politics". In *Indonesia's New Order: The Dynamics of Socio-Economic Transformation*, edited by Hal Hill. St. Leonards: Allen and Unwin, 1994.

Mahrozi, Jonni. "A Local Perspective on Military Withdrawal from Politics in Indonesia: East Java 1998–2003". Ph.D. thesis, Flinders University, Adelaide, 2006.

Mainwaring, Scott. "Presidentialism, Multipartism, and Democracy: The Difficult Combination". *Comparative Political Studies* 26, no. 2 (July 1993).

Malley, Michael S. 1999. "Regions: Centralization and Resistance". In *Indonesia Beyond Suharto: Polity, Economy, Society, Transition*, edited by Don Emerson. Armonk: M.E. Sharpe, 1999.

———. "Class, Region and Culture: The Sources of Social Conflict in Indonesia". In *Social Cohesion and Conflict Prevention in Asia: Managing Diversity through Development*, edited by Nat J. Colletta, Teck Ghee Lim, and Anita Kelles-Viitanen. Washington DC: The World Bank, 2001.

———. "New Rules, Old Structures and the Limits of Democratic Decentralisation". In *Local Power and Politics in Indonesia: Decentralisation and Democratisation*, edited by Edward Aspinall and Greg Fealy. Singapore: Institute of Southeast Asian Studies, 2003.

Manor, James. *The Political Economy of Decentralization*. Washington D.C.: The World Bank, 1999.

Manning, Chris and Peter van Diermen, eds. *Indonesia in Transition: Social Aspects of Reformasi and Crisis*. Singapore: Institute of Southeast Asian Studies, 2000.

McBeth, John. "Dawn of a New Age". *Far Eastern Economic Review*, 17 September 1998.

McCarthy, John. "Changing to Gray: Decentralization and the Emergence of Volatile Socio-Legal Configurations in Central Kalimantan, Indonesia". *World Development* 32, no. 7 (2004): 1199–23.

McGibbon, Rodd. *Secessionist Challenges in Aceh and Papua: Is Special Autonomy the Solution?* Washington: East-West Center, 2004.

——. "Indonesian Politics in 2006: Stability, Compromise and Shifting Contests over Ideology". *Bulletin of Indonesian Economic Studies* 42, no. 3 (2006).

McLeod, Ross H. "Indonesia". In *East Asia in Crisis: From being a Miracle to Needing One?*, edited by Ross H. Mcleod and Ross Garnaut. London and New York: Routledge, 1998.

McLeod, Ross H. and Ross Garnaut. eds. *East Asia in Crisis: From being a Miracle to Needing One?* London and New York: Routledge, 1998.

McLeod, Ross. "Dealing with Bank System Failure: Indonesia, 1997–2003". *Bulletin of Indonesian Economic Studies* 40, no. 1 (2004).

McLeod, Ross H. and Andrew MacIntyre, eds. *Indonesia: Democracy and the Promise of Good Governance*. Singapore: Institute of Southeast Asian Studies, 2007.

Mietzner, Marcus. "From Soeharto to Habibie: The Indonesian Armed Forces and Political Islam during the Transition". In *Post-Soeharto Indonesia: Renewal or Chaos?*, edited by Geoff Forrester. Netherlands: KITLV Press/Singapore: Institute of Southeast Asian Studies, 1999.

——. "The 1999 General Session: Wahid, Megawati and the Fight for the Presidency". In *Indonesia in Transition: Social Aspects of Reformasi and Crisis*, edited by Chris Manning and Peter van Dierman. Singapore: Institute of Southeast Asian Studies, 2000.

——. "Abdurrahman's Indonesia: Political Conflict and Institutional Crisis". In *Indonesia Today: Challenges of History*, edited by Grayson Lloyd and Shannon Smith. Singapore: Institute of Southeast Asian Studies, 2001.

——. "Business as Usual? The Indonesian Armed Forces and Local Politics in the Post-Soeharto Era". In *Local Power and Politics in Indonesia: Decentralisation and Democratisation*, edited by Edward Aspinall and Greg Fealy. Singapore: Institute of Southeast Asian Studies, 2003.

——. "Indonesian Civil-Military Relations: The Armed Forces and Political Islam in Transition, 1997–2004". Ph.D. thesis. Canberra: Department of Political and Social Change, Australian National University, 2004.

——. *The Politics of Military Reform in Post-Suharto Indonesia: Elite Conflict, Nationalism, and Institutional Resistance*. Policy Studies 23. Washington: East-West Center, 2006.

——. "Party Financing in Post-Soeharto Indonesia: Between State Subsidies and Political Corruption". *Contemporary Southeast Asia* 29, no. 2 (2007): 238–63.

——. *Military Politics, Islam, and the State in Indonesia: From Turbulent Transition to Democratic Consolidation*. Singapore: Institute of Southeast Asia Studies, 2008.

——. "Indonesia and the Pitfalls of Low-Quality Democracy: A Case Study of the Gabernatorial Election in North Sulawesi". In *Democratization in Post-Suharto Indonesia*, edited by Andreas Ufen and Marco Bünte. London and New York: Routledge, 2009.

Migdal, Joel S. *Strong Societies and Weak States: State-Society Relations and State Capabilities in the Third World*. Princeton, New Jersey: Princeton University Press, 1988.

Millie, Julian. "The Tempo Case: Indonesia's Press Laws, the Pengadilan Tata Usaha Negara and the Indonesian Negara Hukum". In *Indonesia: Law and Society*, edited by Timothy Lindsey. Leichhardt, New South Wales: The Federation Press, 1999.

Mizuno, Kumiko. "Indonesia's East Timor Policy: 1998–2002". Ph.D. thesis. Canberra: Department of Political and Social Change, Australian National University, 2003.

Morfit, Michael. "The Road to Helsinki: The Aceh Agreement and Indonesia's Democratic Development". *International Negotiation*, no. 12 (2007).

Mununggir Sri Saraswati. "Bribery in Legal System Not Merely Fictitious Story". *Jakarta Post*, 1 April 2002*a*.

———. "Judge Jailed for Graft — Well, Just About". *Jakarta Post*, 23 April 2002*b*.

———. "Justice, Corruption are Merry Bedfellows at AGO". *Jakarta Post*, 24 April 2002*c*.

Najib Azca. "The Role of the Security Forces in Communal Conflict: The Case of Ambon". M.A. sub-thesis. Canberra: Australian National University, 2003.

Nasution, Abdul Haris. *Pokok-Pokok Gerilya* [Principles of Guerrilla Warfare]. Djakarta: P.T. Pembimbing Masa, 1964.

Nazaruddin Syamsuddin. "Issues and Politics of Regionalism in Indonesia: Evaluating the Acehnese Experience". In *Armed Separatism in Southeast Asia*, edited by Lim Joo-Jock and Vani S. Singapore: Institute of Southeast Asian Studies, 1984.

———. *Indonesia Harus Menjadi Negara Federasi* [Indonesia Must Become a Federal State]. Jakarta: Penerbit Universitas Indonesia, 2002.

Noorhaidi Hasan. *Laskar Jihad: Islam, Militancy, and the Quest for Identity in Post-New Order Indonesia*. Ithaca: Cornell Southeast Asia Program, 2006.

Nordholt, Henk Schulte and Gerry van Klinken, eds. *Renegotiating Boundaries: Local politics in post-Suharto Indonesia*. Leiden: KITLV Press, 2007.

Nuraida Mokhsen. "Decentralization in Indonesia". Ph.D. thesis. Department of Political and Social Change, Australian National University, 2003.

Obidzinski, Krystof. "Illegal Logging in Indonesia: Myth and Reality". In *The Politics and Economics of Indonesia's Natural Resources*, edited by Budy P. Resosudarmo. Singapore: Institute of Southeast Asian Studies, 2005.

O'Donnell, Guillermo and Philippe C. Schmitter. *Transitions from Authoritarian Rule: Tentative Conclusions about Uncertain Democracies*. Baltimore and London: The Johns Hopkins University Press, 1986.

O'Donnell, Guillermo. "Illusions about Consolidation". In *Consolidating the Third Wave Democracies: Themes and Perspectives*, edited by Larry Diamond, Marc F. Plattner, Yun-han Chu, and Hung-Mao Tien. Baltimore and London: The Johns Hopkins University Press, 1997.

O'Rourke, Kevin. *Reformasi: The Struggle for Power in Post-Soeharto Indonesia*. Crows Nest NSW: Allen and Unwin, 2002.

Payne, J. Mark and Juan Cruz Perusia. "Reforming the Rules of the Game: Political Reform". In *The State of State Reform in Latin America*, edited by Eduardo Lora. Palo Alto: Stanford University Press and Washington: The World Bank, 2007.

Perlez, Jane and Raymond Bonner. "Below a Mountain, a River of Waste". *New York Times*, 27 December 2005.

Pompe, Sebastiaan. *The Indonesian Supreme Court: A Study of Institutional Collapse*. Ithaca: Cornell Southeast Asia Program, 2005.

Rabasa, Angel and John Haseman. *The Military and Democracy in Indonesia: Challenges, Politics and Power*. Santa Monica: Rand, 2002.

Ramage, Douglas E. *Politics in Indonesia: Democracy, Islam and the Ideology of Tolerance*. London and New York: Routledge, 1995.

––––––. "Indonesia: Democracy First, Good Governance Later". In *Southeast Asian Affairs 2007*, edited by Daljit Singh and Lorraine Carlos Salazar. Singapore: Institute of Southeast Asian Studies, 2007.

Ramlan Surbakti. "Penyusunan Daerah Pemilihan Anggota DPR/DPRD" [Determining Constituencies for the DPR and DPRDs]. *Kompas*, 20 October 2003.

Reid, Anthony, ed. *Verandah of Violence: The Background of the Aceh Problem*. Singapore: Singapore University Press, 2006.

Reilly, Benjamin. *Democracy and Diversity: Political Engineering in the Asia-Pacific*. Oxford: Oxford University Press, 2006.

Resosudarmo, Budy P., ed. *The Politics and Economics of Indonesia's Natural Resources*. Indonesia Update Series, Research School of Pacific and Asian Studies, Australian National University. Singapore: Institute of Southeast Asian Studies, 2005.

Resosudarmo, Ida Aju Pradnja. "Shifting Power to the Periphery: The Impact of Decentralisation on Forests and Forest People". In *Local Power and Politics in Indonesia: Decentralisation and Democratisation*, edited by Edward Aspinall and Greg Fealy. Singapore: Institute of Southeast Asian Studies, 2003.

Rieffel, Lex and Jaleswari Pramodhawardani. *Out of Business and On Budget: The Challenge of Military Financing in Indonesia*. Washington D.C. United States-Indonesia Society and Brookings Institute Press, 2007.

Rifqi S. Assegaf. "Judicial Reform in Indonesia 1998–2006". In *Reforming Laws and Institutions in Indonesia: An Assessment*, edited by Naoyuki Sakumoto and Hikmahanto Juwana. ASEDP Publication No. 74. Tokyo: IDE-JETRO (Institute of Developing Economies, Japan External Trade Organization), 2007.

Rizal Sukma. "Why can't military and police just get along?' *Jakarta Post*, 20 February 2007.

Robinson, Geoffrey. "*Rawan* is as *Rawan* Does: The Origins of Disorder in New Order Aceh". In *Violence and the State in Suharto's Indonesia*, edited by Benedict R.O'G. Anderson. Ithaca: Southeast Asia Program, Cornell University, 2000.

Robinson, Geoffrey. "Indonesia on a New Course?". In *Coercion and Governance:*

The Declining Political Role of the Military in Asia, edited by Muthiah Alagappa. Stanford, California: Stanford University Press, 2001.

Robison, Richard. *Indonesia: The Rise of Capital.* North Sydney: Allen & Unwin, 1986.

Robison, Richard and Vedi R. Hadiz. *Reorganising Power in Indonesia: The Politics of Oligarchy in the Age of Markets.* London and New York: RoutledgeCurzon, 2004.

Rohde, David. "Indonesia Unraveling?" *Foreign Affairs* 80, no. 4 (July/August 2001).

Romli Atmasasmita. *Korupsi, Good Governance dan Komisi Anti Korupsi di Indonesia* [Corruption, Good Governance and the Anti-Corruption Commission in Indonesia]. Jakarta: Badan Pembinaan Hukum, Departemen Kehakiman dan HAM, RI, 2002.

Rueschemeyer, Dietrich, Evelyne Huber Stephens, and John D. Stephens. *Capitalist Development and Democracy.* Cambridge: Polity Press, 1992.

Rustam Kastor. *Konspirasi Politik RMS dan Kristen Menghancurkan Umat Islam di Ambon-Maluku* [The RMS dan Christian Conspiracy to Destroy the Muslim Community in Ambon-Maluku]. Yogyakarta: Wihdah Press, 2000.

Ryaas Rasyid, M. "Regional Autonomy and Local Politics in Indonesia". In *Local Power and Politics in Indonesia: Decentralisation and Democratisation,* edited by Edward Aspinall and Greg Fealy. Singapore: Institute of Southeast Asian Studies, 2003.

————. "The Policy of Decentralization in Indonesia". In *Reforming Intergovernmental Fiscal Relations and the Rebuilding of Indonesia,* edited by James Alm, Jorge Martinez-Vazquez, and Sri Mulyani Indrawati. Cheltenham UK/Northampton MA, USA: Edward Elgar, 2004.

Salim Said. *Genesis of Power: General Sudirman and the Indonesian Military in Politics 1945–49.* Singapore: Institute of Southeast Asian Studies, 1991.

————. "Kontroversi Keberadaan TNI di MPR" [The Controversy over the Presence of the Military in the MPR]. *Republika,* 24 August 2000.

Schulze, Kirsten E. "Laskar Jihad and the Conflict in Ambon". *Brown Journal of International Affairs* IX, no. 1 (Spring 2002).

————. *The Free Aceh Movement [GAM]: Anatomy of a Separatist Organization.* Washington: East-West Center, 2004.

————. "Insurgency and Counter-Insurgency: Strategy and the Aceh Conflict, October 1976–May 2004." In *Verandah of Violence: The Background of the Aceh Problem,* edited by Anthony Reid. Singapore: Singapore University Press, 2006.

Schwarz, Adam. *A Nation in Waiting: Indonesia in the 1990s.* St. Leonards, NSW: Allen and Unwin, 1994.

Schwarz, Adam and Jonathan Paris, eds. *The Politics of Post-Suharto Indonesia.* New York: The Council of Foreign Relations, 1999.

Schuman, Michael. "A Failed State?". *Time,* 21 October 2002.

Sebastian, Leonard C. *Realpolitik Ideology: Indonesia's Use of Military Force*. Singapore: Institute of Southeast Asian Studies, 2006.

Shah, Anwar and Theresa Thompson. "Implementing Decentralized Local Government: A Treacherous Road with Potholes, Detours and Road Closures". In *Reforming Intergovernmental Fiscal Relations and the Rebuilding of Indonesia*, edited by James Alm, Jorge Martinez-Vazquez, and Sri Mulyani Indrawati. Cheltenham UK/Northampton MA, USA: Edward Elgar, 2004.

Sharma, Shalendra D. "The Indonesian Financial Crisis: From Banking Crisis to Financial Sector Reforms 1997–2000". *Indonesia*, no. 71 (April 2001).

Sherlock, Stephen. "Combating Corruption in Indonesia? The Ombudsman and the Assets Auditing Commission". *Bulletin of Indonesian Economic Studies* 38, no. 3 (2002).

———. "Indonesia's Regional Representative Assembly: Democracy, Representation and the Regions. A Report on the Dewan Perwakilan Daerah (DPD)". Canberra: Australian National University, Centre for Democratic Institutions, 2006.

———. "The Indonesian Parliament after Two Elections: What has Really Changed?". Canberra: Australian National University, Centre for Democratic Institutions, 2007.

Sidel, John T. *Riots, Pogroms, Jihad: Religious Violence in Indonesia*. Ithaca and London: Cornell University Press, 2006.

Sinansari Ecip S. *Menyulut Ambon: Kronologi Merambatnya berbagai Kerusuhan Lintas Wilayah di Indonesia* [Setting Ambon Alight: The Chronology of the Spread of Cross-Regional Rioting in Indonesia]. Bandung: Pustaka Mizan, 1999.

Slater, Dan. "Indonesia's Accountability Trap: Party Cartels and Presidential Power after Democratic Transition". *Indonesia* 78 (October 2004).

Snyder, Jack. *From Voting to Violence: Democratization and Nationalist Conflict*. New York/London: W.W. Norton & Company, 2000.

Soepomo. 1970. "An Integralistic State". In *Indonesian Political Thinking, 1945–1965*, edited by Herbert Feith and Lance Castles, pp. 188–92. Ithaca: Cornell University Press.

Soedradjad Djiwandono J. "The Rupiah — One Year After Its Float". In *Post-Soeharto Indonesia: Renewal or Chaos?*, edited by Geoff Forrester. Netherlands: KITLV Press/Singapore: Institute of Southeast Asian Studies, 1999.

———. "Liquidity Support to Banks during Indonesia's Financial Crisis". *Bulletin of Indonesian Economic Studies* 40, no. 1 (2004).

Suharizal. *Reformasi Konstitusi 1998–2002: Pergulatan Konsep dan Pemikiran Amandemen UUD 1945* [Constitutional Reform 1998–2002: Conceptual Struggle and Thought on the Amendment of the 1945 Constitution]. Padang: Anggrek Law Firm, 2002.

Sukma, Rizal. *Security Operations in Aceh: Goals, Consequences, and Lessons*. Washington: East-West Center, 2004.

Suryadinata, Leo, Evi Nurvidya Arifin and Aris Ananta. *Indonesian's Population:*

Ethnicity and Religion in a Changing Political Landscape. Singapore: Institute of Southeast Asian Studies, 2003.

Suwandi, Dr. I Made. "Pokok-Pokok Pikiran. Konsepsi Dasar Otonomi Daerah Indonesia (Dalam Upaya Mewudjudkan Pemerintah Daerah yang Demokratis dan Efisien" [Main Ideas. The Basic Concept of Indonesian Regional Autonomy (Efforts to Establish Democratic and Efficient Regional Government)]. Jakarta (unpublished), 2002.

Syarifudin Tippe. *Aceh di Persimpangan Jalan* [Aceh at the Crossroads]. Jakarta: Pustaka Cidesindo, 2000.

Tamrin Amal Tomagola. "The Bleeding Halmahera of North Moluccas". *Jurnal Studi Indonesia* 10, no. 2 (September 2000).

Telapak. *The Last Frontier: Illegal Logging in Papua and China's Massive Timber Theft.* Bogor/London and New York: Telapak/Environmental Investigation Agency, 2005.

Turner, Mark and Owen Podger et al. *Decentralisation in Indonesia: Redesigning the State.* Canberra: Asia-Pacific Press, 2003.

van Klinken, Gerry. "The Maluku Wars: Bringing Society Back In". *Indonesia* 71 (April 2001).

─────. "Indonesia's New Ethnic Elites". In *Indonesia: In Search of Transition*, edited by Henk Schulte Nordholt and Irwan Abdullah. Yogyakarta: Pustaka Pelajar, 2002.

─────. *Communal Violence and Democratization in Indonesia: Small Town Wars.* London and New York: Routledge, 2007.

Wasingatu Zakiyah, Danang Widoyoko, Iva Kasuma, and Ragil Yoga Edi. *Menyingkap Tabir Mafia Peradilan* [Exposing the Court Mafia]. Jakarta: Indonesia Corruption Watch, 2002.

Weiner, Tim. "American Action is Held Likely in Asia". *New York Times*, 10 October 2001.

Widjajanto, Andi. *Reformasi Sektor Keamanan Indonesia* [Reform of Indonesia's Security Sector]. Jakarta: ProPatria, 2004.

Wilson, Christopher. *Ethno-Religious Violence in Indonesia: From Soil to God.* London and New York: Routledge, 2008.

Wiranto. *Bersaksi di Tengah Badai* [Witnessing the Middle of the Storm]. Jakarta: Institute of Democracy for Indonesia, 2003.

Wirahadikusumah, Agus, dkk. *Indonesia Baru dan Tantangan TNI: Pemikiran Masa Depan* [The New Indonesia and the Challenge for the Military: Thoughts about the Future]. Jakarta: Pustaka Sinar Harapan, 1999.

World Bank. *The East Asian Miracle: Economic Growth and Public Policy.* Washington D.C.: World Bank, 1993.

─────. "Decentralizing Indonesia: A Regional Public Expenditure Review Overview Report". East Asia Poverty Reduction and Economic Management Unit Report No. 26191-IND. Washington D.C.: The World Bank, 2003.

─────. "Combating Corruption in Indonesia: Enhancing Accountability for

Development". East Asia Poverty Reduction and Economic Management Unit, 20 October 2003.

————. *East Asia Decentralizes*. Washington D.C.: The World Bank, 2005.

————. "Trucking and Illegal Payments in Aceh". Aceh: Conflict and Development Program, 2006.

Yudhoyono, Susilo Bambang. *Aceh Perlu Keadilan Kesejahteraan dan Keamanan* [Aceh Needs Justice, Prosperity and Security]. Jakarta: Kantor Menko Polsoskam, 2001.

Zartman, I William, ed. *Collapsed States: The Disintegration and Restoration of Legitimate Authority*. Boulder: L. Rienner Publishers, 1995.

Ziegenhain, Patrick. *The Indonesian Parliament and Democratization*. Singapore: Institute of Southeast Asian Studies, 2008.

Documents

Asosiasi Pemerintah Kebupaten Seluruh Indonesia (Indonesian Association of District Governments), Policy Paper, Rapat Kerja Nasional III. Jakarta, 24–26 Agustus 2002.

Badan Pemeriksa Keuangan. *Siaran Pers BPK-RI tentang Hasil Audit Investigasi atas Penyaluran dan Penggunaan BLBI* [State Audit Board. Press Release on the Results of the Audit Investigation on the Channelling and Utilisation of Bank Indonesia Liquidity Funds]. Jakarta, 4 August 2000.

Cessation of Hostilities Framework Agreement Between Government of the Republic of Indonesian And the Free Acheh Movement, Geneva, 9 December 2002.

Departemen Pertahanan (Defence Department). *Mempertahankan Tanah Air Memasuki Abad 21* [Defending the Homeland at the Beginning of the 21st Century]. Jakarta, 2003.

Government of Indonesia and Bank Indonesia Memorandum of Economic and Financial Policies, 17 May 2000.

Government of Indonesia. *Ringkasan Eksekutif Laporan Penyelidikan Pelanggaran Hak Asasi Manusia di Timor Timur* [Executive Summary of the Report on the Investigation of Human Rights in East Timor], 31 January 2000.

International Covenant on Civil and Political Rights.

Laporan Komisi Independen Pengusutan Tindak Kekerasan di Aceh, Ringkasan Eksekutif [Report of the Independent Investigation of Violence in Aceh, Executive Summary]. Jakarta, 1999.

Laporan Akhir Tim Gabungan Pencari Fakta Peristiwa Tanggal 13–15 Mei 1998: Ringkasan Eksekutif [Final Report of the Joint Fact-Finding Team on the Events of 13–15 May 1998], 23 October 1998.

Laporan Akhir Komisi Kebenaran dan Persahabatan (KKP) Indonesia-Timor-Leste [Final Report of the Indonesia-East Timor Independent Truth and Friendship Commission], 2008.

Majelis Permusyawaratan Rakyat Republik Indonesia. *Panduan Dalam Memasyaratkan Undang-Undang Dasar Negara Republik Indonesia Tahun 1945: Latar Belakang,*

Proses dan Hasil Perubahan Undang-Undang Dasar Negara Republik Indonesia Tahun 1945 [Guide for Explaining the 1945 Constitution to the People: Background, Process and Result of the Amendments to the 1945 Constitution]. Jakarta: Sekretariat Jenderal MPR RI, 2003.

Markas Besar, Angkatan Bersenjata Republik Indonesia (Headquarters, the Armed Forces of the Republic of Indonesia). *ABRI Abad XXI: Redefinisi, Reposisi, dan Reaktualasi Peran ABRI Dalam Kehidupan Bangsa* [The TNI in the 21st Century: Redefinition, Repositioning, and Reactualisation of the Role of the TNI in National Life]. Jakarta, 1998.

Memorandum of Understanding between the Government of the Republic of Indonesia and the Free Aceh Movement, 15 August 2005.

Statement of the Government of Indonesia on Progress of Decentralization in Indonesia, presented at the Twelfth Meeting of the Consultative Group on Indonesia, Bali, 21–22 January 2003.

Undang-Undang Dasar 1945 (1945 Constitution).

Undang-Undang Dasar 1945 (1945 Constitution), First, Second, Third and Fourth Amendments.

United Nations. *International Commission of Enquiry on East Timor*, Report to the Secretary General, January 2000.

U.S. Department of State. *Indonesia Country Report on Human Rights Practices for 1998*. 1999.

Laws, Decrees, Regulations etc.

Laws of the DPR

Undang-Undang No. 5/1974 tentang Pokok-Pokok Pemerintahan di Daerah [Basic Law No. 5/1974 on Regional Government].

Undang-Undang No. 5/1979 tentang Pemerintahan Desa [Law No. 5/1979 on Village Government].

Undang-Undang No. 20/1982 tentang Ketentuan-Ketentuan Pokok Pertahanan Keamanan Negara [Basic Law No. 20/1982 on National Defence].

Undang-Undang No. 14/1985 tentang Mahkamah Agung [Law No. 14/1985 on the Supreme Court].

Undang-Undang No. 31/1997 tentang Peradilan Militer [Law No. 31/1997 on Military Courts].

Undang-Undang No. 2/1999 tentang Partai Politik [Law No. 2/1999 on Political Parties].

Undang-Undang No. 3/1999 tentang Pemilihan Umum [Law No. 3/1999 on General Elections].

Undang-Undang No. 4/1999 tentang Susunan dan Kedudukan Majelis Permusyawaratan Rakyat, Dewan Perwakilan Rakyat, dan Dewan Perwakilan Rakyat Daerah [Law No. 4/1999 on the Structure and Position of the Peoples' Consultative Council, the People's Representative Assembly, and the Regional People's Representative Assemblies].

Undang-Undang No. 22/1999 tentang Pemerintahan Daerah [Law No. 22/1999 on Regional Government].

Undang-Undang No. 25/1999 tentang Perimbangan Keuangan antara Pemerintah Pusat dan Daerah [Law No. 25/1999 on Fiscal Balance between the Central and Regional Governments].

Undang-Undang No. 28/1999 tentang Penyelenggara Negara yang Bersih dan Bebas dari Korupsi, Kolusi, dan Nepotisme [Law No. 28/1999 on Implementing a State that is Clean and Free from Corruption, Collusion and Nepotism].

Undang-Undang No. 31/1999 tentang Pemberantasan Tindak Pidana Korupsi [Law No. 31/1999 on the Elimination of Corruption].

Undang-Undang No. 41/1999 tentang Kehutanan [Law No. 41/1999 on Forestry].

Undang-Undang No. 44/1999 tentang Penyelenggaraan Keistimewaan Propinsi Daerah Istimewa Aceh [Law No. 44/1999 on the Implemention of the Special Status of the Special Province of Aceh].

Undang-Undang No. 26/2000 tentang Pengadilan Hak Asasi Manusia [Law No. 26/2000 on the Human Rights Court].

Undang-Undang No. 3/2002 tentang Pertahanan Negara [Law No. 3/2002 on National Defence].

Undang-Undang No. 30/2002 tentang Komisi Pemberantasan Tindak Pidana Korupsi [Law No. 30/2002 on the Commission to Eradicate Corruption].

Undang-Undang No. 31/2002 tentang Partai Politik [Law No. 31/2002 on Political Parties].

Undang-Undang No. 12 /2003 tentang Pemilihan Umum Anggota Dewan Perwakilan Rakyat, Dewan Perwakilan Daerah, dan Dewan Perwakilan Rakyat Daerah [Law No. 12/2003 on the General Election of Members of the People's Representative Assembly, the Regional Representative Assembly and the Regional Peoples' Representative Assemblies].

Undang-Undang No. 22/2003 tentang Susunan dan Kedudukan Majelis Permusyawaratan Rakyat, Dewan Perwakilan Rakyat, Dewan Perwakilan Daerah, dan Dewan Perwakilan Rakyat Daerah [Law No. 22/2003 on the Composition and Position of the People's Consultative Council, the People's Representative Assembly, the Regional Representative Assembly and the Regional Peoples' Representative Assemblies].

Undang-Undang No. 23/2003 tentang Pemilihan Presiden dan Wakil Presiden [Law No. 23/2003 on the Election of the President and Vice President].

Undang-Undang No. 22/2004 tentang Komisi Yudisial [Law No. 22/2004 on the Judicial Commission].

Undang-Undang No. 32/2004 tentang Pemerintahan Daerah [Law No. 32/2004 on Regional Government].

Undang-Undang No. 33/2004 tentang Perimbangan Keuangan antara Pemerintah Pusat dan Daerah [Law No. 33/2004 on Fiscal Balance between the Central and Regional Governments].

Undang-Undang No. 34/2004 tentang Tentara Nasional Indonesia [Law 34/2002 on the Indonesian National Military].

Undang-Undang No. 11/2006 tentang Pemerintahan Aceh [Law No. 11/2006 on the Governance of Aceh].

Undang-Undang No. 10/2008 tentang Pemilihan Umum Anggota Dewan Perwakilan Rakyat, Dewan Perwakilan Daerah, dan Dewan Perwakilalan Rakyat Daerah [Law No. 10/2008 on the General Election of Members of the People's Representative Assembly, the Regional Representative Assembly, and the Regional People's Representative Assemblies].

Rang Undang-Undang tentang Tentara Nasional Indonesia, 3 February 2003 ["Harmonised" Bill on the Indonesian National Military].

Rang Undang-Undang tentang Tentara Nasional Indonesia, 10 June 2004 [Bill on the Indonesian National Army].

Department of Home Affairs draft of the Law on Regional Government, 26 January 2004.

Decrees of the MPR

Ketetapan No. X MPR/1998 tentang Pokok-Pokok Reformasi Pembangunan dan Normalisasi Kehidupan Nasional sebagai Haluan Negara [MPR Decree No. X/1998 on Basic Principles of Development Reform and the Normalization of National Life as the National Will]

Ketetapan No. XI/MPR/1998 tentang Penyelenggara Negara yang Bersih dan Bebas KKN [MPR Decree No. XI/1998 on State Officials who are Clean and Free of Corruption, Collusion and Nepotism].

Ketetapan MPR No. XV/1998 tentang Penyelenggaraan Otonomi Daerah; Pengaturan, Pembagian, dan Pemanfaatan Sumber Daya Nasional yang Berkeadilan; serta Perimbangan Keuangan Pusat dan Daerah dalam Kerangka Negara Kesatuan Republik Indonesia [MPR Decree No. XV/1998 on the Implementation of Regional Autonomy; the Management, Distribution and Just Utilization of National Resources; and Fiscal Balance between the Central and Regional Governments of the Unitary State of the Republic of Indonesia].

Ketetapan MPR No. III/2000 tentang Sumber Hukum dan Tata Urutan Peraturan Perundang-Undangan [MPR Decree No. III/2000 on the Source of Law and the Precedence of Legislation].

Ketetapan MPR No. IV/2000 tentang Rekomendasi Kebijakan Dalam Penyelenggaraan Otonomi Daerah [MPR Decree No. IV/2000 on Policy Recommendations in Implementing Regional Autonomy].

Ketetapan MPR No. VI/2000 tentang Pemisahan Tentara Nasional Indonesia dan Kepolisian Negara Republik Indonesia [MPR Decree No. VI/2000 on the Separation of the Indonesian National Military from the National Police of the Republic of Indonesia].

Ketetapan MPR No. VII/2000 tentang Peran Tentara Nasional Indonesia dan Peran Kepolisian Negara Republik Indonesia [MPR Decree No. VII/2000 on the Role of the Indonesian National Military and the National Police of the Republic of Indonesia].

Government Regulations, Presidential Decisions and Instructions

Peraturan Pemerintah No. 19/2000 tentang Tim Gabungan Pemberantasan Tindak Pidana Korupsi [Government Regulation No. 19/2000 on the Joint Team to Repress Corruption].

Peraturan Pemerintah No. 110/2000 tentang Kedudukan Keuangan Dewan Perwakilan Rakyat Daerah [Government Regulation No. 110/2000 on the Financial Position of Regional Legislative Assemblies].

Instruksi President Republik Indonesia No. 5/2004 tentang Percepatan Pemberantasan Korupsi [Presidential Instruction No. 5/2004 on the Acceleration of the Eradication of Corruption], 9 December 2004.

Keputusan President Republik Indonesia No. 11/2005 tentang Tim Koordinasi Pemberantasan Tindak Pidana Korupsi [Presidential Decision No. 11/2005 on the Coordinating Team to Eliminate Corruption].

Judgments of the Constitutional Court

Mahkamah Konstitusi [Constitutional Court]. *Putusan No. 995/PUU-IV/2006* [Judicial Commission case].

Mahkamah Konstitusi [Constitutional Court]. *Putusan No. 012-016-019/PUU-IV/2006* [Tipikor case].

Mahkamah Konstitusi [Constitutional Court]. *Putusan No. 5/PUU-V/2007* [Non-party candidates case].

INDEX

www.ingramcontent.com/pod-product-compliance
Lightning Source LLC
Chambersburg PA
CBHW021845020426
42334CB00013B/188